THE
Studio
Business
Book

Revised and Expanded
Second Edition

BY JIM MANDELL

MIXBOOKS

Library of Congress Card Number: 94-073192

Book design by Michael Zipkin.
Production artists: Barbara Gelfand, Karyn Kraft

Production staff: Craig Wingate, Publisher; Andy Jewett, Editor; Barbara Schultz, Editorial Assistant; Georgia George, Production Director; Teri Stewart, Production Assistant.

Special thanks to George Petersen for technical advice and foreword.

Cover photo: BearTracks; Suffern, New York.

Photo credits:
Jim Mandell, pp. 14, 44, 45, 75, 76, 100, 101, 102, 127, 130, 172, 188, 206, 250
Ed Freeman, pp. 13, 15

Thanks also to the studio owners and managers who took the time to shoot and supply many of the uncredited photos which have been printed herein.

MixBooks

6400 Hollis St., Ste. 10
Emeryville, CA 94608
(510) 653-3307

Also from MixBooks:
Modular Digital Multitracks: The Power User's Guide
Concert Sound
Sound for Picture
Music Producers
Hal Blaine and the Wrecking Crew

Also from EMBooks:
Making the Ultimate Demo
Tech Terms: A Practical Dictionary for Audio and Music Production
Making Music With Your Computer

Also from CBM Music and Entertainment Group:
Mix magazine
Electronic Musician magazine
Mix Español
Recording Industry Sourcebook
Mix Reference Disc
MixPlus Directories
Mix Master Directory
Mix Calendars
Digital Piano Buyer's Guide

MixBooks is a division of Cardinal Business Media Inc.

Printed in Chelsea, Michigan

ISBN 0-918371-04-X

Acknowledgements

I'm sincerely grateful to my family members, friends and professional associates who contributed their expertise and enthusiasm during the revision of this new edition.

I especially want to thank my dad, Ed Mandell, who contributed a lifetime's worth of editing prowess and passion, and who braved a forbidding jungle of incomplete sentences, gender-bending and proselytizing, all quite purposely and gleefully included.

And my wife, Terri, whose support and participation lent me much of the strength I needed to complete the process.

My business partner and dear friend Michael Perricone is the model of professionalism from which I've drawn many of my assumptions of how the world of recording should be run. He's also the reason I argue so passionately in favor of partnership. When it works, as our does, it's an intensely powerful union.

Thanks to the managers and owners of studios in the U.S., Canada and the Caribbean who answered some of the hundreds of query letters I sent out for research, and who generously shared their thoughts, interest, materials and belief in the worth of this project. To Dalton Priddy, for reference assistance, and to Joe Gorfinkle, who really went the extra mile.

To my Business and Management students at the Trebas Recording Institute, who contributed new directions, ideas and enthusiasm.

And to Craig Wingate and my friends at MixBooks, who have worked so diligently to redesign, package and promote this major undertaking.

Finally, I thank Joe Csida, who had the bizarre notion to hire me as a teacher at the Trebas Institute of Recording, and in so doing to open up a whole new area of expression in my life, which I have come to love as an integral part of who I have become.

Contents

Foreword

Studios spend a lot of money every year in a seemingly unending quest to attract clients: upgrading equipment, tweaking acoustics, adding that big leather couch for the back of the control room. It's a constant race to keep up with the Joneses. But in the recording industry, the act of merely throwing money at a studio may not be enough keep a facility competitive. As with any other business, a recording studio must to be properly managed in order to be profitable—or even to break even.

Unfortunately, information on the studio business can be difficult to find; it's usually limited to articles in industry journals such as *Mix* and occasional seminars held by SPARS (the Society of Professional Audio Recording Services). Now, the revised, expanded edition of *The Studio Business Book* offers a step-by-step guide to operating and managing a professional recording facility. Author Jim Mandell—co-owner of a multiroom facility in the Los Angeles area and an instructor at the Trebas Institute of Recording Arts—is a seasoned veteran in the art of studio management, and he demonstrates his mastery of the subject in this solid, well-written and carefully organized text.

Appropriately enough, *The Studio Business Book* begins with the basics: formulating a business plan, estimating studio startup costs (from bare-bones to world-class rooms), finding a location, getting funded and making equipment purchases. From there, Mandell takes you through the mundane but necessary details of business operation: accounting, phone and utility services, insurance plans, promoting your venture and increasing revenues. The final chapters cover the fine art of studio management: scheduling sessions, dealing with clients, hiring and firing employees, upgrading equipment and coping with disasters of all sorts.

Interspersed throughout the text are numerous "ProFiles," mini-interviews and advice from experts in every facet of the business, including The Power Station's Zoe Yanakis, noted film-score composer Frank Serafine, remote-recording specialist Bob Skye, post-production ace George Johnsen of EFX Systems and 20 other industry luminaries. These ProFiles reinforce points from the text and paint a realistic picture of the modern studio landscape.

The Studio Business Book is a thoughtful, informative text that will prove to be money well-spent for anyone interested in the art and science of operating a professional recording studio. And at $34.95, its return on investment is a lot higher than that all-important second espresso machine for the upstairs studio lounge. Definitely. —*George Petersen*

The editor of Mix *magazine, George Petersen has written nearly 500 articles on audio technology and operates a 24-track recording facility in the San Francisco area.*

To my son Danny,

who constantly reminds us

how utterly simple love can be

1

Looking Out from the Inside

Book some time in the average professional recording studio, and you'll find a quiet sanctuary with a smiling receptionist who'll greet you at the door, make you feel at home and lead you confidently through the heavy doors into a hushed control room. There, in an atmosphere aglow with console lights, readout panels and the soothing whisper from just a touch of speaker hiss, you'll find a galaxy of possibilities and a skipper who's more than willing to steer the ship for anyone who's got the price of admission. Welcome.

Now that you've arrived, suppose we get started by tearing the place apart? Our aim is to examine all of the nooks and nuances that form this magical ark. We'll take a close look at the personal, managerial and philosophical aspects, and walk through the process of starting and maintaining a healthy studio operation.

One good place to start is with the personnel. When you consider the recording studio business as a *service* business, it's easy to understand why a studio's employees may well be its prime asset. In the service sector, it's been shown time and time again that a client's primary connection is with the *individual* providing the desired service. If the level of trust and comfort is there, then the biggest obstacle to getting the job done has been eliminated.

Find a dentist who makes your visit relatively painless and you'll drive the twenty miles to sit in his chair year after year. The same is true to a great extent with studio clientele: Give them the results they're after and you've taken the most important step towards making them permanent members of the family.

MEMBERS OF THE TEAM

Let's look at the staff positions in a typical mid-sized facility. There's usually a receptionist who answers the phones and makes sure arriving clients are cared for and put at ease. The first engineer runs the session, and the second engineer assists (in artist-intensive facilities, there may be no first on staff—many producers prefer working with their own independent engineers). The staff may be rounded out with an owner/manager, an in-house maintenance engineer and, in especially busy operations, a full alternate staff to work the late shift.

The Receptionist

Assuming a session doesn't grind past the morning rush hour, the receptionist opens the building, puts on a pot of coffee and keeps the phones from becoming too disruptive to others as the place surges into consciousness. However, a receptionist in a mid-sized or small studio may have many more responsibilities than his or her counterpart in a larger facility.

In fact, in many facilities, the receptionist is also the studio manager, in charge of booking and traffic as well as billing and some of the marketing and client solicitation. So in a small studio, a receptionist can have far-reaching duties and responsibilities.

In larger, multiroom facilities, receptionists tend to be just that. Usually, they're kept pretty busy answering the phone, routing requests and making people comfortable. In that case, a separate studio manager will take care of booking traffic, clients and staff management.

The Engineering Staff

Engineers—firsts, seconds and interns—are in full charge of the control and live rooms. The first is the authority, responsible for maintaining the quality of the recording and the flow of the work. It's the first's job to efficiently and accurately interpret the client's game plan for the session and to deliver the highest-quality results possible.

Help is provided by the assistant or second engineer, whose job may include setting up the studio for the session, aligning the machines and keeping track of tapes and takes. Paperwork is an important part of the job; the second will often be in charge of filling out the session work order, which notes the work done, hours spent and materials used as a record for billing later on.

There may also be an intern on hand, who is often unpaid and is there to assist the other staff members. He or she may also get invaluable hands-on training that can lead to a paid position as a second. In large operations, interns usually start out as runners, carrying materials all over town. They tend to fare a little better in smaller studios, where their presence may quickly become critical to the smooth operation of the facility.

The Maintenance Engineer

In larger, multiroom operations, a part-time or full-time maintenance tech is a virtual necessity, because an ongoing program of machine maintenance is essential to help prevent major breakdowns. The tech usually has an office in the studio's shop, which is outfitted with enough equipment to handle most emergencies. Good techs are in high demand and are usually paid as well as first engineers; some of the best make even more.

The obvious advantage of having a tech onsite becomes evident when something breaks down mid-session. In a slick operation, the first may be able to isolate the malfunctioning piece of equipment, and if it's not a major component, the second will bypass it and find a temporary solution. The maintenance tech can then either troubleshoot the malfunctioning piece in the control room or bring it back to his bench in the shop for repairs.

With that kind of professionalism and a little luck, it's often possible to maintain the session without interruption. The client may be well aware that something's wrong, but also equally impressed with the efficiency of the repair process. And for the client, the fewer the technical problems, the more reliable the studio. Obviously, in a well-maintained room, visible problems should be the exception to the rule. But when they do occur, a staff tech is invaluable to have around.

The Studio Manager

Sometimes called the traffic manager, the studio manager's prime responsibility is usually scheduling sessions, both internal and external. Scheduling consists of client booking (also called "traffic"), internal staff scheduling, creation of booking and work orders and ensuring that the studio is prepared on time. Keeping everyone's sessions straight is the great ongoing challenge.

The studio manager is also the in-house diplomat, making sure clients are satisfied with the level of service, settling any disputes over real or imagined problems and acting as a general go-between for the engineering and business sides of the operation. It is often best, for instance, for the engineer to refer discussions about rates and billing to the studio manager. Since money is often a sensitive issue, it's to the engineer's advantage to be isolated from fee negotiations, so that he or she can act purely as an artistic liaison. The client can take out financial frustrations on the studio manager, but in the sanctity of the control room, the engineer's only business should be creating the finest possible recording.

Internal scheduling involves creating and maintaining a workable arrangement with all studio personnel, which can be a little daunting when it comes to Friday nights. The manager also oversees or physically outputs the studio invoices and acts as the employee liaison to the studio owner.

The Business Owner

Many owners participate fully in the day-to-day operations of their facilities by acting as studio managers. They may also be chief engineers or producers, or simply opt to be president and final decision-maker.

As you'll see in many of the ProFiles, an owner often starts his or her career as a musician or engineer. Some then rise to ownership by setting up a simple recording operation at home. As time goes by and their table-top setup begins to acquire more power and flexibility, their outboard gear, instrumentation and wiring start spilling into the next room, and their recorded product becomes more and more professional-sounding.

About this time, the once-muted protests of a significant other sharing the same dwelling may begin to become more vigorous. And so one day, the professional realizes his destiny is to create a proper facility—it's worth taking the plunge to fulfill his or her true passion.

Another commercial enterprise is born.

Corporate Owners

There are many owners who have little to do with their studios' day-to-day operations. Most people in this category tend to be investors in higher-volume facilities. Studios are attractive businesses to those who may be successful in another area of the entertainment industry, such as talent or management.

Ownership can also take the form of an investment group adding a studio to its portfolio. For such a group, the studio is more a business opportunity than a career, and one or two full-time managers will assume most of the hands-on decision-making.

A lot of big-name entertainers own studios as well. They buy them to have a place of their own, out of the spotlight, where they can do their homework. (And because their accountants tell them they need the tax write-off—these are the sorts of problems most of us would kill for!)

Finally, there are the giant orchestral stages owned and operated by major film and TV companies. In Los Angeles, cavernous 10,000-square-foot studios occupy movie lots owned by Warner Brothers, Paramount, Sony, Disney, CBS and others, with histories reaching back to the almost daily orchestral film-scoring sessions of the '30s and '40s. These are the rooms where 110-piece ensembles can stretch out and soar while conductors keep an eye on the theater-sized screens running movie prints in sync to the music. There are few privately owned rooms this size, because the major entertainment companies can best afford the enormous operating deficits (by offsetting them in the context of complete film production budgets).

TYPECASTING

Given the unending variety of sizes, styles and services out there, choosing a studio to work in can get pretty confusing. But among the thousands of operations from coast to coast, some fairly universal char-acteristics become apparent when you step back and gather some perspective.

In the Beginning...

It's been estimated that there are fifty thousand 4-track tape recorders in the world. When TEAC came out with the first Model 3340 self-sync 4-track back in 1971, no one could have imagined the kind of spark it would ignite. Suddenly, multitrack recording was within reach of anyone who could scrape a thousand bucks together.

Those were magic machines. With a little ingenuity, you could coax seven, ten or even 13 bounced tracks out of them before everything started to fade into mono mush.

Then came the 4-track portastudios, and cassettes became a viable tape configuration. When 8-track was introduced in the late '70s, the "home studio" became a serious alternative to going commercial. Fostex unleashed its 16-track, Akai introduced its 12-track, and a universe of creators made a pilgrimage to the medium. Affordable multitrack recording became a new business ingredient in a culture that thrived on innovation. Today, 8-, 12- and 16-track rooms turn out a substantial amount of the broadcast-quality product we hear on disk and over the air.

But the advent of affordable digital technology in the '90s really started turning things around. E-mu Systems' Emulator III added 16 pristine virtual tracks to a 30-second commercial. Then came Digidesign's Pro Tools, the Studer/Editech Dyaxis and the Alesis ADAT. Suddenly, tapeless technology wasn't just opening up new vistas of fidelity and manipulation; it was getting *affordable* (as in "Guess I'll just put it on the ol' Mastercard."). And with it came a whole new realm of cottage and professional applications.

There's no question that as we look ahead, digital leads the charge, and that it has forever changed the face of the "classic" recording studio environment.

Keeping the Human Factor in Sight

But one basic truth still rings true, as it always will: If you've got talent, it doesn't matter what you're using; the message is going to get out there and be heard. You can do great work in virtually any of these configurations. 8- and 12-track setups have launched countless bands and songwriters on the road to success. And digital 8- and 16-track have become the formats of choice for thousands of publishers, dance record studios and serious composers.

Most of the information in this book is applicable to any professional setup, regardless of track capability. In terms of output, artistry will always prevail over technology, because the vast majority of us respond to human expression with feelings rather than logic or calculation.

It really doesn't much matter whether you use a Casio or a Synclavier when the song says something that pulls at our hearts. Taken in that context, it seems pretty silly to compare the relative merits of a Neve console vs. a Radio Shack mixer.

What does matter, regardless of the equipment used, is how well the job gets done. Professionally, that means how successfully you pull out the best of whatever it is you're digging for. And in the studio business, it's about how satisfied you and your clients feel once the job is done.

Facing the Music

The only problem with all these competing formats is that they're incompatible with what still remains the proven, cost-effective world standard in professional recording: 24-track.

The beauty of 24-track studio ownership is that once you take the plunge, you find yourself in the very best of company. You've entered the universe of creativity and parity with everyone else who's done it before. It's also the land of no more excuses. Here, you've got the tools that the world has decreed are prerequisites for greatness. Here, either you can cut it or it's time to fill out the "Make Big Money in Court Reporting!" matchbook cover.

Within the 24-or-more-track category there are many strata of class and quality, ranging from $20-per-hour garages to $5,000-per-day country estates. Yet because of the standardization of the format, all are compatible with one another. With 2-inch master reels in hand, you can walk into any of thousands of pro facilities in the world, toss a mix up on the monitors and get down to work.

The difference between the rooms, of course, depends on the level of investment and specialization. So at this point, it may be a good idea to observe some of the major distinctions between them. In a very broad sense, we can place any 24-track room in one of four definable categories.

The Home Project Studio

First there's the home or garage-variety "project studio." A surprising number of pros have home 24-track studios because they've learned that if they're doing a lot of work with their own songwriting or band or scoring, there's no place like home to relieve the pressure of clock-watching, scheduling, lugging equipment and commuting.

You just can't beat a home facility for waking up from a particularly tuneful dream, trotting out to the garage to get it down on tape in five minutes and still managing a good night's sleep. The setups for these home 24-tracks can be quite elaborate, including some facilities that rival the best commercial studios. It can be quite disorienting to admire a beautiful new room in *Mix* magazine, only to realize it's the finished basement in Whitney Houston's summer house!

The home project studio is a logical tool for professional songwriters, composers and producers who want the ultimate convenience. It's also made life more challenging for a lot of major conventional studios, which have lost significant booking time as a result. At the pro recording artist level, a great deal of the less complicated overdubbing now gets done in converted basements and living rooms equipped with compact but substantial professional setups.

But more often, the garage 24-track studio is an outgrowth of a smaller home studio belonging to someone who has moved up to professional status and has begun booking his or her room. (For a detailed discussion on the pros and cons of project studio ownership, see Chapter 5.)

The Commercial Low-Budget Studio

That brings us to the business-zoned, low-budget, commercial 24-track studio. The bottom line in this kind of facility is getting the most bang for the buck so that you can make the best possible presentation for future deals. These are the places that advertise in the local trades and are available at truly amazing rates, starting as low as $20 per hour and usually topping off at about $60.

Low-budget studios are legitimate businesses and have traditionally been the home for older but still reliable equipment. There's a thriving used-equipment market in most major cities, and these are the places where the lower-end pieces often wind up.

It's a simple case of getting what you pay for. If you don't mind some slightly funky surroundings and, say, an MCI JH16 24-track deck that will give you fine analog results, then you can cut a great-sounding product for a modest fee.

The latest trend in low-budget facilities has been the purchase of newly affordable digital multitracks. By 1994, Alesis had sold over 30,000 ADATs, and a great many of them wound up in budget facilities. Digital has redefined the boundaries of broadcast-quality recording—where just a few years ago, a 24-track digital reel-to-reel recorder sold for $130,000, an ADAT setup with similar specs can now be had for about a tenth of that cost.

Budget studios tend to be good places to get on-the-job training, no matter what position you're looking to learn. In fact, they usually have a very high turnover, due to low pay and sometimes combat-like conditions. Nevertheless, many of the studios at this level have been around for a long time, attesting to their staying power and the continuing need for "no frills" recording workshops.

Logically approached, a facility of this size is a good starting point for developing a recording studio business. With intelligent planning and foresight, equipment can be traded up piece by piece as your business grows. And of course, the risk factor is minimized by starting with a low-priced service.

The Midrange Facility

The midrange facility produces professional, first-class results. It's a well-equipped, large, comfortable facility that caters to a variety of clients and sends them home with first-rate mixes. Midrange facilities cater to the TV and film markets, the professional composer, the dance and medium-grade artist market and anyone else who can afford pricing of around $40 to $125 per hour.

Working in a midrange facility is a satisfying experience. Clients usually don't feel the need to spend more for the very best, because they know they're near the point of diminishing returns and are being treated well.

Consoles are medium- to high-quality and often include automation. The 24-track deck of choice is Studer or Otari with Dolby SR, and a good variety of mics and outboard gear is standard. Amek, DDA, Harrison, Trident and vintage Neve consoles are popular.

Care and money has gone into the design of these larger, more comfortable rooms. Staff members are courteous and highly professional. The atmosphere exudes class and importance, and the facility has a settled-in feel to it.

The studio is flexible in its capabilities and responsive to trends and its clients' needs. For a large percentage of the pro market, this type of facility is all that's necessary to complete the job, however large or small.

The World-Class Studio

Finally, there are world-class studios, the ones with international reputations. They're the most expensive, highest-quality places you can find, the ones insisted upon by top producers and artists and major film and TV companies. The view from the producer's chair in their control rooms encompasses the best there is. Little, if anything, has been left wanting here.

Three major factors set the world-class studio apart from all the rest. The first is money. Most facilities in this category are equipped with custom-built Neve or SSL consoles, often with the latest automation package. The analog recorder of choice often sits next to a 48-track digital machine. The effects racks are filled with eight to 20 linear *feet* of outboard gear, and there is often a sophisticated synth setup on the premises.

The building is big and expensively designed and decorated; it may once have been a mansion, a castle or a cattle ranch. The studios and control rooms are rebuilt as often as every three years to stay current with the latest design innovations and most fashionable trends. In short, these studios reek of luxury, quality and money.

The second factor in a world-class studio is the staff. The house engineers are often rising stars in their own right, having been associated with the recording sessions for numerous gold and platinum albums. They're expected to be the hardest-working people in show biz. And the management is often just as famous, with legendary connections to the great stars of the world and the ability to bring them into the studio on a regular basis.

The final factor in making it to world-class is the reputation of the studio itself. Most are known not only for their style and equipment, but for albums and projects that have been recorded there. So the legends precede them and are often their most valuable asset.

Audio rates vary widely but usually start at about $100 per hour and top out at $350 for music and as much a $700 for a giant film mixing stage. For that kind of bread, you're getting the best there is, with a star staff surrounding you in a glittering, hi-tech playground. All you need at that point is the product to go along with it.

Now, When I Snap My Fingers, You Will Awaken Refreshed...

But let's get down to earth. Although you may have been dreaming for years about owning or managing a studio, the step by step process of becoming a successful businessperson is steeped in heavy doses of reality.

How do you get to there from here? Very carefully. Which is to say that any reasonably intelligent, responsible, motivated adult who wants to own a studio can, even if they're broke today. Assuming you have a steady job, you could be up and running within a year or two from the day you make the commitment to do it.

All you have to do is really want it.

16 Rooms and Up to 40 Sessions a Day

Hank Neuberger was in from the start on one of the most successful facility stories around, constantly investing in new technology but ultimately looking to the client/engineer connection with every new room addition.

Facility Among the largest in the country. Currently operating 16 studios in three buildings: four multitrack music studios, nine audio post-production rooms and three duplicating and transfer suites.

Equipment includes a 72-input Neve VR console with Flying Faders, a 64-input SSL 6000E G Series console and Studer analog and Mitsubishi 32-track digital multitracks.

Post bays outfitted with seven AMS AudioFiles, seven Sonic Solutions workstations, three Synclaviers, two E-mu EIIIs and Pro Tools.

On Building Up Started in one building in 1975 and built five studios there. Moved to a second location in early '80s and now have two buildings a block apart, plus a digital editing suite on the 37th floor of the (giant ad agency) Leo Burnett Building.

"It's been a kind of geometric growth, based on intuitive judgment on the part of the owner, Allen Kubica, all along the way. He very early had a good sense of the need to diversify in terms of the markets that we served."

Hank Neuberger

Operations Manager

Chicago Recording Company

Chicago, Illinois

History "When we opened in '75, there were two mixers: Allen and another assistant. Allen turned out to be an even better businessperson than he was an engineer. We were able to do something that's very hard to do in most cities but that seemed to work very well in Chicago. That was to balance advertising work during the day with record work at night in the same music studios.

"We were able to do that right off the bat. We would do commercials during the day for Kentucky Fried Chicken and then do the Ohio Players at night. We did that kind of work for a long time, and this was in the days before there was an SSL console on every corner. Alan always had a philosophy of providing very top-drawer equipment in top acoustic-design spaces and trying to go after the top of the market.

"We've always tried to be first. We had the first 24-track in Chicago, the first automated consoles. Those things are so common today, but they weren't always there."

Engineering Talent "One of the ways we grew the company was by attracting engineering talent. I think that's much more important than equipment. The way we did this was to set up compensation arrangements with the engineers based on how much work they did. So ambitious folks who wanted to be compensated based on how good they were at their job and how good they were at selling their services liked the way that got set up.

"We don't have reps. Essentially, our engineers are our sales people. When a client calls up to work, nine times out of ten, they're calling not so much to work at CRC as to work with Bill, Tim, Hank, Stan or Mike. That's what they call to do.

"It's the staff that's gonna keep your business going and your customers coming back. It's still a people business; it's still a service business. So as a manager, you want to try and identify people that seem to want to build a long career in your town and hopefully keep 'em there, as well as always cultivating the next guy, so that as people do move on, you're not left high and dry."

Studio Proliferation "It's a little hard to predict what the outcome of all this will be. When we opened our first studio in '75, it had a beautiful console and the first 24-track machine in town. We did records for Styx and commercials for United Airlines.

Tim Butler in Chicago
Recording's Studio C1

"Now we have a half-a-million-dollar console, as opposed to that $40,000 console, and the rates that the record companies and the managers and artists are willing to pay are about $100 an hour, the same as it was in '75.

"Obviously, this can't go on forever. So I think there's less and less opportunity for people to make a good living by providing recording services to the record companies. That's not going to be a good way to make a fair profit on your investment."

Career Planning "I think when people get into pro audio, it's very helpful to look at the whole spectrum of it. The number of chairs for guys to do what Bob Clearmountain or Bruce Swedien do are very few. Broadcasting, audio for post, commercials, film, TV and the explosion of outlets that need to be fed is almost unimaginable. If music is all you live for, great. But be aware that there are a lot of gratifying and challenging opportunities outside of the narrow specialty of recording music."

Predictions "As far as the hardware angle, I think you're going to see pressure from both ends. Obviously the digital 8-track gear is very capable, but if you as a studio can offer something a little different, whether it be a big room that sounds better than a bedroom, or maybe some classic equipment that most people can't get a handle on, there's always going to be a need for that.

"For storage, I think we're going to continue to see lots of digital workstation options, but the beauty of 24-track is that it still sounds great and you can find one in damn near every city in the world."

Upgrading "It took us about 17 years to get to the top of our market in Chicago. Anybody who thinks this business is recession-proof is mistaken. We continue to invest. You can't stop. This is not a business you can clip your coupons in. We've just bought a dozen workstations, expanded a console and added networked computers for all our communication, filing and invoicing. It's very uncommon for us to spend less than a million dollars every year on new investments."

Philosophy "I feel very fortunate I ended up in this business. I think being around creative people keeps you young. This is a very gratifying place to work in. Most of the people in this business like coming to work in the morning, and if you can keep that environment in your facility, then I think you've got a good chance to prosper."

Writing A Business Plan

The most important item you'll ever need to start up a studio (or any venture) is a plan of action. When that plan has to do with setting up a capital-based business, it's called a business plan. A business plan outlines the way the business is going to start up and operate and serves as a presentation document for lending institutions. A lender is going to want to see some detail on this big idea of yours before it decides to invest its money to help you make it real!

A business plan contains a complete outline and projection of what your recording studio is going to look like, how it's going to do business and a forecast of just how beautifully everything is going to work out.

The reason for having a plan is that you and everyone else who becomes involved can look at a hard copy of your whole idea to see if it really looks feasible. The process of actually writing a business plan is quite creative, challenging and time-consuming, but it's also an educational and rewarding experience.

The plan is the most important document you're going to need as you put your studio business together. Fortunately, there are lots of good books on preparing them, as well as complete and affordable software packages, with obvious names like BizPlan Builder, that will guide you through each step and print out a beautiful package in the end. Whichever way you choose, you'll be well rewarded with open doors if you spend quality time in the woodshed first.

Dividing the Plan Into Sections

A business plan for a recording studio should start out with an introduction saying something like, "This is a business plan for a recording studio," and go on to introduce its principals (the chief officers of the company), with a brief biography of each.

Next comes the written outline showing how you'd set up the studio, including a proposed location, an idea of what the studio would look like, a detailed list of the needed equipment and general overview of how you'd see the business working and growing.

Then comes the fantasyland section: the cash-flow projection. This is a detailed spreadsheet or chart estimating how much money you think the studio will make and how much it will cost to operate on a month-to-month basis in the first year or two. Included in the spreadsheet should be a complete list of all anticipated expenses and income broken down into clearly defined categories.

Cash-flow projections are places either to attempt to get real or to go off the deep end and wind up in Disney World. You'll probably find yourself doing a little of both. But if you give it an honest shot and try to be realistic, it's a great way for you and your lender to get an intelligent overview of your whole plan in black and white.

You'll also need to include an extended three-to-five-year projection. This is the place where dreamed-of potential and possibility lives, roughly outlining the spectacular growth you foresee for the business on a monthly or seasonal basis. (By the time Year Four had rolled around in the original plan my partner and I had written for our studio, called Interlok, we'd projected bicoastal offices and had scouts looking for suitable locations in Europe. In Year Five, we proclaimed ourselves joint rulers of our own countries, smallish Balkan states that have since lost their former allure.) You might want to think twice about getting that carried away, however. Bankers don't seem to catch the humor as easily as in the pre-S&L-crisis days.

Finally, you'll need to include a personal financial statement, which is a detailed summation of your net worth, along with copies of your tax returns from the past two or three years. This should cement the realization that you're going to need to have earned income and filed your tax returns.

Taking Your Time

A business plan, as you may have surmised by now, requires a lot of time-consuming work. It can take months to put one together that includes all the proper elements and feels right too. It did for my partner, Michael Perricone, and I when we put our plans on paper.

But we also got a little creative with ours. That's because we knew we were going to have to impress a lender with *something*, and what we lacked in financial strength we would have to make up for in imagination, talent and charm. Unfortunately, to a banker, a great deal of your appeal has to do with your current assets. At the time, the two of us lived in rented apartments, drove five-year-old cars and figured that a good time out on the town included making a drive-through burger stand pit-stop and maybe rolling a few high scores at the local Bowl-O-Drome.

So to make up for our lack of financial strength, we decided to fill our business plan with pizzazz. We packed it with photos, brainy ideas and colorful prose. And because we were dealing with music, an extremely star-struck world, we even included a musical demo tape in our package. We'd put our ties and jackets on, go to each bank on the list and tell that lucky lender about how our amazing and unique business plan would propel us into the forefront of success.

Then, as a final gesture, when we were standing up and getting ready to leave, I'd say to the loan officer, "You know we really enjoyed meeting with you today, Mr. Scrooge. Maybe you'd be interested in getting to know a little more about what we really do." And I'd hand him a demo tape with about 15 minutes of the widest possible range of our best stuff from the last few years.

It wasn't easy getting the loan, but everyone loved getting that tape, and a few people liked it enough to try and help us close in on the right lender.

Do you really need to include a demo tape in your business plan? Of course not. But then again, if you're a *talented* musician, why leave it out?

The Elements of a Business Plan

Here's a list of the components of a recording studio business plan and some suggestions on how to give it a little more sizzle.

1. The Cover and the Title Page
As on a book, the cover simply states the name of the proposed business. You can also include an abbreviated description. The cover might read:

The Jam Factory

A Business Plan
For a Professional Recording Facility

The first page inside is the title page, with the name of your company centered near the top. Below, or down in the lower right-hand corner, names, addresses and phone numbers of the principals are listed. It's also wise to list your accountant's and attorney's names and phone numbers.

2. Table of Contents
Lists each section of the plan with a corresponding page number.

3. Introduction
A brief bio of who you are and what kind of business you want to start. It shouldn't be more than a paragraph or two on each person. Sadly, no one will care about your paper-route Certificate of Merit or your straight A's in dental hygiene. Keep it short and relevant.

4. Financial Package
A single page that lists your equipment and start-up costs, followed by a list of available, on-hand sources of capital. Following that, the loan amount you're asking for. Finally, a bottom-line figure with the amount that will be left the day you open for business. That amount is called your *beginning cash*.

5. Startup and Marketing Plan
This is where you detail exactly how you intend to open your doors, and what your immediate goals are for getting customers to walk in through them. Here, you reveal the research you've done on the existing marketplace and how your business will coexist with the competition.

You should also discuss your marketing strategy, as well as ideas for advertising and specialization.

6. Available Collateral

First, make a detailed list of any related professional equipment you already own that is free and clear of lien. That means all the instruments and electronics you have that you're not still making payments on. You can list those that are partially paid for too, but technically you should also note how much of each is yours and how much belongs to Mastercard.

Then, on a separate page, give another detailed list of the equipment you intend to purchase. Since the loan or lease you're applying for is to purchase this equipment, it too becomes available collateral in the lending company's eyes.

7. Cash-Flow Projection

A 12- to 24-month spreadsheet detailing all projected income and expenses for the first year, listed on a month-to-month basis (see illustration).

8. Detail of the Cash-Flow Projection

A description of the listed items on the projection that clearly defines the reason for each item.

9. Growth Plan

A forecast that outlines your ideas for continued marketing and growth over the next two to five years, with *reasonable* projections of expected income.

10. Personal Balance Sheet

A detailed one-page summation of your net worth. Your accountant should help with this page to make sure everything necessary is included. What, you don't have a personal accountant? Now's the time to get one. A good one will not only help you get to the bottom line, but also help open lenders' doors to you.

11. Tax Returns

Usually the previous three years will suffice. If the business is a partnership, all partners must include their complete returns. This gives the bank an instant snapshot of where you're coming from financially. A healthy income history will certainly benefit you, but low figures won't automatically slam any doors.

12. Cover Letter

This should be clipped to the front inside page of the package with a personalized introduction to the lender and a brief overview of what the business plan is about, along with your phone number and address. Clipping it on will get the reader's attention and give him or her the quickest overview of what the whole package is about.

13. Options and Extras

These are items that can enhance your package and make it stand out from the rest.

Pictures are sure-fire attention getters. Position yourself in front of a long console or an impressive rack of equipment, and a lender may linger over the print, ogling all the sliders and knobs.

Market studies and **comparison charts** show that you're really doing your homework and are aware of the local market. Mention three or four competitors by name and show how your facility will compare, using pie or bar charts for extra visual impact.

Full-blown resumes, including names of people and projects, can make you appear more glamorous and add to your integrity.

Brochures and **ads** from any previous businesses in which you've been involved can be very impressive, because they show the lender you've accomplished other things and know what you're doing.

Advertisement mockups for your new business are a great showcase for your marketing plan. The more visual a picture you draw, the more a banker sees the reality, potential ingenuity and sincerity of your intent.

And a **cassette tape** is something a banker rarely gets or expects. If you're a musician, wait for the right moment and offer a tape of your best material. Involving a non-musician in your life by sharing your music is a unique gesture that will set you apart from the crowd. (Note: Be sure (ahem) that the music is appropriate! Let's be careful out there and not alienate any potential lenders with your late-night cop-killer rap sessions, okay?)

A **videotape** may have an even more spectacular effect. If you're coming off a commercial record with a professional MTV production, use it and impress the hell out of your banker. But if it's something your sister shot for TV class, save it for your relatives.

Another interesting approach might be to make a good-quality video of you at work. If, for instance, you're a working engineer at a busy studio, five minutes of you at the console, taking a directorial role, touring the facility and commenting on its strengths and weaknesses in relation to your vision of your own business could be very compelling. So could a tour of your home setup, a potential location for your proposed facility, or a series of endorsements from friends and community leaders.

But again, be careful with this stuff. Review the material from the standpoint of the banker and ask yourself if this would impress a conservative first-time viewer, or if you're just coming across as a puffed-up pretender. You must present a professional image to be taken seriously. This would be a good time to ask a couple of trusted friends to look at your package and offer some honest feedback. Don't be shy—you need all the help you can get by the time you've reached this point.

Finally, **letters of recommendation and support** from associates and friends add credibility and integrity to your whole presentation, saying that you're known and respected.

Handing It Over

After you've done all that, don't skimp on the package itself: Get it spiral-bound at your copy store or put it in a good looseleaf binder. Give the cover a professional look using large computer type that has been laser-printed. Or buy a sheet of transfer letters from a local art store.

THE LOGIC IN WRITING IT OUT

Working up a great business plan isn't an absolute guarantee of getting the money you want, but it will certainly get you more attention than the average six-page proposal to open a *Socks 'n' Shoelaces Only!* store.

And if you truly are light in the cash department, you're going to need all the sizzle you can muster to take its place. The idea is to come across as a viable business person who at least has the savvy to get the ball rolling and keep it going.

The other thing that happens as a result of pouring yourself into a detailed plan is that *you'll* get a very realistic idea of what your business is truly going to be like. You'll begin to see where your weaknesses are and how to use your strengths to compensate for them. You'll get dozens of ideas, mull over all sorts of situations and have the chance to write them out to see just how good they look when they're down on paper.

The beauty of writing a business plan is that it truly helps you to manifest the goal you have in mind. The plan forces a sharp focus on your once-hazy dream and makes it more real with each hour you spend pulling it out of the clouds. It's a very exhilarating experience, and one that can push you over the edge toward success.

Without a business plan, you're simply going on instinct. And although that approach may work in a flashy detective series, you can bet that the cool dude in the Ferrari's got a nerd sidekick sitting in front of a PC back at the station, working out his partner's next move during the commercial breaks.

Know what's coming and you've got a whole lot better shot at the gold badge.

"I'll Have the 'Two Basically Broke Partners on a Dream Roll,' Please...And Hold the Mayo."

What follows are some of the actual pages from the business plan we cooked up in 1984 when my partner and I went after funding for our studio. We cooked, by the way, on an Apple IIe computer, your affordable state-of-the-art in those days. I mean, this baby could underline *and* do boldface.

But it should be obvious that the equipment you use has little to do with the success of the plan. Whether you buy it at Toys R Us or at Really Big BusinessLand, your computer is only as good as the thought and the time you put into the writing of your plan.

Our plan was chock-full of graphs, photos and letters of recommendation that helped to cast ourselves in a positive and memorable light. And the music cassette we included went over great.

Did we get the money? In a word, yes. In a sentence, yes—after a couple hundred phone calls and 14 sit-down appointments over a two-month period. Our lender was a small leasing company whose president brought us back three times on a 50-mile drive before he finally intoned the magic words, "Tell you what, guys. I'm gonna take a chance on you..."

Pages From Our Original Business Plan

1ST YEAR CASH FLOW PROJECTION

Month	DEC	JAN	FEB	MAR	APR	MAY
Beginning Cash	53,250	56,300	59,800	65,235	71,810	83,110
EXPENSES						
Production Team	1050	1580	2125	2850	2500	3500
Studio time	3600	3200	3150	3000	3000	3000
Video Post	6200	6320	6560	7000	6800	7000
Jingle record	–	300	1000	1000	1000	300
2nd Shift	–	–	500	625	900	900
Equipment rent	300	300	300	300	300	300
Tape sales	400	300	300	300	300	300
Prod. fees	–	–	–	–	5000	5000
TOTALS	11,550	12,000	13,935	15,075	19,800	20,300
EXPENSES						
Rent	3500	3500	3500	3500	3500	3500
Finance pmt	1600	1600	1600	1600	1600	1600
Salaries	2000	2000	2000	2000	2000	2000
Insurance	100	100	100	100	100	100
Telephone	200	200	200	200	200	200
Office/Supplies	50	50	50	50	50	50
Advertising	350	350	350	350	350	350
Attny/Acct.	150	150	150	150	150	150
Maintenance	300	300	300	300	300	300
Misc.	250	250	250	250	250	250
TOTAL EXPENSES	8,500	8,500	8,500	8,500	8,500	8,500
ENDING CASH	56,300	59,800	65,235	71,810	83,110	94,910

TABLE OF CONTENTS

Top left: Every picture tells a story. Here, the partners are professionally photographed in a setting that reeks of success.

Top right: A cash-flow projection charts predictions of income and expenses on a month-to-month basis.

Left: A table of contents makes it easy for the lender to find everything.

```
1ST YEAR FORECAST - Detail


MONTH 1

Do mailing to all established clients and friends a month
before opening the studio, offering special discounts during
opening weeks.
On opening, book lined up clients for studio and production
time.
Finalize booking schedule for video post production recording
of "Mad Movies with the LA Connection" TV series.
Run ad in Music Connection magazine and start meeting with
potential production clients in the studio.
Rent Emulator keyboard and other equipment for outside studio
bookings through professional rental agent on regular basis.


Production Team @349.       10 hours        $1050
Studio time @30. sale price 120 hours        3600
Video Post Production @60.   10 hours         600
"Mad Movies" TV series       package price   5600
Record jingle demo                            300
Profit from blank recording tape sales to clients  400
Equipment rentals                             300
                                           $11,850



MONTH 2

Get contracted to do an advertising jingle demo.
TV series goes into full swing, booking 20 hours per week.
Add to new client list. Host a promotional event for the
studio.
Record commercial jingle demo for ad agency.
Host promotional event at the studio.


Production Team @395.       4 days          $1580
Studio time @40.            80 hours         3200
TV series                                    5600
Video post @60.             12 hours          720
Jingle demo                                   300
Equipment rentals                             300
Blank tape sales                              300
                                           $12,000
```

Top left: Detail pages immediately follow the cash-flow projection, explaining how we came up with the figures.

Top right: Michael posed in front of the longest console he was scheduled to engineer at that month, again adding pictorial credibility to the presentation.

Right: A market study pitting our business against the established leaders shows that we've taken a serious look at the competition.

```
COMPARISON: INTERLOK vs. the Competition


Only three other studios in LA offer comparable production services for
songwriters, singers, and groups. We visited each to evaluate their approach,
and came out way ahead in benefits to the client.
```

features:	INTERLOK STUDIOS	Intelligent Productions	Lawrence Productions	Classic Sound
Number of audio tracks	24	16	24	24
Professional quality studio	YES	no	no	yes
Video interlock recording	YES	no	no	no
Free in-house producer/arranger	YES	yes	no	no
2 pros on every session	YES	no	yes	no
All instruments included free	YES	no	yes	yes
Top rated digital synthesizer	YES	yes	no	no
Top rated analog synthesizer	YES	no	no	no
Top rated sampling synthesizer	YES	no	no	no
Choice of drum machines	YES	no	no	no
Digital sequencer recorder	YES	yes	no	yes
Computer & music programs	YES	no	no	no
Rate per hour	60	70	60	65

STUDIO 2 12 MONTH CASH FLOW PROJECTION												
Month	NOV	DEC	JAN	FEB	MAR	APR	MAY	JUN	JUL	AUG	SEP	OCT
Beginning Cash	0	7800	17450	24925	29025	37800	46450	56675	62075	67125	77125	90225
Income												
Audio to Video	15050	17200	14200	11000	15200	16100	16500	10100	9200	13450	17200	21900
Audio Only	2700	3000	2100	1700	2200	3100	3000	4900	5000	6300	6100	4200
Voiceover	700	900	1200	700	900	1300	1800	800	800	1100	1100	700
Night Rates	400	600	700	1200	1400	700	200					
Total Income	18850	21700	18200	14600	19700	21200	21500	15800	15000	20850	24400	26800
Expenses												
Rent	1200	1200	1200	1200	1200	1200	1200	1200	1200	1200	1200	1200
Salaries + OT	5000	5500	4000	4300	4800	5200	4400	4300	4000	4200	4400	5300
Console	3600	3600	3600	3600	3600	3600	3600	3600	3600	3600	3600	3600
Utilities	350	400	375	350	350	400	425	350	350	400	450	450
Insurance	400	400	400	400	400	400	400	400	400	400	400	400
Maintenance	250	350	300	250	300	600	450	250	150	200	450	350
Petty Cash	250	300	250	250	275	350	350	300	250	350	400	350
New Equipment	0	300	600	150	0	800	450	0	0	500	400	0
Total Expenses	11050	12050	10725	10500	10925	12550	11275	10400	9950	10850	11300	11650
Profit	7800	17450	24925	29025	37800	46450	56675	62075	67125	77125	90225	105375

Left: A cash-flow projection done with more current software imparts a very organized look.

Bottom: Yes, but can he rock 'n' roll? The author in his then-current home studio, attempting a non-threatening, preppy look for the bankers, circa 1984

Signing the Deal

A week later, we returned late in the afternoon to sit at a small desk in a little room, as one multipage contract after another was placed before us. Bank accounts attached. Auto ownership documents pledged. Life insurance valued. Power of attorney granted. Surveillance cameras in our bedrooms...

We kept looking up at the executive and secretary who were producing page after page marked with little red X's denoting where to sign. "More?" "More."

I decided, for entertainment value, to ask the question that was burning inside of me. "Let me make sure I understand this," I muttered, putting my pen down and uncrimping my hand. "All this legalese about you basically owning our souls for the next three years—what if after all the time and effort everyone's put into this deal, if as badly as we wanted this to happen, seeing as we've just spent the last two months setting our whole operation up on a schedule that hinges on this deal (in which you happen to be charging a rather enormous interest rate, based on some silly notion that more new businesses fail than succeed), what if I were to *object* to just *one* of these contract clauses, or refuse to initial some page bottom, or skip one of these little red X's that indicate each place we're supposed to sign? Why, we just flat out wouldn't get the money, would we?"

I looked up and blinked at the executive who was calmly towering over me, up past the Armani suit jacket half-revealing the monogrammed dress shirt, past the thick mustache trying to somehow camouflage the receding hairline of a middle-aged man who radiated comfort and ease, probably anticipating his impending commute home in the gleaming pearl-white-lacquer Porsche Carrera with the ALL MINE personalized plates that was parked outside.

Our eyes met for a second, and I smiled wanly, eyebrows raised in expectation. He chuckled in a fatherly tone, and gave his head half a nod.

"Right," he smiled, calmly pointing at the pen.

Jumping from Demo to Broadcast Services

Squeezing out the biggest bang for the buck, Bob Stark wears three hats while battling for a share of the healthy Portland market, buying ad space and offering extra studio features to help keep the bottom line in the black.

Career Roots Originally a jazz keyboardist and recording artist, he got frustrated working with engineers on sessions because they seemed to act more like producers than engineers working for the artist. Eventually landed at a facility with an owner whose attitude reflected his own.

Facility One room. Otari MX-80 32-track 2-inch with Dolby SR, 26-input Amek Matchless console. "Just to be running as a 32-track studio is a plus in our market." Budget keyboard stack permanently installed with Mac software. Studio 24' x 22', control room 18' x 20'.

House Staff Two first engineers, one second.

Primary Focus Owner Dan Decker estimates a mix of about 70% record work and 30% audio for video, equally divided between pop, jazz and country.

Marketing "The music stores up here are very willing to include ads in their mailers. We get a lot of action from those. We've tried the Yellow Pages with an eighth-page ad, but we're lucky if we get a half-dozen calls from that per year, let alone an actual client. We do a lot of direct mail and usually send out about a thousand pieces. There are six or seven studios in the area, and we're probably the newest 24-plus-track studio in Portland, so we have to offer some pretty low rates."

Billing "We've had a tough time collecting on several accounts in the past. We tried mailings, collection agencies, credit bureaus, etc. But to a great extent, we were unsuccessful in the end. That led us to our present C.O.D. policy.

"We worked up a contract of terms with our lawyer. That led to a slight drop in the number of people who book time here, but the percentage of people who pay on time has increased. We also require a deposit for a percentage of the time booked before hand. Since the average time between booking and the actual project startup is usually about a month, we do the whole process through the mail."

Rates "We have a ten-hour block rate, but if the client goes over that, we revert back to our basic hourly rate, which is about $10 per hour higher. Our rates average about $45 per hour, but we charge $60 for 32-track."

Management "Right now I'm functioning in three capacities, as bookkeeper, manager and engineer. And boy, if I could focus on just engineering, I know our projects would be that much better. Then maybe we could afford to have a studio manager/receptionist. But I also know that in the Portland market, the rates are so low that the budget won't allow for that.

"On the other hand, since the rates *are* so low, it's actually cheaper for bands to come up from L.A., find a place to live for a month and record here. So we wouldn't be getting that work if it wasn't for the attractiveness of the rate."

Image "We originally tried to achieve an art deco look for the studio, but it ended up being really cold. You might as well have hung fluorescent lights up in the room. So we redesigned the control room to move from a sanitary corporate look to a much more homey atmosphere. Lots of wood and softer lighting.

"A lot of times, the studio doesn't have time to get cleaned between sessions. But you

Bob Stark

Engineer/Manager

Sound Impressions

Portland, Oregon

SOUND IMPRESSIONS

**The Sound Impressions
control room**

never know when the corporate people are gonna walk in, and it's important for them to see the place in good shape. The chances are a lot better that they'll book time if there isn't a bunch of garbage and drink cans laying around. It sounds petty, but it's one of the things the clients notice right off."

Problems "Having been a jazz artist, it gets a little intense for me at times, what with all the heavy metal going on around here. But I'm still able to maintain a professional attitude with my clients. Since there's so much metal music in the marketplace, you just have to hang in there, and that includes the high-decibel monitoring. The saner dates tend to be the icing on the cake right now."

3

How Much Does It Cost?
How Much Have You Got?

The key element a potential lender will scrutinize in a business plan is the loan package section. That one page will sum up everything in the book and should spell out exactly what you're after in dollars and cents. It's these figures they'll keep in the front of their minds as they consider your whole proposal.

The chances are that you're going to have a lot better luck getting what you're after if you map out a detailed plan of not only how you'll be successful in business, but exactly how you'll spend your money (this works much better than just approaching someone, suggesting they lend you a hundred grand and promising you'll send them a copy of your first hit record).

So let's talk money. What will quickly become apparent is that over the last few years, the industry has experienced some of the most far-reaching and fundamental changes in basic recordable media it has ever seen.

Buying Into Raging Technology

The technological revolution is as mind-boggling as it is exciting (not to mention scary). No sooner does one fabulous new innovation appear than a half-dozen improvements sprout up, dotting the marketplace with further enhancements and price-plummeting shakeups. And you can bet that a whole new approach to the answer that has just been successfully marketed is already on the way.

Look at the advancements in digital workstations, hard drives, multitrack recorders, and digital and virtual consoles. Or the coming digital superhighway. About the only thing that remains true to form seems to be microphones—the warmth you get from some of the tube

models that were built 40 years ago hasn't been topped yet. But you can bet somebody's working on changing all that, too.

Deciding what to buy in light of all this rampaging progress requires some solid research, informed decision-making and, well, just plain courage. What seems guaranteed is that the pace of change will quicken with time. Stories pop up in the trades about the big equipment shows in which the public views the latest computerized rollout products, while the real insiders get invited into the back room to look at the specs for the equipment already planned to make the current crop obsolete by the same manufacturer!

With that kind of omnipresent change, you need to move back a little to keep your perspective straight. In the early '80s, Bill Gates said the software developers were destined to become the most powerful force in the computer revolution. Back then, a lot of people scoffed, but no one's laughing now.

So buy with an eye to intelligent upgrading. Make sure the equipment you choose has the kind of support that will keep it current and usable for a reasonable period of time, instead of becoming yesterday's disposable gimmick. Be aggressive about researching software support from the manufacturers. Find out what their plans are for the next year or two. Read the trades to keep up with industry trends and then try to look ahead to where and when you think the current wave will land. Talk to as many knowledgeable people as you can find. Go to shows and demos. Ask a lot of questions.

Find out what products other people are buying, and why. There may be a trend or a particular manufacturer that has found favor in your region of the country. For instance, in L.A., most session keyboardists use the same sequencing program, making compatibility a snap. It may not be the best overall program, but it's become the standard, thus making it a near necessity; buying another brand is a potential liability. And interestingly, the choice is different in other cities.

I once attended an equipment seminar in which a questioner lamented, "How the heck am I supposed to know what to buy amidst all this moving-target technology?" *Moving-target technology.* What a great summation of the buyer's dilemma!

The presenter smiled for a moment and then intoned the words, "Study, aim, fire."

A BUYER'S PRIMER

The following plans demonstrate that you really can put together a classic, professional 24-track studio from scratch for a lot less money than most non-owners might think. These examples are exercises in attempting to piece together the smallest amount of the best possible quality equipment for the lowest possible price and still winding up with a real honest-to-goodness facility with professional results.

The equipment lists that follow are just examples of the kind of 24-track studio that would serve a wide variety of demo and low-budget professional needs. There's lots of room for variation and personal preference, but the idea is to prove the affordability of an effective and useful beginning setup.

A key element in setting up a budget room is to take full advantage of the used professional gear market. The beauty of this worldwide bazaar is that there are thousands of used items floating around the planet at bargain prices. Much of this gear is in reasonable to excellent condition, because its former home was a pro studio that maintained high standards.

In major cities like New York, Chicago, Nashville, San Francisco and L.A., there are a number of used-equipment consignment dealers, who represent current owners and sell their gear at a commission by listing them in direct-mail catalogs and calling established contacts. One way to find used equipment is to look up these dealers and call them with specific requests. Often, they'll act as a search service for you if they don't already have the gear you want. To find these dealers, call dealers of *new* equipment and ask them where you can buy used.

Other ways to find gear include looking in the local used-merchandise weekly paper in your area (or even running an "equipment wanted" ad), checking the classifieds in pro publications like *Mix* and *Pro Sound News* and calling local studios to ask if they have (or know of) equipment for sale.

If all this sounds like a lot of trouble, well, it is. But the rewards are well worth the struggle. Buying used can save you 20% to 80% off the original price, and it's a key factor in assembling a pro-quality studio with a limited budget. But you must be aware of what it is you're buying.

Remember: *Caveat Emptor!*

That's Latin for "Let the buyer beware." Above all, be careful out there; if you don't have the technical knowledge to know a good buy from a worthless one, find someone who does. When you buy used, there are no returns, and often the seller is not fully qualified in the operation, nor aware of the compatibility, of the gear. So you're on your own. You may find yourself dealing with the purchase of some very expensive stuff. Give it at least the same consideration you'd exercise in the purchase of a car or, when the numbers warrant, a *house*.

It makes good sense to find an engineer or maintenance person who has first-hand experience with the gear in question, and to convince (or pay) them to come along and inspect each item before you buy. Remember that buying just one expensive wrong piece could force you into becoming a used equipment dealer yourself, which probably isn't what you had in mind. So be sure your choice is an intelligent one. And then make sure everything's right with the equipment itself.

In terms of selection, if you're assembling a studio for hire, try to stay with equipment that potential clients know and trust. Avoid buying esoteric or cheap, off-brand gear. You may make a great deal on it, but you'll be faced with a much more difficult time in selling your *clients* on the idea of working with your marvelous talent in a less than ideal atmosphere. Ask yourself: Will I be able to get a good price for this when *I* want to sell it? And: How come I've never even *heard* of an Acme Atomic Reverb Transducer?

Do some research. Look around when you're in other studios. Notice what gear seems to be common to all of them and consider the validity of those pieces. The less explaining you have to do to potential clients, the sooner you'll be able to get your business up and running on a level equal with others in the field.

Analog or Digital

We've now entered an age of incredible advances. Unquestionably, the most spectacular has been the passing of the torch from analog to digital and the subsequent plummeting prices of digital machines. It's quite amazing to many veterans that a few short years ago, a good analog 24-track would set you back about $35,000 to $40,000, and nowadays a component digital setup with far superior signal-to-noise ratio and dynamic range can be had for 25% of the cost.

For my money, there's no looking back. Digital multitrack recording keeps getting more sophisticated and cost-effective seemingly every *week* or two. But to you purists out there, my respect and admiration. No one can tell you digital sounds as compelling as analog, and there's no question you've got a point there.

The astonishing fact is that you can now acquire a classic 24-track analog deck for just a bit more than a digital setup. So we've included it as an option in the following layout. And even major digital cowboys still give great weight to an analog/Dolby SR setup. It's not affordable in a low-budget permutation but could easily be added somewhere down the road.

The Market for the Rest of the '90s

For assistance in deciphering the dizzying menu of hardware choices in the current marketplace, I asked Joe Gorfinkle, a product specialist at Westlake Audio in Hollywood, to help tailor some lists to particular situations.

Joe has been in sales and product development for the better part of his 20 years in the audio industry. He's been a good friend to many a studio owner in L.A., including us at Interlok, and has always had the time and the resources to handle a wide variety of customers.

One of his more endearing qualities is his droll sense of humor, which gives him a unique take on the studio business. I interviewed him on three separate occasions to get an update on buying trends for various levels of investment, and have included his running commentary on several topics verbatim. The initials *JG* appear when the words are his.

Trends in the Marketplace

JG: "The market at the low end is really fragmented, between Tascam DA-88s, Alesis and Fostex ADATs, narrow-format 24-track machines and this week's newest marvel. The fact is, you can now assemble a digital 24-track system for under $11,000, plus, say, $5,000 for a decent low-cost 24x8 console.

"Since these are compact, rack-mounted units, you can take a rack to the studio and dump it onto whatever is in the control room, or simply bring your ADATs into the studio and mix. It's not just little guys recording surf bands any more. There are major studios doing this. With the advent of virtual tracks, a lot of people don't need 24 tracks any more.

"The line between high-end and low has really become big and blurry, because of the quality of digital and the down-marketing of it. There used to be two or three small suppliers in town [L.A.], selling very high-ticket items that were mechanically complex and very far-removed from the consumer scene because of their high prices. Now other companies have come along who can afford to make far cheaper, smaller versions of this stuff. But nobody ever listens to a record and says 'Oh, that was mixed on an SSL vs. a Neve,' or 'That's a Quad Eight mix, I hate it.'

"Instead of a 24-track room, what it's gotten down to is whatever you can get away with, by either bringing your work in progress into a larger studio to mix it, or just putting it down on DAT. Since so much of the music is electronic—broadcast production at a reasonable rate, local and mid-market broadcast production and source music, inexpensive TV and dance music—all those are primarily electronic media, so you don't have to have a big room. You either layer it in your computer and have a bunch of synths, going directly to DAT, or a combination of items. Often, a person already has some sort of MIDI system and a set of keyboards, then winds up buying inexpensive multitracks.

"The music guys have really jumped onto ADAT. Sales are better than 30,000 units, which is incredible if you consider that Sony has sold over a thousand DASH multitrack units since 1982. So the base has spread pretty remarkably. Now you're talking about a console and a 24-track combination for $16 to $17K.

"But people are still buying analog machines, especially in post-production. Analog is still the format of choice if you need to take things around from place to place. If you're going to mix to DAT, it doesn't matter what the heck you're doing. It's just a question of what you like. But the needs are different if you're going to take a multitrack master somewhere.

"There are a few reasons why analog is still desirable. One is sonic quality. A lot of people grew up with analog and like the way it sounds. So it's what the artist is comfortable with. There weren't as many choices before. Now you have to be careful about what you choose.

"A lot of the post houses are attracted to the DA-88, for its synchronizing capabilities. But you can still lock up an analog machine in 5 seconds, no problem, and take it to lots of other places to work on it. The big issue is qualifying what you want to do."

A LOW-END, HIGH-QUALITY SETUP

This first configuration is for the musician/songwriter/producer who's primarily interested in setting up a project studio that gives the utmost bang for the buck.

JG: "As a solo artist doing MIDI production, all this artist has to figure out is what he wants to put on tape that isn't already on his sequencer. Maybe a solo, a few comp tracks, then vocals and maybe a guitar solo or two, which if he's careful, he can do with 8 tracks. "

2 ADATs (Big Remote Control not needed unless working with time code)	$6,000
2 Mackie CR1604 mixers	1,800
Tannoy PBM-6.5 monitors	300
Hafler Power Amp Pro 1200	425
Lexicon LXP1 reverb	400
Sony DPSR7 stereo reverb	1,165
Audio-Technica single-pattern condenser mic (or used AKG 414)	800
Total	**$10,890**

[Note: All prices quoted in this chapter reflect realistic street prices as of mid-1994. Though it's impossible to predict market changes, a good rule of thumb is that the more high-end the gear, the more value it retains. Other factors that drive down prices include the introduction of new models, new manufacturers entering the marketplace and technological leaps that render older equipment obsolete.]

"Now, that's going to preclude a lot of knobs and buttons and sends, and you're going to have to maybe pay somebody to build you a patch bay. The trade-off is time and flexibility. You have to be careful about what you do. But if you consider that *Sergeant Pepper* was done on two 4-tracks..."

A Non-Keyboardist Setup

Let's assume you're starting from scratch, and you aren't a keyboard player. Maybe you're a guitarist, or your interest is strictly in the engineering or production end. In any case, keyboard players do have an advantage going in to project-type studio setups, because of all the nifty effects and virtual tracks available from their synths.

Without keyboards, you do need to play a bit of catch-up. But assembling a package is still remarkably affordable and is no longer as daunting a task on the technical end as it used to be.

JG: "It used to be that there were musicians and engineers. Engineers were techno kinda guys and musicians were spaced-out kinda guys. Now, you don't have to have that kind of technical knowledge. You don't have to know how to solder or anything. But the ante goes up, since there are no virtual synth tracks."

3 ADATs	$9,000
ADAT BRC (Big Remote Control)	1,500
Panasonic SV3700 balanced DAT 2-track	1,400
Soundcraft Spirit 24 24x8 mixer	6,000
2 dbx 160XTs	650
6 used Shure SM57 mics	300
Yamaha SPX990 multi-effects processor	750
Sony DPSR7 stereo reverb	1,165
6 Fostex T-20 headphones	420
4 Countryman direct boxes	500
Total	**$20,985**

"Here's a way to really improve the quality of the signal that goes down on tape: Spring for a very good-quality mic preamp and equalizer as an outboard piece and then run stuff you're recording to tape to that. For instance:

API 2-channel rack	$650
API 512B mic preamp	650
API 550B EQ	1,000
or Summit TPA 100 2-channel tube mic preamp	1,600

"Use those items as your primo signal chain, bypassing the console, going right into the multitrack and just using the console to monitor the tracks. Which would basically yield the same signal path as what you'd get at a world-class studio, minus the big room and a whole bunch of channels.

"But for that one channel, you're as good as anybody out there. The pitch is to start off with one or two really good channels and move up."

Total Non-Keyboardist System:	**approx. $24,500**

ADDING A 24-TRACK ANALOG LOCKUP SYSTEM

Here's a more ambitious studio, put together for someone doing a variety of projects, including tapes going to and from other places. This studio wants to draw business from other local studios and post-production studios, the vast majority of which are still using 2-inch tape.

Trident 24 console, 36x24	$22,000

Or a used in-line console along the lines of a:

Harrison Raven	18,000
or an Amek Angela	25,000

JG: "The really classic consoles are worth a lot of money and pretty much everything else has fallen way down in resale value, so there are great deals to be had out there. All the midrange consoles seem to have come way down, with the realities of the market. So the bridge between the place you buy your guitar strings and the place you buy your digital multi-track has changed. The gap has narrowed. And in the meantime, the level of capital investment to return has gone up astronomically in the studio business at the upper end of the market.

"On the other hand, at the lower end, with integrated circuits, surface-mount devices and manufacturing economies of scale, very sophisticated signal processing, recording equipment and consoles have become available with lots and lots of features. Ten years ago, a console that was 24 inputs would probably cost about $20 to $30K for something you could monitor 24 tracks on and get 24 mic inputs on with 3-band sweepable EQ.

"Today, you can buy a console like that for five grand new from a music store. On the other hand, you can also buy a 30K console that's 32-input and has moving faders, computer-controlled internally automated group assignment and its own little touchscreen, like the DC-2000 from Soundcraft.

"So a lot of the professional boards on the market that might have cost $40,000 to $50,000 10 or 15 years ago basically aren't worth a whole lot, because the amount of features they have can be eclipsed by the lower-end product, while not being sophisticated enough to be considered upper-end.

"The exception to the rule might be the classic consoles, like APIs and Neves, which are basically discrete-transistor architecture. So those aren't being bought on the basis of features, but on the quality of sound, because they are classic types of boards, much the same way you'd buy a vintage Fender guitar or a '32 Ford coupe.

"That leaves the independent production groups and film scoring composers and artists/producers who can do most of their music production without having a large commercial facility gravitating towards the middle market. They don't need a large studio to record a full band or orchestra, but on the other hand they're not hobbyists or semi-pro users. The quality coming from them extends to major film scores and the like."

Looking for the Right Gear

Finding the vintage consoles or just mining the whole professional used market is something that should be a part of every studio owner's game plan. To find used-equipment brokers, get a trade journal, like *Mix* or *Pro Sound News*, and look in the back.

JG: "There are good and bad brokers. Ask a broker from across the country for references. Never buy something sight-unseen without having a third-party tech look it over. Then decide if this is something that you're going to want as an investment. How long is this product going to last you? Buying in any other way than that is insane.

"The whole key to being successful today is knowing where you're at—knowing what you want and where you want to go with it. Where you're at is, if you're not technical or aren't working with someone who's technically adept, you should avoid the idea of buying a used console or deck.

"With used equipment, as a rule of thumb, you can expect to spend another ten percent of the purchase price right off the bat on service. You have to be an informed buyer when you're dealing with used gear. Even with consoles, capacitors dry out, switches get dirty, power supplies go out of regulation. They do age, some less gracefully than others. If you're not in a position to assess that technically, you're at a disadvantage. Because if you can't assess it, how the hell are you gonna fix it?"

Adding Video Lockup

"Okay, you've already assembled a credible sound recording system. Now let's add the capability of recording music and effects and mixing to video. In order to be compatible with other pro studios, you'll most likely need to choose a 2-inch tape format."

Choose either

MCI JH-24 24-track deck (used)	$17,000
or Otari MTR90 24-track deck (used)	21,000

Then add:

TimeLine MicroLynx 2-machine synchronizer with built-in time code generator	2,600
House video sync card	200
Third-machine expansion card	1,000
Sony BVU-800 Umatic 3/4" deck (used)	2,500
Good quality 27" video monitor	600
Total approx. $26,900	

"And you've got yourself the makings of a professional audio post bay. By the way, the items that hold their value the most are signal processors and mics, not necessarily tape machines or consoles."

Going Commercial on a Budget

"The middle market [in post work] has fallen out," Joe continued. "So that's a tough place to start. The focus of what we've done at Westlake has broadened. So while we've gone very high-tech with things like fiber-optics, we're also going downscale. We've turned one area into two pre-production studios where people can come in and do MIDI stuff.

"There are still successful mid-level studios, but they *become* mid-level. They don't start out that way. Nowadays, there's a lot better places to make money than to lease and build out a 3,000-square-foot building and spend half a million on renovations and equipment. Which means that the existing facilities are scrambling to work hard and stay afloat.

"In the '80s, large console corporations were offering financing as well as machines. They told midrange studios, 'Look, you need to move up to the A level to really make some money in this business. You need to move up, and we'll give you the first few payments for free.'

"So now, there's a whole lot of people out of business, and some big corporation's got a good write-off. It was almost like money laundering. You sell the machines and you sell the financing. Then you repossess the machines and sell them again.

"There were, of course, exceptions: the artist/producer with a built-in market for his product. But those were and are home facilities in which they are not interested in booking time to outside projects. They need a place where they can really do their own work.

"In regional markets, post-production services can do a lot better. Midrange studios can succeed in places where the market isn't already saturated, which is another thing to research and examine carefully."

A PROFESSIONAL MIDRANGE STUDIO

Now let's take a look at a substantial operation. The idea is to assemble a room that is as versatile as possible, will please a wide range of discriminating clients, and will deliver excellent, broadcast-ready music and audio post results.

It's virtually unthinkable to build such a room without including a solid video interlock setup. With dozens of music shows on TV, along with the voracious appetite of the cable and video market and the fact that you have a flexible budget to work with, it would be just plain foolish to overlook this potent area.

We're thinking in terms of a 15' x 22' control room, a 25' x 35' studio, a reception area, a lounge, offices and storage space. The total area would be about 2,000 square feet.

Here, once again starting from scratch, is a plan for assembling a facility that can deliver excellent results in the fields of commercial album production, TV series, jingles and industrials.

By the way, it's still a wise investment to buy a lot of first-class equipment used, when it can be found. And if you're determined, you'll find it. For prices when new, add about 30% to the starred (*) items.

On Building

JG: "Don't ever build a one-room studio without an option to expand. It's suicide. You can only go so far in a one-room operation. What happens is you build it up, you start getting successful, I call you and want to book into your studio and I can't get in. So I get annoyed and I go somewhere else.

"So you need to leave an opportunity for your business to expand. You also want to have economies of scale. For instance, you can have two live control rooms and one live room. Or a dub room and a pre-lay room, so that you can

Interlok's Studio 4 beauty shot used long exposures and careful lighting to capture the actual image on the monitor.

take advantage of all the things and opportunities you've got.

"You're also going to want to diversify, because in a midrange market you're going to be doing a wide variety of stuff: commercials, jingles, possibly radio production, maybe some local-label record stuff, and demos by night. So you want a synchronizer system, and you want a new or used multitrack analog deck. And you're also going to be influenced by what your clients want."

Basic Pro Video Lockup and Laydown/Layback Gear

To offer pro-quality picture synchronization, you'll need to add the following items to the previous list:

4 Lynx 2 modules and TimeLine KCU controller	$15,000

For laydowns and laybacks:

Ampex VPR 80 1-inch video (used)	20,000
BVW 70 Sony Betacam SP video deck (used)	20,000
Sony DVR10 D2 digital video deck (used)	26,000

Plus a digital editing system, such as:

Digidesign Pro Tools with a high-end Mac	15,000
Total	**$96,000**

Outboard, Mics and Accessories List

Now, let's add a proper complement of mics and equipment, capable of recording a full eight-piece group.

(*) *indicates used equipment*

EFX & Processing

Lexicon 480L digital reverb	$7,500
Lexicon PCM70 digital reverb*	1,200
Eventide H3000 Harmonizer	2,500
TC Electronic 2290*	2,500
4 UREI 1176 limiters*	1,600
2 API limiters*	800
2 pairs of Drawmer 500 noise gates	1,500

Mics & Accessories

1 Neumann U87*	1,000
2 AKG 414s*	1,200
2 Neumann KM84s*	400
5 Sennheiser 421s*	1,000
2 AKG 460s*	500
1 AKG D112*	300
4 Countryman direct boxes	375
6 AKG 240 headphones	540

Miscellaneous

Toshiba 6-line phone system with 8 phones	3,000
Studio & office Macintosh systems	4,500
Steinway Model M grand piano*	7,000
Studio and office furniture	2,500
Cords, connectors and professional wiring	6,000
Total	**$45,915**

Business Expenses

Next, you need to add the various expenses necessary to cover the startup of your studio as a business.

Rent
figuring 2,000 sq. ft. @ 1.50 per month — $3,000

Security deposit
1 month — 3,000

Electric, water & gas deposits — 600

Telephone company
Line installation charges and deposit — 500

Legal and accounting fees
Financial statements, dba,
  lease and partnership agreements — 1,500

Security system
Solid, professionally installed,
  central-station hookup — 1,500

Advertising and publicity
First month's print ads and opening party — 2,500

Logo design — 2,000

Stationery, forms, labels, cards — 2,000

Business plan
Binders, printing, postage, etc. — 300

Contracting — 85,000

Total startup cost	98,400
Plus the total equipment cost	190,815

Midrange Studio GRAND TOTAL — **$289,215**

The Business Expense Breakdown

Here's some detail on the preceding list. (These items are also discussed in detail in the "Expense Planning" chapter.)

1. The Business Plan

Once your plan has been written, you'll need to make about a dozen copies and bind them or put them in looseleaf books. Spend a few extra dollars and buy either classy binders or the more expensive printer's covers and paper stock. This is the document you'll be leaving with various lenders. It can't hurt to make a good impression that says "quality."

The cost also includes photo duplication, minimal printer page setup charges and miscellaneous expenses.

2. Rent and Security

In order to figure a reasonable rent on the space you'll need, let's say that a suitable low-cost building has 2,000 square feet at $1.50 per foot per month. That equals $3,000, plus one month's security deposit of $3,000 more.

Bear in mind that square footage charges vary wildly.

3. Power, Water and Phone Lines

Utilities tend to charge fairly high deposits and installation fees for new subscribers. (You would too if you owned one and didn't know who you were dealing with!) If you de-emphasize the amount of equipment and power you'll be using when asked by your friendly local representative, you may be able to talk them into a lower deposit amount.

4. Legal and Accounting

Startup costs would include filing a *dba* (an official city form, short for "doing business as," for setting up a new business), setting up your books with an accountant, getting a *resale number* (which allows you to buy goods that you will resell in your business without paying the sales tax), and writing and signing various legal papers.

5. Advertising and Public Relations

You'll most likely need as much of both as you can get right from the start in order to fill your room with clients. While it may become possible to lower these expenses later on, for now you should spend at least $800 per month to help get the word out and the bodies in.

6. Contracting

Building to suit is usually a necessity to some degree. Your costs could be zero or as high as half a million, depending on the luck you have in finding a suitable location, your resources and your level of courage.

7. Logo and Stationery

Professional artist consultation, design and delivery of a custom business logo. Also, you'll need at least a year's supply of letterhead, envelopes, four-part invoices, work and booking orders, heavy-stock track sheets, crack-and-peel tape box and cassette labels, and business cards.

8. Additional Contracting

Building: Insulated walls, 11-foot ceilings, soffitts for tape machines, custom racks and cabinetry. High-tech track lighting; good carpeting; parquet flooring in the studio; drum and vocal booths; sliding double-glass doors; good hardware; wall fabric and wainscots.

Electrical: 200-amp system, fully grounded and isolated.

Plumbing: Hot water heater; construction of second bathroom with toilet and sink, fixtures and pipe installation.

And Now, To Work

Properly executed, the preceding list should yield an upstanding commercial facility capable of hosting a wide variety of professional productions, from music recording to audio post. Again, this is the kind of room many smaller studios build up to, but at the same time, this is still a modest operation. The console, in particular, is lightweight but cost-effective. Future upgrades would include a more capable (and perhaps automated) desk and an expansion to multiroom operation.

THE ROOM OF DREAMS

Great Grandma Ida—you remember, the one with all the cake makeup and doilies around her neck who used to give you 20 bucks when you were a kid, just for squeezing your eyes shut and giving her a kiss at Thanksgiving? Last month, she passed on, and to your utter astonishment, left you half of the vast fortune your conniving cousins and aunts had been backstabbing one another over for lo, these many years.

The stash comes with a note explaining: "I always looked forward to that kiss each year. Curled my kneehose, it did. Such a *nice* boy. Always seemed to love tinkering with the volume control on the TV.

"See that he gets $5 million tax-free to build a studio in the Bahamas that the headbangers from Jersey will flock to, and make sure you spend it all, or it's no go. Oh, and here's another tax-free hundred grand a month for overhead. In perpetuity. Bye, sweetie. Try to have fun!"

Well. So much for that career in vacuum cleaner sales. Always did like the old girl. Let's see, that'll be a black Mercedes for family trips and a red Corvette for those occasional jaunts to the 7-Eleven. And now, what do you say we go shopping?

Space

We'll buy a 7,000-square-foot villa overlooking the surf on the warmer side of one of the islands, live on the top floor and convert the downstairs to suit.

House and acreage	$2,000,000

Contracting

Gorgeous architectural and acoustical construction of 4,000 square feet, yielding a 25' x 32' control room and 35' x 50' studio with 14-foot ceilings, plus a MIDI pre-production room and lots of space to, like, get in the mood.

Construction costs	$1,000,000
Factor 20% for cost overruns	200,000

Temporary Housing

Allow about six months from start to completion, including wiring, during which you stay in some nearby five-star hotel, in order to be available for ongoing consultations on color schemes and the like.

Per-month living and other expenses	$20,000
Contracting and Living Total	**$1,320,000**

Console

JG: "Good start. The trend is to bigger and bigger consoles." So let's get a:

108-input Neve VR with GML automation, good for both tracking and mixing	$800,000
Installation and wiring, including airfare and hotels for the tech team	60,000
Console Total	**$860,000**

(And another no-cost bonus: genuine expressions of thanks for your inspired business sense and promises of continued ideas for costly future technological innovations from a gaggle of otherwise seemingly hardened industry professionals.)

Tape Decks

JG: "This is the '90s, and people are confused, so you'll need both analog and digital."

Analog:

2 Studer A827s	$100,000
2 Dolby XP24 SR racks	36,000

Digital:

48-track Sony 3348 with meter bridge and updates	200,000

Mixdown:

Ampex ATR 102 1/2" 2-track	7,000

"Something around 80 percent of the music that gets mixed is to a combination of half-inch and DAT machines, running simultaneously. People feel more secure this way, and if there is editing to be done, the half-inch may still be the way to go."

Panasonic SV3700 DAT plus a good set of Apogee A/D and D/A converters to patch into the DAT machine	$1,400
	3,500

"There is still a good amount of insecurity among major artists over mastering on low-cost digital machines. But new systems are popping up all over, like one-write CD mastering and MO drives, which may wind up becoming the mastering disk system of choice in the late '90s. With potential 24-bit performance, MO will actually deliver higher fidelity than consumer-quality CDs for the first time in years."

Sony PCM 9000 master-disk eraseable MO drive, with 20-bit A/D and D/A converters, SCSI interface, memory board, etc.	$55,000
Deck Total	**$402,900**

Outboard Reverbs, Gain Control & Processors

The basics:

Lexicon 480L with Larc and sampling memory	$9,000
Eventide DSP 4000 processor	5,000
EMT plate reverb* (you can't rent these very easily and clients love 'em)	2,000
2 TC Electronic 2290 delay lines with 64 seconds of sampling memory	6,000
2 Sony DDL DPSD7s	2,400
4 dbx 160x mono compressors	1,500
2 Drawmer DS 201s	1,200
Eventide H3000 Broadcast Ultra Harmonizer	2,500
Quantec Room Simulator	15,000
2 pairs of Drawmer M500 noise gates	3,000
2 Aphex Dominator 2 limiters	2,200

Some nice esoteric stuff:

Summit DCL200 stereo compressor	2,400
4 Summit EQ F100 tube EQs	6,400
2 Pultec 1A or 1A3 EQs	5,000
Fairchild 670 stereo tube compressor	10,000

Your classic outboard:

Cooper Time Cube*	200
8 assorted Pultec equalizers*	16,000
8 Lang PEQ2 equalizers*	6,400
2 EMT 140 Plate reverbs *	4,000
2 live chambers, contractor-built	3,500
2 Fairchild 670 stereo limiters*	10,000
2 Teletronix LA2As	4,000
2 UREI 1176LN*	1,400
4 Aphex CX1s in rack*	1,000
Publison Infernal Machine*	4,000
Cyclosonic Panner*	1,500
10-space rack of Gain Brains*	3,600
2 Lexicon PCM42s*	1,600
EMT PDM 156 compressor*	2,500
AMS RMX16 processor*	5,000

And a good parametric equalizer:

Neve GML (including power supply and GML mic preamp)	4,175

More used items:

JG: "Once they stop making good outboard gear, the price goes up."

API rack with 10 spaces for modules	700
6 API 550A 3-band EQs	6,600
2 API 525 compressors	
(must be modified to fit in the rack)	2,000
Neve 33609 stereo compressor	4,000
Outboard Gear Total	**$154,575**

Video Laydown and Layback Decks

Lynx TimeLine 6-module lockup system	$21,000
Ampex VPR 80 1-inch video deck	33,000
Sony DVR 18 D2 deck	60,000
Sony BVW 75 Betacam SP	34,000
Sony Digital Betacam SP deck	65,000
3 JVC 3/4-inch decks	11,000
Barco high-end 10' video projection system	
with electric roll-down screen in the	
control room	30,000
2 Mitsubishi 40" tube monitors	5,400
Techtronics Model 930 house sync	
generator	1,000
Character inserter	1,000
2 Videotek distribution amplifiers	600
Related test & quality-control video	
equipment	7,000
Video Total	**$269,000**

Computers

3 high-end Macs with lots of RAM,	
21" color monitors, big hard drives	$18,000
Emulator E3XS sampler	
with external keyboard and MO drive	7,600
AMS Audiofile editing system, loaded	165,000
Good sequencer like Studio Vision	500
MIDI Time Piece interface	500
Computer Total	**$191,600**

Monitors

Westlake SM1s (with two	
18" woofers, a 10" low mid,	
a 2" high mid, a 1" mid	
high and a super tweeter.)	$35,000
Must be custom-installed into your	
soffitts, plus you need a Westlake	
SM1X crossover system	9,500

Power Amps:

10 Crown PSA 2xs	
(just to drive that system)	$16,000
2 Marantz Model 9 amps	5,000
2 Phase Linear Amps	1,400
"And don't forget a set of Yamaha NS10Ms"	300

Middle Pair Speakers:

JG: "Once something becomes popular, the manufacturer will promptly discontinue it so that they can come out with something better and keep bugging end-users for a few years to move up and spend more money.

"Tannoy, JBL, KRK two-way, midsize monitors will run you about $2,000 per set. You might also want to get a variety of midrange speakers. These days, other than a whole lot of heavy metal (don't forget Grandma Ida's instructions), very few people are mixing on big speakers."

Tannoy System 10 DMT Series II	$1,400
Meyer HD-1s	1,200
Monitor Total	**$69,800**

Mics

We'll get mics for everything from voice-overs to orchestral sessions—a collection to make a producer/engineer get on a plane just to fly down and see all this stuff in one closet (and work on his tan).

2 AKG C12s	$7,000
2 AKG C60s	800
4 AKG 414s	4,000
1 AKG 451	450
2 AKG 460s	900
1 AKG C24	2,000
1 AKG D112	280
2 Crown PZM30s	600
2 EV RE20s	500
2 Milab VIP50s	2,500
1 Neumann M50	3,000
2 Neumann KM 84s	850
2 Neumann KM 82 shotguns	2,000
2 Neumann KM 54s	1,200
2 Neumann KM 140s	1,500
1 Neumann M269	2,500
2 Neumann Stephen Paul U87s	4,000
1 Neumann TLM 170	1,600
2 Neumann U47 tubes	5,000
2 Neumann 67s	4,000
4 Sennheiser 421s	1,400
2 Sennheiser 441s	950
1 Schoeps 221B tube	1,000
2 Shure SM7s	1,000
4 Shure SM57s	360
1 Stanley Church	2,500
2 Telefunken 251s	7,000
Mic Total	**$58,890**

Accessories

12 passive DIs with Jensen direct transformers	$1,800
12 active DIs from Countryman or Simon Systems	1,800
12 cue boxes	3,600
24 AKG 240DF headphones	2,400
30 AKG 201 mic stands	1,200
8 Atlas SB 36W	3,200
4 Starbird booms	4,000
Accessories Total	**$18,000**

Miscellaneous

Bosendorfer 10' concert grand piano	70,000
10-line phone system, installed	10,000
Large maintenance/shop room, stocked & stoked	30,000
Custom designer studio and office furniture	60,000
Best-quality basketball hoop, installed on pole	1,500
Misc. Total	**$171,500**

Extras

Wiring costs can roughly be estimated at 5% to 15% of equipment budget. (The bigger the budget gets, the smaller the wiring percentage.)

Cords, connectors and professional wiring	$20,000

JG: "And most important: An assortment of good-quality vending machines and video games."

6 machines total	$15,000
Extras Total	**$35,000**

"These are the real profit centers for your studio and the main services that clients will come to your place for. Plus a nice kitchen and comfortable chairs. And a receptionist who'll constantly forget your name and ask if you'd like a copy of her demo, and who'll spend the bulk of her time working on her career while doing her job."

Business Startup Costs

Electric, water and gas deposits	$2,000
Telephone company Line installation charges and deposit	1,500

Legal and accounting fees Financial statements, dba, lease, contracting and partnership, agreements, retainers, magnum of Dom Perignon	10,000
Security system State of the art, booby-trapped with legal retainer deposit, pro-installed, central-station hookup	15,000
Logo design	3,000
Stationery, forms, labels, cards	4,000
Business plan Don't need one!	0
Advertising & publicity Three months of print ads in several national mags, PR consultant on retainer, and a grand opening party	30,000
Start-up total	**$65,500**

Total Startup Costs

Real Estate and Contracting	3,320,000
Console	860,000
Running equipment total	1,371,265
Business startup	65,500
Le Grand Total:	**$5,616,265**

Whew!

Uh-oh, we're over budget. "Not to worry," says Grandma Ida's attorney. She just wanted to see if you had the guts to go the extra distance. A check for double the difference is on the way.

So This is Oz...

Actually, we figured a sensible world-class facility could be put together for a million dollars, but it was a lot more fun to dream outrageously.

The best approach, with some really serious money in hand, would be to set up a multiroom facility that offered as much diversity as possible. Spent wisely, that kind of dough could bankroll a very tasty *five*-bay facility. But there's no question that the inherent risks combined with the cost of mounting such an effort would be a powerful deterrent when weighed against the chances for the thrill of success.

Maybe the best way to enjoy an operation like this is to apply for an internship in one that already exists. That way, you get a maximum return on experience, and your biggest worry might turn out to be getting to work on time.

Basking in the Digital, Tropical Domain

With a 32-track digital facility in the middle of the Caribbean, Alfonso Brooks and his wife Margaret attract the cream of the local trade, while they work to entice an international clientele with bargain rates and tropical breezes.

Career Roots He started as a guitarist with a home 4-track setup and then borrowed some money from his family to go 8-track. Moved on to 16 and then took the leap to digital 32-track, offering one of the best facilities in the Carribean. "My wife and I are both musicians, and both Tauruses, and we're very happy running the place together."

Facility One studio at $90 per hour, which attracts acts from the States. Sony MXP-3000 automated console, Otari and Sony decks. Control room 15' x 15', live room 20' x 30'. Mastering room for records. They also offer clients a three-bedroom house with kitchen and satellite TV for $40 per day.

House Staff About 10, including two firsts, plus a full-time house band providing backup for local acts, many of whom are solo singers. "If people don't need the house band, we still keep them on the payroll, because we do so much work with them. It's the only way to keep the best of them around us."

Primary Focus Local talent, focusing on calypso, reggae and soca music. "We get bookings from groups all over the islands."

Booking Policy Half payment up front, half on delivery. "When we book groups from abroad, we usually ask for a deposit in advance. They like to block-book the studio, and we want to be sure they're serious about what they're doing."

Marketing The studio is very well known in the Caribbean, with good PR exposure in local papers. They also record local TV spots and jingles, and advertise in *Billboard* and *Mix*. "Our island is very small, just 39 square miles, so it's like a family here and the word gets around very quickly. We've also begun to send a lot of brochures to both Europe and the States and are now starting to get some action from that."

Problems Musicians who smoke pot in the studio. "We've found out that the resin from the weed, which is very dense here, can do real damage building up inside the electronics in the console and the digital equipment, so we try to discourage smoking in the control room. It's a funny situation. We ask them to please go outside somewhere. It's very lush and tropical here, so they can go out by the palm trees or the fields and come back when they're done.

"We've also had some real problems with the salt air and contact points in some of the wiring. We finally solved that one by consulting with our maintenence experts in New York, who suggested replacing some of the connectors with gold contacts."

Growth Plans "At times, we have been booked 24 hours a day. Now we're planning on building another room on top of our present facility. That's right—we're going to add a second floor to the existing building. I want this one to be 48-track."

Philosophy "Know what you're doing and what you're aiming at. You must have faith, because the minute you lose track of that, everything goes downhill. We really enjoy doing what we're doing."

The interior of the Bronese live room, as seen from the control room.

4
Making It Happen

Before I get started, let me interject a brief commercial message: A personal computer is the first item that should be acquired when starting up *any* business: There's simply no better, faster, more efficient or more inspiring way to plan a project than with a machine that you can use to type, organize, plan and calculate each component of your enterprise, and save an enormous amount of time and effort in the process.

A computer is also invaluable for a number of music applications involving MIDI, the Musical Instrument Digital Interface. MIDI allows the producer and/or artist a wide degree of flexibility in sculpting tracks, adding sounds and programming basic sequences. In the pro studio environment, the Macintosh remains the overwhelming system of choice for the widest variety of MIDI applications. If you buy one at the start, you're that much closer to an integrated system in the end.

Whatever system you choose, try to stay in the brand-name domain to take advantage of the large service networks and software availability a major company offers. If you're new to computing, and you're close to someone who is experienced, put yourself in their hands. Let them recommend their favorite setup, and assuming you buy one, they'll always be just a phone call away with advice and answers during those first tentative weeks.

Another route for less-experienced users is to hire a private consultant to help get set up and hone in on your particular focus. While you will no doubt benefit from cheaper, multistudent class instruction, a few hours of one-on-one direction from an experienced pro should be well worth the $40- to $75-per-hour fee, especially when measured against the amount of frustration and effort it will ultimately save you. The trick is to get a good overview of the soft-

ware you're going to use first, whether by yourself or with a friend, and then to bring in a pro to fine-tune everything for your own best use.

To find a good consultant, start with the store you purchased your system from, or check with friends and associates who are doing similar work.

GETTING FUNDED

There are people who have the means to start up a business as if they were just buying it off the shelf. "I'll take one of those, please. Oh, and do you take American Express?" Wealth does have a way of making miracles happen. If you're one of those people, consider yourself privileged and feel free to skip ahead to the next chapter.

The rest of us are going to have varying degrees of success in going after the things we want in life. However, walking into each situation armed with the best tools and knowledge we can gather is the way to stack up the most favorable odds.

Statistically, far more new businesses fail within the first few years than succeed. Bankers know this, and therefore are going to be extremely interested in the collateral you have to back up your plans.

If you're not a homeowner, or haven't yet built yourself a nice investment portfolio, the chances are that a commercial bank is going to be very reluctant to hand over a cash loan (although recently, credit has indeed become easier to procure). But without a moneyed cosigner or another investor, most banks just don't seem to have much of a sense of humor about those fabled E-Z loan terms.

My partner and I learned that no matter how charming you are, if your financial statement isn't up to snuff, a lender is going to look at it, tell you the bank isn't in the recording studio business, apologize and wish you the best of luck. "Thanks for coming in. You're really nice people and we'd really love to help you, just as soon as your business is successful. So come on back when you're ready to buy some CDs, okay? And by the way, have you considered opening up a business checking account here?"

I'll tell ya what I've been considering, bub...

But wait, put that bazooka away. Because up ahead, there's a faint, glimmering light at the end of the tunnel of doom. And its name is...the leasing company.

LEASING

A leasing company actually *is* in the business of recording studio ownership. Sort of. That's because leasing company reps will look at your needs, and if they agree to fund you, *they'll* buy whatever equipment you want and then *rent* it to you.

What a concept! They retain ownership of the equipment. You sign a three- to five-year lease, which is just like an auto lease, and make monthly payments. At the end of the lease, you have the option to buy out your lease (purchase the equipment outright), usually for about 10% of its original value (in addition to all the payments you've been making). Other leases are structured so that your final buyout is just one dollar.

Or you can simply choose to return the equipment to the company. Needless to say, people tend to choose the buyout option. For the vast majority, the idea is to keep the stuff. "We've been in business specializing in the recording industry for ten years, and we're still hoping that one of our lessees wants to return the equipment," says Doris Tamboryn of JG Capital Corp. in Manhattan Beach, Calif. "But we hedge our bets by buying lottery tickets, because they're a better chance of our winning."

Leasing is a great move taxwise, too: You get to write off your full payment each month, because the government considers it rent money instead of equipment ownership, which can only be written off at about 20% per year. So if your lease is for less than five years, your write-offs save you more tax money.

But the best feature about leasing companies is that they are much easier to deal with than banks. That's because they get to own the equipment while you make payments on it. If anything happens—say, you default on the lease—they just take possession of the equip-

ment and sell or lease it to someone else. Unlike banks, they *are* in the business of owning equipment and have adapted themselves to equipment brokering.

The Personal Touch

There's another advantage to going with a leasing company: They're usually smaller, friendlier, and "meaner and leaner" than banks. The leasing agent who you deal with may, in fact, be the owner of the leasing company. And they are often people who trust their own instincts as much as any corporate bottom line.

This means that all you have to do to get funded is to convince one person in one leasing company that you're a good risk. This isn't easy, but it's not nearly as difficult as getting a similar level of bank funding. In this case, the critical connection you need to make may be on a personal level. And that's where all the research and time and effort you put into your business plan pays off. It tells your lender just how serious you are about making your business a success.

Naturally, the lease company is going to do what it can to offset the risk it takes by providing you with equipment credit. Since it won't have any history on a startup business, the company may ask you to provide some manner of side collateral in return. This can take the form of cash deposits, equipment that you own free and clear or other conventional assurances, like real estate or securities.

Balancing the Risk

The downside is that the cost of a lease package averages 3% to 8% higher than the cost of a bank loan. Some companies may go as high as 15% more. Their reasoning is that the risks are higher; you wouldn't be coming to them if you could get a deal at a bank. Their businesses are much smaller than most banks as well. It's just like the little convenience store on the corner that charges 25 cents more for a quart of milk than the supermarket down the street.

It helps to be a little philosophical when signing an expensive contract. If you look ahead and consider the extra hundred a month as a necessary cost of doing business, and that the company is providing you with a means to a highly desirable end, you may wince a little less.

Leasing is an important financing option, even when a business becomes successful. Most banks will only lend about 75% of the cost of new equipment, which means that you'd still have to come up with $37K for a $150,000 package. A lot of accountants feel that your cash would be better spent on other investments, especially when a leasing company typically requires only the first month's payment and a security deposit to deliver that same console to your door. Remember also that, unlike a bank loan, lease payments are fully deductible. In a profitable tax year, that could mean a substantial savings for the business.

Another positive factor is that, as your business history grows longer and your profitability increases, the lease rate you wind up paying will probably decrease. Some companies are willing to take higher risks, but others will only deal with solid customers and reward them with lower rates.

Assembling a Lease Package

A lease package is a group of items that you assemble and then finance through the leasing company. Choose a few major items that are proven pieces of equipment with strong resale value. Imagine yourself as the owner of the leasing company for a moment. What items would you feel safest about purchasing, if later on you had to resell them on the open market?

The simpler the package, the easier to judge its value. If you're short on cash, keep the package to no more than half of your anticipated start-up expense figure. And try to be conservative in your projections.

To illustrate this point, let's go back to the low-budget equipment list from Chapter 3. Starting from there, you might choose a package like this:

3 ADATs	$9,000
ADAT BRC	1,500
Panasonic SV3700 balanced DAT 2-track	1,700
Soundcraft Spirit 24 24x8 mixer	6,000
Yamaha SPX990 multi-effects processor	750
Sony DPSR/ stereo reverb	800
API 2-channel rack	650
API 512B mic preamp	650
API 550B EQ	1,000
Total	**$22,050**

Each piece is a recognized, professional item. That makes for an attractive list in the lessor's eyes. So by impressing a financial executive with your knowledge, ability, drive and professional presentation, you've just reduced the amount of capital you need to open for business.

Still short of funds? Maybe it's time to buddy up.

PARTNERSHIP

Partnership is probably the official smartest way there is to go into, enjoy and be successful at business, assuming you're not already independently wealthy (or don't like being with other people). Note that if you *are* independently wealthy, or simply have all your funds solidly in place, and you're serious about starting up a studio, the best thing to do at this point would be to hire an experienced professional consultant to get some personalized attention and support.

But back to the buddy plan. To illustrate, look at how a "think tank" works. It's a concept used in government and big business, where a bunch of people lock themselves in a room together and tackle a problem. For several hours or days or months, they throw ideas back and forth and work off of each other's brainstorms and throw in all of their individual points of view, until they finally emerge from this rubber room with solutions. Solutions, one might add, that they could never have come up with separately but that came about because they all put their minds together. Most problems don't have much chance of survival with so many determined minds hacking away at them!

A lot of TV sitcoms are written the same way: Two, three, four or 50 comedy writers handcuff themselves together and straight-man and one-liner themselves into crazed oblivion until they emerge with a 30-minute script that never would have been as funny if one person had tried to write it alone.

The Advantages

Partnership (with the right partner, of course) is a beautiful thing. You play off each other's strengths and weaknesses and come up with ideas and plans and solutions you might never have dreamed up alone. And it *feels* good, because you're connected to someone else who wants the same thing as you do. That's exciting.

Naturally, the other potential advantage is that your partner has money, too. Maybe he or she just inherited a big chunk of cash, or has a savings account, or just won the lottery. Or maybe he or she is as poor as you are. But even so, that's two times richer than you were *before* you had a partner. And with any luck, two times as smart.

No two partnerships are the same; no two people react to one another in exactly the same way. But any partnership that's committed to success benefits uniquely from the contribution each person makes, be it abstract or concrete. What's necessary is a willingness to let down your guard with someone that you trust enough to believe that he or she will respect you for doing just that, and who'll do the same in return.

Granted, finding someone with similar business interests whom you trust and respect may not be easy, but the search is definitely worth the effort. There are few emotions in business that compare to those that come from sharing a dream and the effort to make it a reality with a partner you believe in.

It takes vision, courage and follow-through to put your cards on the table and risk it all in tandem with another human being. But the rewards are in the thrill of turning the key on a place of your own, and in the joy of knowing you've done it together. Once you get that far, you begin to realize that the only limits in life are the ones you set on yourself.

Finding Mr. or Ms. Right

Where do you find partners? Look for someone who complements your strengths and weaknesses. If you're an engineer, find someone with a knack for business, or a musician/composer. Talk to club owners and rock groups. Hang notices in recording schools or in the company cafeteria. Many newspapers have business opportunity classifieds with people looking for and/or offering partnerships.

If you're musical, talk to recording engineers, accountants, lawyers and doctors. Many in the "straighter" professions find the entertainment industry an attractive investment. If you're a business person with capital, you might even start by visiting and getting to know the established operations in your area. There may be several opportunities to walk directly into an existing and thriving facility by simply offering a cash infusion!

In short, keep your eyes open and tell everyone you meet about your plans and ideas—don't just limit yourself to "music people." Depending on your circumstances, that potential partner may be staring you right in the face every day. If your presentation is clear and focused, other people will be interested, and that interest may be the key to building the future you want.

Fear of Flying

To complicate matters, once you find someone you think would make a good candidate, it's easy to get caught up in his or her minor faults. It's like marriage—usually a long search, followed by something resembling a blinding flash of recognition, followed by an avalanche of nagging doubts and suspicions, followed by unimaginable bliss when you know you've picked the right person. (Followed by...ahem...more doubts. But that's really not the point, is it?) The key is to weigh the flash intelligently against the doubts, and at some point, before your dreams turn to dust or you become too old to care, as they say on the carnival circuit, "you takes a chance."

Any number of things can go wrong in a business partnership. One partner might flake out while the other does all the work. Another might turn out to be unfit for the job. Yet another might embezzle the company funds and run off to open a little karaoke bar in Paradise. Or you might wind up just plain hating each other, or worse.

On the other hand, a good partnership *doubles* your chances of success, opportunity and pleasure. And there's nothing like savoring the thrill of a fresh-won victory with someone who's just helped make it happen and who's right there to celebrate with you. (Or commiserating with an equal when you're backed into a corner or stuck for an idea.)

Obviously, you're not going to find out what partnership is like without opening yourself up to its possibilities. And really, if worst comes to worst, the odds are you'll wind up serving any necessary jail time on an honor farm!

The key, as with anything else that's important, is to do it with your eyes wide open. Spend enough time, both socially and professionally, with each candidate until you feel like you're pretty well attuned to who they are. And then, if the balance seems fair—if most of your ideas match and you don't embarrass one another in public—*take that chance!* Win or lose, you'll live to tell about it, and in the meantime, life will most certainly become more interesting.

Avoiding Bloodshed

There are any number of ways to divide up the assets, costs and duties in a partnership. But if you agree that you're both indispensable, that you're both going to give it everything you've got and this thing is going to be a success, then why not split it all right down the middle? A 50/50 split means you agree to share everything: the responsibility, the problems, the craziness, the rewards and, hopefully, the profits.

Start off as equals, and neither partner will blame the other for doing too much or too little because the other is getting a higher percentage. Resentment won't fester when a big check comes in. And respect will continue and deepen over the course of time.

If one partner has more money than the other at the beginning, there are many ways to work out the imbalance. Maybe one will agree to work more hours or come in earlier to help make up the difference, or to defer commissions on future clients he pitches. Or maybe the one who's cash-light has a big client to bring in right off the bat.

That's what Michael had. He didn't tell me about it until weeks after we'd become partners. Then one day at lunch, he nonchalantly said, "By the way, I've got a 30-episode TV series for us to do as soon as we open next month," and took another bite of his tuna melt. My dropping jaw thunked into my soup bowl and splashed vegetables all over my festive paper bib.

You also might be able to work out a cash imbalance in salary trade-offs later, or in any other creative way you like. But if you start as equal partners, you have the makings of a marriage that can work. Choose carefully, be honest with each other and you can have a ball.

Two words there bear repeating: *be honest*. Partnership works on trust. Blow that, and whatever clandestine rewards you think you'll gain will be muted by the growing lack of trust between you. That can only lead to one result: Bust.

So look. If honesty is a new concept for you, now's the time to begin to appreciate it. If it's a concept that makes sense to you, then remember that as time goes by, you'll still find it hard *maintaining* it with the same person. Temptation clothes itself in unending disguises, but it's worth the effort to resolutely deflect each underhanded opportunity as it comes—for your own self-esteem, the invaluable bond that grows between you and your partner, the ease of being together without being weighted down by guilt or fear of discovery, and the knowledge that when the chips are down, you can count on one another to come through.

That's a great feeling to earn, and one that has served my partner and me for nine years running.

Opportunity is Where You Make It

Once you commit yourself to the idea of partnership, a world of possibilities opens its doors to you. With a partner, you'll be working and planning the future together. And that's the best way to get a feel for what your business and interaction as partners will be all about.

Add a relative who believes in you and has the money to prove it. Or a band who makes an outrageous deal with you for 250 hours of album time at $20 an hour for a total of $5,000 up front and an opportunity to break in your new studio with a guaranteed project. Or an investor you meet at a party who comes in as a silent partner and gets a tax write-off to boot. Or a TV production company that not only needs a place to post, but to shoot!

Think about the possibilities that two or three people who really want to start up a pro studio can dream up together. The opportunity is there for the taking.

You really *can* do it, from starting with nothing to opening a great little setup, perhaps even in a matter of months. It's there for you if you're brave enough, if it's what you really want, and if you're willing to focus your energy and imagination on something you want so badly that you just won't take 'no' for an answer.

Going Remote with "Rover"

After years of bringing the studio to the gig, Bob Skye has assembled a multifaceted facility, a uniquely designed mobile unit and a successful partnership that balances both partners' strengths and experience.

Bob Skye

Owner

Skyelabs Mobile Recording

Sausalito, California

Rover's interior, with owner Skye at the controls

Startup Bought a retired Greyhound bus in '83, named it "Rover" and installed a multitrack system and the "world's only certified live-end, dead-end mobile control room."

Facility The bus is based at The Plant, a multiroom facility in Sausalito. Rover is equipped with a 35-input Sound Workshop board and dual Otari 24-track decks, plus a color video camera set up for a stationary long-stage shot to see what's going on.

"We'll probably buy a new console this year; new because we can build it to scale, both physically and acoustically. That way I can go to a manufacturer and say look, I've got exactly seven and a half feet to work with. How can we modify to suit? It's really marvelous what's available now; for instance, in recall, we can now do a soundcheck at a multiple-act event and then go back to each one and remember what the heck we did."

Rates are based on 16-hour days, with overtime charged beyond that.

House Staff The bus normally goes out with an engineer and three crew members.

Marketing "If you're new to a major city, the chances are you're walking right into major competition. So the thing to do is to call around, introduce yourself, and find out who the key people are of, say, the local studios. If they're established, they're going to be getting calls for remote gigs, and they'll say 'Gee, who can we call?' So you want to get on their roster.

"Or maybe you want to be even more clever and let them subcontract your remote so that they can use their engineers and do the whole thing under their own calling card. They make a couple of bucks, but by the same token they may

The Skyelabs mobile unit

feel inclined to push this as a feature that their studio can offer.

"Eventually, however, this method got a little undermined with us. As repeat clients got to know who I was, they'd call a studio to reserve the date, then sure enough, later the same day, the client would find his way to calling me. That demanded that I maintain a fairly rigid cost schedule, so that I knew that my subcontracting rate didn't conflict with what I was offering straight over the board if the client came directly to me. Otherwise the studio would get upset and they wouldn't call me any more, if they knew I would just undercut whatever they were asking.

"So I became one of the first guys to tell people what I charge, and then when they asked me if I went any lower, I'd simply say 'no.' I'd say I had obligations to other studios. Rather than terming it a monopoly, it was a situation of vendor vs. distributor vs. retailer. If you don't maintain a price structure that's respectable, people won't respect you."

Driving to the Gig "We did a U2 concert that was part of the movie *Rattle and Hum*. Here in San Francisco, it was a surprise concert, and I got called at 5:30 the night before asking if we could be ready to do an 8 a.m. call.

"At one point in the concert, Bono was singing. We had a long video shot that was a side view of the stage. It was such a quick setup outdoors at the Embarcadero park that it was the best we could manage with the crowds. All of a sudden, he disappears from the stage, and we begin to hear this sound like his mic is being run through a gunny sack. We couldn't figure out what was going on, so I sent one of the guys to find out. He radioed back that Bono was on a ladder, climbing up the fountain, holding the microphone under his arm.

"So having the camera to use for visual tipoffs is great, except when it doesn't work in the context of the moment. There we were in the bus, exchanging funny looks, wondering if there was something the matter with the board. Looking back, the concert was a lot of fun, the mix turned out very well, and the scene became part of a great movie."

On Partnership "My forte was engineering and management. I needed somebody who was skilled in sales. Partnership is like any other marriage. It's got it's own set of compromises. But when done correctly, it's very potent. One of my financial advisors said to me, in a fit of wisdom, 'Tis better to own a small part of something very big than a big part of something very small.' My criteria for choosing someone was to find somebody who looks farsighted down the road and sees the same basic things as I do. Obviously, you want compatibility. But also, you want to be a smart enough manager to be able to back off and say 'Gee, this guy seems cleverer than I do.' That's okay too.

"I think the diversification and ability of someone in sales is just as, if not more, important than your ability with the equipment. We can have great equipment, we can know exactly how it works and we can get great sounds out of it, but if we can't get the people in the door...

"It's essential to have compatibility between partners. If you're covering one area and you need another to be covered, then you obviously need someone there to take care of it. And you need to feel good about it."

The Business "Record company budgets have changed. Those same media dollars that were being spent on records are now being spent on videos, CD-I and CD-ROM and the other areas they are diversifying into.

"In general there are lower and fewer record budgets. Good music is good music. It doesn't really matter what it was recorded on. If it's good and the record companies get it out there, it'll sell. The public is buying the quality you can get from a $15,000 digital multitrack these days, when just a couple years ago that same capability cost closer to $200,000. Therefore, why spend the money in the record budget?"

The Future "Any entrepreneur or engineer is going to have to specialize to be successful. We're now looking at picture, sound and other fields, which is to say there is unlimited direction out there.

"The remote business is going nuts. There's a lot more live stuff getting recorded. I think that's interesting, inasmuch as it's not formula music. It's real acts playing real instruments in a live situation, with real people who are there to see it isn't a con game. It's really played by real musicians. That always excites the hell out of me. The turnout around here for live musicians and live music is just wonderful. And now I'm waiting for more of those acts to get sucked into the marketing machine and maybe improve our radio listening a bit over the next couple of years."

What You Can Do *Now* to Start Preparing for Success *Later*

1. Partner up. Partnerships are the smartest way for anyone who isn't already financially secure to start up a business. Look around you; keep your eyes open. When you think you've found someone, start spending time together. Cook up a project idea and do it. Work together. Play together. Get close, don't keep secrets and learn to trust each other.

2. Clean up your personal credit. If you don't have credit cards, get a Visa and Mastercard now, and use them when you get them. Be certain to make all credit payments on time for the next two years. It's essential that you have an established credit-bureau history of past credit and timely payments.

3. Start a studio savings or investment account and figure out how to deposit 20% to 30% of your hard-earned pay into it each week. You're investing in your future. Pass on the leather jeans for now and think Porsche for later!

4. Start a directory of names and addresses, a book of clippings of ads and articles, and a notebook of ideas and plans. Get organized and design a system that works and grows with you. It will become a private and invaluable business source in the years to come.

5. Meet and get to know your banker. Stop by his or her desk when you're at the branch, say hello and talk about your progress. Bankers really like this—it makes them feel nearly human. And they can be powerful allies who may want to help you later.

6. Read the industry trades. Subscribe to the local and national magazines and become knowledgeable about the studio business. Check and see if there are local trade organizations that you can join and shmooze in.

7. Clip pictures of the equipment you want and hang them up—it helps make their ownership a reality in your mind. Draw layouts of your control room. Read the real estate and rental classifieds. Start living the dream.

8. Hang out at industry events and watering holes. Tell everyone about your plans. Work on connecting with people who interest you and who are interested in what you're doing.

9. Work on your business plan. Think about what work, projects or research you can do now to gain more experience and to look more professional later.

10. Envision your facility as a busy, successful enterprise. Read some of the classic business and personal growth books: *Think and Grow Rich, In Search of Excellence, Psychocybernetics, Power Shmoozing, This Business of Music, The Richest Man in Babylon*, etc. (see the reading list in the Appendix). Visualize winning!

OTHER WAYS TO FIND MONEY

Of course, partnership isn't the only way to run a business. There are a host of alternative methods for getting the funds you need to start up a studio facility. Mom, Dad, Uncle Sid and Granny Anne account for a surprising percentage of angels who lend or donate seed money. You might inspire them to jump in with a promise of a return on an amount they lend you, or even an equity position that ties their investment to a portion of the profits.

But take care regarding the amount of control you grant them. Unless they're experienced professionals, you may find yourself with a partner who feels entitled to control the way things get run, in spite of your objections to the contrary and their lack of knowledge.

As with any formal loan, spell out the terms of the agreement in writing and then be sure all parties sign the paper. With relatives, there is often a tendency to dispense with formalities because you're keeping things in the family. But don't let that stop you. You'll be glad you've got everything spelled out the first time Aunt Beth insists that she should be entitled to re-record the entire Christmas Fireside Treasury of Songs that she wants her grandchild to have, and never mind that you're busy trying to finish up the score for your first decent-paying industrial.

Outside Angels

The next level of individual investment comes from private venture capital. Traditionally, venture capitalists tend to fund manufacturers or service startups that have the potential for high profit in a short period of time—not exactly the profile of a small recording facility. But the recording business does have a panache and glamour all its own, and if you're a motivated businessperson, there's no reason to overlook this potentially rich source.

The first line to a venture capitalist is probably through your banker, lawyer or business advisor, who may know individuals that occasionally invest in lucrative or appealing startups. The second way is to locate a venture capital network, which is a group of individuals who are actively looking for *you*. You can start the search by contacting your local Chamber of Commerce or other local entrepreneurial groups. "Angel networks," which are often set up by universities and state agencies, can be a great help. They'll also charge you a fee, usually a few hundred dollars, for their service.

You may also find that there are local venture forums being held in your area. These are meetings in which venture capitalists go head-to-head with entrepreneurs in open discussions. You'll want to bring as much impressive material as possible—it's amazing what an impact a good-looking package can have on a potential investor. Just think for a moment about what motivates you to buy, say, breakfast cereal in the supermarket. The look of the package probably has as much to do with what makes it into your basket as the contents itself.

Naturally, there are trade-offs in getting venture funding. Your angel is most likely going to be someone local who will want to keep an eye on you. He or she will also expect to have a say in the way things are run, and of course will expect to get a good piece of the business and the profits, perhaps as much as 50%. Keep in mind that when a venture capitalist chooses you, you in turn are choosing a new business partner. It will behoove you to clearly define the roles each of you will play.

Hopefully, you'll find someone interested in contributing funding, giving some experienced advice, and then, for the most part, keeping out of your way. Otherwise, you may find yourself working for someone else, instead of running the business you thought you were starting!

Sidestepping Cash

More and more, bartering and barter services have become a key factor in running a successful small business. There may be no better way to save on expenses than to simply trade goods or services in lieu of dollars. For instance, Avalanche Studios in Colorado traded a large block of future recording time to a number of contractors and tradespeople who helped build the place (see the Avalanche ProFile, p. 107, for more insight).

In the past few years, barter services have risen to prominence nationwide. Such services work by grouping a large number of companies and individuals together and then listing them all in a directory. As a member, you offer your goods or services (in this case, recording time in your studio), and then wait for someone else to request it. The service supplies your specs and phone number to the customer, who calls you and discusses his or her project. You quote the normal rate you charge, but instead of being paid in dollars, you get barter credit, usually equal to one credit per dollar.

Once you have earned credits through the barter service, you're free to avail yourself of any of the other services available. And most are quite impressive—everything from building contractors, electricians and plumbers to florists, air travel, hotels, lawyers and logo designers.

The service makes its money by charging a commission on the amount of credit you spend, usually around 10%. It's all quite proper and legal, with all transactions being reported to Uncle Sam at year's end. But the beauty of it comes in finding potential clients you would never have heard from otherwise, and in being able to sell blocks of time that you might not otherwise have gotten rid of, including night and weekend hours.

To find a barter service in your area, ask other businesspeople, call your local Chamber of Commerce or check the Yellow Pages.

Getting an SBA Loan

The Small Business Administration of the federal government has been a boon to many small business startups, once they got past the paperwork. The SBA was set up to help small business entrepreneurs get a foot into the door of many banks that otherwise would be out of reach. What it does is to guarantee up to about 90% of the loan the bank makes to the business, thus removing the biggest obstacle to qualifying for a new startup.

But there is something of a gauntlet to run before you get the money. The paperwork comes from the government, which means that there's reams of it and that it's slow and cumbersome to complete. It can take three to six months to finish the process. But if you plan ahead, it may be the way to get funded with the fewest strings attached.

To get the process started, ask your present banker if the bank does SBA loans. A lot of banks turn their nose up at this path, but there are always a few in each city that specialize in it. Those are the ones you want. And of course, you'll save yourself a lot of repeat visits if your business plan is up to snuff when you go to your first meeting.

Loan Programs

Finally, check to see if your city or state offers any special loan programs. Many states have special agencies and funds targeted towards business startups. And many expressly target minority groups (don't forget that some states include women in this category!) for special consideration.

Contact local universities, minority organizations, city chambers and city halls for leads. And watch the paper for announcements of functions and meetings that could benefit you in your search.

The money can always be found, if you're determined, focused and armed with the right information. Stay on top of current trends by reading some of the top periodicals, a few of which are surprisingly entertaining to boot. The *Wall Street Journal*, filled with special feature articles and offbeat insights, is often more fascinating than the daily newspaper. And *Success* magazine devotes entire issues to topics like money sources, while presenting the latest in business trends and entrepreneurial stories.

Simply raising your conciousness about finding money has the effect of opening doors you may never have noticed before. It may take some stamina to walk through several and each time find another closed door. But hang in there. Maintain your focus, keep looking for that elusive welcome mat and watch what happens.

Carving a Creative Niche in a Small Town

Comfortably nestled in the back of a busy professional music store, Blair Hardman's studio has become part of a central scene that includes instant access to the best session players in the area.

Blair Hardman

Owner, Composer, Engineer

Zone Recording

Cotati, California

HARDMAN
PRODUCTIONS
ZONE Recording

Facility   Located in a small town 50 miles north of San Francisco, near a freeway and a local university. The studio is built in the back room of a pro music equipment store. 10' x 20' live room plus small isolation closet for guitar amps, built into an overall space of 20' x 30'. Groups play in the control room space, with the drummer in the live room.

Setup   Mac-based MIDI system with Performer, a Korg 01/W synth, two ADATs, Mackie 24x8 board, and SMPTE lock to picture for industrial videos and TV commercials.

Focus   Electronic media, including training and industrial videos and radio and TV commercials. For hire to bands and songwriters.

Neighbor Relations   "The advantages of having a recording studio in a music store are incredible. The trick of knowing when to buy equipment is being able to read the wave, learning when to buy and sell. I have a good relationship with the store, so I can get good deals and then sell the equipment in the store when the time is right.

"The reps like me because when they come in, they can try out their new gear here, and it makes for a great showcase for the store. They can bring people back here and show them how various pieces of gear work in a real situation.

"We have teaching studios here, and when the students have come up with what the teachers think is a great song, they'll bring them over and I'll contribute an hour of time. They'll multitrack the song and they go home with a tape that's got strings and drums on it and they take it home to show off to their parents and friends. So what we've got here between me and the store is what we call an escalating war of favors. We just try to outdo each other."

Session Players   "Everybody who works here is a professional working musician. It's such an enjoyable place to work, there's very little turnover. So there's an excellent arranger and sequencer expert here, great guitar players, drummers, etc. Quite often during a session, somebody'll say 'Could we get some guitar on this track?' I'll say 'Yeah, just a second. Hey, Randy?' And he'll come in for a half an hour. It's a big pool of talent, so it works beautifully that way."

Getting a Foothold   "The biggest shot for me was joining the local advertising club. I'd go to their banquets and volunteer to be on various committees. I assisted on the judging committee and got to observe what the top execs thought was good and what wasn't.

"The annual awards ceremony is 500 people, so I also volunteered to produce the music for the event. Each year, the show would start with a 5- or 10-minute production number that I'd write (for free), including lyrics that I'd print up and put on each table with my name and address on it. That really got things rolling. I got to know everybody that way. It had a tremendous effect on my business."

Engineering   "Half of engineering is psychology, when you have a room full of people who are trying to accomplish something. You want them to have a good experience. And a beginning band or songwriter is paying as much for that as for the finished product. So I try to be very good at helping people to enjoy themselves here, like knowing when to tell a joke or when to run their voices through the Harmonizer to make chipmunk sounds when they're getting uptight, just for fun."

Clients From Hell "There have been a number of times when I've wanted to stop and say, 'I can't do this. You have to leave now. This doesn't work,' either because I felt they weren't ready to record or I didn't like them. I've only really done it one time.

"Some people were putting together these English/Japanese language training tapes, based on a Bulgarian system where the different phrases would be read with different music in the background: hot classical, cool jazz, etc. And the Bulgarian and his wife, who was a French woman, were fighting a lot. Also, the Japanese business owner was here with a British guy who was his liaison. Quite a group.

"The session occurred at a time before I'd put in air conditioning, and it was during the summer, so everybody was perspiring madly and we were reading these phrases and the Bulgarian was very excited. He

An impressive wall of local ad club awards and trophies in the control room testifies to the studio's creativity.

would say 'All right, now this music, now that music, now this!' It was very weird. They seemed to be totally confused as well and fought continually.

"We got partway into it and spent several hours on this section and he began excitedly saying, "Okay, okay, this is beginning to work!' At that point, I said 'Let me get an overview here. How many different segments like this are there?' He said, 'Well, this is the first one and there are 94 more.'

"I said, 'I have to talk to you. Now.' I said, 'I'm not the right facility for this project.' I sent them away, and a month or so later, another studio called me and said these crazy people are doing a translation tape. Could I help make any sense of the whole thing?"

Philosophy "I do want to keep growing and expanding. I sometimes forget this is a business and that, hey, I should be making more money. But then I think, well, I'm having a very good time, and I'm making enough."

One of several entertaining
marketing pieces

Blair Hardman's List of
ADVERTISING CLICHES
. . . and what they *really* mean

This cliche . . .	*means*
THE BEST KEPT SECRET IN TOWN	business is lousy.
.....AND MUCH, MUCH MORE	there must be some other interesting things to say but we can't think of them.
EXTRAVAGANZA!	there'll be balloons!
THE BIGGEST LITTLE STORE IN TOWN	it's extremely small.
SAVINGS OF UP TO 70%	the big left-handed green paisley one is 70% off.
GRAND OPENING CELEBRATION!!	there'll be balloons!!
FRIENDLY, COURTEOUS SERVICE	they'll talk to you.
DOLLAR UNDER INVOICE	dealer invoice is not actual dealer anything.
PRICE-BUSTER SALE-ABRATION!!!	there'll be balloons!!!
BUY NOW AND SAVE	go figure.
LOOKING FOR THAT PERFECT GIFT IDEA?	it's December 24.
LIMITED TO STOCK ON HAND	there's one left.
PREFERRED CUSTOMER SALE	you must be from Planet Earth.
ON THE QUIET SIDE OF TOWN	they're behind a burned out gas-station.
MENTION THIS AD AND GET.	is anybody out there?
REGISTER TO WIN	welcome to our mailing list.
DON'T MISS OUR ONCE-IN-A-LIFETIME, EVERYTHING MUST GO, SALE-A-RAMA!!!	there'll be balloons <u>and</u> hot dogs!!!
HOW TO TELL A **blair** HARDMAN PRODUCTION. . . .	if it uses these cliches, it's not.

blair HARDMAN   707/664-1213
<u>PRODUCTIONS</u>   msg 795-6536
ZONE Recording   FAX 664-8078

5

The Project Studio

There are thousands of personal recording studios dotting the landscape. For many people, a mini-setup in a corner of the bedroom is as personally satisfying and fulfilling as one could ask for. But many people aspire to larger operations, which inevitably lead to complex layouts and commercial applications.

There's a whole world of economical business alternatives to conventional multitrack facilities, and in this chapter, we'll explore three types: consumer analog, low-cost digital multitrack and high-end home studios.

Two types of people tend to enter this lucrative end of the business: artists (musicians and producers) who want a place to work, and engineers who want to build their own facility for hire. Most find that as time goes by, the distinction between job titles becomes totally blurred. If a one-person operation is your goal, you'll soon find yourself doing everything from crawling around in the wiring and troubleshooting a patch bay to bouncing your own background vocals, whether or not that may have been the original plan.

Many people find that a solo operation is a satisfying, challenging and creative experience. Composers and songwriters tend to build this type of room. Fine-tuning and honing their facilities becomes an ongoing task as their careers progress, requiring better and better product.

Songwriters always need a good facility to demo their material. Since most writers tend to work at home already, the studio becomes a natural outgrowth of this process, if not a necessity. It's great to set your own hours, work when you want to and engineer as part of the creative process. A 12- or 16-track setup should virtually eliminate the need to record elsewhere, and the savings go into upgrading and adding more equipment instead of paying for tracking in a commercial facility.

As for specialties, both film-score and jingle composers have everything to gain from a place of their own. Unfortunately, the majority of non-major film-scoring work now pays at ludicrously low rates. This is market-driven reality, as so many hungry composers now have their own studios and thus have eliminated all hourly charges. But while that's made for a lot of frustration among more established composers, it's also opened the field to a host of eager newcomers. And the fact is that with an adequate setup, you can stop worrying about the clock and concentrate on your art, creating product that gets directly laid back to the final print.

In the field of advertising, many jingle composers divide their time between home and commercial facilities. The nature of the ad agency business often requires overnight demos, which are best done at home, but which on approval may require a live room that can handle an 18-piece big band and a department's worth of agency people (all arguing about the validity of their input).

And so the home has become a viable and vital part of the recording landscape. All of these facilities tend to share some basic characteristics; namely, they are equipped to deliver somewhere between presentable and broadcast-quality results. They're usually designed to be fully operable by one person, and the vast majority of the work done in them is by the owner. Thus, they've become known as personal project studios.

Home Studios and the All-In Deal

The rise in popularity of home studios is in part related to record-company "all-in deal" budgets, which became popular in the mid-'80s. Major record companies, unhappy with the rising and out-of-control costs their artists were incurring on album projects, decided to change the way they did business: They shifted the responsibility for watching the money away from their own offices and onto the producers who were making the records.

Their reasoning was that instead of arguing with artists who insisted they needed another $30 grand to finish mixing, they'd agree to pay the producer of the album a specified amount of cash to deliver a master. The deal carried the stipulation that in exchange for gaining total financial control, the producer would agree to absorb any cost overruns.

Both sides saw it as an amazingly lucrative deal. Instead of doling out the cash to local studios on an hourly or lockout basis, many producers opted to invest the bulk of the record-company money in building their own facilities and then went about recording without the need to keep an eye on the clock. The incredible benefit, of course, was that they then got to *keep* the studio! Once the studio was built, besides the normal fee the producer made on the album, he was appropriating all the per-hour fee money for himself as well, using it to invest in equipment and contracting. And after an album or two, his personal profit opportunities were potentially huge.

It was quite an arrangement. But the all-in deal has undergone a few transformations since then, due to a few unpleasant side effects. For one, some producers, who had once called the record companies cheapskates and demanded more money to finish their current masterpieces in world-class, for-hire rooms, suddenly became tightwads themselves. Now that it was "their" money, they didn't necessarily want to spend it on making a perfect record!

The effect on the high-end commercial studio business was a double whammy. First, the producers, now in the financial driver's seat on each project, began to demand lower rates from their old studio-owner friends who used to be peers and had now inadvertantly become the money-sucking enemy. This forced prices down as producers, feeling the squeeze of having to spend money they would otherwise get to keep, began to call many more studios for each project and created low-end bidding wars.

Secondly, as the producers began building their own studios at home, they stopped hiring commercial studios altogether in some instances. That created an amazing, paradoxical recession in the established Los Angeles studio business, long regarded as ground zero of the the record industry. First, it made mincemeat out of established studio rate cards, sometimes slashing 60% from normal pricing, with the very real threat of a project going to the next competitor if the studio owner didn't stand up and salute.

But the paradoxical part was that as the major studios began to fold and go broke, the market didn't get shaken out. Instead of benefiting the fewer studios carving up the existing work, the fallen studios were replaced just as quickly by the same home studios that had helped to drive them out of business in the first place.

Now the producers were faced with the same problem they had helped to cause: finding bookings to help pay for the cost of equipping and running their *own* studios. But there was another twist: Many of them weren't as interested in making a profit as they were to simply break even on the payments for all their equipment. That created still more competition for the remaining commercial rooms, keeping rates artificially low to compensate for the lower home-studio rates.

A corollary effect, predictably enough, was that creative product began coming back to the record companies that didn't approach the world standard that was expected from the artists and had been achieved in the past. Remember, the producers didn't want to spend the money! The record companies' answer? Hire "clean-up" producers to finish the work the all-in producer didn't deliver, often contracting to the same commercial studios that had been forsaken in the first place! Unbelievable!

The Current Balance

All this has left commercial studios in quite a quandary. Many producers have neither the ability to record a live band nor sophisticated-enough consoles to do 64-input computerized mixing. So they still need the major studios for completing at least parts of their projects. The newspeak term "mothership" has crept into the vernacular to refer to world-class rooms that provide the high-end equipment and expensive live space lacking in most project rooms.

Meanwhile, commercial owners large and small have had to come to grips with this strangely symbiotic relationship. On the one hand, they are competing with the questionable home studios that flourish as they sidestep paying and withholding taxes and providing medical insurance. But at the same time, they are welcoming these same owner/producers as clients when they need to book time at insisted-upon cut rates. It hasn't been pretty for many commercial rooms. In L.A., it's meant a virtual end to the midrange commercial music studio, and hard times or Chapter 11 for some of the majors.

And it's also created a new strata of pro rooms for hire, with home project rooms now competing on all quality levels. Just as in the labor market, the middle class has been squeezed out.

But some record-company execs have finally begun to figure out that all-in deals don't always make sense. Not only is there a problem with the lower quality some producers are delivering, but the interface between the record company and project studios leaves much to be desired from an administrative standpoint. Paperwork is the last thing that many producers want to deal with, and the commercial rooms are clearly the victors when it comes to being professionally organized.

In sum, it's no longer just fun and games running a recording studio. The writing on the wall, which has been large and clear for years now, is that most studios can't expect to prosper without diversifying and/or finding a specialized niche that works for them. That has meant either staying on the cutting edge of world-class technology by creating ever newer and more sparkly high-end rooms, or breaking new specialized ground, like getting into audio post or editing. In the major cities, competition is fierce.

To make matters even more complex, a number of home studio owners finally got the message regarding the practice of skirting the tax and zoning laws when groups like HARP (Hollywood Association of Recording Professionals) loudly protested the burgeoning competition which they saw as unfair. Several home producers moved their operations into the open by building new commercially zoned rooms. The result was even more *legitimate* competition, in a town that has become severely overbuilt with high-quality rooms for hire. "If we'd realized that when we were complaining so loudly," said one well-known major studio owner, "maybe we wouldn't have made such a fuss in the first place."

HOME STUDIOS AND THE LAW

There's no question that home studios are here to stay. They are a great convenience and a satisfying way to work. Add to that the fact that, as each day passes, it becomes simpler and more affordable to own a manageable amount of equipment that can produce broadcast-quality results, and it's easy to predict the proliferation of the species. With the advent of compact digital setups, many people are setting up systems in their family rooms that cater to one specific aspect of the business, like CD mastering or dialog editing, adding a new facet to the home-recording business.

You definitely need to consider the legal and ethical ramifications of running a home-based business, however. What you do with the information is up to you, but it's crucial to be informed on the specific issues. To that end, let's take moment to focus on the legal considerations regarding home-based studios.

Zoning

Communities are structured by city planners to accommodate and organize a variety of land uses. Housing, schooling, industry and commercial applications are just some of the factors that make a city an attractive place in which to live and work. Each of those real estate concerns is mapped out and zoned for the best return, from the standpoints of taxation, location and the resulting quality of life.

Commercial zoning tends to be on major thoroughfares and designated shopping areas. Industrial regions are isolated from housing tracts, and city services are often grouped together—simple logic.

The complexity begins to occur when people attempt to bring mixed usage to a particular zone. For the most part, cities tend to be clear about what they'll tolerate. It's not very often that you see a thriving hair salon, launderette or convenience store in the middle of a residential neighborhood. That would be an obvious mixed use, and thus an illegal operation in a residential zone.

But what about the guy who does astrological readings in his living room, or the woman who runs a resume service out of her dining area? They're not erecting big neon signs and parking lots, they don't have major delivery trucks driving in and out of the neighborhood, and the clients who come in for business don't look much different from a typical visitor to someone's home.

Because of that, city councils tend to look the other way when homeowners do a quiet business out of their residentially zoned dwellings. No one complains, there is no environmental impact and frankly, the city has much bigger fish to fry.

Home project studios occupy a deliciously delicate balance between these two scenarios. You could argue that there's no signage, that foot traffic in and out is minimal and that noise is contained and no one is complaining. But the city could also claim that you've clearly violated zoning laws with a studio for hire in a residential district, that you are illegally collecting commercial fees on non-commercial and therefore non-taxable business property and that you are affecting the quality of life in your community with increased traffic, deliveries and noise in your formerly quiet and serene neighborhood.

Home studio owners cope with these arguments in a variety of ways. If, in fact, the only recording you're doing is for your own work, then you really do define the term "personal project studio." Simple logic contends that you're as guiltless as an accountant who takes his or her work home on the weekend and spreads it out on the dining-room table. The work is being done by one person on a per-job basis. Trucks aren't being unloaded with equipment at midnight, scalawags aren't blowin' weed in the back yard, and smokestacks aren't billowing ashes into neighbors' yards from the giant furnace fires used to power those monster monitors metal rockers love to listen to before they turn 30 and go deaf.

Instead, one person is making a legitimate living out of the home, which, he or she will argue, is good for the environment, gets one more car off the road and increases the quality and enjoyment of the owner's life.

On the other hand, if you are indeed renting time in your home studio to people who are doing their own work, then you've become a studio for hire, just like hundreds of others around the country. If push comes to shove in the eyes of a city inspector, you'll probably be less likely to prevail in the zoning and taxation departments.

In fact, the phenomenon of the full-blown home SSL room has grown into an alarming challenge for major commercial studio owners. The fact that many home facilities can offer cut rates on the same equipment as their larger counterparts has caused real acrimony among commercial owners, who must bear the extra burden of business property costs, plus state and federal taxation.

For every loss of business taxation dollars, a community is either going to have to find a new source or cut that much further back on the services they provide. This makes for spirited debate from all sides when ordinance issues come to the fore, and many cities have found themselves awash in a seemingly endless holding pattern while people continue to run around and do more research on the matter. Naturally, the larger the city, the more the confusion. And thus, home ordinance laws are painfully slow in coming.

As time marches on, city halls across the country continue to grapple with redefining commercial zones, what constitutes gainful employment and how it impacts each area's quality of life. Some have drafted novella-sized ordinances, detailing every potential kind of home employment and ruling on its impact on both neighbors and the city's tax roles.

Both pro and con organizations energetically hail the idea of detailed ordinances as the answer to the home-studio debate. Homeowner organizations lobby to protect the sanctity and relative safety of their neighborhoods, and home-worker groups trumpet the lowered pollution and energy costs saved by eliminating commutes to work. They also point to lower traffic rates and fewer accidents, and stress the tie-ins with the digital superhighway. Certainly, both groups have valid arguments, and hopefully many compromises lay ahead.

In the meantime, there's a lot of recording going on in the basements and garages of America, and a lot of people insisting it's their God-given right. Ask a dozen people about this issue and you'll get a dozen different opinions.

I Fought the Law, and the Law...Shrugged

What's the likelihood of getting shut down by a building inspector? Only time will tell. When the studio owners of L.A. got together to discuss their problems in the late '80s, one of the things they did was to identify the most blatant home studios for hire in town and keep an eye on their interactions with the city. Though HARP drew the line at actually turning in lists of names to the city (HARP board members decided that was a line they did not care to cross, in part because their own clients made up much of the list), they noted the activities of local homeowner and neighborhood associations around town and kept the pressure up on City Hall to draft some pertinent ordinances.

Some operators of blatant home studios were called in by a number of unhappy groups and individuals from their surrounding neighborhoods. City building inspectors showed up, and in some instances actually shut facilities down, padlocking doors and assessing fines and penalties for zoning violations.

But in retrospect, those few home-studio owners were waving their own red flags. They had built full-blown stages and control rooms in their living rooms or garages, kept a staff of employees, and significantly impacted the traffic and parking problems on their streets. Neighbors would complain about drunken or loud conversations on the sidewalks in the middle of the night, multiple FedEx deliveries during the day and amplified noise wafting through the neighborhood at all hours. Who wouldn't get annoyed?

Still, it's a mighty sweet temptation to avoid the high cost of commercial space and its accompanying taxation. This isn't gun-running or mail fraud. "An' if they catch ya," smiled one throaty old blues-jammer, "ya ain't gonna wind up in the joint for jammin' in yer crib."

Well, no. But if all it takes is one competitor or frustrated neighbor making an anonymous call to the local zoning board, then how safe are you? Few of us look forward to unannounced visits from humorless government agents who aren't dressed like postmen.

Meanwhile, the vast majority of small and medium-sized operations have continued to flourish on residential blocks across the country. Owners take care to isolate the potentially objectionable noise they make, admonish their visitors to respect the neighbors, and pay attention to keeping a low profile, eschewing advertising and overt physical indicators of commerce.

Variances

On the local administrative end, there does exist the possibility of a home business getting individually sanctioned. Some project studio owners, tired of waiting for council action that may be years away, apply to their city for a zoning variance. A variance allows a business to operate in a zone that is officially off-limits, giving special permission on a case-by-case basis.

Some people have good luck with this, but many others are reticent about attracting attention by officially notifying the city that they are operating without a variance to begin with. If a variance sounds like a good idea to you, check with your attorney for advice before you contact City Hall.

TAX ISSUES

It's fine to do your own projects in the comfort of your own home. Taxwise, a project studio may be considered a home office, and all the legitimate expenses can be written off over a period of time.

But the hard facts are that if you book outside session work and thus go into business, your business, whatever it is, is supposed to be subject to state and local laws and regulations. And unless your home happens to be in a commercial business zone, you are technically operating outside of the law. Simply put, a commercial business must be conducted in a commercial, rather than a residential, zone.

The loudest complaints from competing commercial studio owners have, not surprisingly, centered around these taxation issues. A commercial studio owner, by definition, must bear the brunt of a slew of special business taxes that can absolutely cripple a business which may be teetering on the financial edge. Consider the following list of yearly responsibilities for which a modest home studio-for-hire would be technically responsible:

1. Property tax

An amount levied on both the real estate value of the commercial property *and* the city assessor's valuation of all the *equipment* owned by the business; typically 1% to 3% of the current value. Example: You own $60,000 worth of recording gear. Your yearly property tax is $1,200.

2. Worker's Comp

Worker's compensation benefits are co-paid by the state and the employer in the form of a yearly tax based on wages. Currently, in California, the amount is computed by multiplying the total taxable wages paid to all employees and owners by 1.37.

Example: You earn a modest $45,000 a year. Your part-time assistant, receptionist and relief engineer make a combined total of $38,000. Your total employer contribution to the state yearly is $1,137.

3. Withholding

Employers pay the equivalent of an extra 10% on top of all employee- and owner-earned wages to help offset the cost of unemployment and other assessments. Our example yields an additional $3,800.

4. FUTA

Federal Unemployment Tax; the federal portion of unemployment taxes. That's right, employers pay twice. Figured on the the amount of salary over $7,000 multiplied by 0.008, which equals a modest $93 in this case.

5. Unemployment Compensation

Based on regular employee time only, and no charge for employer's pay. $1.59 per $100 = $604.

Total Yearly Taxes Due: $6,834.00

This is a sobering amount for a modest operation, working out to $569 per month. Think of what the big guys with 20 full-time staffers are paying! Yes, it's all relative, but is it fair to be in a commercial location and pay tens of thousands in extra taxes while competing home studios pay none? It's no wonder some commercial owners are so worked up about the cut rates homeowners may offer.

GETTING REAL

Home and project studios have become a major and viable presence, and they are certainly the wave of the future. You can't beat the comfort, convenience and budgetary considerations, not to mention the incredible quality you can produce on a table-top.

Many cities are wrestling with the complex questions of regulating home-based businesses and trying to pass new legislation that makes them both legal and operable without hurting competitors or straining neighborhood relations. Some have already passed sweeping new home-worker ordinances that will affect their citizenry for years to come, sanctioning home offices and approving them for a variety of uses. You can't argue with eliminating the stress of rush hour and using the time to be more productive and feel more happy about being alive.

So what's likely to happen is what's already begun: Project studios will become professional operations that benefit their composers and artists in residence, while commercial locations will continue to cater to more complex live dates, large groups, special services and sophisticated mixing chores.

If you take that scenario to bear, then the midsize studio will not be staging a comeback in the foreseeable future. Caught in the middle, these operations will be forced into lower and lower rate structures in order to remain competitive with home operations and will eventually disappear from the commercial landscape as we know it today.

Also, as home-based businesses become more professionally accepted, matters of business taxation will get the focus and fairness they deserve. In the meantime, the present situation is a matter of personal and professional ethics for each individual to deal with.

INDEPENDENT CONTRACTORS

In 1993, the IRS set up one of its infamous audit task forces to check out the entertainment industry in Hollywood. Their mission was to concentrate on the broad use of independent contractors on movie sets and related studios. A whole team of auditors was schooled in the practices of the industry and then unleashed on a wide variety of studio businesses.

The results weren't pretty. The auditors had the power to go back seven years if they chose to, and to pick as many as all seven for intense scrutiny. Their goal was to pull out the taxes due on people who commonly hired themselves out as independent contractors, prove that they were in fact employees, using a set of federal guidelines, and then tax the *employer* for all the back withholding due, plus penalties.

The results were devastating for many companies, most of whom are still going through the courts as of this writing. The IRS, in an unexpected crackdown on employers, determined to change their previous and more lenient stance on independent contractors (ICs).

For many years, there has been a 20-factor set of guidelines to determine each worker's status and to qualify him or her as an IC. Up until this crackdown, the conventional wisdom stated that as long as a worker met at least ten of the factors, that worker qualified for IC status. Now the IRS came along, changed its tune and informed employers that they'd never said that. In the task force's eyes, if a worker violated even *one* of the 20 factors, he couldn't be an IC.

When an independent contractor makes a yearly compensation of, say, $60,000, normal employee tax withholding might run $20,000. But an employer takes no withholding out of an IC's pay. The IC is not considered to be an employee and is therefore responsible for his or her own payment of taxes.

The reasons this is beneficial to the employer are twofold: First, it greatly reduces the amount of paperwork the employer must generate and eliminates any employee benefits he would otherwise have to pick up, like health insurance; and second, all employers have to pay a tax equal to about 10% of an employee's gross pay as their employer's share of contributions to Social Security. That means an extra $6,000 paid out during the course of the year to the government by the employer.

Suddenly, the IRS was saying that regardless of what the IC's had paid out themselves over the years, the employers were responsible for the entire amount of withholding, plus penalties for any and all years they were inspecting. That's roughly $33,000 per IC per year. If the IRS prevails, this could quickly bankrupt any small or medium-sized business that has employed multiple independent contractors!

Undoubtedly, some court-assisted compromise will rise from the fury all this business has stirred up. But the message from the IRS is clear: Your IC's had better stick to the letter of the law, or we'll make life miserable for you later on. Have a nice day.

Determining Independent Contractor Status

For years, engineers who worked freelance for multiple studios were treated as independent contractors. It was the custom of the business community to do so, and one of the key factors that attorneys are now arguing in tax court. It seemed simple enough to assume that since the engineer only showed up once or twice a week, or sometimes not at all for a couple of months and then for a week at a time, that such a person was not a regular employee of the company. But those assumptions are gone. Now, in the eyes of Uncle Sam, anyone who works for a company which schedules their workers' hours is most assuredly an employee, even if those hours occur only once a month.

Here are some of the 20 factors the IRS uses in determining the potential independent contractor status of a worker:

1. No instructions: Contractors are not required to follow, nor should they be furnished with, instructions to accomplish a job.

2. Services don't have to be rendered personally: Contractors have the right to hire others to do the actual work.

3. Work not essential to the hiring firm: A company's ongoing business should not have to

depend on the services of outside contractors. An example would be an architectural firm that used on-call project architects as independent contractors.

4. Setting their own hours: Contractors set their own work hours.

5. Job location: Contractors must have control of where they work. If they work on the premises, their work should not be subject to that company's direct supervision.

6. Paid by the job: Contractors are paid by the job, not by the hour.

7. Have own tools: Contractors should furnish their own tools.

8. Can't be fired at will: Contractors can't be fired so long as they produce a result that meets the contract specifications.

The rest of the 20 regulations are less relevant and easier to bypass for recording engineers. So in the past, it was easy to meet half of the factors. But how many of the above regulations can you dodge in the studio business? Remember, the IRS now claims that violating any *one* is grounds for employee status.

Taking Your Medicine

This is clearly a signal that times have changed on the tax front. Many commercial studio owners have heeded these warnings and changed nearly all of their worker relationships from independent contracting to employee status. It's a small tax bite to swallow now, as opposed to potential disaster or ruination later on.

It may take years for all this to shake out in court. And as of late 1994, still more revisions were afoot. A committee of CPAs and tax regulators announced that major changes were on the horizon, which could possibly lead to an overhaul of the IRS formula for independent contractors. Ultimately, it may become much easier to qualify, because specific guidelines were being drawn for the entertainment and production industry in light of the hue and cry raised after the preceding years' witch hunts.

But nothing had been decided, and the committee had been meeting for something like two years. Sounds like the government, doesn't it? Consult with your accountant before deciding what to do, and be sure that he or she looks into whatever newly formed rules for our industry might emerge from the IRS.

Qualifying for IC Status

Naturally, there is some light at the end of this tunnel. Independent contractors have a legitimate place in the audio world, and with the current trend towards more project-studio output, there is at least one area in which the concept makes good sense: music and dialog editing.

Many creative musicians, engineers and producers have embraced the incredible potential of desktop nonlinear editing systems, setting up a Pro Tools, Dyaxis or other affordable workstation at home. These rigs are extremely powerful and compact, capable of producing completely professional results. They excel for music editing, dialog cleanup and assembly, time compression and even film and video sweetening. And there is a good and productive relationship to be had between commercial stu-

dios and these professionals working at home.

It fits nicely into a multilayered film project, for instance. The facility gets the project and farms out a few of the components. It may handle the Foley, music recording, ADR and final mix. But there is still dialog and music editing to be done, and in major cities, independent contractors are a ready and convenient asset for the job at hand.

They take the work off the premises, do it for a flat fee per reel or per project, deliver within a specified period and handle the job using their own tools, location and personnel. That makes them independent contractors, pure and simple, which means that the studio saves taxes, time and space. And the IC gets to work at home on a purely professional basis.

As the technology progresses, more areas of specialty will no doubt open up to project studios, which will help bridge the uneasy gap that now exists between commercial and home-based operations.

Creating an Ultimate Destination

Frank Serafine has become a respected composer and electronic sound effects artist in the L.A. film, TV and advertising market. Using his studio exclusively for his own projects, he offers a prime example of the project studio carried to the highest professional level.

Career Roots Started as a composer and at age 22 was hired to do the sound effects for the first Star Trek movie, working out of his apartment with headphones. For his next film, he moved into a space at a major film recording studio complex and collaborated on projects for years in trade for studio space. From there, he moved first to a home facility created in a four-car garage, then spent nearly five years planning, building and finishing his present, permanent facility.

Notable Projects Sound effects design on *Star Trek I* and *III*, *The Day After* and *Lawnmower Man*. Touring SFX performer with Peter Gabriel. Multiple-speaker-array sound and music for simulator rides in theme parks worldwide.

Facility Multi-use building, zoned for living and commercial production. Custom-designed and built for over $3 million. First floor: offices for rent; second: high-ceilinged suite of four studios, plus reception area and a 30-foot waterfall; third: permanent home; roof: lush garden with Jacuzzi.

Studios total 2,200 square feet. Music studio, Foley/ADR stage, effects studio, mix stage to THX spec. Otari 24-track with Dolby SR, Otari Premiere console with DiskMix 3, tons of keyboards and outboard effects.

Staff Five full-time employees. "Everybody is an all-around person. You've got to be a combination sound designer, mixer and engineer."

Marketing Nothing formal. "Once you do something for a film company, their promotion department creates documentaries and articles. If the film becomes a success, then everybody gets to ride on it. So I've been very lucky in that I haven't really had to go out and pound the pavement. I just do the work, and get calls for articles and more projects.

"I do have to get out and see people. It can get isolated here in a home studio. So I go and find out about projects that I'd like to work on. I hear about things and think, 'Wow, I'd like to work on that,' and then I have to go and find out who the people are. Sometimes I get 'em and sometimes I don't.

"In the freelance world, there's a certain amount of interaction with directors and other people—parties, trade shows and the like. I do a lot of trade shows as an exhibitor, presenter or panelist. I just did one last weekend. Several producers were there to see the show, and I got a call on Monday to come down and screen something as a result of that. So a lot of it is showing the industry how I'm doing my work and getting a response that way."

On the New Space Everything is to code, including installing and reimbursing the cost of new telephone poles and transformers to meet electrical codes. "I've gone through two years of hell with Plan-Check [in L.A., every time you make a change, it has to be approved by the city], and that's why so many people go bootleg in their own homes. They know how difficult it's going to be if they want to do it legally. There's one major roadblock after another when you do it by the book.

"Here in L.A., there are only two zones that allow artists to live and work in the same building. And I still had to go meet my potential neighbors and get signatures on a petition to help get final approval to build."

Frank Serafine

Owner

Serafine Inc.

Venice, California

SERAFINE

This impressive building houses several city-sanctioned studios and offices, plus complete top-floor living quarters and a rooftop garden.

Financing "The musicians' union has a credit union, which got real interested in what I was doing. I met the treasurer and the next thing I knew, they had agreed to finance the building.

"It was a great situation that I managed to get in before the door slammed. They're not planning to do that again for quite a while. The union wants to see it happen and they want to be a part of it, so I was very lucky to get such a unique deal."

On the New Building "Right now, I just need to keep everything under control. I got this whole thing done and it's pretty expensive to keep up. Now I just wanna keep doing the really cool gigs and get as creative as possible. The last few years of just getting this facility done, I did it out of necessity of getting to this point where, man, I'm just doing what I've been wanting to do my whole life."

Doing ADR "A huge part of what we do is ADR. We bring in a lot of actors to re-loop lines. The actors are in another unconnected room, so we train a camera on them and put them up on large screen on the mix stage. You can see them as if they're on screen. It's even better than if you look at them live. So the producer sits back here on the dub stage and watches it in a very unique presentation."

Living In a Box "I don't ever go out. I occasionally go out for a cup of coffee or with clients, but a lot of the time people are dropping in. I'm located at the beach, so it's very busy here all the time. The only drawback is that people can get a hold of you a little too easily even when you really want to disconnect.

"But it's cool living upstairs. I can watch TV for a while or make a sandwich and lay down for 15 minutes and get away, close off my working environment, then come back feeling so different, having a new perspective on everything just because I was able to, like, touch my home for a second. I can kinda go and rejuve."

6

Expense Planning

It costs money to run a business, and a lot of it changes hands in a recording studio. Rent, salaries, utilities, tape, bank and lease payments, taxes...and don't forget the guy who comes around every two weeks to wash the windows. Then there's the merchant and rental accounts, petty cash disbursements, office supplies and unexpected expenses that just show up out of thin air.

There's also a very definite element of keeping up with the Joneses, which in this case means staying informed about the latest equipment on the market and how it's affecting the way you and the guys down the block are doing business. And finally, let's not forget that gleaming new piece of outboard gear that you never knew you desperately needed until some client announced that without it, your whole operation was basically unsuitable for his latest project.

Finding a Break-Even Point

A critical part of your planning has to do with deciding what your monthly break-even point is going to be, from when you first start acquiring equipment and space to a year later and beyond. If you're about to do this for the first time, you may be in for some pretty sobering news: It takes some heavy dough to maintain the music flow, bro.

But knowing what's in store before you go in and buy everything in sight is the key to maintaining an efficient operation. So it's a good idea to start with a template that lists the monthly expenses you're likely to incur. The Monthly Expense Worksheet on the next page categorizes the main areas of professional studio outlay. You may find it helpful to make a few copies, so that as the picture of your operation comes more into focus, you can make the necessary changes.

There's also some extra space in each category to add other items that only *you* know you need. Once you've filled in all the blanks, you can use the subtotals as a categorical summary on the expense column in a cash-flow chart.

You may not need everything on the list, at least not in the beginning. And if you're putting your place together in a home or garage, you may already have an adequate phone or security system. If you do, you may now be able to write most or all of those expenses off of your taxes as the cost of doing business (ask your accountant about that—don't just take it for granted).

Many commercial spaces offer janitorial, water, power and even reception services to their tenants. And if your business is a sole proprietorship, or just you and a partner or two, you may be able to get by without paying any salaries for a while, let alone establishing a medical plan.

But as your business begins to grow, you'll most likely find yourself signing monthly checks for everything on the list, as well as a few extra items like psychiatric consultations or physical therapy. Okay, I'm half joking and half serious. We actually did a marathon session one time for which the client enlisted the services of a chiropractor/massage therapist. She arrived at about midnight with her own portable massage table, oils and towels. The project had just gotten into several hours of electric guitar overdubs, and the producer and musicians were working together in the control room recording direct through the console.

Casandra set up her table in the studio behind the rolling gobos surrounding the vocal mic for a modicum of privacy, and for the next three hours took on all comers with superlative back massages at a dollar a minute. Nobody could resist her, and she left at about 4:00 a.m. with a good $200 in her pocket.

Charley-horses and rejuvenated guitar

Monthly Expense Worksheet

Fixed

Rent/Mortgage	
Power & Water	
Phone Service	
Misc. Utilities	
Security	
Loan Payments	
Lease Payments	
Health Plan	
Commercial Insurance	
Life Insurance	
City Permits	
Misc.	
Total	

Variable

Equipment Purchases	
Spare Parts	
Computer Hardware	
Computer Software	
Blank Tape/Disks	
Furniture	
Studio Supplies	
Office Supplies	
Advertising	
PR	
Petty Cash	
Total	

Pro Services

Accounting	
Bookkeeping	
Legal	
Equipment Maintenence	
Equipment Rental	
Equipment Repair	
Studio Cleaning Service	
Piano Tuner	
Air Conditioning Service	
Copier Service	
Total	

Salaries

Owner	
Partner	
Studio Manager	
1st Engineer/s	
Maintenence Engineer	
Assistant Engineer/s	
Salesperson	
Interns/Runners	
Receptionist	
Total	

Total Expenses $

This kind of expense sheet can help you keep track of spending. Note the blank spaces for additional expenses.

elbows aside, the grand total at the bottom of the expense chart should equal the bottom-line cost of running the studio, and can range from $15-40,000 per month with a staff of five or six. But cheer up—the only way to get into those kinds of figures is to be doing the volume of business that supports them, and that should mean that your studio has become a success.

The rest of this chapter goes into detail on the nature of each of the itemized expenses.

FINDING SPACE

In major cities like L.A. or New York, rent will most likely be the largest single expense you have. You can save a lot of money by renting unfinished warehouse space and building your own studio, but you should bear in mind that contracting charges on pro interior studio construction run from a bare-bones $30 to an ultra-luxurious $250 per finished *square foot*. Unless you're an experienced carpenter with time on your hands, you can expect to pay at least $20,000 for a 1,000 square-foot control room and studio setup that potential clients will take seriously.

But in cities where the studio industry is well-established, there are some very attractive alternatives. The first one is to find an existing recording studio that has been vacated (or is about to be) and is for rent. This is a great way to start up a business.

To get started, call several major real estate companies in your area and tell them you're interested in leasing commercial space that would be suitable for a recording studio. If you've never considered that real estate brokers would be in the leasing business, you'll be amazed to find that many have full-scale leasing divisions. Those that don't will refer you to the companies that do.

A major benefit at this point is that time is on your side. If you aren't overburdened by a self-imposed killer deadline, you'll get a fascinating education in the local commercial real estate market, and you may get to see some wonderful spaces. And with a little time on your hands, you won't feel so pressured to take the first deal that comes your way. Instead, you'll be able to go home, do some rough figuring and sketches and learn more about the kind of space and layout that works the best.

Planning Ahead

The trick is to develop a relationship with a few brokers while you're midway into planning your business. If you can tell an agent that you're looking seriously but have a few months to find something, they'll stay in touch with you regularly as new listings come up.

With perseverance, it's possible to become the leaseholder of a once-great studio that previously housed a full-fledged, expensively built operation. There's just no way a former tenant can take a soundproofed control room wall or a drum booth with them when they leave, which

can leave you standing in the middle of a gorgeous, lovingly designed and well-executed vacant studio for lease, just waiting for a few machines and a console to be rolled in and wired up.

Incredibly, about half the time the landlord would just as soon tear the insides out and turn the space back into offices or stores. But those are the times to make your best deal, because this type of property owner doesn't know what he's got, and can usually be talked into renting the space "as is" with no added premium, or at a bargain rate.

Brokers usually know better. They know that developed rooms, in this case recording studios, are more valuable than just plain raw space. They'll often advertise special spaces in the local trades, and the rent per square foot may be appreciably higher. You may even find yourself occupying a studio that you formerly worked in as a client and that originally cost $100,000 or more to build.

But whether you out-and-out steal it or have to pay a premium for the privilege of refitting a

A flyer advertising a studio space for lease.

former studio, the extra time and money you save should be well worth the effort.

Bigger Challenge, Bigger Reward

The second alternative to leasing raw space is a little further out, and a good deal less likely, which is probably why it worked magically for my partner and me.

When we first started working on our business plan, we obtained a directory of all the pro studios in L.A. Then we called each one, and asked if they might have a spare studio in their building that wasn't pulling its earnings potential. We offered to lease such a room on a long-term basis.

This was something of an outrageous idea. We called everyone, from the smallest places in town to some of the world's mightiest, and came on to the owners like land barons. I think that was the origin of our rallying cry "Coconuts!" as in "balls as big as..." To this day, it's a theme that we continue to live by.

Anyway, the interesting part of this little adventure was that since we were calling studios with rooms to hire, many managers and owners were somewhat intrigued with the idea of what in essence was a three-year lockout deal. They listened with interest as we made our best pitch.

Our nagging problem, however, was two-fold. One part was that there were very few existing studio complexes with a spare room just sort of lying around that could be leased. And second, we simply couldn't bluff our way past the, uh, money issue. At the time, we could squeeze together maybe $3,500 a month for a fully equipped 24-track studio, subject of course to our stringent standards of approval. (Never mind that $3,500 normally bought a couple of *days* in these places. Remember: "Coconuts!")

Putting Your Coconuts on the Table

About midway through our search, we got into a few very intriguing conversations with the owner of a well-established, cutting-edge Hollywood studio that had three great rooms. This friendly, easy-going, successful guy was amenable to discussing our idea of leasing his smallest room out. By this time, we'd gotten pretty good at skirting the money issue on the phone, making references instead to the kinds of plans we had and the projects we'd done, etc.

We set up a meeting at the studio, and for an hour, toured this beautiful facility, got cozy with the owner and started falling in love with the room that could be ours. Even though it was the littlest of the three, the control room had an API console, loads of outboard gear, gorgeous quarry-rock walls, and a studio that could accommodate a 16-piece orchestra. The owner had even found a little private office upstairs for us.

After a lot of notetaking, good conversation and planning, he finally discreetly raised the subject of the monthly rent. We all walked out of the control room and began to move slowly down the dimly lit hallway, lined with gold and platinum records, toward his office at the other end. I knew the moment of truth had come. I glanced at my partner, took a deep but tentative breath, looked him straight in the eye and told him we were prepared to go as high as four thousand a month.

There was a brief moment of dead silence as the three of us shared the same intake of breath. The only emotion that showed through the smile that didn't crack on our deadpan host was a slight quivering and reddening of his neck muscles, as he put his arm firmly around my shoulder, half-whispered that he had a figure closer to *40* thousand in mind, and propelled us with adrenaline-powered force out through a magically appearing emergency exit door in the middle of the hallway, pulling it firmly shut behind us.

Fifteen seconds after I'd made our offer, we found ourselves standing completely alone outdoors, squinting under the blazing noonday sun in a back alley strewn with garbage and broken glass, and looking at an old bolted metal door with no handle on the outside. As the sound of an approaching garbage truck filled our ears, we exchanged stupefied, glazed stares for a moment and slowly shuffled down the alley trying to figure out where the hell our little kingdom had just disappeared to. The only element missing was the comic underscore that should have swelled up to remind us that it was only a movie.

It was the most disorienting (and looking back, the funniest) negative turn of events we ever experienced in our quest for space.

Staying With the Program

And what a range of emotions there were, as we continued to work our way down the alphabetized list of L.A. studios. Between us, we had first-hand knowledge of about half the places in town, and when we came to one, we'd feel rushes of excitement, anguish or just plain disbelief that we were actually calling, say, Stevie Wonder's facility with the intention of moving in. "Yo, Stevie! Check it out! We'll trade riffs after the session. Later, homes!"

That experience alone was a unique kind of training, talking to all the professional owners and managers in town and getting a feel for what our eventual peers were like. Putting an idea like this across on the phone in a few seconds and getting a positive response was a real challenge.

But it wasn't until we got to the U's that the magic happened, and therein lies the point of this whole exercise. Because about 150 phone calls into our adventure, we finally found a sympathetic ear and, lo and behold, an empty and available room.

A peach of a guy named Dean Austin was the senior manager of a legendary studio in Hollywood called United Western, which had been around since the '50s and had been a major player on the recording scene during the '60s record business years. Groups like the Beach Boys had cut albums there. But now the original managers had retired, and things had slowed way down in this once top-rated facility.

The building housed four rooms, and two had already been leased to another production company that specialized in jingles. That left the enormous main room, which could accommodate a 70-piece orchestra; and the smallest room, into which you could squeeze a rhythm section and maybe a couple of horns (if they were careful and didn't do steps).

The Payoff

Mr. Austin apologized and said that was all he had, but that he'd be amenable to a fair deal. We slammed the phone down, barreled over to the building, jumped out of the car, ran to the door, stopped dead in our tracks, straightened our ties, fixed our hair and sauntered inside at one mile per hour, copping our best Joe Cool attitude.

When we saw the studio, it looked like a palace to us. We dropped most of the fake pretense, and bit our lips to keep from screaming when he told us he'd not only give us the room, but could outfit the place with virtually everything except a console. For that kind of deal, he'd have to get $2,500 a month!

We moved in three weeks later and started up our business at a prestige address, sharing

the hall with a building full of seasoned pros and blessing this one man we'd dug out of thin air who had changed our lives.

Our year and a half at United Western was a tremendous experience. We shared the client lounge with some of the great artists of the world, sauntered down the hall late at night to hang out at other sessions or borrow tape, and made some unique connections. It had all come from persevering with this crazy idea, and finding just one person who had the power to help make it all happen.

Sometimes that's all you need to find: one person who opens the doors of opportunity and change. When you operate from that standpoint, you find that the world doesn't seem so intimidating, because the ultimate connection comes down to a simple one-on-one.

The point is to clearly visualize your goal and stay with it. If you can do that, the chances are that something or someone will align with you. And when that happens, you'll find it's time to start visualizing your *next* goal.

A Unique Alternative: The Tenant/Landlord Venture

As successful working musicians progress from one area of career focus to another, their circumstances can change dramatically. For Tom Seufert, an L.A.-based guitarist/composer/producer, that meant running three separate studio operations over a ten-year period. But the most intriguing situation he was able to arrange demonstrates how unique each individual business can be, given enough thought and imagination.

When he decided to move up from a home 24-track setup to a full-fledged commercial enterprise, Tom, like us, went off in search of an existing multiroom facility with some available space for rent. After a lot of effort, he found a complex that had an extra studio that was, for the most part, vacant. The exception was that it had a decent monitor system (since the room had formerly been used as a mastering facility) and some permanent equipment racks already installed. The owner had been using the room just for songwriting and had planned to develop it slowly as time went on.

When Seufert approached him with the idea of leasing it, the owner hesitated, wary of abandoning his plan. He couldn't quite let the place go for just a monthly rent check. So Tom offered instead to set up a profit-sharing deal that would depend on the amount of business that passed through the room.

The two sat down and figured out what sort of business Tom could bring in, based on his past experience and contacts. Then they figured out what the value of his tenancy in the building would be. The owner would provide not only the studio space and monitor system, but also a receptionist, parking, electricity and even a phone system.

Once they agreed on the monthly value of all those services, they determined that it would be a good bet to trade them, along with free rent, for a profit-sharing deal that amounted to a split of 60% for Tom and 40% for the owner on all the billing, after the costs of engineering personnel, phone bills and other miscellaneous items were deducted.

The advantage to the owner was that he was getting a piece of the earnings from a studio's worth of equipment that he didn't have to buy. The advantage for Tom was that in return for moving in all his equipment, he could forgo all the usual monthly expenses incurred in operating the business.

The deal was a great success. Tom did well by bringing in a lot of business, and the owner got a piece of a second room at virtually no extra expense above his existing overhead.

It worked so well that three years later the studio owner exercised his contractual option to evict his tenant. He'd made enough to be able to buy his own equipment and keep a hundred percent of the billing.

Seufert was shocked when he received a legal notice of eviction in the mail. He'd been doing well there, but he had no choice, and he pulled his equipment out, wondering what to do next. But when you're that resourceful, you usually wind up landing on your feet.

"I was very disappointed at how he handled the situation," he told me. "But by kicking me out when he did, I was forced to rethink my career and figure out what to do next. And that turned into a whole new area that I never would've found without having been forced to. I was very comfortable in that setup. But as a result of the abrupt and unwanted change, I stepped into working on film scores and commercial production, which moved me up into a whole new league. I could kiss that guy today."

PHONE SYSTEMS

There's no question that the act of simply ordering up a multiline telephone installation can be enough to make you rethink your whole dumb idea about going into business for yourself. But while it's a hassle to get just your lines installed, the real dilemma comes in choosing a phone *system*.

While it's true that you can fake it with conventional phones, the obvious choice is to install a multiline system that can grow with you. Although it may seem like overkill in the beginning, a six-line system gives you the space to grow.

With a phone system, you can start with just two or three separate numbers and add more as time goes on. Your receptionist can screen your calls before they interrupt the flow in the control room. And you can do some interesting tricks, like dedicating a line to use as a combination door intercom and electric entry buzzer. Then, as the need arises, more lines can be added for just the cost of the service itself. And that may become necessary sooner than you think.

The savings come in avoiding an expensive upgrade a year or two down the line when you outgrow your original two-line system and have to discard it (it's very rare that a two- or three-line system can be upgraded past its original capacity). On the other hand, the cost can get serious. A rough rule of thumb is to figure about $250 to $800 per line capability, so a six-line system with eight phones may run somewhere in the $2,000-$4,000 range. That's partly because what you're really buying is a substantial computer setup.

Advantages Over a Normal Telephone

The heart of the phone system is the KSU (short for Key Service Unit), a wall-mounted computer in a box that can be programmed to handle all of your communication needs. Modern phone systems come with a host of programmable features allowing you to decide which phones will ring on an incoming call during the day and which will ring after hours.

They also provide privacy on each line with individual intercom paging, and usually offer restricted dialing, which means that they can be programmed to allow direct dialing to only one or two area codes (you haven't lived until you get a long-distance bill with a 30-minute call to Tokyo that was made the day that Japanese production team came in to look at the control room).

Most also have message-waiting lights, conference calling, speed dialing, music on hold and hands-free speakers. Sounds like a bit much, but once you get used to all the features, you'll wonder how you ever lived without them.

Virtually all of the phone-system companies carry their own leasing and purchase programs, and offer extended service contracts, which are pricey (or is that *piracy*?) but often worthwhile for the first year or two; depending on the quality and reliability of your system, you'll probably need at least a couple of service calls to the original company, which tend to be very expensive. That's because the phone company that bills you for the line service has nothing to do with the actual phone equipment. They will send service people to fix the lines leading up to the phones, but their obligation stops at the end of the connecting cord. With a phone-system contract, at least you know that the price includes the full extent of your service costs.

Other sources for good deals on a system include good discount appliance or business stores. Many now sell complete, brand-name starter systems at discount prices. Just be sure that you understand their service agreements and that you're covered for on-site support. Even simple systems can develop major operational problems, and your phone service is something that you really need to depend on, so don't be tempted to save money now and worry about any service hassles later. Pay the fee, cuss the company out and relax. Later on, you'll be able to indignantly demand the level of service you paid for, and will most likely need.

Finding the Right Equipment

It's hard to choose the right system. There are dozens that all claim they were built with *you* in mind. Try to avoid gimmick-laden or cute-looking phones; they're usually cheap and trouble-prone. Trade the appeal of an LCD readout through a pink Cadillac windshield mockup for a phone that won't crack open when it falls off the console for the twelfth time.

One good idea is to notice which systems look professional when you're in other offices, restaurants or studios, and then call each company for an on-site demonstration. They will send a salesperson to your location with a complete demo setup and take you through the system. Take the time to book two or three systems that seem to be attractive and affordable for an office demo.

A good test for quality is to have the rep plug a phone into your existing line and then let you call a friend and ask how the sound quality is. There is a wide difference between systems,

and you're undoubtedly going to have clients holding the receiver up to the speaker to play back a mix for someone on the other end of the line. So it's important to sound good.

It's also important to know you're dealing with a reputable company. Ask them for a list of customers who have bought the system you're considering and call them to find out whether they're satisfied. You'll be able to hear what the sound quality of the system is like for yourself, while you get some direct feedback on the actual performance of the whole package as well as the performance of the company you're about to buy it from.

The Phone Company

Once you hook up your new telephone gear, it's ready to carry all your communications over the telephone company's lines. Then all you need to do is pay for the service itself.

No matter what size studio you are planning, if you're going to cater to the professional market, you must have a setup that doesn't intrude on your ability to work. That means that at the very least, you'll need an answering machine to pick up calls while you're in sessions. It's simply unacceptable for a phone to ring in the control room and to answer it there every time someone calls. You'll also need at least one line available to your clients for calling out, which means you should start with a minimum of two separate lines.

The telephone company, you will find out, is a proud, healthy and somewhat stern government-regulated monopoly, in terms of local service. You don't have a choice there. You have to take what's offered to you, play by their rules and like it.

Being the heavily regulated industry that it is, the phone company is compelled to give private citizens the best possible rates without going bankrupt, which is why the rates are still affordable in people's homes. The two ways the company makes up for those relatively lean private line charges are with long-distance service and billing for the business sector.

Business vs. Private Lines

You're going to find that business rates are a lot higher than private rates, and that phone-company reps aren't in a position to cut you a bargain. One learns to accept that what the phone company wants, the phone company gets.

There's nothing to gain in trying to con

them into a private line rate. The installation will be made at your place of business, and when they realize what a cad you are, they may politely triple your deposit to make sure you behave in the future.

You'll need to pay a deposit of a couple hundred dollars for your new lines, maybe a hundred or two more for installation, and another hundred just because they're the phone company and they say so. Then, of course, expect a pretty hefty bill each month.

If you have a lot of client traffic, your clients will no doubt make a lot of calls. One major difference in billing is that for businesses, there's no such thing as unlimited local calling. All calls are individually charged to your account. Local calls may be only a few cents, but each one is documented and added on. The further the distance, the higher the charge.

One thing to try to avoid are clients who slip in a quiet ten-minute conversation to an old buddy in, say, Stockholm. That's one of the very worthwhile features of owning a phone *system*: You can restrict the outgoing calls on each phone in your studio to only one or two area codes. When someone tries to dial a more distant area code, the system simply kicks the dial tone back in on the fourth or fifth digit, preventing the call from being made.

Your system KSU can be programmed so that only certain designated phones can dial out beyond local area codes. Then, if a client needs to make a long-distance call, your receptionist can dial the number for them along with their credit card number, or you can add a charge on their final bill for long-distance calls made.

And now that most areas are offering features like special service blocking, you may want to opt for that one-time charge as well. It's frustrating getting a $50 charge a month after a late-night session in which a room full of chortling party animals just couldn't resist repeatedly partaking of the vocal charms of 976-LOLA.

Choosing Your Number

It's a plus to have an easy-to-remember phone number. You'll find that the added charges for business lines bring with them a somewhat higher level of service and cooperation from the phone company. If you're friendly and don't come across as angry customer #27 for the day, your rep will try to find you a number you like. But remember, it's still your responsibility to ask for what you want and to not settle for less than what you feel is fair.

One thing to bear in mind, by the way, is that you only need one "good" number for your phone system. The next numbers don't have to be consecutive. The phone company will include *hunt group* service, which routes different numbers together to your location, where your own system's KSU will sort them out. That way, you can always give out the same number, and it will ring through to all of the lines.

There is also the option of requesting a specific phone number. Lots of companies arrange for numbers that spell out a message, like 24-TRK-4-U or HITS-R-US. As one might expect, there are extra fees and surcharges for these special services.

For normal service, plan on at least $50 per line per month for phone company charges, exclusive of long-distance carrier bills. When the joint starts jumpin', that figure may triple, but the shock of receiving a $500 monthly bill can be offset by the fact that the studio billed 300 hours of time that month. Looking at it that way brings the cost of providing phone service down to $1.50 per billed hour.

This isn't to say that you can't save substantial amounts by being careful. Don't dial information a dozen times a day. Leave phone books where people can find and get to them. Take care in picking the right long-distance carrier and avoid the temptation of making cold-call pitches to potential clients in neighboring countries.

TURNING ON THE LIGHTS

When you move into your location and apply for electrical service, the power company will ask for a detailed description of the interior layout of the space and for an estimate of your anticipated electrical usage. Based on your answers and their projections, they'll require you to pay a deposit up front along with any standard startup costs. To that end, you may want to carefully consider what kind of answers you give.

You should be prepared for a deposit of several hundred dollars, and may want to downplay your anticipated actual usage to save a little money going in. Depending on your answers and the attitude of the utility employee, the difference could be substantial.

Bear in mind that a majority of your equipment may run 24 hours a day and that your monthly bills may equal the deposit amount. There isn't much you can do about that, except to remember to turn off the lights at night; this is small comfort when you walk out the door leaving recorder and console lights ablaze to promote their longevity. But the majority opinion remains that turning your equipment on and off with any regularity causes the most internal damage from power surges, and that good maintenance includes running the juice steadily for months on end.

Don't Forget to Write

Remember to be careful about paying your bills. Power is one of those things that's good to avoid losing; you can't hand-crank a multitrack.

If the company actually does turn off the switch, they'll usually insist on *another* hefty deposit in addition to the one they've already got to get you back online again. But there are several warnings first. Even when the date on the "final notice" delivered by mail lapses, most companies send a live agent to your door with a 48-hour notice of impending doom. If that's your local district's policy, it may be the last warning you'll get.

LEGAL AND ACCOUNTING SERVICES

Every serious business needs at least some help from both an accountant and a lawyer. It may only mean filing papers or signing a partnership contract to begin with, but don't be foolish and try to save money by doing the legal work yourself. Dealing with the law is serious stuff. Using a pro means getting the job done right and having someone to lean on if problems occur later.

Lawyers and accountants are expensive, but they take the responsibility of putting the heavy, fundamental building blocks of your business together. After that, you can pretty much wave goodbye and make them disappear until you need them again.

It should only cost a few hundred dollars to file your new business papers, set up your books and receive some valuable advice on how to get started and stay clean in the eyes of the government. Then, when you sign an act to a production deal or file your year-end taxes, your legal and accounting support team will be just a phone call away.

Granted, it's easy to file a dba ("Doing Business As," the papers you file to form a company with a fictitious name) yourself and walk through the basic steps of filing and starting up. But many counties have peculiar codes or regulations that you may be unaware of. You should,

at the very least, check carefully with your local government to make sure you're not missing anything if you opt to file on your own. The advantage of using a pro, who may well advise you to go ahead and do it yourself anyway, is that you'll be setting up a proper business that won't come back and bite you three years later for having misfiled or forgotten something.

Finding the Right People

Again, a good way to find a lawyer or accountant is to ask people for referrals. Then go and interview *them*. If you tell them you're interested in discussing their potential representation, ethical professionals won't charge you for a first meeting. If they do, it's a good bet they'll charge you a rental fee on the magazines you read in their waiting rooms as well.

We interviewed three attorneys and three recommended accountants before we made our final decision. Each had a good track record in the entertainment business and was affordable, and, not surprisingly, the three were all as different as people could be. Knowing they were all capable, we simply chose the ones we liked the best.

As for the trappings of power, don't be intimidated by titles, fancy offices or gold-trimmed Mercedes. Attorneys and accountants are just people who want and need your business. Insist on fair treatment, discuss and thoroughly understand their fee structure and don't settle for anyone you don't like, no matter how highly they're recommended.

Your attorney and accountant may become longtime and important members of your business support team. Pick the ones you feel the most comfortable with, both as people and as professionals. If you start out that way, trust and confidence will soon follow.

THE INSURANCE MAZE

Insurance is a many-headed beast that you eventually learn to tame and live with. If you have employees, worker's compensation is usually required by law. The next most important coverage is for fire and theft, but following close behind are complete commercial policy packages, plus business interruption, disability, partnership and medical and life insurance. Not to mention an umbrella policy to protect *them*. It sounds overwhelming, and it is.

There's a lot of discussion involved in choosing a plan that works for you. If you're just starting out, you may want to begin with a minimal insurance package and work your way up. But a key factor in figuring this all out is to find the right insurance agent. A good way to get started on that is via word of mouth.

Finding an Agent

Ask businesspeople you know about their insurance policies and agents. Talk to other studio owners, or call local musician's unions or professional organizations. Sooner or later, someone will rave about their agent and give you a number.

Collect two or three of those names, and you ought to be able find someone you like and trust. Your agent will then bury you in a blizzard of promotional paperwork touting necessities, options, confusing terminology and endless premium payments. But the big advantage of going to an agent is that he or she is connected to a wide range of companies and plans, and will assemble a package that's right for you.

Later, when questions, problems or claims arise, your agent will be your personal representative, making sure that the business at hand runs as smoothly as possible. That's when a good pro is invaluable. Instead of dealing with a secretary at the company who couldn't care less, you've got a seasoned expert on your team to open the doors for you.

Another criterion for choosing the right person: Try to settle on an independent agent, not someone who works at a brokerage or insurance firm. While brokerage people may have a variety of companies to choose from, they are usually third-party companies with restrictive agreements. An independent will be able to choose from a much wider variety of carriers.

Separating Options From Necessities

There are several different types of policies to sift through. A *commercial insurance policy* provides overall fire, theft and general liability in a wide range of standard situations. If you are buying or leasing equipment, your lender will insist on fire and theft at the very least, and will require a certificate of insurance as proof from your company.

The trick is to find a company that will insure you. Historically, the entertainment business has been known to cause a fair amount of lip-biting among most (read "conservative") suppliers, and recording studios often get lumped into this unfairly labeled "high-risk" category.

For this reason, it may: a) take you a while to find an agent who can underwrite your business, and b) pay you to shop around and get several different quotes from agents who can. Once you find the companies who are willing to take the risk, you may be amazed at the disparity among their rates.

Acting Like a Grown-Up

Once again, a tactic to bear in mind is that your attitude should be conservative and professional when dealing with others of the same ilk. Serious businesspeople may not wholly approve of your lifestyle or humor, and you're much better off playing by their rules than risking their disapproval and subsequent turn-downs.

An insurance company wants to know that you're a good risk, which means that there are obvious subjects you should play down when applying. Don't joke or make references to all-night jams, performing or touring, equipment blowing up or even the merest hint of recreational drug use (blood tests are often mandatory prior to getting coverage approval).

Come across as a responsible businessperson and you'll save yourself a lot of headaches. And who knows? Maybe you'll start believing your own hype.

Worker's Compensation

Worker's compensation is a low-cost form of insurance that is required if you have even one employee on your payroll. The premium is based on the amount of salary you pay and covers you for any potential injury that might occur to your employees while on the job.

Worker's comp is serious stuff. The true story of a healthy young second engineer at a major post house provides a good illustration. He worked for the company for two years, until one day he tripped and banged his knee on an equipment rack. To his surprise, he broke a couple of tiny bones and was bedridden for two months.

When he could finally walk, he returned to find that his position had been filled by a new employee. To make matters worse, the studio hadn't listed him on their worker's comp policy, and then asked him to lie on the insurance application form, saying he'd been an independent contractor. The studio then promised to pay his medical expenses on the sly.

The poor guy, who had lost his job and major source of income in the process, called his lawyer, who advised him that should he sign such a form, he risked going to jail for perjury in any ensuing actions. When the studio subsequently balked at covering the $12,000 in medical expenses, he opted instead to sue for half a million. The case continues to drag on, with the employee left in semi-permanent limbo.

Everyone hates paying insurance premiums, until something terrible happens. It is inevitably at that point that they're able to at least breathe a financial sigh of relief, knowing that the years of prior payments are about to do their job. So go ahead and hate 'em, but don't forget to pay 'em.

A World of Options

With basic coverage firmly in place, your agent will begin to casually mutter about the convenience of a host of other policies. All have something worthwhile in them. It's just a question of how much you're willing to pay in the interest of business paranoia.

1. Business interruption insurance is a desirable option. In case of fire or some other disaster that forces you temporarily out of business, it pays all your normal monthly bills up to a set limit while you rebuild.

Take a look at your operation and figure out how long you could stay alive if a giant foot came out of the sky and stomped it into the ground while you were all out to lunch (hopefully, the foot waits until you're hungry). If you couldn't afford to stay afloat on your own for more than a few weeks, you may want to find out more about this valuable and somewhat pricey policy.

2. Partnership insurance is a form of life insurance that compensates the surviving partner in the event of the death of the other. It can be as simple as buying an inexpensive term life policy and listing one another as beneficiaries. It's never a pleasant thing to consider, but should one of you die, such a policy can act both as a buyout for the deceased partner's surviving family and as a cash infusion to help the company find and hire a replacement.

You could, for instance, buy a low-cost term life policy with, say, a $250,000 death benefit. If, *God forbid* (a phrase my agent is fond of inserting into most of his paragraphs of policy-speak), the worst does occur, you could agree that

$200,000 would go to the beneficiary, which would also function as an automatic buyout of the business by the other partner. The other $50,000 would go to the business to help cover the costs involved in finding a replacement to help the surviving, and now sole, owner of the studio.

You should draw up some simple papers with your attorney clarifying your agreement. There are specialists in this field who make a lot of money fashioning impossibly complex buyout agreements. That simply shouldn't be necessary with a relatively small studio business. Ask your attorney if he or she feels comfortable assembling a simple form, or better still if they can refer you to someone who does buyout contracts as a specialty. Then request a simple boilerplate letter that they can tailor to your own conditions.

When we did ours, our insurance agent set us up with a law firm that gave the nuts-and-bolts work to an intern. We went over it with him, made a few changes, and before signing had his boss go over the final draft, which he tweaked for half an hour. We wound up with a good standard contract, tailored with a few special clauses, and saved about $3,000 in legal fees in the process.

3. Disability and **supplementary hospitalization insurance** covers you in the event of an injury or sickness that prevents you from coming to work. It's expensive, but it gives you peace of mind in the event of a serious accident. Most plans pay benefits for two years or more, and if you're the sole breadwinner in a family, you may find the cost acceptable.

The most affordable kind of disability insurance is group disability, which covers all full-time employees and supplements worker's comp. It usually provides coverage and payments until you reach age 65, meaning that if someone gets into a truly disabling accident at the age of 25, he's got 40 years of supplemental insurance payment income to count on. Group coverage is surprisingly affordable, in part because the percentage of people suffering long-term disability is low.

Life insurance, be it whole, reverse-split, universal, term or otherwise, is about as confusing an option as you could ask for. It's an important item for a family breadwinner to have. On the other hand, if you're single and without dependents, one well-respected consumer magazine did a study that concluded you'd be better off spending the intended premium payments on vacations at Club Med.

But if you are the head of a household, some policies are very cleverly crafted and can become the basis for your retirement portfolio, as long as you're willing to pay in through age 65. Those are the ones that seem to make the most sense. Your agent will be happy to shower you with flashy brochures and computer projections.

Just bear in mind that many companies charge a high premium for what is ultimately a fairly low payout—don't base all your retirement projections on low-interest-bearing insurance. If you're under 50, buy the coverage you need and then investigate the payout difference in stocks and mutual funds.

There are a lot of good arguments for buying straight-term life insurance instead of more fancy and costly alternative plans. And with the savings you reap, you can buy into a nice portfolio of mutual funds. Even the conservative asset-allocation funds have a history of doubling or tripling the eventual payout 20 years down the road when compared to most insurance policies. And that could be the difference between being a hundred-thousand-aire and a millionaire, come gold-watch time.

MEDICAL PLANS

It's a good bet that with the horrendous cost of medical care, your employees are more than likely going to march into your modest little office one day, shoot daggers from their eyes and demand some benefits of their own.

If you're in business for yourself, you're going to need a health plan for yourself to start with. You're crazy to be alive and not have one. Being in robust health simply won't pay the $20,000 hospital bill when you slip in the shower right in the middle of a rousing chorus of "Losing My Religion" and break your gluteus in half.

Outside of paying your employees' salaries on time, health insurance is probably the most important responsibility you'll have as an employer. It's true that individuals can buy their own, but as costs skyrocket, the best deal for everyone, including yourself, is in a group. And there are plans that are willing to call two people a group.

There are two approaches to putting a health plan together. One is to provide coverage as a pure benefit that is included free, and the other is to offer inclusion in the group to any employee who's willing to pay the premium, which should be much lower than an individual can get.

At Interlok, everybody gets free health insurance. It costs us a lot, but we believe it's an absolute necessity. It's also a good bargaining tool in talking salaries, and our employees feel that we are doing something special and extra for them. And that helps to boost morale and loyalty.

Besides, we *are* doing something special. You can't help but feel good about yourself when you're helping protect the people you work with. It helps build confidence and pride in a small company, and it's truly important to everyone's well-being.

If you're an organizational type, one potential way to lower premium payments for health insurance is to put a large group of people together. Call other studios and related businesses in your area and discuss the idea of assembling a large group to buy one policy. Arrange a meeting in which your agent addresses the group. If you can put 50 or 100 people on one plan, you may be able to save thousands for your businesses. An added side benefit is all the networking that happens as a result of meeting other professionals in the area.

Of course, all the above advice may change once America figures out how to insure everybody. But in the meantime, health insurance is probably the most important insurance for any individual to have. The risks of operating without it are just too great to justify the interim savings.

Doing it Right

One more word of advice: Don't even *think* about trying to compare companies and put a plan together without the help of an independent agent who specializes in health insurance! You'll need an agent's help just to understand what's being offered in various plans, but their real value shows up when a claim is filed. That's when your agent will be your company expert and representative, and really go to bat for you.

It may, in fact, be wise to get a separate agent just for your health plan. Ask your business insurance agent if he or she is fully qualified in the health field. If not, ask for a referral.

Don't be intimidated into staying with the same person just because you've become buddies, or because it's embarrassing to speak up. This isn't just business; it's your *health* we're talking about. Speak up, and ask for what you're entitled to—the best help you can get.

Umbrella Insurance

Just one more kind of coverage to consider: umbrella insurance. This is literally insurance for your insurance. It's designed to kick in when your other insurance runs out. Depending on the amount of your investment, you may need more coverage than most of your policies provide at a reasonable rate.

For instance, if you were to get into an auto accident and your auto coverage maximum was $100,000, you could easily be sued for far more and be held liable for the difference. When that happens, in our orgiastically litigious society, the first thing most lawyers with 800 numbers do is go after everything you own to help pay off the difference. How else are they gonna stay in those sharp Armani suits? So if that difference happens to be a studio's worth of equipment, they'll find a way to take it.

There are two ways to protect yourself. One is to increase your auto and commercial insurance to higher levels—say, $500,000, which seems like a lot but isn't. And the second is to purchase an umbrella policy that kicks in after $500,000 is paid out by your other insurance company. A $1 or $2 million umbrella policy is relatively cheap—just a few hundred a year—and can potentially protect you all the way up to its limit, which should satisfy the most bloodthirsty of claimants.

You really needn't worry about umbrella policies until you have some substantial assets to protect, like a paid-off console or other heavy equipment. But once you have reached that level, it's wise to protect it with this kind of policy. Once again, discuss your individual situation with your agent for sound advice. It's probably the best way to avoid the third option, which takes guns and ammo to pull off with any real style.

SUPPORT SERVICES

In 1988, there was an organized crime ring in L.A. that used the same M.O. over and over again. Someone would call a studio, talk up a demo project they were doing, say they had their own engineer and book a block of late-night time at a bargain rate. The person was knowledgeable and friendly on the phone, and would promise to pay C.O.D.

They'd show up around midnight, and the one or two staff members who were there to second or watch the phones would let the group in. As soon as the door closed, the group whipped out revolvers and shotguns and then tied the stunned staffers to water pipes or file cabinets. Over the next few hours, they would professionally and methodically empty the entire contents of the studio into a waiting trailer truck that had pulled up and parked outside.

The moral here isn't about hiring armed night guards, although that may not be a bad idea if you're in a truly dicey neighborhood. It's about being careful about whom you choose for a client, and making sure your insurance is adequate and paid up.

Knowing your neighborhood and your local police makes common sense. But there are situations like our "late-night jammers" where it's best to just stay cool, make yourself comfortable handcuffed below the bathroom sink, and start figuring out what new equipment you'll be buying with the insurance money.

It's also a good idea to set a studio policy that in the unlikely event of something like an armed robbery, no one is to try any Clint Eastwood-style moves. Just cooperate and concentrate on staying alive.

Insurance Company Requirements

Your insurance company will do its part in requiring you to take certain reasonable measures to keep the lower-profile thieves at bay. Because you're insuring a lot of valuable equipment, they will require a burglar alarm and smoke detector, and probably insist on a central-station alarm service as well. That means that when the building alarm is tripped, it will automatically communicate with a professional security service, which will then take further steps.

Typically, a central station will first call the studio to see if the alarm's been tripped accidentally. If you're there and can give them the proper ID numbers or codes, they'll reset and forget. But if there's no answer, or the person who's there doesn't know the code, the next step is to either to dispatch their own private security guards or call the local police, or both.

They'll also call one or two phone numbers that you've supplied (for instance, your home) to tell you the alarm has gone off. This only happens, by the way, when you've just come home from finishing a 24-hour marathon session and have finally fallen asleep for half an hour.

The Joys of High-Tech Surveillance

When that call comes, the following emotions race through your head: 1) rage, that this has to happen now, of all times, 2) panic, that something awful has occurred, 3) resignation, dragging your clothes back on and starting out for the studio, 4) anger, realizing that you'll beat the cops there by an hour, and finally 5) cold fear, that not only will the place be trashed, but that the bad guys will still be there and will kill you, or worse. It's a beautiful world, hmmm?

Chances are a mouse has scampered across the lobby floor, tripped your motion detector and ruined your first opportunity for sleep in a week. But the sigh of relief you breathe will almost make you forget how much you're paying every month for the alarm coverage you've been compelled to carry. The hard fact is that virtually every system in existence is flawed in some way, and you'll be victimized by your own high-cost, high-tech system at least once in a while.

Finding the Right Service

The security business itself is one of the fastest-growing and highest-profit businesses extant (are you sure you want to own a *studio*?) and a little shopping around will reveal an incredible disparity in prices and services offered. Ask around and find someone who hasn't had any problems with false alarms, or better, who boasts of a security guard service that arrives less than an hour after the alarm goes off.

It will pay to take the time to sort through several different companies, comparing rates and services. The range of charges we found went from a high end of $7,000 for equipment and installation plus $150 per month, to *free* installation and $35 per month!

We checked out the "cheap" company by calling a few of their other clients, looked over their simple but effective equipment, got an okay from our insurance broker, signed a contract and saved a mint. True, we didn't get a fancy digital readout, but the insurance company was satisfied, and the mice only come down from the attic to roust us out of bed about once a year.

STUDIO SUPPORT PROS

Choosing a Piano Tuner

Every studio with a live room still needs a piano. It'll always be a classic rhythm section instrument, and singers, composers and producers will use it to work out parts between takes during sessions.

The piano you buy should be a grand or baby grand, not a spinet or an upright. There's just no comparison, soundwise, and with a grand, you have an elegant piece of furniture that doesn't have to be pushed flat against a wall and can be miked properly.

Your tuner can be a valuable asset when you're buying a piano. Before you sink a few grand into the grand you found in the local Pennysaver, hire your tuner to come with you to check the instrument's condition. Just like a mechanic checking a used car before you buy it, he'll be able to detect any potential problem spots, like a cracked sounding board or loose tuning pins, before you buy. He's also the best source for determining the instrument's true value. Many tuners are craftsmen in their own right and may buy, rebuild and sell pianos themselves, making them great sources for good buys to begin with.

The best way to find a good and experienced tuner is, of course, to call other studios and ask them for recommendations. The reason for finding someone with studio experience is that they'll be easier to work with when you call and leave a message that there's a 30-minute time window open at 9:15 a.m. before the 8-piece horn section starts up at 10:00.

Find someone reliable and recommended, and you'll have another support team member who'll take the pressure off, send his own subs when he can't make it and be just a phone call away whenever he's needed.

Maintenance and Repairs—A Prevention Program

Smiling announcer: "Join us now, as we enter the unpredictable, irrational and maddeningly chaos-prone world of disasters that invariably occur at the worst possible times: breakdowns!" Breakdowns tend to occur either 15 minutes before the most important new client of the month shows up, or 15 minutes and one pass away from the end of a 12-hour mix.

Either way, there's nothing you can do to prevent problems, aside from making sure they occur as seldom as possible. You just have to be ready when they do.

Every studio needs a maintenance program designed to stay a step ahead of foreseeable disasters. If you're experienced enough to be knowledgeable about the intricacies under the pro gear hood, you can do much of the preventive stuff yourself. If not, you're going to need help.

And since a good maintenance engineer is hard to find, the hourly fees can really sting. The best maintenance people either work on staff in the top studios at very high pay (often on a par with the studio's top engineers) or start up their own independent businesses to service many facilities.

If you're just starting out, an independent is the way to go. If you take the time to call around, you may find a few guys who have their own contract programs wherein you agree to pay them a set fee each month, and they stop in once every few weeks to give the room a once-over.

The value of these people is that they can spot a problem before it gets serious, and are usually well worth the $100 to $400 a month they charge. Many will also make themselves available for emergency repair on a 24-hour, per-day basis as part of the ongoing deal, and will become instant heroes the first time your master deck goes down.

Trading Services

If a monthly contract sounds difficult to afford, there's another alternative to safe and sane maintenance: Find a pro who's also a musician or producer (and many are) and offer a trade-out deal for studio time.

Trading for time is an idea that should come to mind again and again. Remember that you have a valuable commodity in your studio. It's a service business that you're selling for a substantial fee to any qualified taker. But all studios have down time to contend with, and there's no better way to fill it than to get someone else's valuable services in exchange.

Put the word out that you're looking for someone who's interested in trading services, and with a little luck you may be able to make a deal. Make one that's attractive to your maintenance pro, and they'll not only go for it, but they may take a little more care in keeping your equipment up to snuff. After all, they'll be recording their own projects on it, and they'll want the best possible mechanical performance.

Rental Companies

You're also going to find yourself in occasional situations when your deck doesn't just stop working, but goes "thud," "thoing," "grind" or just plain "uh," followed perhaps by a little wisp of smoke. When a major breakdown occurs, you need more than just a maintenance tech—you need a rental company. They're the ones who'll zip out with a piece of replacement gear

```
      The following is a brief list and description of
      the various service plans offffered by TECHCRAFT.
-------------------------------------------------------------------
SCHEDULED FIELD SERVICE (SFS):  On site monthly  maintenance at a price
and support level to fit your exact service requirements!
With this service,  you choose the particular type and amount of routine
maintenance your facility requires.  A convenient service  day  will  be
scheduled  at  the beginning of each month and promptly performed on the
appointment date.
The following is a brief description  and price list of the four  levels
of the SFS plan:
   SFS EXTENSIVE:................................................$300.00/month
        Full day component level technical service including
        troubleshooting  and  repair  of all audio equipment
        and interface problems.  Also may include  equipment
        installation, wiring, and any SFS BASIC servicing as
        described below.
   SFS EXTENSIVE (brief):.......................................$155.00/month
        Same as EXTENSIVE level except only half day service.
   SFS BASIC:...................................................$230.00/month
        Full  day system check and cleaning.  Includes audio
        aligning,  transport align and  tension  check,
        degusing,  and  overall  machine  performance check.
        May include light soldering (connectors,  patch  bay
        repairs,  etc.) and general fault finding (interface
        problems, general machine diagnosis, etc.).
   SFS BASIC (brief):...........................................$125.00/month
        Same as BASIC level except only half day  servicing.
-------------------------------------------------------------------
EMERGENCY TECHNICAL SUPPORT (ETS):   Immediate  technical  help  and
information  is  just one phone call away!  With this service you choose
the level of emergency technical support you will  be  most  comfortable
with.  No matter which plan you choose, TECHCRAFT will provide immediate
qualified  technical  assistance ANY  DAY  (including  weekends) during
normal business hours to aid in urgent  problem  solving, manufacturing
information,  etc.
The  following is a brief description and price list of the three levels
of the ETS plan:
   ETS LEVEL 3:.................................................$190.00/month
        Includes Technical Support Hotline plus 1  emergency
        callout (up to 4 hours) per month.
   ETS LEVEL 2:.................................................$50.00/month
        Includes  Technical  Support  Hotline plus emergency
        callout service available at  a  reduced  rate  of
        $37.50/hour.
   ETS LEVEL 3:.................................................$30.00/month
        Includes Technical Support Hotline only.
-------------------------------------------------------------------
DEPOT SERVICE (DS):  Monthly shop service at a price  that's less  than
half  the  going rate!  With  this  service you receive 2 hours of shop
repair per month at no additional charge.  The plan also provides for  a
reduced  rate of $28.00/hour on all additional depot services including
equipment repair, interface fabrication, and patch bay wiring.
   DS Price:....................................................$45.00/month
   Free pickup and delivery*:...................................$20.00/month
       *If Depot Service is combined with one of the SFS plans,
       pickup and delivery is available free of charge.
```

for the day or two or three or the week it takes to get your own machine fixed.

Don't wait for a disaster to happen to establish a relationship with an equipment rental company or two. Ask around, find out who the most respectable ones are, call and say hello. They may require an application with references and bank information before they'll be willing to drop off a $100,000+ deck at your door at 3:00 a.m., and when that time comes, you'll congratulate yourself for having thought ahead to avoid being turned down.

But the real value in a rental company is that it can provide the piece of gear you need to make the session work right. Typically, audio rental companies have a wide range of mics, outboard gear, recorders, keyboards and cables, all available on very short notice.

To find out who rents pro equipment in your area, try your local entertainment business commercial directory. These are private directories that are compiled in many major cities where business is substantial, and can usually be found at better local newsstands. If there aren't any in your area, call neighboring studios or your

Some technicians solicit studios via direct mail. Virtually all are willing to tailor a program for each studio's needs.

nearest pro equipment supplier or music store and ask them for help.

Once you locate the right people, call a few places and request their brochures and price lists. When the need arises, you'll have them ready and in front of you, so that in the heat of a session, you can have someone call the appropriate place without wasting any further time. A good rental company will usually try to deliver whatever you need within about an hour, assuming you're centrally located.

Most rental companies charge their rate card price per 24 hours. In major cities, the standard discount breakdown is to get a week's time at the daily rate times four, meaning that you pay for the first four days and the last three are free. The monthly rate is figured at the weekly rate times three—you pay for the first three weeks and the fourth is free.

In highly competitive cities, like New York, Nashville and L.A., you can sometimes swing an even better deal on a weekly or monthly rate, and some of the meaner and leaner companies will offer a week's rental at the daily rate times three instead of four.

Mark Napier of Audio Affects, a major L.A. rental company, tries to tailor each deal to his clients' needs. "This is a small town, and everyone knows everybody," he says, referring to the quake-prone megalopolis. "If you get one guy who needs you and you stick him good, he's not gonna be back." Napier has the latitude to wheel and deal and believes that his strong repeat business is based on both trust and mutual respect.

If you believe you're going to need the equipment longer than a month, take a serious look at buying or leasing the piece yourself. Rental rates can run as high as 50% of the value of the equipment per month, which means you could be better off buying it outright, even if that means reselling it later on.

OTHER OFFICE EXPENSES

Janitorial Services

Your facility can probably get by with as little as one good cleaning per week, if you keep an eye on things. But someone is going to have to do the dirty work: cleaning the bathrooms, emptying the trash, washing the windows, vacuuming, etc.

A janitorial service will come on a regular schedule, usually in the late evening or early morning so that they remain virtually invisible, and smile apologetically when they walk into the control room wearing elbow-length rubber gloves at 6:00 a.m. and you're still mixing. Unless you're real busy, two or three times per week is a good norm, which means you're probably looking at $200 to $400 per month in charges.

For that, you should expect professional results. That means the place looks good and the bathrooms are shiny. They'll usually provide all the cleaning brushes and chemicals and bring their own vacuum cleaner as well. It's legitimate to charge extra for trash bags and other disposable items you request. If you're unhappy with the results, let the service know, have them come in during the day, and show them exactly what needs improvement.

Obviously, your cleaning team is going to require complete access to your facility, which means giving them all the necessary keys and security codes. So check them out carefully. A referral from a business friend for a trusted company or person makes a lot of sense. So does a request for additional references. Your landlord may have someone to recommend. Make some calls and don't settle for less than positive responses from all.

At the least, deal only with fully bonded services. And don't beg for trouble: Put the hundred-dollar bills away before you go home, and consider taking your Nikon home with you.

Drinking the Water

A lot of your clients, especially singers, are going to be fussy about the water you use for coffee and tea. If your live in an area with good-quality tap water, you're one step ahead of the game. But if you reside in a city like L.A., in which the water is best left for dishwashing, you're going to have one more psychological plus on your side by providing filtered or bottled water. A leased hot and cold water cooler can become the cornerstone of a mini-kitchen. The cold will provide good water for drinking and making coffee, and the hot spigot delivers instant tea and soup water.

Bottled-water companies usually offer a lease plan that keeps the monthly payment under $20 for the hardware, which may also include a small built-in refrigerator. (Actually, you're better off buying a small refrigerator at a discount appliance store and paying the hundred bucks once, instead of an extra $10 per month forever.) Put a microwave beside it, and you can give the local 7-Eleven a run for its money. Most clients expect this, at the very least.

But there are some minor problems. You're at the mercy of the delivery person, which means that at times you'll have either too much or too little water. And the bottles can really get in the way.

One alternative is a filtered-water, "bottle-less" cooler. These companies claim that their filtered stuff is every bit as good as the bottled stuff. If you agree, then they offer some pretty logical inducements.

For one, the cooler is installed by tapping into your existing water lines. That water then goes through the filter and comes out the spigot, which means no more deliveries and no more bottles. And second, after a few years of paying the same amount you were getting bottled water for, you own the whole system free and clear, which means an end to all the charges that would normally go on forever. Check the Yellow Pages.

Staying Cool

If central air conditioning is your own responsibility, get someone to take regular care of it. Recording equipment builds up a lot of heat, which puts added strain on the system. And air conditioning tends to go down at the worst possible time, like on the hottest day of the year with a 20-piece orchestra in mid-session.

A maintenance agreement with a professional company serves you in two important ways. First, they'll set up a schedule, say every two to three months, when they'll send someone out to change your filters, check the unit and do regular preventive maintenance. But even more importantly, a good company will get a service person out to you within hours of a breakdown if you're a regular customer.

If you've ever tried to plead with an air-conditioning repairperson to come and fix your broken unit in the middle of a heat wave, you probably remember the sound of your own disgusted groan as you put down the phone. But if you have an ongoing contract, when disaster strikes, you'll be first on the list.

When that moment comes, you'll forgive all the maintenance bills from the last two years and be able to look into the eyes of a sweaty client and say, "Don't worry, they're on their way."

Copier Service

Unfortunately, you need a photocopier to send copies of bills to clients, to make copies of checks and purchase orders, and to deal with clients who bring in one typewritten sheet of announcer copy or song lyrics, realize they need five, and ask you to make copies.

You can get by with the copy shop down the block, but what do you do during night sessions? You shake your head, say "Sorry, we don't have one," and the client has to write out the extra copies by hand. Next time she needs to book a session, she'll remember how much extra work she had to do at your studio.

Copiers appear to be a constant reminder that man has not yet perfected machines with moving parts. They're expensive, and no matter how good they are, they break down with depressing regularity. The best deal for service is to buy a contract from a third-party repair service that covers virtually anything that can go wrong. For best results, ask other businesses for referrals. The companies that sell copiers usually have extended deals also but tend to be a lot more expensive than the independents. Sometimes though, the service contract is the best way to shop for a copier. Watch for special promotions that include three-year, in-house service on the copier you buy. Because no matter how good the salesman says this copier is, you can be sure the damn thing will go down time after time.

So, assuming that all copiers are mechanically inept, the most important thing is having professional service at the ready. The contracts are expensive, and the maintenance people don't always know what they're doing. Think of all the stories you've heard of how the copier broke down 20 minutes after the service person left for the third time this month.

Try to find a machine with a good warranty. Often, the independents who sell service contracts also sell used machines that they'll maintain for you. Ask around and see if *anyone* is the slightest bit excited about their reasonably priced copier. They probably won't be. This is depressing. Let's move on.

Recording Tape

It's difficult to judge how much tape you'll use from month to month. If you're in a major city with a ready supply nearby, you can probably get by with a box of master reels and a few software blanks in reserve. Shop around for the best pro prices and don't rule out mail-order; often, the best deals are on bulk quantities.

Then apply for or have your accountant get you a *resale number*. They're issued to companies who buy goods and resell them to their customers. That way, you don't pay tax on the tape when you buy it. Instead, you charge your clients the proper sales tax on the tape they buy and forward the money to the government at regular intervals.

There's good profit in selling tape. The average pro markup from studio to client is about 40%, which can add a nice bump to the month's profits. Find a brand and series that you like and stick to it: You'll save yourself a lot of headaches by reducing the amount of time you spend aligning your machines, and you'll become very familiar with the characteristics of the tape.

There's also a lot of used tape floating around for sale. It's a great way to save money, but be on your guard. If you don't know who you're dealing with and it's open-reel stock, insist on running the tape through a machine and check for splices. Even one or two splices in a used tape makes it basically worthless to a client who figures his or her project is at least worth a clean roll to begin with.

Also, if you're going to lock up to SMPTE or some other form of sync to picture or computer, avoid used tape altogether. The code is too fragile to handle imperfections on a used reel, and one tiny dropout can cause an unfixable wow or computer skip, ruining an entire take.

But there *are* advantages to used tape. It works just fine for demo projects and other non-critical applications, especially if the stock is relatively new. And prices on used tape run one-half to two-thirds less than new. Just be straight with your client. Making an extra 60 bucks on a used roll isn't worth the hassle of being found out later and losing their trust or the project altogether.

Embracing the Digital Explosion

First adding digital equipment rentals as a sideline, Gene Shiveley has carefully planned and built a major rental and mastering business with a unique style that makes it stand out from the pack.

Career Roots Started as a staff and independent engineer. Original partner John Cadenhead was a musician and recording artist.

Business Roots "We were both working as engineers in '82 when digital recording started happening. We thought it would be a good idea to offer our services with digital mixing, so we got some backing and bought a processor. It worked out really well, and then we started renting the equipment when we weren't using it ourselves. It became an instant hit as a rental item. Nobody else had them, and within the first year we bought two more. Next came a van and a driver, and we were in the business officially.

"The big buzz on the street was CD, and we did some research and decided to invest in a compact-disc mastering system. We ran the whole thing out of my living room, having no idea what we were doing. Our backer convinced us to take some business management courses, which turned out to be immensely helpful. We've continued taking special business classes ever since. If you expect to survive in the business world, it's a definite requirement. We live by business plans."

House Staff 11 full-time employees.

Primary Focus Rentals, CD mastering. "Other people rent auxiliary equipment, but we rent only digital recorders in all formats. Rentals will stay strong because every form of entertainment in L.A. is using digital recorders. And most of those places will rent rather than purchase, because of the ongoing format wars and changing technology. It's much more reasonable for many people to rent rather than purchase."

Now introducing magneto-optical mastering, which will completely take the place of tape in the facility.

Mastering Trends "Mastering has changed in terms of the storage format. The CD one-off is now a reality and is becoming a reference standard. It's the best form of a reference, because it's played back on the same medium that's going to be manufactured. With CD-R [compact disc reference], the primary use is for the artist to take home a disc after the mastering session, just like the old ref disks from the vinyl days."

Staff Management "It's more vital than ever to not only continually study and work with business plans but to pass them on to our employees as well, to get them to understand more about how our business works. We constantly give them little snippets to read, giving them reports to do and showing them why and how they work and how we can work and focus from these activities."

Facility A converted train station and historical landmark, combined with the fixtures installed by the previous tenant (an antique ceiling fan company), have made the interior stunningly unique. The entrance is still marked "Ladies' Waiting Room."

Once inside, digital processors sit atop an ornate turn-of-the-century bar, amidst a collection of antique telegraph equipment and penny-arcade machines. There are two digital premastering bays, a tape transfer room and several offices in various corners.

On Rentals "We move a lot of equipment around town on a daily basis. We actually have one item that's been out on rental in the same place for three years, on a daily rental basis. One reason for that is that a digital processor is probably going to be upgraded about every 18 months, and every manufacturer has their own unique format. They're non-compatible systems—they don't talk to each other. So clients wonder, 'Is this a good system to buy? Will it be outdated soon? Will I need another kind?' So a lot of people feel safer renting than buying.

"The other reason is that we give great service. And we have the best-maintained equipment in the world. And we service for cosmetics as well. We'll buy a new faceplate or cover whenever something starts looking worn. If the equipment looks beat-up, it's going to be the first place the client looks when something goes wrong."

On Mastering "The 'prosumer' market has come into play. You can now get a mastering system at a very reasonable price. But professionally, it still takes $200K plus, vs. $8 to $10K, to be considered real mastering. It looked as though the low-end systems might have been a threat for a time, but most of those places have fallen aside, in spite of people being able to go there and get mastering done for as little as $35 a side.

"But it's not just the equipment. It's the engineers. It's still the last creative step in the recording chain and must be looked at that way. Most labels and major artists are very conscious of the importance of the mastering step. For a while there, it was misunderstood by the prosumer market.

"But without the knowledge and experience of Somme, who's been doing that for several years, I don't see how you're gonna come out with a really good product. Most of the clients who had tested that area to see if they could save a few bucks there have all come back. "

Marketing The company publishes a complete list of commercial studios and support services in the L.A. area called "The Studio Menu." They distribute copies to all the businesses listed and take the only advertising space available to gently stand out from the rest. The Studio Menu is so valuable as an up-to-date information source that most places use it all year long.

"We've found that people will call us up to ask for the Menu. Once they're on the phone, we try to establish a professional relationship with them. It's a nice way to help expand our client base."

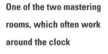

One of the two mastering rooms, which often work around the clock

SOUTHERN CALIFORNIA
STUDIO MENU

cms
DIGITAL
(818) 405-8002

The Studio Menu is updated and reprinted every year. Sealed in plastic like a restaurant menu and distributed free to all the related companies in the area, it has become an dependable resource and a unique promotional vehicle for CMS.

CMS DIGITAL RENTALS
STUDIOS

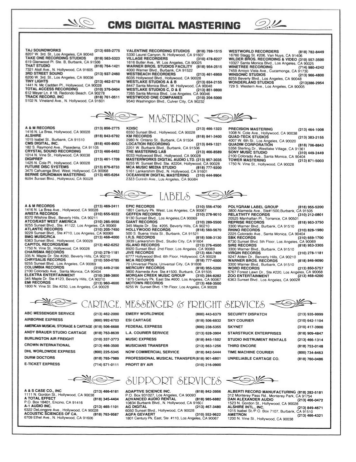

CMS DIGITAL MASTERING

MASTERING

LABELS

CARTAGE, MESSENGER & FREIGHT SERVICES

SUPPORT SERVICES

7

Putting a Price on Value

Once you've figured out the cost of doing business, all that's left is figuring out a way to *pay* for everything. You do that by convincing potential clients that your studio is the place where they really want to be.

The amount of a studio's income is determined by the rates it charges. The key factors in determining rates are the value of the studio's equipment and services and the amount the competition is charging to deliver the same results. Let's take a close look at each of these, plus some other important elements: Location, size, the quality of the equipment, the expertise of the staff, ambience and comfort, and reputation.

LOCATION

There's an old real-estate adage that says the three most important things to consider when acquiring a piece of property are location, location and location. It figures that the studio business would be the one to break the rule.

In fact, successful studios have been built in cheap warehouse spaces in the seamiest parts of any given city. The obvious draw is that you can rent a large space for a small price in areas like this and not have to worry about attracting window-shoppers.

But the drawback to leasing this kind of space is that while you're in the process of becoming one of the best studios in town, you're likely to make people think twice about the extra travel time, not to mention the danger level inherent in your "offbeat" location.

Is there secure parking, or will your clients have to park on the street and hope for the best? Does the neighborhood look barren and foreboding? How will women feel about walking up to your outside door alone? How long will it

take for the majority of your potential clients to get there? Are there restaurants or convenience stores nearby? And will *you* be happy working there every day?

There are lots of questions and no firm answers. If your location is funky, maybe your reputation as a first-rate studio will override that consideration. People may think it's worth the hassle. And you may also be able to offer a lower hourly rate. Set up shop in a deserted warehouse district and fortify the place with electric fences, security cameras and gun turrets with some of the rent money you save. Maybe the spike-collared Dobermans will lend an air of chic to the place.

But logic dictates that you're better off in a safer neighborhood. It's crazy to pay high rent on a trendy street, but a good test might be to imagine whether or not a female client or employee would feel comfortable driving to the part of town you have in mind. If you do good business, a lot of important execs are going to be showing up with regularity, and many will have a powerful say in where the recording for their company gets done.

Obviously, where you draw the line is also going to have a lot to do with what kinds of commercial spaces are available and how much you can afford. So planning ahead and allowing yourself enough time to scope out the market as well as the neighborhood vibe are approaches that should work in your favor.

And please don't get me wrong: The necessity of keeping rent and taxes down has spawned a veritable nation of studios in low-rent and warehouse districts. It just has to do with finessing your particular market and determining whether such a location will fit into your own criteria. (This is another good reason to have a detailed business plan in hand; as Maxwell Smart would say, "99, I want you to check the business plan for our criteria and read it to me out loud...")

So look around. Where are the low rents in your area? Some cities have industrial zoning right in the middle of town, with an established (dare we say trendy?) commercial zone inside them. Of course, by the time a section gets trendy, the rents have long since gone up for newer inquirers, even if it still becomes a jungle after dark.

In New York, many studios are located on upper floors in office buildings. Maybe that'll work for you. Mini-malls seem to be growing in popularity as locations. And try abandoned churches, historical landmarks, strip-mining pits, etc. Once you've found a place that excites you, ask everyone you know what they think of the idea. The feedback will help you decide, as you gather a list of pros and cons. Just try to keep a clear concept of the image you will be presenting. This may not be the fashion business, but when people have choices to make, image carries a surprising amount of weight.

Bringing the Neighborhood
Up to World-Class

Turning an 8-track studio in a dicey location into one of L.A.'s premiere world-class facilities, Buddy Brundo's vision and energy have toppled the kind of urban obstacles that stop most businesspeople cold.

Buddy Brundo

Owner

Conway Studios

Los Angeles, California

Career Roots "I was a musician. My dad owned a music store back east. We used to have jams upstairs. I moved to L.A. in '72 and started working for a little house with an 8-track room called Conway, right here at this location. When the owners got disenchanted with the place, I bought it in '76. It was pretty scary. At that time, our rent was our biggest expense. A year later we bought the property, and gradually bought the adjoining lots.

Facility Three studios in four buildings, all in a lush, resort-like setting. Two Neve VRs with GML automation and recall, modified with Conway Discrete Monitor VCAs and summing amps. Studio C: Focusrite 64-channel console with GML automation. Decks: five Studer A-827s, three Mitsubishi X-880s, an upgraded Sony 3348, four heavily modified Ampex ATR 102s and 104s, two Mitsubishi X-86HS 20-bit-capable digital 2-tracks.

Mixing to DAT "We never do DAT mixes. There's no sense coming here and spending all this money and then mixing to a DAT with minimal error correction. You spend three months making a record, you put it on a DAT, it doesn't make sense. I don't understand these professional guys that put their trust in them. Well, if you're mixing on NS-10s, I guess it doesn't matter.

"We mix on 30-ips analog on half-inch. Or 15 half-inch SR, or 48k Mitsubishi 2-track, 96k Mitsubishi 2-track, or 48k Mitsubishi with 20-bit special converters. It seems nuts to me to come in here with all the audiophile stuff we have and simply mix to DAT. Nuts."

House Staff 15 full-time employees, counting the three gardeners. "All of our seconds are really firsts. At this level, you have to be."

Primary Focus Records, with some music-for-film work.

Clientele U2, Barbra Streisand, Kenny G, Rickie Lee Jones, Lyle Lovitt, Simple Minds, Black Crowes, Linda Ronstadt.

Location Across the street from Paramount Pictures, in a low-rent neighborhood on the non-fashionable end of Melrose Avenue.

"Every great star in the world has driven past this studio. The [lower] land values in the neighborhood were what allowed me to buy so much space. We've been here 17 years and have never had a danger problem. This is a residential neighborhood. There are families here.

"We had a bar across the street that was really bad, with drugs, shootings and stabbings. So we got together with the neighborhood and brought the Guardian Angels down here when they first came into L.A. We really put ourselves on the line. There were a lot of fights outside of the gates for a while. We took pictures of the buyers and sellers outside.

"After we took pictures of everybody, hassling the buyers and the sellers, we finally got some politicians involved, who brought the police and the Liquor Authority in, and we got 'em to close that place down.

"The Guardian Angels were protecting us while we exerted the pressure to close the bar. We hosted block parties with the Angels and the politicians, we bought the Angels bullhorns, we fed 'em, we paid for printing leaflets to distribute...it was a very exciting time.

"We didn't really feel scared. In the meantime, I got to know all my neighbors and was astonished at how many wonderful people there are living around here. We got the families together and shut down Melrose Ave. and picketed the Hollywood Police Department with the little kids carrying signs that said, 'We want you on the streets, not in the donut shop!'

"A TV show about communities came down and did a whole special about what was going on. It was great. It was on the news for months. The problem was that the Liquor Authority and the police weren't communicating with each other about that bar. So we introduced them to each other. That fixed it.

"In some businesses, location is everything. But musicians, including myself, have traditionally worked in the worst neighborhoods imaginable. So we're all kind of used to it. You can't make any money if you're getting killed with high rent. My dad taught me that.

"I tell everybody I know that it's better to buy in a less desirable location than to rent in a nicer neighborhood. I walk into a leased facility and think, 'Wow, look at all the money they put into this place. Eight years is gonna go by, and then what are they gonna do about the 300 grand they spent here?' You can't take it with you. For me, the pot of gold at the end of the rainbow is probably gonna be the real estate we're sitting on right now."

Changing Times "We've worked with the top groups in the world. Nobody uses drugs any more. It's great. People are educated and healthy. The worst thing the young rockers do is drink beers. I think they've learned something after watching us older guys all check into detox clinics."

The Record Biz "The record companies are making billions, but you call them to collect your money and it's like you're asking them for their last nickel. Few of them pay their bills in 30 days, and they get away with it. The ripple effect is how it impacts everybody's credit.

"It may be that the record companies are subsidizing their conglomerates' other subsidiaries. So now, you talk to them and ask for your normal rate, it's heart-attack time for them. From a businessman's standpoint, it seems the A&R people are trained to moan and groan when they hear a quote over a certain amount. All while the execs are raking in millions in bonuses.

"I know we're going to get paid by the record companies eventually, but it seems like they're playing some sort of game of delays and excuses. In the meantime, the project coordinators are after me to save fifty dollars a day on studio time, and maybe another fifty on extra machine rentals, and then turn around and approve unlimited party budgets for their artists. It just doesn't add up."

On Success "I didn't have any special connections. It was just a matter of providing what people were asking for. In this business, you have to be so insecure that you work yourself into the ground until your hair falls out. Because the guy next door to you is gonna do the same thing. I don't even remember my 30s!

"Years ago my uncle, who was an auto mechanic working in a garage back east, came out here to visit. When he saw people working on cars *outside*, he moved here. I build my studios with views of lush gardens to look like you're working outside. I found a niche because I have the real estate to do it."

Philosophy "People say, 'That's a good piece of equipment for the price.' But what does that have to do with reality? It's either good, or it's not. To me, good for the money doesn't mean anything. People make a little money and they spend it right away. You can't do that here. You just have to keep putting it back in and live at a moderate level. It's very tricky.

"People never know what to expect when they come here. I'm always working on something new to make the music sound better. I like loud music that's clean. That's my Jones."

On the Future "What I'm pouring money into is real estate. To go out and buy the world's largest console in 1994 is a joke. The current rates won't support it. In L.A., there's been an unbelievable expansion of major studios. Without a doubt, L.A. is overbuilt. I'm personally kind of up in the air about what to do. Everybody's business is down. In the scheme of things, we're holding our own, but we're all expecting a shake-out.

"I feel fortunate that I have a totally different facility to be able to offer clients a unique experience. All that's left for us is the very top end.

"California is still the only place to live, problems or no. I think that anybody that has the drive and courage and can find a niche for their business is going to survive. I don't care if you're a big or a little studio. There's still so many opportunities here, I still think this is the greatest place to be. "

SQUARE FOOTAGE

With the advent of MIDI in the early '80s, an old trend began to reverse course: Live rooms started getting smaller, and control rooms began getting bigger. This is to accommodate the stacks of MIDI keyboards, outboard and computer gear and electric instruments that can go direct to the board or are miked via an amplifier in the studio, therefore eliminating the need to be sonically isolated. Communication between engineer and player is a pleasure when you converse normally instead of having to deal with a talkback system through a wall of glass.

A large control room also makes for a very comfortable environment, allowing enough space to accommodate clients, players and engineering staff. While the technology of the 1970s often supported little 9' x 12' control rooms, today, a 15' x 20' area is much more of a necessity. And studios specializing in keyboard music production or video interlock are being built with control rooms as large as 40' x 50', often with an accompanying studio the size of the old control rooms!

On to the Subconscious Level

The size of your working environment also plays a strong psychological role in a client's mind. He may not think about how he relates to the space, but may still be affected by it, feeling either comfortable or somehow uneasy.

Consider that a particular artist or executive may wind up spending several long days and nights on a project in your control room. When he needs to book more time, will the environment you've created be a factor in attracting him to come back? If he's comfortable, the answer may justify the rate you're charging and a return visit.

Remember that the larger the room, the more air there is to go around, which is an important consideration when smokers are present (if you're allowing smoking in the studio, that is). Ideally, you should be able to accommodate a substantial synth/computer setup and still be able to offer an area that seats a few clients in relative comfort, without affording a forced undercarriage view of somebody's towering keyboard stack.

Working together in close quarters can be a bonding experience or a very uncomfortable one, depending on the mix of people. Having a room that's large enough for clients to function

in separate groups or to feel comfortably apart from others is preferable to one that forces people to squeeze together.

Another trend that has evolved in recent years is to involve clients and visitors in the control room with what's going on around the console instead of out in the live room. Whereas in the '60s and '70s visitor seating was most often on a couch placed between the front end of the console and the control room glass facing the live room, now larger rooms are placing seating *behind* the console, affording visitors a means of observing or participating in the action along with the engineer and producer.

This is particularly effective for TV, film and jingle projects, where several people may be contributing to the creative effort (often by driving each other crazy with too many conflicting opinions). Their proximity to the action may play a key role in whether they choose to return, especially if a competing studio is offering the same level of service but isn't as hospitable.

Obviously, space is a luxury when money is tight, but there are still ways to maximize its use. Make the room look larger by choosing lighter paint colors. Use track lighting to create two or more separately lit areas of focus. Choose furniture that's less bulky or cumbersome. And see if there's a way to let some natural light into the room. Daylight can have a powerful effect on people's feelings of well-being.

Just bear in mind that nowadays, more than ever, a control room is a *living* room. It's where people will spend many, many hours doing their best to produce the highest-quality results they can. Making your living room as inviting and as comfortable as possible means that they'll have a place that's all the more conducive to achieving their goals, and that one of the reasons they'll choose you again will be to enjoy that same atmosphere.

Studio Dimensions

The second ponderable is the size of the *live* room. You can get by with a small booth if the primary focus of the business is audio post or voice-over work. Many studios that choose this area of specialty do so because the field is lucrative and the vast majority of the recording is done in the control room.

When *sweetening* (adding sound effects, music and mixing to picture), the primary sound sources are tape, CD and digital samplers. The booth is used for announcer overdubs and/or

ADR (Automated—or Actor—Dialog Replacement), which require only a small space.

There are fabulously successful studios with single live booths that measure a paltry 5' x 8'. There's even a company that offers prefabricated isolation booths that can be delivered to your door ready for quick assembly, allowing you to tuck a 4' x 4' announcer booth in the corner of a control room, or install an isolation booth in a hall or entryway.

But outside of vocal or instrumental overdubs, there's little else you can do musically within that sort of claustrophobic situation. So the next category would be a room capable of accommodating a four- to six-piece group in relative comfort. You can do that with as little as 12' x 16', assuming the drum kit doesn't come with any timpani.

A healthy-sized group, one with a fairly extensive keyboard rig and a couple of guitarists with racks of their own, is going to require about 400 square feet, or roughly a 20' x 20' room. And that's still squeezing them in a bit. In this case, you'll also need isolation booths. Without at least one, it's all but impossible to record a simultaneous vocal that can be re-recorded or punched in on later.

Less necessary, but very desirable, is a separate room for an acoustic piano, allowing for perfect isolation, and to a lesser extent nowadays, a drum booth. Drum booths were a must in the '60s and '70s; there was no other way to get that perfectly clean Steely Dan sound. But today, as often as not, producers elect to set the drum kit up in the center of the room for maximum presence. In fact, they'll often seek out a studio with an especially large, reverberant, high-ceilinged live room just to get closer to a natural-sounding big hall reverb. An average size with these specs might run 25' x 40' with a 12-foot ceiling.

Going Orchestral

At 20' x 20', you've got a fairly versatile and nicely designed room. But there's no way you can comfortably seat more than ten players, and now the producer is talking about adding full string and horn sections to the existing track. For that, you'll need to start at about 30' x 30' and work your way up.

The higher the square footage, the more creatively the room can be designed and laid out, and the more comfortably a larger group can work. A 30' x 35' room can handle a 25-piece group, as long as the concertmaster gets the violin section to bow their instruments in the same direction all the time. A 35' x 40' room can begin to be broken up into some interesting configurations, with live and dead zones, iso booths and risers.

The really massive rooms start at about 40' x 50' and can get as cavernous as 80' x 130', big enough to seat a 90-piece orchestra and still have enough space left for a couple of bowling alleys. Skywalker Sound, in San Rafael, California, boasts a space about that size, with ceilings about 20 feet high. The space is at once gorgeous and huge, and features two iso booths, each the size of a small studio, designed to accommodate complete *sections* of instruments when desired.

Imagine what it would feel like to be a solo singer and do a vocal overdub in a place that size! The challenge is to be able to justify the need for the amount of space you decide upon. The giant rooms are most often owned and operated by major media companies that can absorb the upkeep by writing it off against a wide variety of other sources of corporate income.

A large room is a great asset, but can push you right into bankruptcy from just paying the rent on time. Unless you're quite sure that an orchestra is going to set up housekeeping at your place, a 600- to 800-square-foot studio will serve you well, and will appear spacious, impressive and versatile to most people when they come to look you over.

CONSIDERING THE EQUIPMENT

Equipment is obviously a big factor not only in setting a rate, but in the kind of work you'll attract. It's also a bit of an unknown, depending on the specialty you've chosen. If you're just starting up on a low budget, you'll be going after the best deals on the lowest-cost equipment that can do the job without breaking down every Thursday night.

As we've discussed, there are many levels of overall studio quality (and corresponding rates), ranging from low-end demo studios to world-class mixing rooms. But your hourly rate will also depend on what brands or specific pieces of equipment you choose.

For instance, a hot piece of effects gear can be a powerful draw to a client who's used to paying a daily rental on it at other studios. If it usually costs $100 through a rental company and you're offering it for free, the client sees an immediate benefit.

One high-end mixing room in Chicago uses this technique: They only sell time on a per-day, lockout basis, but all the gear you're likely to need is included. They have about 15 *feet* of the trendiest outboard gear of the year permanently installed in the room, along with a big SSL console and two Studer 24-track machines. Ratewise, they are about $200 to $400 per day higher than many other high-end rooms, but those rooms don't offer nearly as much of the exotic outboard gear. These other rooms arrange for daily rentals and charge their clients extra, but the slick brochure on the first room proudly asserts that yes, the rate is higher, but they include everything you'll need and then some.

A heavy investment in extra gear? Definitely. Does it work? They're often booked two months in advance.

Audio Post: A Notable Exception

There is one mighty interesting twist on the equipment quality/rate ratio, however. In the field of audio post, equipment variety and quality can carry much less weight in the creation of the product and, consequently, the client's choice of studio.

Audio post is a complicated and skilled art that requires an experienced and knowledgeable engineer. It's the final step in the chain of a television or film production: Often, the music has already been recorded and all that's left is to create the sound effects and to record dialog replacement, narration and final mix.

The fact is, you don't need much exotic equipment to do any of that. And instead of record producers, composers and artists, your clientele is primarily drawn from directors, editors and film producers. These are professionals who, by the time they get to the audio, have reached the final step in a long and arduous picture-making journey, and they're more interested in getting the job done than insisting on exotic mics or mixes.

That's not to say they don't care what the end product sounds like. But in this case, audio is only one element in a project that may have been going on for two years and will wind up being broadcast through a 3-inch TV speaker.

A couple of limiters, a decent mixing board, a good multitrack system, a digital reverb and delay and a pair of bookshelf speakers can form a passable (and for the job at hand, a *reasonable*) system. Add to that a good-quality synchronization system, a 3/4-inch video deck, a 16-bit sampler, a sound effects library and a couple of video monitors, and you're in business at a relatively low cost, compared to high-end music mixing.

The anomaly is that the rates for audio post often surpass those of top-end album studios; the reason is that the process itself is what the client is paying for, not the equipment. Audio post is one of the most difficult and challenging forms of engineering, requiring great patience and knowledge, because each project comes to the studio with its own set of sync and production problems that have accumulated over the course of its development. It's also a very creative endeavor, since much of the effects building and sound design is up to the engineer (dependent on the producer's personality and agreement, of course).

But getting into the field isn't easy. A good post engineer needs a lot of experience, which means getting it somewhere else first. Then you have to attract the clientele to justify the service, and film and TV producers tend to cling very stubbornly to the studios they know and depend on. Audio is their area of *least* expertise, and also the last step in their (probably extremely tight) production chain. So on top of bringing the work in, you've got to get it done fast.

The best way to attract serious audio post business is not to have the equipment, though of course that's a necessity, but to have an engineer on staff with a solid professional following. That is, someone who's worked long enough with the kind of clientele you're after to be able to attract them to your place simply because that's where he or she is now working.

If you do find someone with that kind of experience and pulling power, be prepared to hand over a piece of the store. Top post engineers are in great demand, because there are so few really good ones, and yearly salaries approaching $100K (or more) often come with the territory. A way around that may be to offer profit-sharing or an out-and-out partnership. However you work it, a successful arrangement could mean a successful business.

Choosing Vintage Gear to Create a Unique Facility

As a longtime tech editor with *Guitar World* and technical consultant for some of the world's great studio players, Perry Margouleff helped many other owners find equipment and build facilities before he decided to assemble one for himself.

Perry Margouleff

Owner, Chief Engineer

Pie Recording

Glen Cove, New York

PIE STUDIOS

Career Roots Guitarist and tech aficionado. Special consultant to Jeff Beck, Jimmy Page, Joe Perry and Ted Nugent, helping to create custom guitar sounds in sessions. Decided to build a facility that would be especially conducive to ensemble recording.

Choices "I've chosen my equipment based on its audio performance level and not necessarily on its ease of use. When studios first began to proliferate here on the East Coast (which is why New York used to be referred to as Radio City), every place was different. Owners were very technical, involved in the design of the rooms and equipment and very hands-on.

"Today, people are more likely to buy the best-reputation equipment, which leads to cookie-cutter operations. All that led me to do things in the original school of thought. In my mind, if you really have something to offer that no one else has, you can create a niche or specialty market. And once you develop your client base, they'll be a lot less likely to decide to go down the street to record.

Facility Neve 8078 console with 32 additional API EQs. Two Studer A80RC 24-track decks. Live room: 30' x 35', with an 18-foot ceiling. Control room: 19' x 24'. Two Studer A800 master decks. Very large collection of tube and vintage compressors and mics. A great collection of guitar amps. No MIDI equipment.

"So a guy will ask, 'What sort of amp do I need to use to get this sound?' and I'll actually have it. Basically, my studio inventory is a product of what functions best in a particular application, so I do have some of the hot digital outboard gear as well."

Location A commercial cement-block building located about a half-hour's drive from New York City, also accessible via train.

"One of the things I realized was that once you're inside, you're here to work. So my choice of location was based around the fact that people can make as much noise as they like day or night without bothering the neighbors.

"But the location makes things incredibly difficult. I've had a hard time convincing people to come out and see the place, because a lot of the music business is based on how quick and easy you are to get to. It's a real trade-off, the overhead consideration vs. the accessibility."

Clientele "The kind of clients I'm attracting are those with similar mindsets: older, more knowledgeable engineers and people who grew up using Neve consoles, who want to record in a big acoustic environment. You can't do that in the city except in a couple of the most expensive rooms. It's kind of tough for groups that want to play together to find this kind of environment."

Rates About half the price of competitive studios with similarly-sized live space in Manhattan.

On Expenses "Overhead and reality is extremely important. What I've done is to amass a huge collection of killer vintage equipment that I was able to purchase at auctions for pennies on the dollar. I didn't decide to build a studio and then approach a leasing company to

Owner Margouleff poses with some of his vintage equipment.

buy new. That's part of what makes it viable for me. I don't have $15,000 a month in lease payments to make. I can work with my own band and do my own projects at a cost of something like a hundred a day. Then, when I get booked, I can let other projects churn some money back in, so I can keep doing what I want to do."

Direct Marketing "The only way to develop contacts is via direct marketing. A studio is much like a doctor's office. So when you put your shingle out, all the people in the neighborhood talk to one another and ask, 'Have you been there yet?' Nobody wants to be the first to stick his tongue out for the new guy.

"So calling up and tracking down a specific engineer or producer has been the way to get things rolling. It's like with the doctor. Once Mrs. Jones goes there with her kids and everybody's happy and the kids are fine, the neighbors start thinking, 'Well, okay, everyone's all right, so I guess we'll try it.' Before that, you could stand on your head and offer to give the place away for nothing.

"I don't think advertising works, unless you're doing demo-level work. You need to reach the engineers and producers and go one-on-one with them. If you know a great engineer, for instance, you have to let him become part of the creative process.

"When I tuned my room, I had a couple of heavy-duty engineers I knew come down and participate so that the room got tweaked up to their liking. That makes people feel like they're part of the whole process and, in fact, they came back to work here.

"Then again, you never know where it's going to come from. I did one ad in the Village Voice and made friends with a Brazilian artist, who I'm now producing children's records with for the Smithsonian."

THE QUALITY OF THE STAFF

The right house engineer can bring in a lot of clients. Conversely, an engineer who has problems and produces unsatisfactory work may cause a studio to wither and die with the ensuing word of mouth around town.

An established engineer can also command a premium rate, both on the studio rate card and in his or her paycheck. But the right person is worth it. That's because the studio business is a service business, which in nearly every case means that the human element is what makes it all work. For that reason, it's safe to say that for a recording studio with an engineering staff, *the single most important factor in repeat business is the connection between engineer and client.* Read that line again. Because surrounded by the world's greatest gear in the most gorgeous environment, a client makes the ultimate do-or-die connection with the engineer who's in the driver's seat.

Whether it's you or the person you hire, a first engineer must be a tireless politician, creative artist, goodwill ambassador and trusted arbitrator. The first engineer is the embodiment of the studio: If the producer's chair crashes through the rotting floorboards in the control room, but the engineer is a hero, that producer will pick himself up, dust himself off, make some remark about getting that thing fixed and then come back to the same room over and over again.

The People Connection

Your whole staff sets the tone for the way people perceive your operation. We'll get into this more in Chapter 13, but people who come off both professionally and personably contribute to winning repeat business, and to the willingness of clients to pay your rates.

It sometimes takes years for a staff to really click together as a group that makes magic. And by that time, if you haven't done a good enough job of taking care of each individual, they'll have already left for another gig.

It doesn't take a lot of smarts to figure out whether a studio team is working smoothly. Does the client who calls get put on hold for two minutes by a rude receptionist who's on another line? Do the assistants sit in the control room and read the newspaper? Is the engineer diplomatic and truly responsive to requests that are made? Does the whole operation feel like it's just lurching ahead, step by halting step?

Your clients will know if the magic is there in the space of a single session.

Another extremely important link in this chain is the studio traffic manager. Whether one person will be dedicated to this job or everyone will work at booking clients, the rapport between your studio and the people who call to book time is a key element in smoothing the path to repeat business. It takes charm, eloquence and some thick skin to make a good studio booking person. But a talented individual will be able to sell a whining client on taking a time frame that isn't exactly to his liking, negotiate the right rate, and smooth any ruffled feathers in the process.

Some clients put great stock in that connection and specifically request the person they want to talk to on the other end. And for many people, the person who handles their regular booking becomes someone they develop a close working relationship with. That carries a lot of weight in the day-to-day workings of a good studio business.

CREATURE COMFORTS

Comfort is a very personal concept. It includes breathing space, ambience, color, facilities, temperature, even odor—anything that makes you a little happier to be somewhere.

Every studio needs a lounge or some kind of space to use as an escape from the control room. Artists and producers need a place where they can get away and relax or make important calls. Or maybe someone just needs to zone out or clear his head.

If you create a room that's comfortable and removed, people will unconsciously associate your studio with comfort when they're deciding where to book their next session. And if your location, equipment and staff are comparable to another room, comfort could well be the deciding factor.

At Interlok, clients know that the kitchen in the lounge is stocked with soft drinks and munchies that are on the house. A lot of places install vending machines, but we feel that the few dollars worth of food that gets consumed each day makes a lasting statement about our hospitality.

Rolling Out the Goodies

Some studios go as far as arranging to have a tray of fruit and cheese placed in the room at the beginning of each session. That's a very special feeling to impart to a client: We care enough about you to really do something special for you.

The difficulty in a policy like that, however, is keeping it up. Not only is it an expensive bill to pay at the end of the month, but it means someone is going to become the produce person on the staff, making runs to the supermarket every two or three days and spending time arranging baskets and washing dishes. But if you're up to the logistics, the effort may pay off in real client appreciation.

We decided on a sort of middle-of-the-road policy. There's a bakery near the studio that makes the best bagels this side of the Hudson River, so we opted for a fresh basket with some cream cheese in each studio every morning. While someone has to pick them up fresh every day, our clients really seem to appreciate the extra effort. And since bagels come in six or eight varieties, there's always a nice assortment to choose from.

Finding Your Own Comfort Level

My partner and I have struck an interesting balance in terms of comfort. As the chief engineer, he's most concerned with a layout and design that makes for an efficient operation. As a composer and the senior manager, I'm more concerned with our clients' perspective. Together, we've come up with a working combination that merges both form and function.

I tend to look at the studio setup as a client would: How are the sight-lines into the live studio from the producer's control-room chair? Is the phone within easy reach? Are the chairs comfortable for long periods? Is the room light washing out the video picture? Is the coffee fresh? Is the parking taken care of? Does anybody *need* anything?

The most comforting thing I do is to be at least marginally involved in every session. Most of our sessions are booked by clients who work with my partner and our staff, and I'm usually in my office taking care of the day-to-day business. But I try to stop in at least once to say hello and ask the client if everything is going well. "Hi, nice to see you. How's it going? Is there anything else we can do for you?"

I find that walking in out of the blue and asking something like that gives the client a chance to breathe for a second and to take an overall look at how everything is proceeding. Occasionally someone complains that there's

been some annoying down time or that something isn't going right. Most often they just appreciate a fresh face checking in.

Either way, the goodwill adds to the level of comfort in the room. If everything's okay, then I've just reminded them of that fact, and maybe the feeling will become a little more deeply ingrained. But if something's wrong, I've given them an opportunity to tell me, and I try to do something about it. For example, I make a point of verbally instructing the second to log in a half-hour of non-charged time on the work order if a client has had to sit through an equipment problem.

What I believe is that by doing that assertively in front of the client, I'm freeing them of worrying about a billing problem later on. And I think that adds to their overall comfort level, by ridding them of the problem on the spot. In making that kind of effort, our clients know that we're concerned about their comfort. And nobody's ever complained about that.

THE CARE AND FEEDING OF YOUR REPUTATION

Nothing sells services better than word of mouth. If the word on the street is that your studio is hot, people from Mozambique will call you and book you for days on end. But if your room gains a reputation for being a place where everything seems to go wrong, just try to convince your best friend to record there.

You can't control word of mouth once the mouth leaves your premises, but you *can* influence it. You can make sure that every finished project that leaves your studio is being carried out by someone who's satisfied and who knows that they've been treated well. And who hasn't been overcharged, or over-hyped, or taken advantage of.

Experiences last forever in memory and can be retold and related countless times. Take a client who may have sat through an hour's worth of down time while the multitrack got repaired, but got an hour and a *half* in credit on final bill. Or someone who didn't have to ask for everything that they needed because the attentive staff second-guessed them nearly every time. And who loves the sound of the mix when it's played at home, where it really counts.

A studio's reputation can be a long-term asset or a real monkey on your back. Think about the last time you were at a session somewhere and things went badly. People left unhappy, and they decided to go somewhere else the next time. Most likely, when that studio came up in a conversation a few months later, you added your negative story to the buzz. The crazy part is, that lousy session experience may have occurred *five years ago*! But it was the only time you were there, so that remains your permanent impression of the place! That's why every session is important.

Making Each Day Count

As the years go by and you start moving up into the major leagues, your image will be enhanced by the projects that were recorded in your room. It's *nice* to own a room with a dozen platinum album credits, and to have "problems" like Electric Lady in New York, which is block-booked for months on end and has to deal with crowds of fans lining up on the sidewalk to get a glimpse of superstars as they come and go.

People will book time at a hot facility just to get the vibe of being in the same studio where The Carpet Stains cut their quintuple-platinum album. But that kind of rep is only earned after you've done a lot of homework.

SETTING RATES

Determining your hourly rates is as difficult as being a manufacturer trying to set a price for the new "Mr. Soapdish." You should expect to go through a certain amount of trial and error before you're likely to find a comfortable level of acceptance in the marketplace.

First off, you're going to need to know what the general rates are at the other studios in your area. If you're unaware of that, it's time to get to work. Check the local publications for ads. Also, check in your regional edition of *MixPlus*, a directory of pro audio facilities and services from the publishers of *Mix* magazine (available through Mix Bookshelf; call 800/233-9604).

Real Life Research

The *MixPlus* listings will give you an idea of which studios have comparable equipment to yours. When you find them, you might try calling a few and telling them you have a project you're thinking of recording there.

Your imaginary project should include as many of the services that you plan to offer in your own studio as possible, because you're trying to zero in on your own rate levels. This way,

you can find out about live and overdub tracking rates, mixing, the cost of cassette copies, etc.

Some good studio managers will try to persuade you to come by to discuss prices in person or to see the facility. Don't turn them down— go! There's no better way to check out the competition than to meet them face-to-face.

A tour through a neighboring studio will fill you with insights and ideas for your own facility. Just hang onto your project cover, be polite and don't take unfair advantage of another unsuspecting business person. And who knows—you may wind up becoming friendly competitors later on and enjoy a chuckle over your original visit.

Maybe such tactics sound a little sneaky. But bear in mind that studio staff people give nickel tours all the time and usually enjoy showing their place off. And in the more cosmic terms of payback, you'll undoubtedly give unsuspecting guided tours to other enterprising entrepreneurs later on when *you've* become a success.

So let the adrenaline flow and give it a try. And be sure to ask for a rate card. Most of the services and tape costs should be listed, although many studios either use cards simply as a starting point for negotiations or dispense with them altogether.

Rate Cards

Rate cards are a good item to have in your negotiation arsenal. They're an official way of saying, "Don't just take my word for it. Here it is in print."

There's something about a typeset price that carries a lot of weight. I guess it has to do with the historical fact that somewhere back in time, we North Americans decided that printed prices were exactly what things were supposed to cost, as opposed to buyers in dozens of other countries around the world who'd never even *consider* paying a merchant's asking price.

There is, however, a modern practice of negotiating price for services, and you are most certainly going to wind up bartering with many a cost-conscious client. Each time you present a rate card to someone, you'll find they tend to turn into one of two types of customers: Either they thank you and proceed to ask when their session can be scheduled, or they thank you, smile and say, "But what kind of rate can I *really* get?"

Either way, the card is a benefit. In the first instance, you've immediately sold time to a dyed-in-the-wool, what-you-see-is-what-you-get customer, who, based on the piece of paper you've just handed him, has just unflinchingly agreed to pay your highest asking price. Thank you, oh God of Ingrained Conditioning. May the years pass blissfully by while you deliver deals this easily to my door...

Dealing Adroitly

In the second (and far more common) instance, with an experienced shopper, your rate card effectively starts the bidding on a formal level. And you've hopefully left yourself enough breathing space to come down to a comfortable price that convinces your client he or she is getting a bargain.

For that reason, your rate card should list prices of 5% to 20% higher than you're willing to settle for. Most savvy producers will expect you to come down, especially if they're talking about booking substantial amounts of time. The amusing part is that one producer will base that kind of reasoning on 40 hours of time, and another will base it on four.

Here's a list of the standard services that might be included on a studio's rate card.

Parsec Sound
We Go the Distance

Rates:

24-track recording and mix time	($) per hour
24-track to 2-track DAT	($) per hour
2-track DAT recording	($) per hour
Lockout	($) per day
Block booking rates	on request
Special services [list what they are]	on request
[Brand name] 2" tape	($) per reel
Other sizes of tape	($) per reel or cassette
Disks/cartridges	($) per piece

(Add house policies, including overtime rates, billing time and property disclaimers.)

Balancing Income and Spending

Rate cards come in all shapes and sizes. Often, they are printed as part of a brochure for the studio. But the best approach is to print them separately, or to insert them into a brochure folio. That way, when you overhaul your price structure, you'll only have to reprint one page.

Another factor to consider when setting your rates is to calculate whether they will support the cost of operating your business. You should expect to sell at least 25 hours of time per week once you're up and running, and average at least 100 hours per month. Hopefully, you'll do a lot better than that, but if your bottom line can't support 100 hours a month, you'll need to do some careful thinking about how to balance things out (unless you're really focused on your own projects; if so, see Chapter 5, on project studios).

Returning to the low-budget operation outlined in Chapter 3, let's consider a hundred hours at an average 24-track rate of $45 per hour. That would yield a monthly income of $4,500, which may not net you a Lexus after your first year of operation but is a realistic number to use when figuring your cash-flow projection.

If you work hard and run a quality operation, chances are you'll book twice that time and bill twice the income. But experience teaches that at least some of the good months will be offset by some pretty lean ones, which is why the 100-hour-per-month figure is a realistic one to use.

It's generally thought, by the way, that a studio is considered successful if it's billing about 2,000 hours per year, which translates into about 40 hours a week. Sure, there are studios that burn around the clock and turn in 150-hour weeks, but the challenge of keeping the momentum up month after month is quite formidable. Think conservatively, and you shouldn't have too much trouble sleeping nights.

Block Rates

Precious few clients with big projects on their hands are going to settle for your normal hourly rates. And they shouldn't. They're offering you a lot of time and money and should be compensated for having had the wisdom to come to your place.

A block rate amounts to a lower per-hour rate for a client who is interested in buying a block of time. You can either advertise and list your block rate on your rate card or negotiate each project separately. Some low-priced studios advertise block rates very successfully. If you've got a funky garage filled with creaky equipment, a $20-an-hour block rate on an 8-hour booking ought to get you a lot of interested phone calls.

But a decent-quality operation should involve individual, one-on-one negotiating sessions between the owner/manager and clients. That gives managers the opportunity to size up clients and tailor a deal to each project.

Block rates are easy to negotiate, if you can afford to stick to your guns once you've come down to the bottom-line figure you had in mind. It gets a little tougher when that figure won't do for your client, who says he's got a better deal waiting at another place and wants another $30 off the hourly rate.

Whatever happens at that point is entirely up to you. How has business been lately? Can you afford to let this one go if he isn't bluffing? If the answer is no, you need to agree to his terms in a way that maintains the integrity of your future business.

Protecting Your Rates

You should bear in mind that agreeing to a low rate is, in effect, making an unspoken agreement that this client's future rates will remain at the same low rate. It's very difficult to talk someone back up once they've enjoyed the savings from a special deal.

To prevent that from happening, you should look for a plausible reason to lower the rate on this project alone. Maybe you can say that you've been told this is a low-budget project and are of a mind to agree to a special rate just this one time. Or you can cut a special weekend or evening rate. Or you can just say that the time happens to be open, and you'd rather sell it than watch it go by unused—normally, the rate would have to be higher.

You don't need to spread it on thick; people know you're handing them a line if you overdo it. But it's important to make an effort to maintain a certain price point in your operation, or you'll find your standards quickly vanishing as the word gets out that your prices were low for one project after another. Be flexible, but be vigilant as well.

Maintain a reasonable rate, say "no" a few times, and clients will know you mean business (and that your business is worth it). Of course, delivering that "no" with a certain panache is an art all its own. There are some great books and tapes on the art of negotiating listed in the "Recommended Reading" section of the Appendix.

42 Years at the Same Location

A SPARS past president who continued to engineer right up to his retirement, Mack Emerman has focused on building up a facility that boasts over 150 gold and platinum records as a constantly evolving labor of love.

Career Roots Started as an engineering hobbyist in the '50s and set up a home operation with a lathe. His family helped buy a small building in '57, which opened with a 3-track operation. Built a scoring stage in '67 and met vacationing Atlantic execs Tom Dowd and Jerry Wexler, who began bringing in big stars, helping the studio gain an international reputation. Went 48-track in 1978.

Facility Five studios. SSL consoles, Mitsubishi digital 32-track decks. Three natural live echo chambers, eight echo plates. Studio A: 46' x 67', Studio E: 50' x 50', control room 23' x 26'. Completed the latest addition to the building in 1981, for a total of 25,000 square feet.

House Staff 11 full-time staff people. About 20 on-call first engineers. "It's remarkable to think that our studio manager has been here for 19 years. Another person who started with me hit 20. My assistant has been here for 15. Eight groups of siblings have worked here. And I, as one of the two senior citizens who work here, still engineer some of the larger orchestral and big-band jazz sessions myself."

Primary Focus Music.

Notable Projects Derek and the Dominos' "Layla"; all of the Eagles' albums; the Bee Gees' "Saturday Night Fever." A total of 150 gold and platinum records to date.

Marketing "It was a joke when we built in Miami. Everybody said, 'Why would you want to build here?' There were no record companies, and there was no reason to have one. But it was all that I wanted to do. I was very driven, and I just turned out to be in the right place at the right time.

   "We don't do much to bring business in. We do send out press releases. Video and film is a lot easier to market, but the best way to market a music studio is to record more gold records. We're planning to do more now that we're getting ready to open our new film and video facility. It's strange to say, but our reputation as a music facility is so strong that we have to market the film end very aggressively."

Comfort "We know how to create the kind of ambience that makes people's creative juices flow. We make people very comfortable, and people know that they can get anything that they want here."

Trends "Back in the sixties, we were the drivers. We knew what would work best and how to keep it that way. Nowadays, our business is client-driven. It's much more what *they* want. 'Gee, I wish you had one of these,' or 'I'd give you a lot more business if you'd just do this.'"

Problems "I think people get tired and stressed out doing endless patching and programming of synthesizer setups. It's not like the old days, when there was continual interplay between the musicians. And due in part to that, it's become much more difficult for producers to predict how long a project will take. That makes for some difficult booking problems."

PROFILE

Mack Emerman

Founder & CEO

Criteria Studios

Miami, Florida

criteria recording studios

GROUND FLOOR

SECOND FLOOR

Criteria includes a layout of the huge facility in their promotional package.

Growth Plans Building a new theater-sized, multi-use room with rollaround consoles and screens, which can accommodate music, scoring, dialog replacement, Foley and mixing. "But I think that could turn out to be the best tracking room in the world. The film console will be the last to come.

"I don't think about retirement. I can't imagine doing anything else. How many other people get to do their lifelong hobby as their business? I'd just as soon stay connected with the people I love the most for as long as I possibly can."

BIDDING ON PROJECTS

Instead of charging an hourly rate, one can also bid a price on an entire project. Bids come in two forms: verbal and written. Either way, a bid is your estimate of what you think you can charge for a project and simultaneously make a profit while attracting business. It can either take the form of an hourly rate or be a detailed outline of a complicated piece of work, such as a film.

The idea is to protect yourself against losing money by going overtime, and then making as much money as possible without losing the client. You rarely know if he or she has gone elsewhere to compare rates, and at the same time, you don't want to underbid and lose money while you win the work.

One great way to find out if your client has been shopping around is to say (ahem), "By the way, do you have any other quotes on this project?" Blinding logic, that.

If they do, ask how much and from whom. You can then discuss the relative merits of the competing bid and yours, and hopefully come up with a few reasons the client should work at your place. Some potential clients are very resistant when it comes to showing their hand, and may not want to divulge the quotes they've received from competitors. You can usually loosen their tongues by looking them in the eye and calmly saying something like, "Well, the reason I asked is so I can weigh the merits of the deal you want to make. If I know where else you've been considering, it may help us both decide if working here makes sense."

If that works, you'll find yourself discussing the merits of your competitors vs. your own studio. That's an advantage for you because you'll know who you're competing with. You may

Negotiating Your Best Rate

1. Make a firm and confident offer, at least to begin with. Set the stage to maintain some control over the negotiations.

2. Don't joke about how badly you need the work or the money. Even if it means the difference between the lights staying on or being shut off, act as if business is solid and you can live without this project.

3. If you do need to lower your figures, make the circumstances sound special, as in, "Well, if you could begin tomorrow night, I've got a cancellation that I need to fill." Or, "Tell you what. I understand your money problem here. How do you think you'll be fixed on your next project?" Producers are always optimistic about the money just around the corner and will readily promise you a spot on their next artist's world tour for a lower rate now.

4. Another effective way to hold your ground is to agree to a lower price with a different first engineer. That way, you come off as willing to play ball without compromising too much on your price. Your client will usually understand that you're flexible in some ways, but not necessarily in the way he or she wants, and may eventually settle for a higher rate.

5. When discussing the attributes of your facility and staff, avoid criticism or outright denigration of a competitor. You may inadvertently insult your prospect for considering them, and it's also very unprofessional to throw stones in the first place. Rather, acknowledge the competitor congenially and then proceed to extol your own studio's virtues.

6. Don't joke about your client's money. A lot of people fail to see much humor when discussing allocating their own funds.

7. When you reach an agreement, end the discussion on a firm and positive note. Avoid any further dickering or changes of mind. Project an image of surety and professionalism.

know of specific reasons that booking your place would help your client. And then, there's the warm and fuzzy approach: talking about a higher level of service, the comfort of your place and how it relates to the overall value, etc.

The other advantage in finding out who you're up against is that you'll get to learn more about your competitors. And that's a mighty important aspect of doing good business. Knowing your competitors will inspire you to find ways to set yourself apart from them, and to thus attract more business. But bear in mind that it's easy for a lot of people to look you in the face and quote you a competitor's rate as 30% below the actual offer. Or simply to lie to cover up the fact that they haven't been anywhere else at all.

The bottom line is twofold. First, the more experience you acquire, the better a negotiator you become. And two, learn not to panic in the face of real competition. Maintain a specific bottom line on rates and conditions, and don't go below it. Stay calm and professional as you discuss money, and learn how to politely refuse an offer that's too uncomfortable.

Often, you'll get into negotiating over price on the phone. This is a touchy situation. You need to retain the upper hand and not sound too hungry. People like to work with people who appear to be strong, not weak or needy. That's why it's so easy to get a loan from a bank if you're rich and you don't need one: The bank's *impressed*.

About Album Projects

If you're bidding for an album project with a record company, all you need to settle on is an hourly rate and who'll be engineering. *Never* make an unspecified-length album deal; 99% of all albums take longer to complete than their optimistic producers think they will. If you pull a number out, like $10,000 for the entire project, which may sound like a lot at the moment, you may wind up selling studio time at eight bucks an hour by the time you ship the final mix.

What you *do* need from the record company is a P.O. (purchase order) that specifies what the project is, when it will get started and what the hourly or daily rate will be. A P.O. is really a mini-contract without all the extra paragraphs, and should be sent to you prior to the first session.

Often, the record company will issue a series of P.O.'s over the course of the project, each one stating the company's order for, say,

another 30 hours of time. Make sure you get them! If they're promised and don't come in time, you carry heavy weight in demanding one before the first note gets recorded.

If it's an album deal, or any deal of some length with a legitimate company, you shouldn't begin without one. Your P.O. will stand up in court and help win you a judgment, while a handshake won't. But don't consider P.O.'s money in the bank! Unfortunately, many record companies consider them to be a way to simplify the process of stalling or reneging on payment.

Among world-class facilities, several major record companies have a reputation for consistently "losing" P.O.'s when payment comes due, insisting that studios resubmit them two or three more times and taking months to pay up. It is a maddening dance for studio owners, who rely heavily on the record company's business, to be thrust into the role of alternately demanding and begging for payment due, and at the same time attempting to maintain a cordial relationship with a company they will probably be dealing with for years to come.

As for taking a client to court, the road is a long and expensive one, with one exception. If the amount owed is $5,000 or less, and thus qualifies for small claims court, you may be able to get a date within days or weeks. This is a far sight better than the length of time needed to get to a U.S. Superior Court, which can easily be a year or more. This doesn't even *begin* to address the problem of paying attorney and court costs, not to mention finally collecting the money after you win.

As you'll read several times in this book, the only *sure* way to get paid for services rendered in the recording business is to get paid in full *before* you begin a project! The next best bet is to get regular payments as you perform services, with the final bill getting settled before your master tapes leave the building.

Any other arrangement carries a much higher risk of getting burned. I've always had great faith in my own instincts in money matters and in the better part of human nature in general. But the sad truth is that people are unpredictable and untrustworthy, especially in business and money matters. So the chances are, if you decide to trust your instinct on a regular basis, you'll learn some hard lessons. Protect yourself as completely as possible, and you will minimize your losses.

Teach your client that he or she will get all the services you've agreed to, as long as he or she plays by the rules. Insist on this the first time it happens, and it's likely it won't happen again.

In business, people constantly test one another, and money is often the biggest issue. Demonstrate your willingness to play by the rules, and then demand that your client respond in kind.

As for the flakiness of some major record companies, the caveat that seems to emerge is that quite often the larger the corporate client, the longer the wait for payment. Chalk it up to organizational indifference, mega-bureaucracy or effete snobbism; however one attempts to explain that kind of predictability, it inevitably illustrates the importance of maintaining clean books and a vigilant watch.

BIDDING ON FILMS

In the field of audio post, feature films are among the most sought-after projects because they represent the biggest single-project deals you can make. They also pose a great creative challenge for the engineer.

Doing audio post for film, which is often referred to as sound design, involves several complex procedures that demand a real sense of artistry. In a typical feature, hundreds of sound effects must be laid in, dialog edited, muffled lines re-recorded (ADR—Automated Dialog Replacement), live action mimicked (Foley—recording the sound of people's movements), ambience created, music added and finally, a complete mix assembled.

To do that, and to bid intelligently, the film is first *spotted* (viewed with an editor who discusses what's needed) by the engineer and studio manager. Then the work is divided into sections on a chart, and an estimate is made as to how long each part will take.

Once a reasonable estimate of hours is determined, that number is multiplied by an hourly rate, along with tape, talent and miscellaneous costs, to reach a final number (since a facility typically values each of the services at a different rate, common practice is to quote a package rate). You can then agonize over this total, trying to second-guess the competition while staying afloat in the sea of problems that may arise later on. When you submit a firm bid, you're agreeing to live by it no matter what.

The challenge of assembling a film bid is that you can only guess at how long each part of the process is going to take, and hope that the producer(s) you wind up working with won't slow you down with unreasonable requests or difficult behavior.

Actually, the behavior factor can be addressed in a number of ways before you make the deal; namely, find out if the director will be at the studio all the time, or just for the important stages like ADR and mixing.

Have you ever seen those signs in auto garages quoting three different hourly mechanics' rates: $35 an hour if you drop it off, $50 an hour if you watch and $75 if you help? There's really something to that! If a producer or director attaches himself or herself to every aspect of the audio post process, the task will no doubt take longer to complete. The producer will not always agree with the engineer's choices for effects or ambience and will ask for alternatives, at least to audition. They will discuss edit points, point out differences in crossfades and want to sift through your entire library of tropical bird sounds.

They will do this because they are a) creative individuals, b) determined to maintain a certain level of control, and c) bored out of their skulls sitting in the producer's chair hour after hour while your engineer tries to perform the hands-on part of the moment's tedious task with someone breathing down his neck.

You can avoid this kind of trouble by gently negotiating with the producer, demonstrating how much money he'll save by letting the studio do a portion of the job without his having to be there. The truth is, a producer will never hear most of the minute changes he would have asked for if he isn't in the room when the work is being done. Instead, he'll be presented with a cohesive work in progress that will be far easier to listen to and critique from a broader viewpoint.

It's every producer and director's right to be as involved as they would like in the final step of their production. But many will already know the logic of letting the cook prepare the beefstock first and then getting involved in the taste-testing later. Suffice it to say that all this makes the involvement part of the negotiation an important one, from the standpoint of trust among the parties and the length of time it will take to accomplish the task at hand.

Making the Deal

Once you make a bid and it is accepted, the film company may send a signed P.O. along with a check, usually for half or a third of the full amount up front and the rest on an agreed-upon schedule, culminating with a final check on delivery. The trick is to survive the complete experience and collect the entire amount.

Some studios assemble multipage contracts that cover every legal nuance, from completion date to unnatural disasters. And some keep it simple, with minimal paper work and a lot of eyeball-to-eyeball agreement.

A simple bid for a job includes a short cover letter and a separate sheet outlining the proposal. The bid lays out the proposed hours, notes services and supplies that will be included, guarantees a completion date and states the terms of payment. (Since your facility usually will value each of the listed services at a different rate, it is common practice to quote a single cost for the entire package.) If the bid is accepted, the receipt of a company P.O. may indicate that the deal is sealed. It's also a good idea to have the client sign the bid to indicate her agreement to the terms and return a copy for your files. That way you have a record of the agreement in case someone tries to dispute it later.

Here's what a bid might look like:

2/1/96

Mr. Rush Limbaugh
American Way Productions
1010 5th Ave.
New York, NY 10028

Dear Rush,

Enclosed is our bid for the complete audio post-production for the feature film *Attack of the 50-Foot Woman President*.

This bid presupposes that the locked version will be 100 minutes or less, and be delivered to us on 1-inch or 3/4-inch videotape. Materials include all audio tape and one 3/4-inch videocassette.

We're excited about the prospect of working together and have some interesting ideas on how to handle Hillary's chase scene around the Pentagon.

If the attached bid is agreeable to you, please sign where indicated and return a copy to me. Feel free to call me with any questions you may have.

Sincerely,

Abigail Jones
Manager, The Right Stuff Studios

P.S. This *is* supposed to be a comedy, right??

Audio Post-Production Bid for "Attack of the 50-Foot Woman President"

Laydown	2 hrs.
Spotting	8 hrs.
Dialog editorial	90 hrs.
Effects design and pre-lay (includes digital fx and programmer)	40 hrs.
Foley, including talent	30 hrs.
ADR recording	16 hrs.
ADR & dialog editing	10 hrs.
Music lay-in	8 hrs.
Pre-dub & final mix	48 hrs.
Total	**252 hrs.**
Materials:	included
Total fee estimate:	**$46,680**

Production audio must be delivered to us on 1/2-inch 4-track with sync pops and SMPTE time code corresponding to telecine transfer. This estimate does not include editing time or music composition. Final delivery format will be 1/2-inch 4-track, with SMPTE time code and sync pops.

Studio will supervise all aspects of audio post-production and guarantees completion 24 days from delivery to the facility.

Terms: Signed P.O. and $23,340 prior to commencement of production. Cashier's check for $23,340 on delivery of the final mix and all elements.

Agreed to and Accepted:

_____

Production Company

Rewriting the Book on Film Sound

Working entirely in the digital domain, George Johnsen has devoted his career to revolutionizing the process of recording and transferring sound to film with a studio that he designed from the ground up.

George Johnsen

Owner

EFX Systems

Burbank, California

Career Roots Started as a floorsweeper at Capitol Records, then as a second when someone called in sick. His fondness for TV paired him with a composer who had a home studio, and from there moved into studio design and synthesizer sound effects production, using a Moog Model 55.

"I was getting really frustrated with cutting on mag, which only offered three or four tracks. In the '70s there weren't any studios that could lock a 24-track machine to picture with feet and frames. So I started this place."

Facility 10,000 square feet, leased with an option to buy and set up for both film and video. Both mediums are available in the mixing theatre.

"We tend to *micro*scope on video and *macro*scope on film. Somehow, the mind perceives that film is better than video, so we do all the digital stuff to video and then, with the flick of a switch, we flip it over to the film projector and watch a larger chunk [laughs]—another piece of custom software by EFX Systems! It's one of those things where you have to do a lot of thinking to make it work, but the whole point is that we're trying to make the technology absolutely 100% transparent to the user."

46 full-time employees. Seven all-digital studios: a Foley/ADR stage with an interlocking system of movable pits, a film mixing room with a Harrison SeriesTen 256-input console, two TV mixing rooms, two effects editing suites and a dialog editing room. Six complete Synclavier systems, all Sony 3324 digital multitrack recorders.

[Laughs again.] "We're proud to say that we have more Synclavier systems and have spent more money on them than anybody on the planet. And yes, I drive a nine-year-old car."

Primary Focus TV and feature film sound and sound for theme parks.

Notable Projects TV: *Thirtysomething*, *Freddy's Nightmares*. Films: *Torch Song Trilogy*, *Talk Radio*. Parks: King Kong attraction at Universal Studios.

Marketing Nothing but phone calls. "In the film market, it doesn't really matter what your ad says. It matters what you're working on and what image you present to the people you're working with, and if they've had a good experience. It's an extremely small community. You're constantly updating your reputation. That's because there's such a high turnover of personnel in the film business.

"So as each project gets completed, your reputation tends to hang on the quality of the work you did on it. Unfortunately, the phrase 'You're only as good as your last picture' actually applies. It's real funny. You have to avoid squeezing in a low-budget project.

"In the beginning, we were selling a new technology and did take that kind of work. It's very tough to break out of that mold. For instance, if someone doesn't have enough money to do a project right, and you do what they ask you to, you're taking care of your client but hurting your reputation, because people are going to say 'Gee, they didn't do any Foley here. What's the deal?'"

On Innovation "People have been making films in exactly the same way since 1942. But we're finally looking at a completely digital chain now. What I'd like to hear is what the guy recorded in the field, not something nine generations down. What I'm trying to bring to the theatre is clarity."

Analog Equipment Several sets of dishes, a full set of carpenter's tools and anything that makes an odd noise. "We have about a garageful of Foley props that we keep here to add to whatever the artists bring themselves. And then whenever anybody at work wears out a pair of shoes, it goes straight into the pile. I think we've got ten or 15 different new and rusty pulleys, maybe eight different kinds of rope and half a dozen swords. Garage sales are the places to find them, because what you want is junk. So we have people who say 'Hey, I found this the other day and it makes a really great sound. I don't know what we're going to use it for, but let's put it in the closet and figure it out later.' That's where you get your best props.

Billing "The saying goes, 'Budget, speed, quality—pick two.' Which is reasonably true."

The studio does bids on some projects and bills hourly on others. "We bid complete projects in most cases when the client is putting something in our control and it's a closed-end bid. If they're retaining control of something like mixing, then we leave it open. When the clients are in direct control of the session, we'll tell them how long we think we can do it in and give them the guidelines. Then it's up to them as to whether or not they want to go that way. If they want to do more, we'll be happy to help them."

Interns Full program with eight weeks unpaid full-time commitment, plus the option of another eight, leading to possible regular employment. "We work directly with four or five of the schools that actually have degree programs in sound engineering. So they know the basic idea, but it's real hard for students to walk in off the streets and actually edit anything. And it's gonna be at least a year learning Synclavier programming before they're ready to be left alone to make their own decisions on what to program to play back for the director. "

Challenges "Sometimes when something really difficult comes in, me the business person says, 'We can't do this.' But me the artist says, 'That's all we're here for.' Right now, we're working on a project for Lockheed which is essentially a commercial for selling the new fighter they're building.

"So I've sent a team upstate to record a Lockheed P-38, because it's the only one in existence that's still flying with the right engines in it. The guy remembers the right sound; it *is* the right sound and we *have to have it*. I'm not charging him for that. That's just what we want. You just say to yourself, 'I'm doing this because I have to,' and there's no explanation for it.

Philosophy "We don't like to say no. We like to figure out how to say yes so that it works for both the client and us. You have to guard against giving away the store but you

The central machine room

want to make sure your reputation stays intact once the project gets finished. So the philosophy of the business is not having to say no, except just once. And that's at the initial outset of the project, where you look at something someone's brought to you and you just can't do it. And that's the hardest no to say. Because you look at it and say, 'Okay, you've got 20 thousand for this project but it's 40 thousand dollars worth of work. It's really a great project—but the answer's still no.'

"You may have a situation where you've got tumbleweeds blowing through the studio for the next five weeks and you figure, well, geez, at least I can put people to work. But you still have to say no in order to protect your reputation for the future and in order to be able to deliver a product that you're proud of. Otherwise, a year from now, you're not going to have the business that you want. It was very difficult for me to realize that even though we had to do low-budget pictures in the beginning because that was all we could get, we had to *stop* doing them because no one in an upper-budget level would take us seriously if we continued to work on low-budget stuff.

"Money's always the great justifier. With employees, with clients, it's always the justification. But it's never the reason. I feel real strongly that what we have to build here as a facility is a team spirit in the sense of not all working for the company, but because we just plain love what we're doing."

GETTING PAID

Every studio owner has a story about the band that came to dinner and waltzed away with the finished master. The vibes were great, the music was righteous, and the camaraderie was beautiful. Then they got in their van, promised a check and drove off into the sunset, never to be heard from again.

It's difficult to describe the sense of frustration and anger you experience when something like that occurs. It's akin to having a computer disaster: You're doing a complicated sequence on a tune you just wrote and the going is maddeningly slow, but you know the groove is starting to get tamed and it's going to turn out great. Suddenly an electrical spike shoots through the system, and in an instant, the file blows up. You're shocked and surprised for a second, and then in the next second, you realize you haven't hit the SAVE command for over an hour.

Everything is gone, irretrievable. You've just lost something you can never quite bring back. It's the most helpless kind of rage. And the only positive way you can deal with it is to try to learn something from the experience so that it won't happen again, while you try to keep from putting your fist through something.

Protecting Yourself

Unfortunately, you need to do that in business as well. There's a host of reasons why payments can be slow in coming, or why they may not come at all: The record company insists the deal was different than you know it was (here's where a P.O. will help). The artist claims you delivered unacceptable quality. The production company declares bankruptcy. Or the client just plain stiffs you.

As an owner, you're entitled to a reasonable amount of assurance that the charges your clients incur will be paid. One way to guarantee that is to insist on full cash payment up front. That's actually an acceptable demand in the case of a deal where the studio is granting an extraordinarily low rate for a one-shot project, or when it's offered by a client in an attempt to use the cash as a bargaining tool.

But it's more likely that you can set a general policy of cash (or check) on delivery. Many studios insist on this, but the problem is that in doing so, they wind up turning away solid citizens who aren't equipped to pay on such a tight schedule. The reason they're so insistent is that they're inevitably the ones who've been burned the worst in the past. In no way are they going to let this happen to them again. From now on, it's cash or crash.

This is real head-in-the-sand reasoning. Established producers and companies can't always deliver like that, and when pressed, may come through and resent it, or just plain find another studio with a more reasonable policy. These policies can be derived from good business sense and some simple paper work.

The Credit Application

Whenever you apply for a credit card, or for a bank loan or an auto lease or anything else that requires extended payments, the first thing that's always required is a credit application. The application is the method by which the lender can find out about your past credit history as well as your present financial health.

When a new client asks for credit on studio time, the first thing to do is to smile, hand him the studio credit application and ask him to fill it out. Legitimate people won't object to this; shifty ones might. At that point, you would be wise to ask them to shift on over to another studio.

The credit application simply asks for some personal legal information, such as who the client banks with and, more importantly, vendor references (other merchants and suppliers who have accounts with the company).

Get the application filled out with enough advance time to follow up on it. Call each trade reference and ask them the amount of credit your new client carries, as well as how prompt they are in paying their bills. In a few minutes, you'll know if you're dealing with someone you can depend on or a potential new problem.

Then call the client's bank. Say that your business is contemplating taking the client on as a credit customer and ask how long they've been banking there and if there have ever been any problems with the account.

The bank will either tell you on the phone or ask you to have the client call them and authorize the release of that information. Call the client and tell him you're following up on his application, and could he please cooperate. Your client will know you mean business and should okay the inquiry. Again, if he doesn't, there's obviously something he's trying to hide.

You will often get straight answers and a feel for how trustworthy your new client will be from those reference companies. If they give you a reasonable thumbs-up, extend a charge privilege. If the references are uncooperative or

NEW ACCOUNT CREDIT DATA

Date _____

Name _____

Address _____ Phone No. _____

City _____ State _____ Zip Code _____

(Check one)   Corporation _____   Partnership _____   Proprietorship _____

Division or Subsidiary (If so, name of firm) _____

Names and Titles of Officers and/or Principals:

_____   _____

_____   _____

Date Business Established _____

Federal Tax ID No. _____   Anticipated Monthly Requirements $_____

CREDIT REFERENCES: (BANK & 3 TRADES)

Release of Bank Information (Signature) _____

Account Number _____   **Contact** _____

Bank _____ Branch _____ Phone _____

Address _____ City _____ State & Zip _____

Trade:

1. Name _____ Phone _____

   Address _____ City _____ State & Zip _____

2. Name _____ Phone _____

   Address _____ City _____ State & Zip _____

3. Name _____ Phone _____

   Address _____ City _____ State & Zip _____

The undersigned hereby certifies that the foregoing statement is a true and correct statement of the undersigned's financial condition, and that it is submitted for the purpose of procuring credit. In the event that any material representation set forth herein should prove to be incorrect or untrue, the same will constitute an event of default in any agreement in writing between the undersigned and

_____

Company Name

By _____ Title _____ Date _____

A typical credit application. Handing one to a client produces varied responses; often they will fill in a portion of what's asked for, leaving the rest blank. It's a matter of judgment whether to press any further. The trade references will provide the most useful information.

not forthcoming with account information, so be it. It may be that the company has a policy not to divulge their private business dealings to other businesses.

Unfortunately, such policies are becoming more of a trend, due to the seemingly endless spiral of gratuitous and greedy litigation choking our legal system. A growing number of employees and companies have been suing anything that moves after a mishap; for example, someone who slips on a sidewalk and breaks a bone may be inclined to sue not only the property owner, but the contractor who poured the sidewalk and the factory that mixed the cement!

A reference that divulges private information about another company's business dealings can potentially be held liable for slandering that company's good name. We can all thank the

S   O   U   N   D

TERMS OF BUSINESS

PRICES

Prices on brochures and advertising subject to change without notice. Prices do not include tape stock unless otherwise specified. Prices to be charged shall be the prices in force at date of invoicing. Transportation of tape and equipment to and from Comfort Sound Recording Studio shall be at customers' risk and expense.

SALES TAX

The customer guarantees that the sales tax exemption numbers (if any) listed on the invoice are valid for the work done by Comfort Sound.

TERMS OF PAYMENT

All work is accepted on a C.O.D. basis unless other arrangements have been made in advance and have been listed on the invoice. Overdue accounts will be subject to interest charges of 2% per month. The customer agrees to pay all costs and expenses including legal fees incurred by Comfort Sound in connection with the collection of amounts owing to Comfort Sound. Any claims for adjustments in connection with an invoice must be presented to Comfort Sound in writing within ten days from the date of the invoice in question. Customer hereby waives any claim for adjustment in billing which is not timely presented according to the provisions of this paragraph.

BOOKINGS

The Customer is responsible for time and services booked and is not entitled to any extensions of the scheduled time without the approval of the senior Comfort Sound staff member on duty. Bookings are one half hour minimum, with quarter hour increments thereafter.

CANCELLATIONS

Cancellation of any work or service ordered will be charged 50% of cost of services scheduled if cancellation takes place within 24 hours of scheduled start of session.

TERMS REGARDING USE OF FACILITIES

Comfort Sound will use its best efforts to ensure that all equipment will be in working condition. Should time be lost due to equipment failure, Comfort Sound agrees to credit the customer for that portion of the time for which the use of equipment was denied, or should the customer so request, Comfort Sound will furnish the equipment for an additional period equal to the time lost due to equipment failure, subject to Comfort Sound's obligations to other customers. Except for such obligation, Comfort Sound shall have no further liability in connection with such defective equipment.

SEVERABILITY

Each term of the Terms Of Business is severable from every other and shall survive the nullity or unenforceability of the other.

MODIFICATION

These terms of business can only be modified by an instrument in writing signed by an authorized representative of Comfort Sound.

RETURN OF CUSTOMER'S MATERIALS

Customer's materials left on premises six months after completion of work become property of Comfort Sound.

CUSTOMER'S LIABILITY FOR INFRINGEMENTS

The customer shall indemnify and save Comfort Sound harmless of and from all suits, claims, demands, and other liabilities and expenses, including legal fees and disbursements arising out of the production, distribution or exhibition of any films, tapes, or phonograph records or equivalent in connection with which Comfort Sound shall have furnished any goods and services.

LIMITATION OF LIABILITY AND WARRANTY

Comfort Sound warrants that it will take every precaution for the safety of clients' materials in production or storage, however Comfort Sound assumes no risks and makes no guarantees unless such loss or damage is caused by the wilful negligence of Comfort Sound or any of its employees acting within the scope of their authority. In no event, however, shall Comfort Sound be liable for more than the replacement value of the unrecorded tape or any other unprocessed materials. In no event shall Comfort Sound be responsible for any loss incurred by its customer as a direct or indirect result or consequence of any of the foregoing.

Comfort Sound assumes no risks and makes no guarantees concerning the content of materials prepared for customers or delivery schedules, arrival times or air-dates of materials prepared for customers. All risks for content and delivery are assumed by and are solely those of the customer. Comfort Sound shall not insure any of customer's materials while in the possession of Comfort Sound or while in transit.

LIENS

In consideration of Comfort Sound performing work for the customer, Comfort Sound shall have a lien on all customers' tapes, cassettes, and other materials and on all tapes and cassettes made from them until full payment for any due and outstanding accounts is received. Comfort Sound is and shall be entitled to sell, lease, or otherwise dispense of any tape or other property upon which such lien is granted in its absolute and unfettered discretion upon giving 30 days notice in writing to the customer of its intention to sell, lease or otherwise dispose of the tape or property. Such written notice is duly given to the customer if sent by prepaid registered mail to the customer's last known mailing address.

In disposing of the tape or other property referred to in the preceding paragraph, Comfort Sound shall not be required to obtain the best price available. Upon disposing of the tape or other property, Comfort Sound shall retain from the proceeds an amount equal to the amount owing to it together with all costs of the disposition and the balance, if any, shall be paid by Comfort Sound to the customer.

The customer has the right, at any time previous to the actual disposition of the tape or other property, to discharge the lien, by paying to Comfort Sound the amount claimed in the notice of disposition, and all reasonable costs and expenses incurred by Comfort Sound as a result of the customer's failure to comply with the terms of this agreement.

ENTIRE AGREEMENT

These Terms of Business and the written contract signed by the customer constitute the entire agreement between the customer and Comfort Sound, and no evidence of any oral agreement or representation whatsoever shall be admitted to vary, modify, waive, or add to any or all terms of this agreement.

Comfort Sound prints its contract on the reverse of its invoice, referring to it as Terms of Business. No signature is required, but the legality is implied as a condition of doing business with the studio.

legions of lawsuit-happy, 800-number law firms for that, as well as the general pervasiveness of the I'm-gonna-get-my-piece-of-the-pie-no-matter-who-I-have-to-ruin attitude that's poisoned our legal system.

Plugging Into the System

Another extremely effective way to check out the credit-worthiness of your client is to reference him through a local trade organization. Many cities have professional groups made up of businesses in the same field; these are a great way to get connected, and stay connected, with businesses in your community.

The entertainment field is no exception. In post-production, for example, there is the International Teleproduction Society. It's a group

EAST COAST SOUND LAB   -3-

IN CONSIDERATION OF THE MUTUAL COVENANTS HEREIN MADE IT IS AGREED AS FOLLOWS:

1.   Recordings. As used herein the terms "recording" and "recordings" shall mean and include any recording or recordings made by tape, wire,film disc or any other similar or dissimilar method, whether now known or hereafter developed.

2.   Compensation. The Artist shall pay the Company full compensation prior to the date of the recording unless other terms,stated in writing and signed by a Company representitive, have been agreed upon. Said payment shall be in full and received in either cash, certified check or money order.

3.   Property Liability. Company shall not be liable for loss of, damage to or impairment of the value of any property furnished by the Artist for use in the connection with any of the programs or recording.

4.   Force Majeure. In the event any recordings or broadcasts contemplated herein are not performed by reason of fire, casulty, lockout, strike, labor conditions, unavoidable accident, riot, war, act of God or by reason of enactment of any Municipal, State or Federal Ordinance or Law or by issuance of any Executive or Judicial Order or Decree, whether Municipal, State or Federal, or by any other local constituted authority or by reason by any cause not subject to control of the Company, no compensation shall be due Artist for the broadcasts or recordings so prevented.

5.   Changes In Scheduled Time. In the event of changes made in one or more of the series of broadcasts or recordings herein provided for from the scheduled time to another time, or another day, or from one broadcasting or recording system to another system, this contract shall nontheless be performed in all respects at the new time, providing two (2) days written notice of such change is given to the Company, in which the day of the week and the hour and place of such broadcast and recording is stated. In the event of such time and/or day conflicts with Company's prior contractual obligations, this contract shall stay in effect until such new scheduled time is made. Under no circumstances shall compensation be repaid to the Artist for a delay or change in scheduled times.

6.   Indemnities. Artist shall indemnify and hold harmless Company against any and all claims, damages, liabilities, costs and expenses, arising out of the broadcast and recording.

7.   Effect Of Breach. Company reserves the right to cancel this contract at any time upon default by Artist in the payment of bills, or other material breach or part of the Artist or any of the conditions herein; and upon such cancellation all broadcasting and recording done hereunder and not paid shall become immediately due and payable. In the event of cancellation by reason of material breach by Artist, Artist shall pay to Company, as liquidated damages, a net sum equal to actual out-of-pocket costs to the Company incurred through the cancellation of this contract, together with the amount owing at the earned rate for recordings and broadcastings performed hereunder prior to such cancellation.

8.   Exclusion Of All Warranties. THERE IS NO WARRANTY OF ANY KIND, EXPRESS OR IMPLIED, AND SPECIFICALLY THERE IS NO WARRANTY OF MERCHANT ABILITY OR OF FITNESS.

9.   Quality of Recording. Artists understands that recording quality is not guaranteed and that any defects must be verified in the studio. Artist understands that if quality is not verified in studio upon completion of recording and broadcasting, Artist is barred from being reimbursed for quality of broadcast or recording.

10.   Attorneys Fees. Artist understands that if his account is referred to collection, the Artist will be liable for all reasonable collection expenses, including but not limited to, court cost, reasonable attorney's fees and compounded interest.

11.   Severabilities. The provisions of this agreement shall be severable so that the invalidity , unenforceability, or waiver of any one or more of its provisions shall not affect the remaining provisions.

12.   Entire Agreement. No oral statements or agreements shall be valid or binding on the parties hereto. This agreement may be modified or extended, or the promises or covenants hereof waived, only by written instrument executed by the parties.

13.   Assignment. This agreement is personal to Company and Artist shall not assign or transfer without the prior written consent of Company.

14.   Additional Cost. Artist agrees to bear any additional costs in broadcasting and recording. All additional costs shall be paid to Company within forty-eight (48) hours after broadcasting and recording is completed. Payment shall be made by cash, certified check or money order.

Company representitive:_____

Artist................._____

East Coast Sound Lab's contract is signed by the client before the project begins.

that welcomes all manner of teleproduction people and is primarily composed of video and audio post studios. One of its key offerings is the credit manager's group, which meets once a month and reviews the payment of history of every account that comes to any of the local chapter's facilities. If a client is slow in paying, his or her name is added to the database. Then, when an inquiry comes in, the manager who has had the problem relates it to the inquiring studio. It's a great tool to have in a credit manager's arsenal, a sort of you-can-run-but-you-can't-hide deterrent to errant clients.

The ITS has chapters in many U.S. cities, including Chicago, San Francisco, Denver, New York, etc. If your studio does the majority of its work in audio post or TV or film-related projects, you can obtain more information on this excellent organization by calling 212/629-3266.

To find other local professional groups, look through the pages of local papers and check the news sections of *Mix* and *Pro Sound News* magazines. Membership is a great way to plug into a whole society of people who are doing the same things you are and who are interested in sharing knowledge and experiences.

Keeping Close Ties With the Community

With a little help from their friends, Linda and Harry Warman have built a beautiful facility. And with a little help from their lawyer, they've built a solid client base with a steady accounts-receivable flow.

Career Roots With husband Harry, started with a 4-track home facility for eight years, and now has occupied commercial space for the last five years. "A hobby that got out of hand," she calls it. Harry played with touring bands for ten years and then wanted to get off the road.

Facility One studio, 30' x 44', control room 20' x 30'. Soundcraft 2400 automated console. MCI JH-24 24-track plus 24 tracks of ADAT, yielding 48-track lockup. A second suite is used for MIDI production and editing.

"We joined forces with an existing company that did music productions, who moved their existing equipment into our facility. It's been a real positive link."

House Staff Manager, two firsts, three seconds on call. Interns from the local schools.

Primary Focus Albums and original music by local artists, commercials and film scores.

Financing "We built the studio with the help of a lot of local musicians. The way we got financed for labor was by offering free studio time in return for people's help: electricians, carpenters—any musicians we could find who were qualified to build the place. In Colorado, most of the local musicians depend on outside income to support themselves, because the music industry isn't as strong here as it is in the major cities.

"So we offered to compensate them for their labor. It helped us to get the job done at a much lower cost. Some musicians racked up 200 hours of recording time, and that was based on two hours of labor equaling an hour of studio time.

"The one mistake we made was not being clear on a time limit to collect on the hours earned. We still have people showing up five years later claiming that we owe them more time. But I did keep careful track of the hours.

"Outside of that, there were no other problems, and one surprise benefit was that we ended up with a lot more interest from the community. In all, 40 or 50 people participated over a six-month period.

Partnership "We brought in a third partner when we moved. It was just a case of finding someone who was interested in investing at the right time. The extra money meant the difference between opening our new place with 24 tracks instead of 16."

Equipment "We've considered buying a Neve board, but we realized we'd price ourselves totally out of the local market and would have to go national just to make the payments. Nevertheless [sighs], it's still a consideration."

Rates "I try to keep them pretty consistent. We have to keep them reasonable and in line with the local economy. I have a hard time justifying raising my rates, because I know how tough it is for the people who live in the area. But as the economy has improved, we've been able to increase them very marginally."

Marketing Some local magazine print ads. PR releases when a good album project comes in. "My best advertising is by word of mouth."

The view of this large 20' x 30' control room is enhanced by an expansive wide-angle shot.

"Colorado is a beautiful place to live, and we're all working hard to make it more of a music Mecca. It's the kind of place where people feel it's worth their while to be here, and in the last several years, some great talent has emerged.

"I think the goal of all the studios in our area is to support our local talent and to help them get their product out there and do something good for themselves and the region.

Comfort "We have a strict no-smoking policy in the control room. We found that the connectors were getting caked up, the lingering smell was a problem, and the cleaning was very difficult. Most of the local studios have similar policies. And it's no problem in terms of upsetting any smokers in the group."

Philosophy "We'll go out of our way to make people feel as comfortable as possible, because we feel that's when they become the most creative. We try to do everything we can to contribute to the local music community, because that can only help us in the long run."

On Contracts "We have a contract that all our clients sign, and it does make them responsible. We put it together several years ago when we started losing too much money from people not paying their bills. We'd have groups come in not paying any money up front, and they'd do all their recording, saying they'd pay in the end. Then they'd take their cassette and leave, and we'd never see them again.

"So we decided we needed something binding that would stand up in court. We had the contracts drawn up with the help of our lawyer, and it covers everything from payment guarantees to malicious damage.

"It has worked wonderfully. Our clients know exactly where everything stands. It covers all the costs, what I'm responsible for, what they're responsible for, when they're coming in, when their payments are due, how much they're paying in advance, everything. And I tell them that this protects *them* every bit as much as it protects me.

"All in all, the contracts have really helped us. We haven't had to go to court since we started using them."

R E C O R D I N G

10650 Irma Drive, Suite 27
Northglenn, CO 80233
(303) 452-0498

Date:

Proposal/Recording Agreement/Invoice:

Work Order No.:

Client No.:

Client:

Artist:

Producer:

Project:

Master tapes to be released to (any) (all) the following individuals:

Work orders may be signed by:

Recording Date and Specifications of Project:

Hourly Rate for Studio if balance of invoice for studio and materials is paid

on or before_____, 19_____: $_____

Deposit Required on or before_____, 19_____; $_____
Deposits are not refundable credit will be issued.
Subject to all terms and conditions set forth on reverse side.

Avalanche Recording Studios, Inc.

By:_____
             Studio   Date

_____   _____
Street   Client   Date

_____   _____
Town   State   Zip   Client   Date

_____   _____
Phone   Client   Date

Avalanche Studios developed a two-part agreement that each client signs at the start of a project. It has virtually eliminated their accounts-receivable problems.

8

Income Sources: Getting Creative

In the previous chapter, we discussed the various ways that a recording studio usually handles its main source of income: selling time. A good mix of different clients with various needs and projects is the basis for a healthy ongoing business. Yet there are a host of other areas that can not only represent a source of income but offer some real creative challenges as well. Even a successful operation is prone to periods of unused "dead time." But if you've got the drive and the energy to jump in, there are plenty of projects you can generate to wake up a sleepy schedule.

Consider that you have not only a studio for hire, but an incredible machine that is ready to respond in kind to whatever level of talent and imagination that's put into it. To begin to see all the potential is to "get out of the box" that may be limiting your view of possibilities. The idea is to gain more perspective on what may only be a narrow view of what you think are your boundaries.

There are always more ways to solve a problem than are immediately apparent. The two steps to finding them are to stop for a moment and remember that 1) more choices always exist, and 2) the way to uncover them is to simply give yourself the extra time and perspective needed to find them.

The Lesson of the Nine Dots

I once took a music-industry seminar that dealt with unleashing your creative potential. There was a fascinating challenge that was put to the group in the form of a brainteaser.

"Here's an interesting exercise for you," said the leader. "Draw a square box that is made up of three rows of three pencil points each. Now see if you can take a moment and find a way to connect all the dots *without your pencil leaving the paper,* in just four straight, connected lines."

Here's the box. Give it a shot. Four straight, connected lines.

Did you figure it out? Good thinking! Didn't get it? The answer is on the last page of this chapter—check it out.

Armed with this newly broadened perspective, we can now get into some interesting ideas for developing a multifaceted business approach that removes some of the stress of simply selling studio time.

GETTING INTO PRODUCTION

A record company is a business that finds talented performers, records and produces their music, then packages, distributes and sells the finished product. A *production* company does the same thing, except that it leaves the final steps – those of physically packaging and distributing the product – to the record company.

Anyone with enough interest can start a business as a production company. You don't need a fancy A&R office in a lofty high-rise with a staff of secretaries and gofers to be successful at finding and developing salable talent. All you need is the drive, ambition and personal talent to put the elements together.

The major expense in record production is,

of course, in recording the material. That's where owning or managing a studio comes in rather handy: The only hard costs you're going to incur in the production of an $80,000 album will be engineering time, musicians and tape (and food, if you're a pushover). Handled creatively, most of that can be pared down to the bone.

Setting Up Your Company

With a studio operation in place, you have just about everything you need for your production company already laid out in front of you. You should discuss with your attorney whether you need to incorporate or create another company name for your production division.

Incorporation is usually a good idea, because of the increased liability in doing contractual business with other people. There may be tax advantages as well. However, laws and regulations can vary widely from one state to another, so it isn't wise to attempt to incorporate on your own unless you're truly qualified to do so. A brief phone conversation with your attorney may be all that's necessary to start off on the right legal foot.

So don't just count on friends or stories about other deals—spend a little time and money on a pro. This is important legal stuff, and if the groundwork isn't solid, you run the risk of suffering some major headaches later on. If incorporation looks like a smart idea, take a deep breath, invest a little money and have your attorney file the necessary papers.

Store-bought incorporation kits or do-it-yourself storefront services are an intriguing, money-saving idea and may work if you've got a legal background. But the potential for making a simple mistake that comes back to haunt you later is a compelling reason to pass on the home-brew approach.

An attorney not only will make sure that the proper steps are taken, but also will assume the responsibility of dealing with any state or federal problems that may arise later on. It makes good sense to spend a little extra now to be secure later.

Bang, You're a Record Company

Got your paperwork straight? Then it's time to become a mogul. Get out there, find an artist and make a deal. *Into a handheld bullhorn:* "Attention, all you musicians hanging out in this rock club! I'm interested in talking to those of you who would like to be stars. Please form a line to the left of this barstool!"

You now qualify to do what thousands of other companies have done for lo, these many years: find a magical, one-in-a-million super-talent who the record companies and the adoring but fickle public will find simply irresistible (at least for a few minutes). Record, package and sell your star, and you can grin all the way to the bank. It's a piece of cake.

But on the serious side, owning or operating a studio gives you a certain amount of clout in the music world. A studio is the key element in translating and bringing the performer's message to the masses. With a studio of your own, people will line up for blocks if offered the chance to be signed for a recording contract.

That's exactly what you're offering as a production company. And there's relatively little difference between you and, say, Warner Brothers in the kind of contract, services and attention you can offer a struggling artist at this beginning level.

Okay, there *are* differences—Warners can sign the artist for a hundred grand and fly him to a castle in France to record an album with a producer who charges the company a quarter million for his services. And that's just for three sides.

But it just isn't very likely they're going do that for someone completely unknown. What an established record company *will* do is everything that you're about to do in your own business: sign the artist to a multiyear contract, promise to record a number of tunes in a professional studio, make sure he has a good producer to oversee the whole project and get as much of a piece of the action as possible.

It's true that a production company can't guarantee that an album will be released when it's done, but you may not realize that a record company rarely guarantees a release either. Thousands of albums have been recorded that have never seen the light of day, because for one reason or another, the record company decided it wouldn't be in their best interest to spend the money to go any further. Talk about artist heartbreak!

Doing the Same (or Better) Job as the Record Company

Once the production company records an artist, its next job is to convince a record company to get involved, by either releasing the master the production company has brought them or recording a new one based on the material they've heard.

Given enough time and ambition, your production company has the same tools and ability to create the next musical sensation as anyone else does. All you need is enough talent to produce an artist yourself or enough smarts to hand the job over to someone who can. You've already got the studio, the know-how and the time. With those elements in hand, you'll find no shortage of artists who are just "Dyin' ta meetcha!"

Signing Talent

TALENT SEARCH

Serious production company with professional recording studio seeking a star-quality pop, rock or heavy metal band for exclusive recording contract. We're for real. Are you? Send current tape, bio and photo to:
The Platinum Mine
P.O. Box 32115
Bayonne, NJ 07002

All you have to do to get inundated with tapes and pictures is run an ad like this in your local music gazette. As you probably know, record companies are buried under an avalanche of pleas from the self-proclaimed Next Superstars of the World, but never actually solicit tapes. When a notice is run for fresh talent, the seas will spew forth an incredible variety, and with it an equally incredible demand for attention and consideration.

Which is why you should use a post office box with an anonymous name for a mailing address. You'll be spending plenty of time listening to and reviewing material, and a constantly ringing telephone will only slow you down. When you find a tape you like, call the artist or manager yourself and arrange a meeting, and you're off to a running start.

Alternative Methods

Of course, there are several other ways to find an artist or a group that excites you. Running a recording studio means that a wide variety of talented people will be walking through your door regularly. That's a great way to make friends and contacts, to develop trusting rela-

tionships, and to find a project that interests you.

It can be a lot more pleasant to get intimately involved with an artist or group you've known for a while than with one that just walks in from out of nowhere. But you shouldn't settle for anyone you feel is anything less than truly exciting and first-rate. The odds are incredibly high that you won't net yourself a star in the first place, so signing nothing less than star-class talent should really be your most important consideration.

It's also wise to get a few other opinions. If you think you've found the next Madonna, ask a few people whose opinions you trust to take a listen as well. Keeping a secret too closely guarded can give you a bad case of tunnel vision, not to mention a potentially distorted view of the bigger picture. Getting feedback will invariably result in a multifaceted war plan that may help you greatly in choosing the right direction to pursue.

Signing, recording and producing talent is a great adventure and, with the right people and material, a real labor of love. That's the way you should look at a project like this: as something that is going to be an exciting and rewarding experience just in the making of the final mixes.

There's nothing sure about making a deal. There's no guarantee that you're going to be successful in placing your group with any company, or ever seeing the actual product in a store's disc bin.

But the world belongs to dreamers who are *doers*. And of course, life can be awfully dull without taking a few big chances now and then; both artists and producers know this. Sure, the odds are against you. But if *doing* something brings you excitement and satisfaction, then the unlikely event of its success will be the icing on the cake. And that's the best kind of chocolate there is.

Protecting Yourself

If you're trying moguldom for the first time, be sure to start out with your training wheels on. Try to keep your excitement from sending you overboard with your investment. Your primary cost is going to be time, but don't discount its value; as a studio for hire, your main source of income is derived from just that. Remember, when choosing an artist or project, be realistic. You're hoping to make money on this, so be sure you choose someone whose music can sell. You have to pick someone great, not just some band that you want to impress with your God-given production talent.

Doing a good job on a record is a time-consuming effort. So it makes sense to take it easy when planning the amount of recorded output your "sensation" needs to make a deal. Start with your sights set on recording two or three smash sides, rather than a whole album.

If you can't sell a record company on two or three great tunes, the overwhelming chances are that a whole album of tunes isn't going to change anything. What's worse is that you'll have wasted a couple of hundred extra hours that could have been devoted, at the very least, to producing *another* group.

Making the Deal

Once you find an artist or group that has a handful of songs you just can't get out of your head, the next step is a contractual agreement. As beautiful and organic as your friendship may seem at the moment, it is, shall we say, "unwise" to expend a great deal of time and effort on recording a project that you believe in without first signing a contract that clearly spells out the terms of the deal.

A contract is a prerequisite, expected on both sides and essential to making the agreement between the parties understood. You can write anything you want into your contract, anything at all that's important to you. But best friends, partners, brothers or mothers are no exception. *Get it in writing before you get to work!*

Although a contract can say anything you want it to, there are two major areas that need to be addressed. The first concerns the actual recording and production of the music, and the second focuses on the publishing. As a production company, you are entitled to express an interest in both. Although every deal is different, a boilerplate agreement usually includes certain basic elements (see below).

Signing the Material

As a production company, in light of the fact that you're expending a substantial amount of time, effort and studio services, you are also entitled to negotiate for the publishing of the material that gets recorded. Publishing contracts are separate deals, and the split is endlessly variable, depending upon how many writers are involved, whether or not another publishing company already has rights to the material and whether the artist is willing to give up a piece of publishing at all.

The 200% Split

Publishing often becomes a major bone of contention. Artist and company may both be very adamant about how it's to be divided. One fact to bear in mind is that when a publishing contract is signed, the rights to the material still go to both parties. That's because 100% of the publishing royalties actually equals only 50% of what the song earns. The other 50% always goes to the writer.

Elements of a Production Agreement

1. The production company signs the artist to an exclusive contract for a certain length of time and/or guarantees to record so many sides (recordings of songs) within that period.

2. The company promises the artist X number of points (percentage points, based on the retail price) as a royalty on whatever is sold. This usually includes a 10% deduction from the gross, written off to promotional copies and expense, so points are then based on 90% of gross sales.

3. The producer of the album is specified and given X number of points.

4. The agreed-to details of marketing and shopping the product and further responsibilities of the artist and company are spelled out.

5. Everybody signs on the dotted line, smiles for the camera and agrees to get to work.

Many new writers find this a difficult concept to deal with. The normal assumption is that 100% *means* 100%. But for every dollar that comes in on a given song, in a 100% publishing deal, the company will get 50 cents, which is equal to 100% of the *publishing* money, and the writer will get 50 cents, equaling 100% of the *writer's* money.

If the writer insists on a 50% publishing deal, that means the publishing company will net 25 cents on each dollar. Retaining all the publishing means, of course, that the writer gets a dollar for every dollar.

But for writers who aren't interested in doing their own business and promotion, giving away the publishing makes sense. That's because the publishing company will then absorb all the costs of administration and, hopefully, will plug the material to other artists and projects and try to get it into films, TV and other recorded packages.

Royalties on a hit song are substantial. For that reason, as well as the fact that signing the song means giving up only a portion of its potential earnings, it's reasonable, as the production company, to feel entitled to a percentage of publishing, at least on material you record.

Many production and record companies insist on both a signed artist deal and a publishing contract. They feel that the risk and expense they're taking justifies their getting both. Getting the publishing, or a portion of it, could mean the difference between losing money and breaking even. It's also another potential source of income for your studio. Here are the major issues that get covered:

Elements of a Publishing Contract

1. The material to be published is specified and becomes subject to the terms of the agreement.

2. The split on the division of royalties is spelled out.

3. The length or scope of the contract and what performance is required of both the publisher and the artist is detailed.

There are some excellent books that cover the finer points of contract negotiations; check the Appendix in the back of the book. Then there's your attorney. Make sure his or her number is in your personal Rolodex and be sure to dial it when you get serious about signing someone.

When contracts are involved, don't be penny wise and pound foolish. Find an attorney who's smart enough to believe in your talent and future earnings potential, in light of which he or she will be willing to invest some time in helping to make the project a success, rather than billing you for every moment on the phone. There are plenty of attorneys who'll do this because they're smart enough to see the potential in their own future business. Take the time to find someone who responds emotionally to your presentations and ideas, and you may make a friend for life.

Forgoing the Advance

The major difference between an established production company and one that you start in a small studio is that you're probably not going to be in a position to offer a cash advance (a sum of money paid as an incentive upon signing and credited towards future royalties) to your artist. Advance amounts are extremely unpredictable in the music world. True enough, every so often some artist signs for a zillion dollars, but most often, when they are offered, advances are more a token of the seriousness of the company's intention to get behind the artist. Typically, they hover at around $10,000 to $20,000.

Granted, to a struggling artist, that's enough to live on for a year, but many deals are made with no advance at all. And as a studio owner and good negotiator, you should be able to explain that what you are offering in terms of attention and opportunity is potentially far more important than a cash advance.

Many artists will understand this and agree to forgo the cash. Those who don't will obviously continue their search in wealthier pastures. Often, obtaining a voodoo doll of the artist and chopping its little head off provides a certain level of comfort and solace for the frustrated studio owner/producer following such a loss.

But it just isn't a good idea to hock the farm in order to come up with a demanded advance. The odds are too high against success in the first place, and in the second, such demands are portents of more disagreement to come. It's far better to sign a deal with someone who supports the idea of your impending partnership, instead of attacking it.

Coming to formal terms with an artist is a great opportunity for the two parties to get to know each other better. How your negotiations go should be a pretty good indicator of the chemistry you'll have to look forward to in the studio once you get to work (assuming you get that far, that is).

Negotiating the Deal

Although you can do a lot of the bargaining yourself, you should be in close touch with your attorney on each point. This will most likely be the most expensive part of making the deal, but don't underestimate the value of working with an experienced pro on your team.

Because each deal is unique, no two recording contracts ever come out quite the same. There are just too many personal variables that get written in along the way. But your attorney should have a standard contract to start off with, and from there, you can refine the agreement to suit the circumstances without having to start from scratch.

In the event that the attorney who put your business together isn't an experienced music professional, it's quite acceptable to ask for a referral to someone who is. Don't think you're married to someone just because they're the person who got your business off the ground. It makes sense to tailor the job to the right professional, just as you would pick the right engineer for a specialized session.

Jumping In

Okay, you've got a hot group, a signed contract and a professional studio. As the head of the production company, you'll have discussed who's to be in charge of producing the material. Some groups insist on self- or co-production, and some on a producer of their choice, while some production companies insist on a producer of their own liking.

Often, if the studio owner feels they have the talent, the experience and/or the guts, they will want to produce the material themselves. More power to 'em; who's to say just exactly what it takes to be a great producer?

Bear in mind that once you get rolling, in most cases, the studio is going to have to leave time available to other clients in order to make enough money to stay in business while you bring your Frankenstein to life. Your artist should understand going into the agreement that a condition of the deal is that the group may need to be flexible in its bookings, so that when paying clients request time, the studio can accommodate them.

In-house production is definitely both a great adventure and a heck of a gamble. You'll have the luxury of not having to worry about the clock ticking the hours away, but that shouldn't make you lose sight of your bottom line. Approach your production project as an investment of time and effort that complements your regular business, rather than displacing it, and the end results will be pleasure, valuable experience and maybe some glory (and money) as well.

Contests and Promotions

If you've put together a production company, there are plenty of ways you can use it to your advantage. For example, you know that offering a recording deal will get you a lot of attention. Why not promote your studio name and make a contest out of it?

Run this ad in the local trades. Make an 8-1/2" x 11" poster, photocopy it and put it up in clubs, music and record stores. And send it out as a promotional piece—this is real news! Just make sure to be prepared with facts and information for the people who call in. It's a great way to get a lot of attention, and with a little luck, some good new bookings.

One Studio's Success Story

Dee Robb is one of three brothers who own and manage Cherokee Recording, an industry-renowned, world-class complex in Hollywood, California. "With the advent of the '90s and the ensuing alternative music styles, live recording and live bands made a big comeback," he said, referring to his new focus on production.

"As we started seeing acts just beginning to make a name for themselves in that genre, we got on the phone and began talking to labels and managers who we'd worked with in the past, and ran across this band from Boston that had made a record for Atlantic. We went in on a pretty limited budget, used our own facility and made the best record we could.

"What really got us into thinking we could do something was that the leader of the group had made a little 4-track cassette tape in his kitchen on acoustic guitar. We heard something there, broadened the sound and came up with something we really liked." The group, The Lemonheads, wound up with a gold record for their efforts on *Come On Feel The Lemonheads*.

"Atlantic came to us, because we'd told them we were looking for something to do, so several people there that we'd known personally kept us in the back of their minds. We made a basic normal deal, but it was all-in, so we as producers were just paid a lump of money to deliver a product."

But while many producers who do all-in deals opt for going the cheapest route possible in order to walk away with the most amount of money, the Robbs budgeted the whole amount to studio time in their own place and looked at the project as a crucial investment.

"To a great degree, we've continued to do this," Dee continued. "And with each project, we've gotten better and better deals and fees. We also had another great advantage in choosing who we were going to work for. As studio owners, we had this frame of reference of working with people on the other end and seeing who was ethical, who fulfilled their obligations and who tried to shave everything every-

where. So we had a good sense of the kind of people we wanted to align with."

While at a clear advantage with their experience and connections, the brothers have demonstrated that opportunities are out there for anyone with the wherewithal and the talent (not to mention the studio) to become producers in their own right. "The fact that we've been in the business for better than 30 years certainly helped with our connections, but I can't really say that our recent success is because of all of that. We decided that we really wanted to do this and started looking for acts, but we'd been in [production] hibernation for about ten years.

"What really made the difference, I think, was the fact that we could take a little alternative group that had a very small sales base and take the time to make the best possible personal investment into that record. Had we not owned the studio, we'd never have had that luxury.

"Now we're talking about developing a label of our own. The great thing about that is that I wasn't sure I'd ever be able to recapture the creative end of the business again. But all of a sudden, there was this change in the music, and all the things that used to be important to us back in the '60s were back again.

"As artists ourselves [former recording artists The Robbs], we all went through the same stuff: the pressure to perform, what new artists are facing in the industry and all. Do you ever get a chance to really use that knowledge? Well, not that much, because by the time you learn it, it's passed you by. So all of a sudden, you get to put all that stuff to use and it really makes you feel great."

The brothers are now spending a substantial portion of their time seeking and producing acts, and in doing so, have revitalized both their facility and the creative side of their individual careers.

SPECULATING ON SUCCESS

A long-standing and fairly universal practice in the studio business involves what is called *spec time*. In this situation, a studio finds itself looking at a fairly large amount of time in which there are no bookings in sight, or at a time period that is rarely used, such as the middle of the night. Here's a typical scenario.

A group or artist who's working in the studio on a project begins to run out of money but has a long way to go before anything that looks like a product will emerge. Or maybe a manager simply approaches the studio out of the blue with a deal offer.

Either way, what they're pitching is a deal based on speculation. They want to convince you that the artist is so good, and the material so strong, that there's label interest already, and that the buzz on the street is just, well, phenomenal. They say, "Here's an offer you'd be a fool to turn down: Let us record the rest of the project at your place for free, and when it's done and we get a label deal, we'll pay you at your full rate for all the time we owe from the first contractual monies we receive."

"Hmmm. Well, that's not an entirely abhorrent proposition," you think. "But there goes the money for the new reverb. Welllll, I dunno...They really are a good-sounding group, and the material is strong Top 40 stuff. They're going to need about 50 more hours of recording time, and they have their own engineer, so all we need to supply is the room and a second. And they're willing to work nights. It *is* an interesting proposition. Maybe we can sweeten the pot a little. How about throwing in a piece of the publishing, or a point on the album, or a guarantee that the next release will be recorded here as well?

"I should call Jake and ask him about this. I'm glad we've got an attorney I can really talk to. I know he's done these kinds of deals before. It sure beats the studio just sitting alone in the dark all night, and these guys are pretty flexible about scheduling.

"I bet we could do this with a one-page contract. And I wouldn't have to do anything but relax and enjoy dropping in on the sessions to see how they're going. And if they make it, we'll get a nice chunk of change. Yeah, I *like* this group. They're good people. Good tunes. Let me run this past a couple of people, and I'll get back to you."

Be Realistic

As with all deals, *get it in writing*. Approach the bargaining table with the knowledge that the odds are against seeing any money in the future; far more spec deals fizzle than fly. But if you go into negotiations with the attitude that this isn't the deal to save the business, and if you genuinely believe in the artist, you stand a chance of at least having a good time hanging out and watching or participating in the making of good music.

And if your ears are good enough, and you make enough deals on unused time, one of them may just take off. For that matter, you may find yourself in a position to insert your good ears into the production. If owning and/or operating a studio is part of your plan to become a successful producer, why not deal yourself in on the action? "Yes, you can have the time, provided you make me a co-producer and are willing to listen to my input."

You've got nothing to lose by asking for this kind of arrangement, and everything to gain. Even if the band breaks up midway through, you'll have realized a substantial benefit for yourself by gaining valuable production experience. And after all, it's your ball.

GIG BAND ALBUM PACKAGES

There's a long-standing tradition among unsigned performing groups of selling their own custom-recorded albums at the gigs they play. Many road groups earn substantial extra income selling cassettes and CDs at $7 to $15 a pop that are essentially good recordings of their best live sets.

So a lot of studios have found that putting their services together and fixing a package price on the entire process, from recording the masters to arranging for the artwork and duplication, can be a profitable sideline.

Advertising in the local trade publications, in music stores, on campuses and with a selective direct mailing list can bring some real results. These are also fun projects. The simplest packages offer the biggest bang for the smallest buck, meaning that recording time is pretty limited.

Normally, 20 hours of studio time is barely enough to do a good job on one carefully crafted tune. But a well-rehearsed gig band can run through a dozen songs a couple of times, overdub some extra vocals and still have time for a decent assembly-line mix in that same 20 hours. And that kind of pace can make for some welcome excitement after spending all of last Tuesday night digging into an edit window on a sequencing program to change selected note velocities.

Do a good job, and the word will go out on the street that your place is promoting a good deal. You can also offer duplication yourself, or network with a duplication service in your area and include their regular price plus a small commission in the package. The duplication service will undoubtedly refer potential business to you in return.

PLAYING ON THE SESSION

If you're a good musician, there's a host of opportunities for your services in the studio. As a keyboardist, you can offer your expertise as both a player and a programmer. Makes a good case for getting on more intimate terms with the resident synth gear in your studio, doesn't it?

You can make your availability known in several ways. The first is to be sure that when the need for a keyboardist arises, the rest of your staff will recommend you to the producer or artist who's looking. Very often, by nature of the fact that you're a player who's immediately available, you'll get a shot at the part.

Decide on the hourly rate you want to charge and stick to it. That way, the rest of your staff can quote your price, and the client will figure it in for future gigs.

'Boards Rule!

Keyboardists seem to have inherited much of the one-man-band recording world. They're the ones who are going to be the most likely candidates to call when there's synth programming to do or a drum-machine part needs to be laid down. Once you develop a relationship with a client, you can be on call for whatever their needs are, whether it's five minutes of drum-machine riffs or a full day's keyboard comping.

With composers and songwriters, a keyboardist can be the central figure in an entire production, and offering your skills and expertise can be a powerful inducement in putting a production package together for an industrial, jingle or cartoon. Building your rate or package price into the studio rate is one less bill for a composer to worry about, and the savings in cartage (the fee paid to professionally move, set up and tear down equipment), along with the convenience of having you around for a quick touch-up, are substantial benefits.

But keyboardists aren't the only players in demand. An in-house guitarist is a godsend to a producer with a synth-heavy track, a bass player may be the cure for a pseudo-keyboard riff, and a drummer whose setup lives in the studio means no delays and no cartage fees for a budget-conscious client.

If you're serious about playing, list your services on your rate card. Something like "Please ask about our in-house keyboard, programming and vocal services" may help get you the gig you might otherwise have never heard about.

SCORING TO PICTURE

If you offer picture interlock in your studio, you may find many opportunities to pitch various clients on composing original music (this process is called "scoring," as in a musical score) for their projects.

Trailers

Trailers are the "coming attractions" previews in movie theaters, and also the previews run as commercials on TV. They got their name in the old days from being spliced onto one end of the feature film the theater was showing.

Trailers are often edited from the still incomplete film so that they can be shown before its debut. Often, the film's composer hasn't written the score yet, and so a separate company is contracted to produce the trailer. That leaves the music up for grabs. Budgets are usually low, which is the perfect opportunity to build in a bid with the studio's audio services and do the music production in-house.

Getting scoring work requires submitting a demo tape to the producer, who then determines whether your style and ability are appropriate for the gig. So a good demo tape is the composer's calling card. Putting together five to ten minutes of widely varying music is a good way to cover as many bases as possible, so that at least *something* will sound good to the producer.

Got an outdated tape? Don't have a tape? Why not find (ahem...) an available studio and put one together? It's a lot of work, but it's also creation of the highest order, which makes the end product mighty satisfying. What better way to fill your scheduling voids? And there's a lot of work to be won out there, if you want it.

Industrials

Industrials are short films produced specifically for businesses that want to depict a new product, development or marketing campaign. They're shown at trade shows or special in-house presentations, or used as sales presentations to potential customers. Industrials also include employee-training films.

Producers have a maddening habit of opting for either *needle drop* or *production library* music for many industrials. Needle drop means using a commercial recording as a soundtrack. Because industrials are not offered for sale or for commercial exhibition, many producers feel it's perfectly okay to use anything from Gregorian chants to the latest Travis Tritt single if the music is appropriate for their soundtrack. After all, who's gonna know?

Production library music is a little more kosher. There are several companies that offer vast catalogs of custom-composed music on a per-use basis. Major cities often have branch offices of these companies, which offer their expertise in selecting the right music for each project. Others sell multidisc libraries to studios, with the stipulation that each time a piece is used, a licensing fee is paid by the producer.

The obvious advantage of using production music is that it's the cheapest legal way to score a film. You can license 10 minutes of music for as little as a couple hundred dollars. But the disadvantage is that pre-existing music can rarely cover specific *hit points* (the exact frame of the picture where something needs special musical emphasis) as effectively as a piece of original music can.

For that reason, composers are still very much in evidence on industrials with moderate or better budgets. But here, there's a drawback to being an in-house composer in a commercial facility: More and more, the competition comes in the form of outside composers who have sophisticated home project studios. Their advantage is that they have no interest in selling studio time, so they can afford to create a finished score for the price of their individual time, instead of their creative fee *plus* studio hours.

Each situation is different, but you may have to substantially cut or eliminate your studio rates in order to stay competitive. You can test the waters in each potential bid by talking numbers and getting an idea whether composers are bidding.

Staying Competitive

Even if it means eliminating the studio rate altogether, the fee that you earn can be split between you and the studio and is money that you wouldn't otherwise have had. Just be sure that there's enough open time available so that you're not turning down bookings that might otherwise have been profitable.

Another way to meet the competition is to set up a small work area outside of your main studio. A medium-sized office can accommodate both a desk and a simple MIDI setup, and having one could be the way to keep your paying clients in the studio while you do the composing in your office. Then, when you're ready to rock, the impact in time lost to other clients will have been substantially lessened.

Feature Videos

Feature videos include an unlimited range of made-for-video special interest subjects, from aerobic workout tapes to zoology travelogues. The challenge in video is that you may be looking at up to 90 minutes of original music, which is enough to cause an anxiety attack in the right brain of John Williams, let alone a hot and rising talent like yourself.

Be sure to watch the tape from top to bottom with the producer in order to get a clear understanding of what's required. Then you'll be able to make an intelligent bid based on how many minutes of music are needed, and how many hours of work you think it will take.

In summary, industrial and video scoring is a highly creative endeavor, with the trade-off being less than stellar wages. But the trick is to offer the music in a complete package so that the producer pays one fee for everything from conception to the final mix.

Adding studio time and musician session fees is a potential way to come out ahead, assuming everything goes according to plan. Writing well and making the producer happy, however, is a case-by-case process, and a good topic for another book; see the Appendix, p. 262, for further reading.

Student Films

Student films are short features produced and directed by college students majoring in film production. These projects are invariably shot on the slimmest of budgets but offer a way for both the studio and the composer to get a foot in the door of the film world.

If you're just getting started as a composer, and you happen to be driving distance from a film school, student films are a great way to get some practical experience. Contact the school and offer low-priced audio and scoring services. You might even go so far as to offer the studio free when they hire you for the score. Or vice-versa—offer the score free when they hire the studio for audio post! Why not? Create a placard that advertises your services, and get permission to hang it in various locations on campus.

Then be ready for anything. You may wind up viewing a film by the next Scorcese, but it's more likely it'll look a lot closer to Roger Corman's first efforts. Either way, a student film lets you flex a little and see what happens. And therein lies the beauty of the deal.

Working with Composers

If you're not a composer yourself, operating a studio means that opportunities are going to arise in which you'll be able to recommend one. Maybe the producer of the project who's currently working in your studio will express dissatisfaction with the present music, or maybe wonder out loud who he's going to use for this or the next project.

That puts you in the position of being able to procure work for other people. (An agent does the same thing, except it's a full-time job.) Composers often approach studios with demo tapes in search of work; between tapes that come in off the street and the ones from people you know, you should have a number of contacts from which to draw when asked.

Striking a Deal

There's something that doesn't feel right about extracting a percentage from a composer as a commission fee for stumbling onto some work for him or her. But given the choice, it does make sense to expect the composer to record the score in *your* studio. So by being in a position to recommend the work you can't do yourself, you can benefit by becoming the studio in which the ensuing work is done.

Most composers will have no quarrel with this, assuming your facility can accommodate the type of work that needs to be done and that they do not normally record in their own home. Make it a friendly but clear understanding that you have an agreement, and you'll both come out ahead.

Marketing to the Max

Chock-full of ideas and the drive to turn them into reality, Blaine and Wayne Wilkins have created a multifaceted business that's thriving in an area where no one had thought a studio could exist, much less turn a profit.

P R O F I L E

Career Roots Started with a background in TV, sales and management. With brother Wayne, started Studio West as a 24-track studio retreat. At that time, there were no other major studios anywhere near them. "So we felt like pioneers. We thought if we opened as a 24-track, we'd make the biggest splash."

Facility Two studios, one 24-track and one 8-track. The 8-track is set up for teaching and in-house demo work.

House Staff Three full-time first engineers, receptionist, bookkeeper and two salespeople on salary/commission. The two brothers are doing the management and marketing.

Blaine Wilkins

Partner

Studio West

Primary Focus Album production and in-house jingle, film and video production.

Saskatoon, Saskatchewan

Marketing "Here in the Midwest, we're semi-isolated from the major centers. So we've had to be resourceful and diversified. We have two studios and two record labels; we offer recording courses, a film and video division and a commercial production house. With the studio, we've deliberately gone a different route, which is to market it as a retreat.

"The province wasn't ready for us when we started up. Most of the production was going outside to the major cities. It was quite a challenge turning the local attitude around to look at us. So we hired salesmen who went out and actually sold production packages to retail clients.

"When we became successful, we didn't see any reason why we couldn't be successful in video and film. But we also wanted to avoid the enormous cost of the equipment. So we sent our existing salespeople out with complete packages and began subcontracting cameramen and technicians and using local facilities on a rental basis."

Virtually every Studio West photo features people involved in the action.

Some examples of
Studio West's marketing
campaigns.

Promotions "We made our latest contest a sweepstakes. We're getting a large volume of entries back from people we've never been in contact with, who we'll add to our mailing list and contact later. Even though the prizes are substantial, we feel we can afford to give them away because we're only running about 60% booked. So it's a good use of time."

Recording Workshop "We use an independent teacher who we split the fees with, and graduate about 35 to 40 people per year. It's made very good use of the 8-track facility, and it's a good promotional tool for the studio. We then encourage the grads to intern with us for 30 days in both studios. Through that program, we've found some good assistants."

Organizing Started the Saskatchewan Recording Industry Association, now with 225 members provincewide. Publish a newsletter with the intention of raising the profile of the recording industry and local talent.

Local Promotion With two local radio stations, produced a CD featuring local talent that was sold in stores for $5.95.

Production Work "We've gotten creatively involved with several local groups, and one in particular has been pretty successful. We recognized that there was a very alive and vibrant local scene, and tapped into it. We've really tried to take the role of spokesmen and champions of Saskatchewan talent."

Package Deals "These packages have been very successful. The people who use them don't care about getting a record deal or becoming stars. They've just always wanted to come into a good studio and get their songs on tape. Then they have some product that they can bring back home and sell locally if they like.

"Our engineers usually give them a lot of help. Since the most popular package is 20 hours of time, they will typically come in and set up and run down a live set of 10 to 12 songs two or three times. That leaves them enough time to pick tunes and get a pretty good mixdown. The groups love it. They walk out of the studio five feet off the floor and go home heroes."

CorporateCommunicationsFilmMusicVideosAdvertising Music Soundtracks Audio/Visual Jingles Multi-image

Communication is a powerful tool. It can create images, sell products, or change perceptions. Communication skills have become a discipline requiring a comprehensive understanding of motivational psychology, market strategy, and production technology. Whether you are concerned with industrial public relations, advertising commercials or employee training programs...**studio west** can help you achieve corporate communication goals. From market research and analysis to effective implementation of your message...**studio west** creates communication products that work.

Technology doesn't have to be complicated. In experienced hands modern technology provides simple, precise solutions to the most demanding production requirements. At **studio west** we start with state of the art recording facilities and the unparalled quality of 16mm and 35mm film production. Add broadcast quality video, multi-image production, and our experienced production team and you have Western Canada's most comprehensive package of production services...

Crisp, clean images and startling sound reproduction is guaranteed. Leave the latest post-production techniques to us...like digital mastering and computerized editing. We keep it simple. Listing equipment specs, names and numbers only confuses the issue. We use technology where it counts — adding production values without breaking the bank. **studio west...** Superior technology to create superior products.

Creativity and good business sense are terms rarely spoken in the same breath. In fact, the most compelling corporate advertising and promotional campaigns are clearly the product of imaginative minds at work. Whether working with creative concepts developed by leading advertising agencies or by our own in-house production department... Writers, producers, artists and technical craftspeople work together to create distinctive effective messages that make sense for your business.

Production is a straight forward process with us. We respect deadlines and recognize the cost of time. We work with you to establish objectives and set priorities...developing production timelines to meet your schedule...consulting with you throughout the project stages. Over the past ten years, **studio west** has earned its reputation by making sure what hits your desk meets your expectations...no delays, no surprises. On time and on budget means something at **studio west.**

studio west productions

502 45th St. W., Saskatoon, Saskatchewan, Canada S7L 6H7 (306) 244-2815

With aggressive marketing, Studio West has expanded to become a full-service production company. By contracting out the camera and editing work, they've successfully avoided the tremendous investment normally required for video production.

CASSETTE DUPLICATION

A lot of clients are going to want multiple copies of their finished masterpieces. Although there are well-established dupe houses in most cities, offering to keep all the services your client needs under one roof is another way to trumpet your facility's ultimate convenience.

You can start with as few as three or four good-quality cassette recorders and build up if demand warrants it. Or, you can make duplication an important adjunct to your business, buy 20 machines and advertise in the trades.

By offering dupe services, a lot of business that began elsewhere will walk through your door for this final process. That's the time to make friends, find out what sort of work they're doing and offer a tour of your place. Maybe you'll need to offer a special rate to someone who's satisfied elsewhere to switch over and give your place a try. But if that means landing a new client, it's a smart move.

You can get into some special services in duplication. Blank tape and disk sales are a natural outgrowth, and you'll most likely have a resale number from your existing operation, allowing you to charge tax when you sell retail.

Also consider offering labeling services. You can sell label stock sheets, the crack-and-peel type that come 12 to a sheet, in sets of 50 at a good profit. Many laser printers handle this thick stock well, providing you with a complete print service for clients. Or, you can set up an arrangement with a local printer, referring your customers to them for their label printing, in return for discounts on work you need done for your own business.

Going Retail

If you do your homework and begin to see your business grow, you can start offering more retail items in a display area. Blank reels and boxes, recording accessories and industry books are always interesting to clients and customers.

And how about a T-shirt or a baseball cap with the studio logo on it for sale at cost plus 10%? What a great way for your clients to help you pay for your own advertising!

DAT TRANSFERRING

With magnetic tape technology reaching back to the '50s, there exists a truly staggering number of old and aging analog master tapes. Many artists, producers and companies have since unearthed their old products for remastering for CD re-releases. With the average time to remaster a old album clocking in at about one day in a digital mastering room, the process has been a gold mine for the record companies, even at so-called "budget" CD prices.

A trend that goes hand in hand with all these re-releases is that many people are becoming aware that the oxide coating on their old tapes is in danger of decomposing (interesting use of the word, eh?) and becoming unsalvageable. For them, the idea of transferring their old masters into the digital domain is a very attractive one.

The easiest and least expensive way to do that is to transfer from analog 2-track or multi-track to DAT cassettes. All the investment that's necessary for a studio is to buy a good DAT deck and to let people know you've got a service to offer. Some places charge a flat rate per album or song, while others bill for studio time.

One engineer who's done many of these sessions has watched it become a profitable sideline for his studio. He's also worked with old masters in such bad shape that they've fallen apart during the first playback, giving him just one shot to capture the material on cassette and comfort a panicky but grateful producer.

MUSIC & DIALOG EDITING

There's a whole world of opportunity in music and dialog editing, now that nonlinear editing has become the norm. These systems are so called because all the sound elements are stored on disk and therefore one can almost instantly access any point in the program. Nonlinear computer systems have revolutionized the way traditional editing is accomplished: Instead of handling, cutting and splicing tape or mag reels, one simply loads all of the elements onto the system's hard disk, and from that point they are manipulated and assembled onscreen, entirely in the digital domain. All of these systems share many superior characteristics: You never lose another generation, fades and EQ are programmable, tracks are cleaned of noise graphically and all cutting and splicing is accomplished digitally.

The beauty of nonlinear editing is that all you need is a tabletop and a small room to set up a complete and extremely impressive system. Prices start at as low as $3,000 and top out around $150,000. Because of the space and price advantages, thousands of systems now exist in basements, garages and dining rooms, and in small editing bays in major facilities worldwide.

A nonlinear bay excels at several tasks. First, you can assemble scores and music libraries for TV and film. Second, you can eliminate the analog bay for TV and film dialog editing, which involves a great deal of cutting, cleaning and splicing. Third, music assembly, such as album ordering or editing, is far more efficient and creative. And finally, TV and film sweetening, in which several tracks are used to record and load sound effects and ambience, is growing in popularity.

All this can be comfortably done in an 8' x 11' room, although many facilities choose to add larger mixing boards and make the editing system a part of the whole audio operation. Nonlinear editing continues to improve in terms of capability, speed, reliability and affordability on a continual and nearly, well, nonlinear basis. It's a great service to offer both for its gee-whiz appeal (many systems have stunning color interfaces) and for its price/performance ratio—for a relatively small investment, it's possible to charge a healthy hourly or per-project fee. For this reason, it's become as popular in project studios as it has in commercial rooms.

The only downside to this hot field is the dizzying speed in which it is developing; this is truly moving target technology, meaning that you aim and take your best shot when buying and hope that your brand stays current with the technological developments that ricochet down the road...next month!

That's not to say one ought to wait until then. What we've all begun to learn and expect is that the smarter we all get, the faster things change. (Which sometimes means the dumber we look a short time later.)

But standing still on the sidelines isn't the answer. Go to shows, read the trades, join local and national groups and keep abreast of what's happening. Then jump in, hang on and paddle like crazy. Things certainly aren't going to slow down, and you just may find yourself enjoying the hell out of the race.

RENTING OUT EQUIPMENT

With the explosion of home project studios, as well as the growth of commercial facilities, there has been an accompanying rise in the need for spe-

cial rental equipment. Rentals are convenient for studios when buying the gear would be too costly in relation to its frequency of use.

The most likely candidates for rental are digital tape machines, hard and M.O. drives, outboard effects gear, and synths and samplers. But you can get into the rental business by buying just one in-demand piece of gear and marketing your service effectively.

The advantages are twofold. First, you get into another aspect of the business that pro-

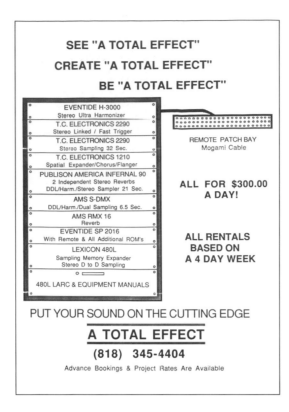
A Total Effect packages one super-stack of outboard gear and rolls it into your room wired and ready for mixdown.

duces potential income, and second, you get to own a piece of gear that can benefit your own studio as well.

If you pick a standard rental item—one most studios don't usually include in their normal rates—then you can charge a daily rate when it's used by your own clients. Price the gear at something under the going rate and point out the convenience and lack of cartage charge when it's used internally.

Standards for Pro Gear Rental Rates

Daily rates include delivery, setup, teardown and pickup.

Weekly rates are calculated by multiplying daily rate times four (the fifth, sixth and seventh days are free).

Monthly rates are calculated by multiplying weekly rate times three (the fourth week is free).

Some competitive companies will offer a weekly rate based on a three-day instead of a four-day rate.

Choosing the right gear means looking for developing trends, following up with inquiries to make sure of your information, and then making your best deal on something with the widest potential appeal.

In the mid-'80s, we bought Interlok a used Mitsubishi X-80 2-track digital tape machine for mixing down masters. It cost about $14,000, more than we would have spent to equip our own place, especially when the practice was to charge clients for each day's rental on digital mixdowns.

But that was the point. We reasoned that if we could sell a couple of days' time per month to our own clients, we'd be halfway home. With payments at $600 per month, we just needed to to rent it out for a couple more days to break even. With a bit of effort, it worked.

Devising a Campaign

We advertised via direct mail to all the studios in town, undercutting the going rental rate by about 20%. Then we advertised in a trade classified section to find equipment roadies who owned vans. We interviewed a couple of guys who came with references, and taught them how to pack and unpack the two-piece recorder in its road cases. Then we put them on call. When a call came for a rental, we sent the first driver we could get a hold of with the recorder over to the studio that wanted it.

At that time, the X-80 was the hot deck, and there were only a few others available through the other pro rental companies in the area. And when a couple of artists happened to be in town mixing down their albums, they'd create a real shortage by tying up the few available machines for weeks.

Something else happened that was pretty surprising as well: When the other rental companies got wind that we had the deck for rent, they started calling us when they got requests *they* couldn't fill. They'd act as the agent, renting the machine from us to rent to their client. We would split whatever rate they charged 50-50, but they'd send their own driver to pick up and deliver the deck, saving us both money and hassle.

It was a great arrangement. We lucked into picking the right gear at the right time, had the prestige of owning it and using it ourselves and had more profitable than negative months. Two years later, as digital recording technology advanced and better models began to appear, we sold the deck through a consignment deal-

A 30' x 35' room can comfortably accommodate 75 people with theater-style seating. Rent chairs from a party supply company that will deliver and pick up, and pass that cost on to the client in addition to the negotiated room rate. Here, a drum booth becomes a presentation stage for a speaker and a projection TV.

er and wound up with a few thousand dollars profit to boot. The ongoing benefit was that we had the use of a premium piece of cutting-edge technology at our own facility pretty much whenever we wanted it.

Keeping Covered

If renting sounds interesting, be sure you do it with your eyes wide open. Make sure your insurance includes both on- and off-premises coverage for the specific piece that's traveling. Rent only to qualified professionals who have a permanent address, with a clear understanding of the charges.

You also need to supply a contract that states the exact inventory of equipment rented, the period of time that's been agreed to and coverage for any loss or damage. Your driver makes sure that it's signed when the equipment is dropped off.

Check other rental companies for the variety of contracts that go out and make sure your attorney goes over the final draft of your own before you use it.

RENTING OUT THE ROOM

One way to fill up an empty room at night is to turn it into a rehearsal hall. Use a separate sound system that the group can control from inside the live room, rather than rigging the control room console and the room monitors; they're just not built for that kind of abuse.

One advantage to the group may be that they can remain set up over a period of several days, if you're not anticipating any other live work that week. The other obvious ploy is that for just a few dollars more, you might be able to talk them into recording their material. That is, if they don't talk you into throwing it in first!

Expand Your Horizons

If your facility has enough room to comfortably accommodate a group of happy people, it may be a prime location for hosting large special occasions. Bar mitzvahs are probably best left for the local Moose Lodge, but an industry-related function can generate extra income and valuable publicity.

A recording studio is the perfect setting for a party celebrating the culmination or release of a musical project. No other location is more conducive to listening in a well-tuned environment.

Summa Studio markets its mega-array of outboard equipment by comparing its rates to the cost of outside rentals.

COMPARISON OF SUMMA STUDIOS IN-HOUSE OUTBOARD GEAR "PACKAGE" VS. MAJOR L.A. AUDIO RENTAL HOUSE PRICES

	SUMMA DAILY PRICE	AUDIO AFFECTS DAILY PRICE	DESIGN FX AUDIO DAILY PRICE
LEXICON 480L DIG PROCESSOR		$150	$150
FOCUS RITE EQ/MIC PRE'S - 4 CHANNELS		NOT AVAILABLE	$200
GML/MASSENBURG EQ		$75	$75
LEXICON PCM 70 REVERB		$50	$50
(2) TC ELEC 2290 W/32 SEC SAMPLING		$300	$150
AMS RMX-16 REVERB		$150	$150
(2) DRAWMER DS201X GATE		$40	$40
EVENTIDE H3000-"ULTRA" HARMONIZER		$100	$75
(2) UREI 1178 DUAL PEAK LIMITERS		$40	$40
(2) VALLEY PEOPLE 430 DYNAMITE		$60	$60
(4) VALLEY PEOPLE 810 KEEPEX II'S		$80	$60
PAIR -LYNX SYNCRONIZERS & CABLES		$250	$275
PULTEC EQP 1A		$30	$20
SONY DAT RECORDER		NOT AVAILABLE	$50
TC SPATIAL XPANDER		NOT AVAILABLE	NOT AVAILABLE
(2) DBX 165 A		$40	NOT AVAILABLE
(3)BARCUS BERRY 802'S		NOT AVAILABLE	$60
(2) YAMAHA SPX-90 II'S		$60	$60
TOTAL PER DAY*	$400	$1,425	$1,515

A teaching program can be both profitable and personally rewarding.

An album-listening party, catered at your facility with special decorations, is a prime promotional vehicle. The studio looks its party best, the atmosphere is relaxed, finished product pumps through the system, and guests who've never seen your place fill it with admiring interest.

You can encourage affairs like this by suggesting them to your clients and offering the studio at a special reduced rate. Just make it clear that they are to handle all the catering and cleanup, or that extra fees will be added if you provide the service. Use the fee to pay any overtime to ensure that the room is well-staffed and secured throughout the evening.

Screenings are another prime opportunity. If you're doing audio post, you may already own one large screen monitor. You can fill a 30' x 30' room with 75 rented folding chairs and host a screening for the project you just finished scoring. Better still, convince the producer to rent the room and fill it with industry people. Co-host the party and meet some new friends (and potential clients).

TEACHING SCHOOL

Several studios across the country have become centers for the growing recording institute industry. There's a wide range of programs that you can offer in terms of depth and time, but a six- to 12-week recording workshop that emphasizes an intense, hands-on learning experience for beginning students may attract a lot of interested inquiries.

Merel Bregante, who manages Vintage Recorders in Arizona, saw the potential in this field and helped develop a major program, taking full advantage of the facility's two studios (one analog and one digital). Known as the Southwest Institute of Recording Arts, the school features a 16-week course with over 300 hours of instruction. Students start as beginners and work through two major recording projects at the rate of about 20 hours per week. The rest of the time, the studio functions as a pro recording facility.

To get started, the management wrote a curriculum, talked with the state board of education and hired a couple of experienced instructors. By looking closely at what other schools in the area were doing, they fashioned a course that they felt could compete effectively. The school runs three semesters per year.

Getting Involved with Local Schools

You can also contact schools in your area and offer your facility as a hands-on training site. Although most schools can't afford to pay top dollar, reaching an agreement could mean 40 weeks a year with a steady six-hour booking every Saturday afternoon. Having something like that to count on can help brighten up a dark scheduling book.

Finally, you may be able to get more into the picture by becoming a teacher yourself. If you're confident and experienced, many schools will be glad to talk to you about taking advantage of your personal areas of expertise. Adding that to a weekly contract for time could make the deal much more attractive. And many people who may have never considered teaching before (this author included) find it to be a very enjoyable, rewarding and, dare one say, educational experience.

ART FOR ART'S SAKE

John Wood, the son of Dot Records cofounder Randy Wood, is the co-owner and manager of Studio Masters recording studios in Los Angeles. A jazz pianist whose roots and purist ideals make him a compelling anachronism in the studio business, he recently gave up performance in the outside world in favor of a unique idea: entertaining paying customers by putting on live performances in his own facility.

Wood's musical roots go back to the heady days of the '50s record industry, right to the center of the action. His dad opened a record shop in Gallatin, Tennessee in 1945 and sponsored a Nashville radio show that showcased black rhythm and blues music. They advertised on the air and sold records via mail order; at the time, they were one of the only places in the America that made R&B accessible to the general public.

The station's high-powered signal was beamed all over the world and was tremendously successful and influential, particularly for African-Americans in the '40s. In 1950, Wood founded Dot and assembled an artist roster that included Pat Boone, Billy Vaughn and Lawrence Welk. The label eventually produced 27 number-one records with 37 million-sellers, all of which were recorded live with no multitracking. John remembers Elvis Presley and Tom Parker coming to the house to discuss a distribution deal in 1954, when Dot was the biggest label in the South and Elvis had just recorded his first sides. His dad, on top of the charts with Pat Boone, turned them down.

John loved the business and the music, playing in clubs and making his own records, selling them out of the trunk of his car. The studio, which he now manages with his brother, was built in 1972.

"One night, I was at a club and realized how tired I was of playing on bad pianos in noisy rooms. With rare exceptions, the owners are insensitive to what we do, and at that moment, I realized I didn't want to do it any more. Our studio building had this extra room and I decided I'd bring my Steinway from home, add some comfortable furniture and that would be my concert room.

"So instead of playing at some restaurant for $75 a night, I got this room listed in the local paper, charging $10 per person and offering a recording of the night's performance for $20. If I play for three people for an hour and sell a recording or a CD or two, then I've made close to what I was making playing for four hours at somebody's club. And it keeps me around the studio, which I think is the key to being successful. Being there, in my mind, is 99% of the battle."

Wood typically plays for two or three people a few nights a week. He turns down the lights, takes requests and plays some fine, mellow jazz. His showroom is a medium-sized former disk-cutting room with an adjoining lounge.

"I play in here because I don't want to tie up the studios on a regular basis, although with larger groups, we've used Studio A, which also has a great piano in it." Each night defines its own personality. He interacts with whomever is there in whatever way feels right.

Some nights evoke an almost therapeutic atmosphere. "One thing I like to talk about is how things in the recording business have changed. For instance, in the old days of the three-hour session, where three hours rendered your four finished songs, they'd hand the studio owner a check for the time and walk out with their next four sides for release. These days, with mega-multitracking, people find it very hard to say they're finished with what they're doing, and consequently, we've suffered a continuing problem with people constantly owing us money.

"I think this multitrack process makes monsters out of people, because there's no totality. There's no beginning, no middle and no end—just this amorphous thing that goes on and on, and no one can really recognize what it is that they're a part of. In looking back, there was a simplicity and a way to comprehend things for everyone, both for the people who rented the studio and for the studio owners. They came and they lived or died in those three or four hours they booked in the studio. And then they walked away. And the guys who played knew that it was a complete entity. Today they've all lost that control. So it's therapy for me, as well.

"My hope is that what I'm doing here will point my studio in the direction of music and live recording. I believe that from the beginning of the human race, music has played an important part in the quality of life. So if American music began to lose its humanity, as it did starting in the late '60s, then essentially there's been no music in America for 25 years.

"Sure there'll always be a live-music niche, and there's a perception and desire to get back to basics, but I think we have a huge distance to go. In the early days, artists released five and six albums a year. *Per year!* That is the nature of music and of the days when *music* drove the music business."

To book John for an intimate performance, call 310/391-7986.

H ere's the solution to the puzzle at the beginning of the chapter.

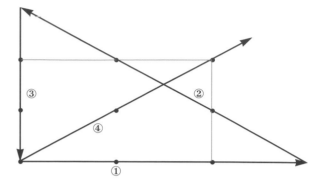

A cheap trick? Cheating? No way! It's the *answer*. It's just camouflaged, because people tend to look at things head-on without stepping back a little to get some more perspective.

By increasing your perspective, you expand your horizons. No one said you had to stay *within* the box—the only rules were to draw four connected, straight lines.

The answers to so many of the challenges we face in life, be they in relationships, careers or business, are often hidden from an obvious head-on view. But where some people shrug and give up on a challenge that isn't immediately solvable, others step back and widen their vision.

So get out of the box! When you come up against your next challenge, remember: The solution may come a lot more easily if you first *get outside of the nine dots*.

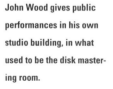

John Wood gives public performances in his own studio building, in what used to be the disk mastering room.

From Songwriter Setup to Commercial Co-op

As friends and associates began crowding him out of his home basement setup, Scott Parker realized he had enough friends with enough projects between them to form a successful and profitable collective.

Startup Originated as a basement project room for his songwriting/composing work. Looked for a niche that was unfilled and found there was a real need for a quality mid-market room in Portland.

Songwriter, formerly with Warner/Chappel; also writes with his wife, Carol. Now involved with artists at the ground level. "Old-style song pitching is no longer as valid as it used to be. I'm trying to develop a number of original projects, which figures directly in my need for the studio."

The Transition "The turning point came when I watched the Super Bowl one year and heard an ad spot that had been done at the house. I thought, there's not a soul in the world that knows that spot was cut in my basement. And I know the budgets on the some of other stuff that we were listening to, and we sounded just as good. So there was something to be said for the producer's ability to be able to take some time and care in creating a final product.

"One day we're sitting in the basement and the laundry's going, and there were two executives from major agencies in San Francisco and New York sitting on the floor and I pulled the producer aside and said, 'Hey, I'd be glad to rent you a room somewhere with a more kosher and professional environment.' He said, 'These are, like, cutting-edge ad guys, doing the outside kind of stuff and in that kind of environment all the time. They like tripping over the dog and being away from that kind of thing to be creative.'

"That really keyed something in my mind, because it was the same thing I was finding as a producer at that time, that people wanted to be comfortable — that 70 to 80 percent of the battle of getting a good sounds was getting good performances. I'd been in so many rooms that gave no emphasis on making you feel good. Musicians grew up playing in garages and in bedrooms and nightclubs, and to put them in a place that looked more like NASA and expect them to perform was just not ideally conducive. So my dream studio was just a place that was going to be as comfortable as being at home."

Facility One studio, 1,300 square feet, converted from an old beauty parlor, with occasional older ladies inquiring as to their hairdresser's whereabouts. Trident Series 24 board with Tascam 1-inch 16-track deck with dbx and 2-inch 24-track on a daily basis.

House Staff Part-time studio manager/receptionist. Co-op members have keys and assume responsibility when there.

The Co-Op Concept "We cater to just a handful of professionals. It's kind of a virtual studio to these other production entities. I don't really have the infrastructure to deal with a lot bookkeeping, security and reception, so what I've done is to stay out of the studio listings."

Producers do their own scheduling via modem, interfacing with a Mac program called Datebook.

"We work with about six different producers who collectively control about 50 different projects. They all have keys and codes and are pretty much responsible for logging their own hours and taking care of the place. We've found that when you empower the producer with that level of responsibility, they're almost harder on security and neatness and maintenance than you are."

PROFILE

Scott Parker

Owner, Songwriter

Dead Aunt Thelma's Studio

Portland, Oregon

Choosing Equipment "I'm a real gear-hound and love all the latest technology but there's a point where it really doesn't make financial sense to invest in the newest, latest thing, because your capital costs are so high, and there's also the debugging time.

"I'm very purposeful in trying to stay about two or three years behind the technology curve. For instance, one of my clients needed video sync capabilities for music for video. So he called me up, advanced me the money against his account and enabled us to equip him and the rest of our clients for video by splitting the cost of the gear and the studio 50/50.

"Regarding multitracks, we use several formats, so we've pre-harnessed the room for five-minute changeovers. One guy leaves his MTR-90 here, and we rent it out on a daily rate for him. Others bring in their ADATs, hard disk recorders or 1/2-inch 16-tracks. So in being flexible, we've become an augment room for people working up from their home or down from more expensive rooms."

Designing the Room "I worked with one of the best designers in the country in designing the studio. I met him through a friend of a friend, for lunch in Dallas when I was on my way to Nashville. I thought maybe I could get him to spend an hour looking over my plans to see if I was making any big mistakes.

"He got back to me and said, 'Scott, I feel like you're the guy that's gonna come back to me with a million-dollar room in ten years. We'll do it and make it cost-effective for you.'

"They wound up saving me thousands in construction that I was going to do but didn't need to—materials, ways to do things with less expensive common building materials. And the credibility of having that name gave people a confidence when they walked into the room. It wasn't just like some songwriter trying to build a room."

The Name "My wife brought down some pound cake when we were in the basement, and someone said, 'This is really good. Where'd it come from?' I said, 'Oh, it's my dead Aunt Thelma's recipe.' And everything that night was dead Aunt Thelma's this and that, and it started showing up on album credits.

"I told the designer, who needed a working name, and he loved it and talked me into keeping it. I think that irreverence about the name and about the recording process is part of the vibe that makes people feel comfortable. Almost an irreverence towards the recording process that makes it seem less like you're walking into some kind of technological temple. More like, 'Let's walk into someplace where we can make some music.'"

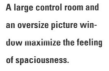

A large control room and an oversize picture window maximize the feeling of spaciousness.

A little money and a lot of style dress up the lobby.

9
Developing Contacts

Success in business is based on communication. Whether your studio is a vision or a reality, one of your prime directives should be to constantly give it *presence* by getting it out from inside your head and into the fresh air.

Talking about your studio helps bring it to life by keeping it in the front of your mind among your top priorities, and by making the vision real in others' minds. Don't worry that your friends will steal your "top secret" plans (the chances of that are virtually nil, and even if it were to happen, their final version would be entirely different than yours). What you need now is to put together an informal support network of people who will give you interest and feedback, and who also know others that they'll recommend you talk to. Start this process early on, and you'll build a wide circle of acquaintances who may become important allies as time goes by.

Tell them your ideas about specialization, the equipment you've been thinking of, your location and your target date. People are fascinated by other people and what they do, and a recording studio has an especially glamorous image to project, even to industry professionals. What's more, people *like* to help, especially if they catch some of the excitement emanating from you.

You'll find that they may also help you avoid making some big mistakes, because when you talk about your specific plans with others, it gives you the opportunity to literally listen to your own thoughts. So discussing them out loud becomes a practical way of seeing how your ideas fly on their own, and often the ensuing conversation will yield more important detail and refinement right then, rather than later.

Talking up your studio is also a great way to find a partner. And you never know where one of those may come from, so don't just limit your conversations to industry-related people. Everyone is connected to someone else, and their interest in your project may lead you toward some totally unexpected turns in the road.

MAKING NEW CONNECTIONS

In the working studio environment, connections play a major part in finding business. Your best advertisement is a satisfied customer, and on subsequent visits or telephone conversations, there's nothing wrong with first making sure the client is happy with your work and then asking if they might know of anyone else who'd be interested in your services as well.

If something actually comes of a referral, be sure to drop the person who helped make the connection a note of thanks. A phone call will do, but these days, a letter without a bill or a come-on attached is rare and memorable. The studio business is a repeat business, and little touches like a note that says, "I just wanted to thank you for referring BrainDead Records to us. They gave us a try last week and seemed to really enjoy working here," will make a tremendous positive impression on your valuable client. He or she will not only appreciate your thanks but will also know that he or she looks good in the eyes of the client who was referred.

The Trades

In case you haven't noticed, the entertainment industry is positively choked with professional papers and magazines that fall all over themselves to find out what every business in town is doing so that they can write about it and sell more copies.

The music industry bible is *Billboard*, which is published weekly. In the film and TV trade, there are the *Daily Variety* and *Hollywood Reporter*, plus a passel of monthly magazines, including *Post, Film & Video* and *Millimeter.* Recording studio business is the prime focus of *Mix* and *Pro Sound News,* to name a few. Once you have a legitimate dba (for "doing business as") and address, you can get most of the studio magazines free—just write to them on company stationery and tell them you're a new commercial studio. The dailies and weeklies are another story, due to their up-to-the-minute information, with subscription prices in the $150-per year-range. Depending on your area of interest or specialty, at least one of them should be very valuable to you and worth the cost.

Staying Current

You should make it a point to read trade publications regularly. First of all, there's no better way to see and understand what's happening in your chosen field on a week-to-week basis. Second, you need to get to know the names of the companies and the executives you'll be dealing with. And third, you'll get where you're going a lot faster if other people perceive you as someone who knows what's going on, rather than someone who's just asking a lot of questions.

There's no better way to make an impression than to be knowledgeable about chart movements or label acquisitions, using facts and figures gained from the music trades, or studio news that's reported in the studio magazines. With that kind of credibility, people will take you much more seriously.

Learn to read the trades with an eye on how productions, signings and executive appointments can affect your own business. An announcement that someone has been promoted to, say, head of artist development at A&M Records means that person could potentially steer a project into your studio.

When the trades announce job promotions, those spotlighted executives expect to make an impression around town and may receive dozens of calls from a wide variety of friends, associates and services who have read about their promotions. It's also a good opportunity to try to make a new contact.

So is the announcement of an act being signed, a staff being expanded, a singer signing a management contract, a movie starting production or a trailer company winning an award. When something happens in the industry, and the media reports it, you can get a perfect foot in the door by calling that company and saying, "I just read that you've signed the Vienna Boys Choir. Totally tubular, dude..."

Connecting by Phone

There are a million reasons why none of these executives would ever want to waste time talking to someone as unimportant as you, you're thinking. But with that kind of attitude, you shouldn't have much of a problem standing still in your career.

So drop the attitude. Take a chance and swallow your fear. Don't be afraid to pick up the phone and try to contact a "big executive." You never know when your timing may be truly opportune. You may think of yourself as a little fish in a big pond, but that doesn't mean that you don't have just the service that your target exec needs at the moment.

Usually, a receptionist or an assistant will answer the phone and either put you through or take a message. The chances for success in just getting through will be heightened because the exec may momentarily be more open to talking to new people, many of whom are calling because they have read the same article. Just be sure you're ready with an intelligent pitch (sales jargon for your best shot at selling a prospect on an idea) when they do pick up.

Make an effort to acknowledge the importance of the rest of the people in the company. When someone picks up, tell them who you are first, and then ask to be switched to the person you're after. If your call is intercepted by an assistant or secretary, tell them why you're calling. Don't keep it a secret, or insist on only talking to the boss. Executives do get barraged with cold and unexpected calls; it's legitimate and reasonable to be screened first and expected to provide an honest answer. You may be surprised by how many times you get through, simply by explaining that you wanted to introduce yourself and your studio. Some people will be relieved simply because you're not a securities broker or an irate customer.

Remember that executives, no matter how high up they are, are just folks. If you get into the habit of making a number of calls per week, you'll be successful in getting through to some of them, and in the process, open doors for yourself you may never have dreamed were there in the first place.

Make Friends With the Support Staff

Often the most powerful allies you can have in a company you want to add to your client list are its support staff. They may take dozens of boring calls a day for their bosses, but they'll remember you and try to help if you treat them with as much respect and importance as you would the person you're really after.

Be friendly or charming to a secretary or receptionist, and they'll go out of their way to track down a busy exec or let you in on the latest happenings in the company. Ask them their names, write them down on your Rolodex next to the company's phone number, and say "Hi, [name]" each time you call. Take an extra five seconds and ask how they are, or comment on the action you've heard about in the company. It's just like anywhere else—if you treat *them* right, they'll treat *you* right, and you may wind up with an inside ally who can open doors.

THE COLD CALL

For most people, making cold calls is about as appealing as an Eskimo pie in a snowstorm. You pick up the phone, dial the number of someone who's too busy to talk to you and who wishes you'd go away, you mutter some feeble drivel about how they really ought to be working at your place, try to sound confident, hang up and want to run away and hang yourself.

But wait. Here's the good news (and also some more bad news). The good news is that if

Points to Cover in a Telephone Pitch

1. Get your overall message out in the first 10 seconds. People respond better when they know what's being pitched at them. They'll also be able to tell you right away if you're talking to the wrong person and can then steer you to the right one. There's nothing like screwing up all your courage, pitching your heart out for a full two minutes and being unceremoniously zapped onto hold while you're switched to the right listener so that you can begin all over again.

2. Include some interesting information in your opening. Mention an offer or a piece of current news that is calculated to elicit a response from the person you're pitching. The sooner you're conversing, the less awkward the one-sided emphasis.

But avoid the immediate canned intimacy, like "How have you been?" or even, "How are you doing today?" Many people react negatively and suspiciously to a stranger eliciting responses without their knowing who they're talking to.

3. Get to the heart of the matter. You're dealing with professionals who usually know what they're after and will ask detailed questions if they're interested. Lay out your presentation first. You can talk about the weather later, after your prospect responds favorably.

4. Anticipate questions and objections and be ready with answers and positive arguments. Practice playing telephone with someone else at your studio. You play the caller and make them the client. Have them think up objections to your offer and then work out the answers.

When you play, simulate the conditions of a real cold call. Work in separate rooms, or if you're both in the same office, don't look at each other. Have your "client" simulate different personalities each time you hang up and try again.

Take this game seriously and you'll be ready for the real thing ten minutes later. Done right, this is a very powerful exercise!

5. Don't sell too hard. You're selling a service, not a product. People are going to have to like you later on if they're going to work with you face to face. So don't come on like a used-car salesman, and learn to back off if you're getting a lot of resistance.

6. Practice reading until you sound natural and relaxed. You mustn't sound like you're reading a script. This is another good reason for the telephone game in point 4. If you're alone, read your lines out loud several times until you find the right conversational tone.

you get into the spirit of the challenge and learn how to do it right, you really *can* generate new client interest, make more connections and actually get people to come in and work at your studio.

The bad news is you still have to make the calls.

Enter the Script

The best way to avoid falling all over your words when you first try your hand at "pitching" is to start out with a cold call script. Scripts are used in a wide variety of businesses, including those infamous "boiler room" mail-order companies that try to sell you merchandise over the phone. Have you ever been tempted to pay "just the $59 shipping charge" on a complete portable home sauna and Jacuzzi—you're among the 20 lucky winners to be notified! Hands, please.

Well, live and learn, but whether they're legit or not, you may have noticed that those salespeople are never at a loss for seemingly brilliant reasoning, retorts and reassurances. And that's simply because they are sitting in a large room in cubicle number 16, row 4, with a detailed script book in front of them that's filled with color-coded response pages they've been trained to read back with genuine human conviction.

So when the customer says she doesn't really think she's interested in a lifetime subscription to Biker Leather Monthly, they just turn to the page about the free tickets you'll receive to their annual Hurt-the-One-You-Love Ball and then read the well-written answer that also includes the complimentary girlie-tattoo gift certificate if she acts *now*.

But this is different. We're not selling merchandise here. We're talking about a recording studio, offering a service that thousands of industry people and artists need. So let's take a serious look at how a well-tailored script can help you come across as a confident professional.

How a Script Can Help

Scripts offer a great opportunity to test your resourcefulness, and to have the "If I'd only thought of saying *that*" answers ready at your fingertips. They're also a way to beat the jitters in delivering that first opening paragraph. And once you get used to making calls, you'll be able to throw the script away and improvise on your own.

But until videophones become widespread, good scripts are a great tool (as long as you sound natural), and no one will be the wiser.

Here's the kind of script I wrote when we went after a few hundred film producers, offering audio post services. (By the way, we landed a grand total of one client in two weeks of calls. But the company booked better than 20 grand worth of projects over an eight-month period and went on to become our biggest client for four straight years.)

Cold Call Script: Production Company

— *to reception, if we know the exec's name*

Hi, this is Ace Greenburg from Digital Madness Studios.
    May I speak to [name] please?

—*to reception, if we don't know anyone's name*

Hi, my name is Ace Greenburg, and I'm calling about Digital Madness Studios, a place that specializes in audio post.
    I wonder if you could tell me who'd be the best person to speak to about post-production...

— *switched directly to exec*

Hello. My name is Ace Greenburg, and I manage an audio post studio in downtown Wilmington called Digital Madness. We specialize in locking up 24-track audio to video at pretty competitive prices, and today, [beat (pause)] I'm specializing in locking *in* some new companies as clients.
    So, are you folks currently in production?

[conversation]

— *after talking about projects*

Anyway, [name], I'm following up on a mailing that we sent you last week, called the Madness Monitor *(note: see Chapter 10 on advertising and publicity)*. It's a chronicle of some of the more recent adventures we've had around here working with clients like [names of recent people who've worked at the studio].
    Did you receive it?

— *Yes/no/don't remember*

Well, it also included some material on our latest promotion. You see, in an effort to expand our current client base, and to try and get your attention, we're offering our first day of services at a special rate: just $X an hour.

And that includes just about every service we offer, from custom digital effects to digital laydowns and laybacks.

[With a little hesitancy in voice.] Does... something like that sound...interesting to you?

— No, we do everything somewhere else.

Well, I understand what it's like to keep working in a place that feels like home. A lot of our clients feel that way about working with us. For instance... [launch into a clever anecdote about a big-name client that loves your studio].

But the day may come when your regular place is booked solid and you need to book another place in a hurry. Maybe if you knew about us, you'd think about Digital Madness at that time. If it's all right with you, I'd like to send you some rate info that you could refer to at your convenience.

— Well, that's not very likely. Look, I'm really busy...

OK, but please don't hold it against me for being excited about what we're doing here. Nice talking to you. Have a good one...

[Don't hang up! Wait for possible reply!]

[If the person hangs up: Keep working on the mailing list, but don't try calling this person for another 3 months.]

— I'll bite. Tell me more.

Well, we've worked on a wide variety of projects over the years, everything from TV specials to music videos and film soundtracks. We have a huge custom-sampled library of instruments and effects, and a great staff who perform all our services in-house to help keep our rates down.

The studio, by the way, is big and private and comfortable, and it's located in a very unique setting that's a bit off the beaten path, but right in the center of town. We think of it as our quiet little oasis, with lots of trees and open space.

Anyway, if any of this sounds good to you, I'd like to send you a little more Madness propaganda. Then if you're interested, I'd be glad to come by to say hello, or to have you visit our place to see how it feels. That way, I won't just be this drone voice on the phone, and maybe

we can discuss what it is that *you're* doing and how we might be able to help...

— Well, I don't know...

Tell you what. Why don't I just send you some more material for now, and let you form your own opinion.

— Do you work to film?

No, we don't. We work strictly to video. It's much faster, and it's *much* more economical. But if film is your normal medium, we'd be glad to take care of your telecine transfers.

— Well, I prefer mixing on a stage.

Fair enough. But you could be saving a couple thousand dollars a *day* by doing your prelays and effects here with us first.

Then, you could do your final expensive film mix wherever. Which is just to say that we have a lot of creative solutions around here.

— Well, we don't have anything going on at the moment.

That's okay, we're not going anywhere. And it's been nice talking to you. Would it be all right if I check in a month or two and see how you're doing?

Take it Easy

Get it? Be real. With a little practice, you'll sound spontaneous, like you aren't reading at all. And yet, the responses are right there in front of you.

A key factor in a good sales call is to stay calm and friendly. Don't come on like a locomotive—that kind of approach rarely works when you're dealing with professionals.

The more calls you make, the more natural you'll sound. And as people ask more questions, you can add them to your list. That way, when you hire someone else to do the cold calling, they'll have the whole scenario laid out in front of them with your script.

Remember to practice reading your lines out loud several times before you try calling a real prospect. It's best to work with a friend or partner. (Once again, here's a personal situation where, if you let your guard down a little and ask for help, you'll get all you need. Too many people get ulcers by keeping all their pride and anxiety locked up inside; you don't have to be one of them.)

After a while, the reading style will become your own (that's why it's good to write out your own scripts in your own words), and soon you won't need to read at all. And cold calling won't seem like the scary monster you made it out to be in the first place.

Working Hard at Making Friends

Doing his own aggressive marketing, David Platt has made a success out of a creative partnership that keeps the income flowing from studio-for-hire projects while concentrating on a variety of creative in-house productions.

David Platt

Partner, Manager

The Room

Weston, Ontario

THE ROOM

Career Roots   Started an 8-track room as a keyboardist with an Emulator in 1984, in a basement rehearsal space. Outgrew it and partnered up with the engineer he hired to run the equipment. They built the present facility in '86.

Present Facility   One 24-track room, Amek Angela board, Otari MTR 90II 24-track, MIDI keyboard stack, 3/4-inch video lockup.

House Staff   Manager, engineer, assistant.

Primary Focus   Record production, TV music production.

Notable Projects   Just completed their first record with a band they signed.

Rates   "We don't cut our rates just to attract business. We've been able to hold steady and maintain a certain clientele, which hasn't been easy but has definitely paid off. It's important to maintain a level of integrity, especially concerning price."

With groups the production company signs, rates are negotiated within the contract. For instance, they may charge half of the rate in exchange for half the rights to the recorded product.

Marketing   Actively soliciting record labels for record deals. Strong results from an impressive full-color brochure. Primary advertising: cold calls, direct mail. "We're heavily MIDI-based, which has been a great drawing card for us."

Cold Calls   "I hate 'em with a passion. But I've learned to feel better about them. I've had enough smokers on the end of the line to have developed a thick skin, and I know that nine out of every ten calls are gonna wind up nowhere, but that tenth one can really make your day."

"I wasn't born a salesman, but in this business you have to be. I make at least some calls every day, without fail. And when I reach someone who doesn't need our services, they usually know people who do."

Client Relations   "I try to convince a potential client to actually visit the facility before they book a date. I'd rather deal face-to-face than over the phone. If that's not possible, I do the best to sell myself and then let the facility speak for itself when they get here.

"One time our assistant put up a roll of 2-inch and blew away half a tune. Luckily, it was all programmed material. We immediately pulled out all the stops and re-recorded everything on the house. If it had been live musicians, I don't know what I would've done. But if you show your clients that you're willing to go the extra distance to satisfy their requirements, they'll not only return for business, but because of friendship."

Growth Plans   The partners are planning to move to downtown Toronto, buy a building and start up a production facility in cooperation with other service companies, including audio/video duplication and video post-production. They've looked into setting up a "small business corporation development" program. This is a nonprofit service, run by the Canadian government, that consists of a computer-based matchup program so that like-minded investors can find one another.

The immediate goal is to start their own record label.

This single-page color flyer showcases the whole facility at a glance.

The Room's brochure features a pull-out card offering a free hour of time when a session of six hours or more is booked.

TELEMARKETING AND COMMISSION SALES

There is an alternative to filling your once peaceful and creative existence with cold-call cacophony: Hire someone else to do it. Believe it or not, there are people out there who love this kind of work (it's not *that* bad) and make a good living plying their craft. They're called telemarketers, and if you'd rather be doing other things like engineering a session, you may want to consider setting up another desk and a phone and hiring someone to work part-time.

A telemarketer is usually paid both a salary and a commission, so that he or she can be sure of a minimal draw and a bonus for any work brought in. You should be able to get an experienced pro for a reasonable hourly fee or administrative-level weekly salary, plus a 5% to 10% commission on billing.

It's true that the commission can get pretty hefty—if a telemarketer finds a client who brings an album project in and the studio bills $20,000, they'll make a nice bit of change. The justification for this, of course, is that without them the work would never have existed. And it's hard to argue with that.

The best way to find telemarketers is through referrals or by running job classifieds in local entertainment papers. Be sure to get resumes, and follow up on the candidates who interest you by calling some of the people they list as references.

Another way to stretch your employer dollars is to find someone who can telemarket part of the time and help you with other tasks as well, such as engineering, tech work or bookkeeping. Over the years, we've experimented with people who are willing and interested in doing a variety of tasks, and we've had fair results. Our last telemarketing person was also an experienced post-production supervisor. He actually helped bring in film projects and then stopped making calls to supervise the work we would do for the client full-time. It was an interesting and creative arrangement.

Talking Terms

Find out what your telemarketer wants and negotiate the rate he or she will receive. A fairly standard practice is for the salesperson to continue to receive a commission on all subsequent work the same client brings in for a specific period of time.

Sometimes the deal stipulates that they'll receive half the original project commission percentage for as long as they are on staff with your company. They may also request a guarantee of a continuing percentage for at least six months, even if they leave before the time is up.

Everyone has different ideas about terms, so a good way to get started is to ask your rep what kind of deal he or she has in mind. Once you both agree, you should get the terms written down in a simple contract you both sign. And don't forget to have your attorney give it the once-over; it's always smart to spend a few dollars to get a legal opinion on an employee agreement. There may be one phrase to insert or delete that could save you huge potential grief later on—think of it as an insurance premium payment.

With a signed and sealed paper between you, your rep can get down to business. Just don't expect a sea of new projects to come pouring in. Remember, you're in a service business, not merchandise.

You should expect a good salesperson to work hard, make a lot of calls, keep a detailed record of contacts and report his or her progress on a regular basis. A pro will eventually get results and earn his or her keep, but it usually takes some real perseverance and patience. You may want to hire someone to just work a quick promotion deal for a few weeks, but a good salesperson will need several months to prove his or her worth.

Working Together

Work closely with your rep; don't just hand over a list and close the door. Make sure the right topics and important details are being covered. In the beginning, your rep will relay a lot of questions the prospects are asking; explain the answers carefully and have them added to the notes or script.

You might start by trying out your marketing person on a part-time basis, working on the best selling days (Tuesday, Wednesday and Thursday) to see how it feels. Try to give him or her enough space and privacy to work in a way that creates the best results.

Within a month or two, you'll know whether you've got a star or a dud on your hands. And you'll have learned a lot more about this whole creepy solicitation business in spite of yourself. Who knows—you may even turn out to be one the weirdos who likes it yourself!

SHMOOZING YOUR WAY TO SUCCESS

There are contacts to be made everywhere. But you can increase the odds of making successful ones by making an effort to look in the right places.

Find out where the industry "watering holes" are in your area. And on your way to the bar, remind yourself that you're going there to work as well as play. Read the trades and walk in with a few good news events in mind that you can use to turn a smile into a conversation.

Keep an eye out for special events, like album-listening parties, gallery openings and charity benefits. All are gatherings that draw artistic people who are likely to be connected with the audio world in various ways.

Watch for the glitzy special evenings that honor a local performer or national personality. They may be expensive to attend, but they're filled with people on the fast track, and are a great way to make important connections. Most of these events are charitable, which means they're tax-deductible. They're also a legitimate business expense, if your objective is to promote your business. And they may be the only opportunity you have to rub shoulders with some movers and shakers who are otherwise well-insulated.

If It Were Easy, Everybody Would Be Rich

There's a trick to making contact with powerful people. You have to work at it. But it's not impossible, and the rewards can be substantial. Try a black-tie evening and see what a special opportunity it is. One tux or evening dress will see you through a dozen functions (okay, one evening dress with revolving accessories).

If you're cash-light, there are killer deals in used tuxes and formal gowns at second-hand stores. And once you put one on you'll begin to feel as special as you look.

Then all you have to do is to be incredibly brave, walk up to Ms. Megabucks at the charity ball, and say hello without your voice cracking. Act naturally, tell her who you are and what you do, and anything can happen. She may even turn out to be human! The next day, drop her a line and a brochure, and you're on your way.

Some Additional Ideas

Take a batch of business cards on each trip out of town (in fact, never be without them, anywhere). Talk to the person next to you on the plane. Eavesdrop on conversations at the hotel. Give a card to the folk singer in the lobby bar. Host small parties at your home and get to know your own clients better, while you mix them with other prospects.

Go backstage at the concert and meet the band. Linger in the lobby during intermission at the show. Call the guy your mother told you about who plays the saw. Ask yourself why you didn't talk to that person an hour ago who looked interesting. And don't get tired of talking about your work. It's fascinating, and people want to hear about it. Be interested in what *they're* doing, and they'll remember you even better.

Look for the opportunity of the day. If there isn't one, figure one out. Hang out at record stores and comment on the album someone is buying. Tell the guy in the entertainment section of the bookstore about another book you read and would recommend. Talk to the guy in the Guccis sitting on the bench next to you at the car wash. Look for a seat on the train next to a group of people who know each other.

Pick up and butt in on an industry conversation at the next table in the restaurant. Go to the songwriter showcase of the month or start one of your own on your studio premises. Introduce yourself to the owner of the local disc shop. Throw an anniversary party at the studio and invite everyone on the mailing list. Look deeply into the eyes of your significant other and say that you're in a position to be able to offer a great deal on studio time.

You can fortify yourself with a great book on the subject called *Power Shmoozing: The New Etiquette for Social and Business Success*, by Terri Mandell, available from Mix Bookshelf (800/233-9604). It's a high-flying manifesto on tearing down the walls of old-fashioned politeness and making the kinds of connections that can dramatically change your life.

Reach out and grab someone! Do it!

Jammin' Down the Digital Highway

Embracing both the human and technological networking opportunities that continue to open up, Carlos Chafin has built a vibrant production company in a location that is thousands of miles from some of his clients.

Carlos Chafin

Partner/Composer

In Your Ear Recording

Richmond, Virginia

IN-YOUR-EAR

Startup Started as a music production company with partner Robbin Thompson. Robbin was a singer/songwriter, and Carlos was an engineer/producer. Wrote a few pieces together and clicked, choosing ad music as their focus.

Began as a production studio, but then quickly became a room for hire, as well. "Our clients wanted a place to do all the ancillary work that they did around our music projects...recording the voice-overs, doing the mixing, etc."

Facility Located in an old Depression-era bank that still includes a wall of the original safe-deposit boxes that have never been opened. "It's too expensive to open them, and to break them open would be a crime, because they're beautiful, so we've just left them there and they make for a great visual effect."

Setup Studio A: Euphonix CSII 56-input automated console; NED Postpro 16-track recorder. Studio B: 24-input DDA console and a second Postpro system. Two MIDI studios include a full keyboard complement, tethered to a high-end Mac running Opcode's Studio Vision.

Business Focus "In this market, there are a variety of recording facilities out there, and most of them aren't doing that well because there's not a big enough business in town to record, say, bands only. But there is a good amount of voice-over and audio post work, which is where we try and stay. The rates are much better, and we're pretty self-maintained, which is part of what's rolled into our premium rate.

"One philosophy we have is once you pay the rate, you don't pay for anything else, except materials. So we roll everything in, from Dolby to D2, at no extra charge. We keep a very, very straight rate card. Fits on half a page. And it works. We've found that the simpler you make the invoice, the faster you get paid."

Home Studios "We don't feel that we're in competition with the local home studios. In fact, we encourage them to go digital 8-track and to bring their playback machines in for overdubs and mixing. Usually, we'll figure out a package price or even take a couple of points on the project to try and stay as flexible as we can."

Marketing "We work with agencies all over the country. The thrust of our marketing has been to get to the agencies that win the awards shows. And we've worked with top agencies in many different cities. As a result, a lot of our production is done outside of this studio.

"A lot of times I'm buying studio time elsewhere. Let's say you've got a dog-food campaign coming out of an agency in Minneapolis. It may make a lot more sense for us to fly up there. They've got some great facilities there. So we may carry some of our key equipment, hire musicians up there and do it. It's just like the record business, the way they move around the country and take advantage of the resources as they find them. We do the same thing."

"We have relationships with studios all over the country. Since the agencies are buying a creative product, they may send a call out to several companies and then pick the best idea. So the agency picks us and then thinks, okay, these guys have the best idea for the job, but they're located in Richmond, Virginia, and getting our team there is gonna be a pain in the butt if we have to fly ten people there. So instead, we go there. And we do it at least once a month.

"And you know, it keeps us fresh too. It gives us a chance to see what other studios are doing, what equipment they've got, what musicians there are...Sometimes, we'll even work with another music supplier in the city and split the project. I'll remain the writer, they'll help me produce it, we'll all have a good time and leave. Sure, I'm not making as much money as if I'd produced it here, but I'd rather do good creative work out of the better agencies than just sit in Richmond and take everything that blows in the door."

Networking "I'm looking to expand this idea of creative alliances with people. I'd like to become more connected with people in other markets that are doing what we do and work in a cooperative way. It's fun, it's profitable, it keeps you fresh, it's great.

"I'll stay here. This place is a great place to live and raise kids. I'd like to develop a building space here in town with a video post facility, a couple of different graphics houses, maybe a small agency, and turn it into a production mall. We've already got an old tobacco building picked out. That's what makes the major cities really tick, and there's no reason we can't do that here."

Connecting Digitally "We're members of EdNet, using T1 and ISDN lines, which allows us to get a lot of data around very quickly. It delivers full-quality stereo digital audio sent across ordinary phone lines, instead of doing satellite feeds, which is a lot more difficult. So you dial up into the network, dial the subscriber studio of your choice and you've got a direct link. We work on a regular basis with a voice-over guy who lives 120 miles from us at the beach, who's got a setup in his bedroom.

"Our clients love this stuff. It's the most popular thing I've seen since multitrack. The other day, we had live talent in Atlanta, Dallas and New York. The producer was in L.A., and we recorded the whole thing here. It's just amazing.

"I think you're going to have to be more open-minded about who you're working with and where they are. The digital network's opened up whole new vistas to us. Next week, we're doing a live radio show with worldwide dial-up. So people will call up the artist in L.A. and then bounce it through the service to us, because the band happens to be here this week."

Vision "Our philosophy has been to try and figure out how to integrate terrifically talented people into what we do and then to try to help further their own careers in the rest of the world. I think cooperative relationships, those that don't involve us necessarily being the owners of the product or equity, aren't necessary. We're willing to work in many different ways. And that's what's kept us alive and happy: being open-minded from a business attitude.

"People sometimes ask me how you do that profitably. I tell them you've got to seek business out. They're not going to come and beat down your door. But if you tell them, 'I want to really work with you,' and you know they do good work, then it's just a matter of time to convince them, and pretty soon you're working together."

10
Advertising & PR

I f you've spent half your life yelling with righteous indignation at the TV every time a commercial comes on, you'll be amazed at how your attitude changes when you become a business owner and start spending money on advertising.

As omnipresent and objectionable as it may seem, advertising is an essential element in a free-enterprise society. With a seemingly limitless number of companies offering the same products and services, ads are one sure way to catch consumers' attention and convince them to remember you. The tricky part is to find a way to do it effectively.

Your studio's area of specialty dictates a lot of your choices in designing a *campaign* (advertising-agency parlance for a theme used to create an overall direction for a client). If you have a demo studio that specializes in singer/songwriter packages, you might choose print space in the local songwriter newsletter. If you're going after the album market, you're probably better off using direct mail to producers, artists and the record companies. And if you're into picture lockup, you might want to buy space in the local trades, national magazines and yearly directories of film and video publications.

USING DIRECT MAIL

D irect mail—sending advertising directly to people or companies that are most likely to use it—can bring real results. This is another reason a computer is essential in managing and running a business: Using a database, you can input thousands of names and addresses and generate lists, labels and reports by category, location, frequency of response and so on.

As your business grows, so will your mailing list. Important sources for your master list can be found in local directories of organizations that publish lists of members of performance groups, production companies, editors, union musicians, record companies and the like. To these, you should also add your growing list of clients, personal relationships and prospects.

A mailing list can quickly grow to several thousand names, and when you realize that each piece will cost you first-class postage plus printing and materials, you can begin to see the wisdom of keeping it current and weeding out the deadwood.

Please don't even think of managing a list like this by hand. Your time is simply too valuable, and a decent computer and printer can address thousands of updatable peel-off labels per hour, with no errors.

Using the Mail Effectively

So now, what to put in the envelopes? Maybe something as simple as an announcement that you're open for business. Or a limited-time special on low night rates. How about an open-house cocktail hour invitation? Or another in a series of newsletters about the goings-on at the studio.

The best direct-mail pieces are like the best cold-calling scripts: They get to the point quickly, have something interesting to say and come across professionally. Here again, your computer becomes the centerpiece for a successful promotion. With a desktop publishing program like Pagemaker or Quark Xpress, you can create professional-looking, typeset-quality pieces on your screen and print or copy them at your friendly neighborhood 24-hour copy center for peanuts (there's nothing quite like the thrill of whipping out a couple hundred flyers at Kinko's on a Saturday night around 3:00 a.m.).

Once they're in the mail, all you have to do is wait by the phone and pick the fattest responses, right? Well, serious mail-order houses that sell merchandise tend to rate the success of a piece by the percentage of responses they get—a 2% to 3% response indicates a pretty respectable showing, and is usually considered the business's break-even point in terms of paying off the cost of the mailing in the first place.

But in the recording-studio business, you're not trying to move merchandise. You're selling a service, and the response to your mailing may be a good deal lower than you'd hoped.

The difference with service-oriented mailings is that each time you send out a direct piece, you're making an impression on someone that will get stored away in their "For Future Consideration" brainfile, which is what direct-mail advertising is all about. It may take four or five mailings before someone with a project in hand thinks, "Maybe I'll try that place I read about last month," and calls in. Or, you may get lucky and catch someone in the middle of searching for a place to work.

Getting "Lucky"

People *do* respond to good advertising; we found our best client through direct mail. We worked for a week at creating just the right look with our own desktop software and sent a two-page, low-priced "first time only" deal out to about 1,200 local companies whose names we got from an assortment of industry directories. One of them just happened to be under the gun and without a studio when they got our piece in the mail. Six years and hundreds of thousands of dollars in billing later, we're still longtime friends with this company, and we're also working with several other clients they've referred to us over the years.

By the way, we got a total of three responses from that mailing, and only one other company booked some minor work. It's impossible to predict the kind of response you're going to get, but in our case, that one company showed us that direct mail packs a giant wallop.

Brain Games

Repetition is an important factor; so is follow-up. If you do two to four mailings per year, you'll be making that many impressions on each potential client who receives them. That builds up recognition, respect and trust.

Think about being on the receiving end of the process: You get a single piece of literature in the mail. Assuming you open and read it (which is another problem in the age of junk-

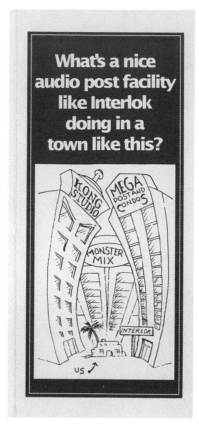

mail inundation), it makes an impression. Unless there is a pressing need, it more than likely gets stored away into the drawer in your brain marked "So What?"

But as months or years go by, you receive additional input from the same source. More ads come from the same company, which seemed mildly interesting six months ago when you read their first piece. You begin to become more familiar and comfortable with the new image of this company, which is beginning to work its way into your "General Knowledge" file with its logo and events.

Your brain notices that the "Elephant Breath Recording Studio" image from last year is still here this year. And maybe it takes that old image from the "So What?" file and puts it into the "This is Something That Appears to Have Weight and Matter" file. Later, when you need a place in which to record your brilliant ideas and songs, which file do you think your brain will scan?

Following Up

The other way to enhance the impression you make with your direct-mail promo piece is to follow up in a couple of weeks with a phone call. The beauty of this follow-up call, which is what our cold-call script was based on, is that you have a legitimate reason to call your prospect.

One of five Interlok mailers to go out to selected producers over a six-week period. Each took a humorous approach to getting new business and aimed at generating positive word of mouth.

You want to make sure they received your direct-mail piece!

Whether or not they received one, you still get the opportunity to work on building familiarity and trust by talking about your studio, and you'll be well on your way to making the kind of multiple impressions that national advertisers pay millions for on network TV.

Bulk Mail

You should send direct-mail pieces via first-class mail, for three very important reasons. The first is that although you can arrange to set up a bulk-mail system, it's a lot of work. To take advantage of the very attractive-looking bulk-mail rates, you must buy a permit from the post office and have special envelopes or postcards printed to exacting specifications. Then, when you're ready to mail your ads, they must all be presorted. That means you're responsible for bagging and banding your pieces in separate stacks for each different zip code (which *can* be done with certain software programs) and drop-

Triad Studios created and printed the expensive front side of this postcard by the thousands several years ago. Now, when they need marketing materials for a fresh promotion, they spend about $75 to print 1,000 to 2,000 back sides to send out.

ping them off at a special window at the post office.

And if your friendly postal professional isn't satisfied with some aspect of your sorting procedure, they'll send part or all of the shipment back to you, along with a possible charge, giving you the grand opportunity of starting the process all over again. This is pretty clearly a practice that should be reserved for businesses with big lists of 10,000 or more names, and really works best for the Publishers Clearing House folks.

The second reason bulk mail is a mistake is the physical look of the envelope. Bulk mail is the clear choice of businesses that are trying to reach as many addresses as possible at the cheapest rate, to get the highest possible return. The ploy is quite obvious to the addressee.

Think about it. As you look through your day's mail, you see both stamped envelopes and letters with Bulk Mail Permit numbers printed where a stamp should be. That permit stamp is a loud announcement that whatever is inside the envelope is a nonpersonalized, unrequested, more-or-less intrusive, same-as-it-ever-was, all-American, USDA-certified hunk-o-junk mail. Not exactly the impression you want to make with your personal, professional one-on-one recording service.

Why They Call It First Class

But the final and most persuasive reason for mailing first-class is that this is the only class that the post office will deign to forward to a new address or return to the sender if undeliverable. As your mailing list grows, you will appreciate the large number of pieces that come back to you, which if bulk-mailed would simply have wound up on the Planet of the Undelivered Mail (according to latest reports, this planet is full and not accepting any further deliveries).

By getting the returns brought right back to your Earth address, you'll be able to keep your database current and accurate, making the most out of each piece that goes out in the first place. That alone ought to save you nearly as much as if you kept mailing hundreds of undeliverable pieces at bulk-mail prices.

Finally, your letter will arrive looking like a letter. It may have a mailing label on it, but it will also announce the fact that the sender thought enough of the recipient to put a first-class stamp on it. Minor psychological value? Maybe. Worth it? You be the judge.

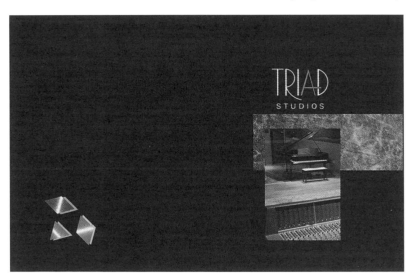

TOP TEN REASONS WHY BANDS SPEND THEIR HARD EARNED CASH AT TRIAD STUDIOS

10. They are blown away when the moving faders "do the wave" on the most excellent Diskmix automation.

9. They get a big kick out of their drums with our naturally rockin' acoustics.

8. They trip out at about 3:00 am when George does his tricks with the vintage compressors, TC2290 digital delay and the Panscan.

7. They feel like kids in a candy store when they see the mic selection.

6. They squint their eyes and move their heads around really fast while looking at the tiny red lights after sniffing new 2" reels of Ampex 456.

5. They like to see the dimples on the Sub Shop #22 delivery girl.

4. They recorded at Triad 10 years ago and are still entranced by Larz's *musico cum technibus.*

3. They want to see if Dave can edit faster with a razor blade or with a DAW.

2. They like the way the afternoon sun shimmers on the gold and platinum records on the wall.

1. They demand the best 24-track recording in the Seattle area at rates they can afford.

Free 46 minute DAT when you pay for 10 hours of time in either studio. While supplies last. This offer may not be used in conjunction with any other promotions or specials.

PRINT ADS

Print (or display) ads are advertisements that appear in print, in newspapers, magazines, directories and phone books. A good print ad can make a strong impression on a lot of people. That's why it's worth taking the time to create both a good-looking and effectively worded piece.

As opposed to direct mail, you need to be a lot more careful when using DTP (computer desktop publishing) for your ad. Amateur DTP tends to look a lot different in the context of a professionally printed magazine. Often, the high quality of the rest of the publication will make the DTP piece look very cheap.

So it's a good idea to have an artist help or simply put the whole thing together. Bear in mind that a good ad can run for months or years, so what may seem like a high cost at first can amortize itself into a very reasonable charge.

The good news about art in most newspapers and magazines is that the publisher's in-house art department will usually do a simple but professional piece of artwork for you at a low charge (or even free, in some cases). All you have to do is bring in the copy and/or photos you want to use and leave the rest to them.

They will, of course, consult with you and make absolutely sure you don't agree to an ad that doesn't make you happy. You're paying the publication a serious chunk of change to run the ad; at least feel good about how it looks.

If you do decide that the world needs to be exposed to your own desktop self-expression and do up your ad yourself, bear a couple of simple design rules in mind.

Looking Good in Print

One area that you *should* spend some time and money on is photography. One good photo shoot can result in some great-looking artwork that you wind up using in print and PR for years. Do it right, and your ad will exude confidence and class.

That means a professional shoot—a snapshot won't do. A single flash results in hot spots, where the picture is overexposed and washed out, and cold spots, where the area blackens and disappears. Your room should be professionally lit with multiple light or flash sources, photographed with a wide-angle lens to include the most area and shot in the largest film format possible to deliver the finest detail.

Most control rooms have several angles and banks of equipment that look the most impressive when they're all properly lit and highlighted. The wide-angle lens gives the room width and depth, making it look bigger. And using a larger-size film negative, say 2-1/4" square, preserves much finer detail in all the

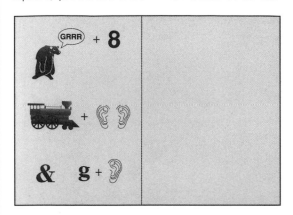

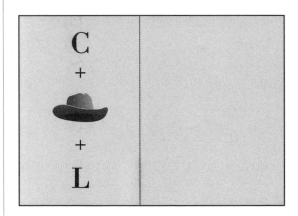

Triad devised this clever campaign using the same artwork shown earlier on the postcards' fronts, creating multiple impressions while recipients enjoyed decoding each message.

Interlok Studios · 1522 Crossroads of the World · Hollywood, CA 90028 · 213/469-3986 · Fall '91

Spielberg's "Family Dog" at Interlok

With the completion of "American Tail 2," Steven Spielberg and Warner's again chose Interlok for the pre-recording, editing and mixing of the new CBS animated series "Family Dog." Although once again in production limbo at press time, the series utilizes the different strengths of Interlok's individual suites.

The show is first pre-recorded by the entire cast to script on the live stage in Studio 1. This allows the director to record and choose from multiple wild takes. Once the decisions are made, the episode is then edited in Studio 3 on the Dyaxis 2 + 2, our digital editing work station. The assembled episode is then animated to sync with the now existing dialog. Weeks later, when the picture is delivered, music and efx are then mixed together digitally in Studio 4. *(continued on p.3)*

New Studio 4 Features Digital Audio Mixing at Analog Rates

It's no secret that digital mixing has become the audio post format of choice. Using it, sound can be bounced, processed, edited, mixed, minced, sliced and diced ad infinitum, and still retain all its original punch and vitality.

Our newest room offers clients this unparalleled quality of sound at truly affordable rates. And as usual, we've done it with smart equipment choices and creative design.

The heart of the system features a separate machine room with both a Sony PCM3324 digital 24-track tape deck *and* an Otari MTR-90 analog 24-track deck. This gives our clients real service flexibility. Many have opted to work in Studio 1 or 2, which are both excellent analog deck rooms, to benefit from their lower rates. Then, to avoid any generation loss and to take advantage of its added capabilites, they mix to digital in 4.

Studio 4 also adds the luxury of 48 available tracks. That leaves plenty of room for extra effects, overdubs and mix stems.

The room features a custom-designed Quad Eight Screenstar console, fitted for Dolby Surround Sound. Conceived for mixing down the Family Channel series "Zorro," the room has proved equal to the challenge of everything from high-tech trailers to high-price amusement park soundtracks. Many of the projects feature a variety of effects coming at the viewer from all sides.

Other clients have opted to book their project from start to finish in Studio 4, which offers a digital sampling workstation, 35" video monitor and latest outboard and effects processing gear.

Designed by supervising engineer Michael Perricone, we think you'll find the room as fast as it is affordable.

Interlok Studios uses desktop publishing software to produce an updatable eight-page newsletter. The "Times" has become a requested item among clients and is sent out to the studio's 1,500-name mailing list. Many projects and people are mentioned and credited by name, along with "advertising" that trumpets special deals and promotions. It also serves as an updated brochure, working specs and pricing into the news stories and photos.

A shoot like this could wind up costing $1,000, but the impact the photos make and the uses they can be put to are often well worth the cost.

Naturally, there's a perfect way to get around the professional fee: Trade your photographer for a fair amount of professional studio time and engineering services! Many music and video industry professionals do photography as a hobby, and lots of photographers are serious about their entertainment-industry pursuits.

Ask around, or run an ad offering to trade services in a local paper. Don't settle for anyone whose work doesn't fully impress you. Then propose a day of studio time for a day of studio shooting. A fair compromise is to pay for film and processing in return for their picking up any tape costs.

Choosing the Right Publications

Perhaps the most important rule in the ad placement game is to be sure you know your market and the competition. Assuming money is important to you, the expense factor in print advertising can get pretty scary. Know who it is you want to reach and how to reach them. Then see how your competition is doing it.

The best research method is, once again, to talk to people about your ideas for advertising. Call friends and associates and ask them what they think they'd do. Speak to professional organizations like musicians' unions or local performance-rights offices and ask them what they think. Try calling some of the other advertisers in the publications that interest you and ask what kind of response they've gotten.

If you're brave enough to call strangers on

buttons and meters you're trying to show off when you blow the picture up to 8" x 10".

A good photographer may take four to eight hours to get just the right combination of elements together in a studio photo shoot. You must pay great attention to the cleanliness of the room and the equipment setup for best results.

Creating Effective Display Ads

1. Don't succumb to the temptation to use multiple fonts and type styles in one piece. Use one font for your headline and one for the copy.

2. Avoid lengthy or wordy ads. Use language economically.

3. Always use the same company logo. Build multiple-impression recognition.

4. Print your camera-ready copy on the highest-quality laser printer you can find, preferably one with at least 600-dpi (dots per inch) output.

5. When you're done, laser-print the ad to the exact size you want to run and then carefully cut it out and paste it over a similar size ad in the publication you're buying space in. Now you can realistically judge how it compares to other ads running in the same book.

the phone and wise enough to put yourself across as someone sincerely in search of help, most people will fall all over you with answers. Why? Because that's the way we are. We are a social, familial, caring and nurturing species, in case you hadn't noticed, though many of us are shy or judgment-sensitive.

If you're one of the shy types, the studio business is a great place to break out of your cage. It's an exciting and social atmosphere, filled with people who are bursting at the seams with creativity and vision. Interface, communicate and play with them, and more things will come to you.

Now that you've determined who reads what and where, you should be ready to put your ad together and buy space. Here are a few suggestions to follow:

1. Make your ad concise and to the point. Remember: Less is more.

2. Use simple headlines, like "NOW YOU CAN PAY LESS AND GET MORE," and then follow them with a few lines of copy (the body of your text).

3. Don't lie or make promises you can't keep. If you do, you'll wish you hadn't later on.

4. Use photos or illustrations. One picture is worth an awful lot of hype.

5. Unless the publication you're going into is really homespun, don't try to do your own ad layout and artwork unless you've really got the knack. Most magazines and newspapers have art departments that will work with you, and include this service in the cost of the ad. Bring them your ideas and let them help you.

6. Give your ad enough time to work. One or two exposures may have little effect. Figure out what you can afford, and then buy smaller sizes, if need be, to appear in more issues. Try four to six times to start. You'll also find that advertising rates fall as the number of insertions you purchase rises.

7. Negotiate to get the best rate; publications always print their ad rate cards and base their charges on them. Sound familiar? The rate card should be viewed as a starting point for your negotiations! Often, you can get a better deal simply by asking for one, just like your own clients do.

8. If you plan to advertise in more than one publication, list a different contact name or phone number in each different paper. When people respond, you'll get an instant analysis of how well each publication is pulling in readers for you. This little "market study" may lead you to the conclusion that one publication is better for you than another, which can save you a lot of money and help maximize the impact your advertising makes.

9. Get your *ad representative* (the person selling you space in the publication you've chosen) interested in your studio and then get your rep's editor to do a feature article about you in their paper! When you're paying their bills, you have considerable muscle with the press (just listen to how Paul Harvey boosts his sponsors on the air, pretending they're legitimate news stories). It's perfectly legitimate to do your own publicity at the same time as your advertising, especially if you've been working on something especially newsworthy.

10. If you don't get a good response to your ad, talk to people and figure out why. Maybe what you're saying is wrong, or you're not reaching the right market, or your competition has got you beat. Try testing a mockup of your ad on your friends, and get their comments. If something's wrong, find out what it is, then fix it and try again.

Triad Studios combines humor and information into a hip ad for band packages that runs in local trades.

11. Finally, if your response is good and business goes up, don't mess with your ad! Remember the motto, "If it ain't broke, don't fix it." Let your ad do its magic for you, while the impression that it makes on people sinks in deeper and deeper.

GETTING PUBLICITY

Publicity works hand-in-hand with advertising. The difference is that with publicity, it's your job to get someone else excited about your business without paying them for their attention.

There are many outlets for studio publicity. The trades thrive on press releases describing just-signed or completed projects, and are constantly gossiping about people and announcing appointments, migrations and promotions. Trades are a great source for exposure for your business, and they are constantly in need of more to write about.

As a studio manager, you should either write your own press releases or hire someone to do them, and then mail them off to the local and national trade publications every three or four weeks. You'll be delighted to see news of your studio popping up in the "studio news" columns, and the exposure will help you get your name known.

The Difference Between PR and Advertising

The key element in writing a press release (also called a news release), is to remember that

Rules for Writing a Publicity Release

1. Put the news on your own stationery. On the top of the page, type: For Immediate Release [current date]; Contact: [the name and phone number of the person who would talk to a reporter who might call with a question].

2. Start with a non-hype headline, like "Crusher Productions Signs Reggae Artist Jack Hammer" and then follow with the body of the copy.

3. Keep it all to one or two double-spaced, typewritten pages.

4. Include Who, What, When and Where in your first paragraph:
"Chicago – Crusher Productions has signed Zelmo Crudemore to an exclusive singer/songwriter contract. Crudemore, a 12-year jackhammer construction veteran, will record his first album at Crusher's Electro-Shock Studios this spring. The zydeco artist has developed a unique style that combines sensitive love songs with an insistent, machine-gun-like rhythm."

5. Don't write "laundry lists." They won't get printed. Spread multiple news items over several releases. Pick no more than one or two items of interest to write about in each release.

6. Close your release with a short "tag" that sums up the identity of the studio neatly. Use this tag on every release you send, to impress the identity of your business on the editors over and over again. A sample tag might say: "Crusher Productions has been specializing in emerging music trends since 1989 and is located in Chicago's historic O'Leary's Barn District."

7. Unless it's a really big story, let your release do its job. Don't bother column editors with follow-up calls, unless they continue to ignore your releases—then your unwelcome calls can't make things any worse!
But here's a tip: Call the trade magazines that mean the most to you, ask for the editor who covers recording studio news, and find out how they like stories presented to them—what they'll use and what they won't. That ought to get you on the inside track to getting some regular ink.

you're sending *news* to *newspeople*. Don't confuse PR with advertising. Hype—the kind of salesmanship used in paid ads—has no place in PR material.

Every magazine has a staff person whose job it is to sift through all the releases that are sent in each month and then write a column that reports the goings-on in the industry. What they need from you are *just the facts*.

A lot of people starting out in business are confused by this difference. Their PR releases tend to read like badly written ads:

"Boise is sure to find its place in the sun, now that Giant Thud Recording has opened its doors. With its beautiful control room and magnificent sound quality, Giant Thud is the promise fulfilled. Come one, come all, to the grand opening party on October 15."

This is a nice party invitation for your friends, but it isn't a proper news release. With a notice like this, the folks at Giant Thud have just informed 40 magazine editors across the country that they don't know what they're doing.

Writing Right

All an editor wants is a clear, direct and simple news piece that they can read in half a minute and to decide how best to use it. And what you can expect in return is some regular "ink" (PR jargon for exposure) and an open phone line when the time is right.

What you will usually end up seeing in print is a couple of sentences that briefly report what's happening at your studio. This should act as a model for the kind of release you send in the first place.

A typical blurb, filled with the news from studios in the Northwest area, might say something like this:

The Grapevine

January/February, 1989

DANCIN' THE NIGHT AWAY

GHERKIN RECORDS artist GALIFREE put the finishing touches on their latest 12" single "Don't Walk Out On Love". Produced by LARRY HEARD and RILEY EVANS, the cut features a wailing vocal by MONDAY OLIVER sung in the finest Deep House tradition. Tommy White was the interface between the ideas and the equipment.

CAPITOL RECORDS producer LARRY HEARD tracked, overdubbed and mixed his latest offering "Twilight". In addition to the mixes by Larry, the song was has re-mixed by TEN-CITY. Capitol Records New York A&R rep KEN ORTIZ attended the mixes. Mike Konopka handled the equipment.

M RECORDS new release, an album titled "Sweet House Chicago", has been completed and is on its way to the pressing plant. Produced by MICKEY OLIVER, the album features songs by 8 different artists in both the Acid and Deep House styles. If the activity at Seagrape is any indication, there will be a pitched battle between Acid and Deep House for control of the dance floor this summer. Mike Konopka and Tommy White worked together separately on the engineering.

HOT MIX 5 RECORDS artist RALPHI ROSARIO, has completed his 4-song E.P. Included is a rocker called "Daddy Daddy" which is about parental mis-deeds. Ralphi produced, Tommy White and Mike Konopka engineered.

Producer DEZZ CHRISTIAN mixed 2 songs for NEW POWER RECORDS. Mike Konopka engineered.

IN THE CATEGORY OF BEST POP OR ROCK PERFORMANCE BY A DUO OR GROUP W/VOCAL

Hard Rockers PEGG LLEG, with screaming lead vocals by ANDY HAVIAN and twin guitars by RUSTY and AL ALDRICH. CINDY BEDNARZ produced while Tommy White engineered.

Pop rocksters NEVER ENOUGH led by guitarists JOEY LYNCH and GREG GREITER, for their single "True Emotion" which was produced and engineered by Mike Konopka.

Blues rockers EDDIE & THE PIZZOLAS, with lead vocalist LIEF CAMP and axe man DON MUENCH for their album slated for indie release. Tom Haban engineered.

Bi-lingual pop crooner JESSE RODRIGUEZ for his single called "Come A Little Bit Closer" engineered by Mike Konopka.

5740 North Western Avenue Chicago, IL 60659 (312) 784-0773

"**Joe Johnson** was at **Hardball Studios** working on his new EP for Transfixxed Records. The studio just installed a new Lightspeed Digital Workstation which features an 98-input zygote sequencer and a ZX starpitudinal analyzer."

That's *it*. Which is to say, "Hey—we got our name in print, and people will see it." That's what basic PR is all about.

Seagrape Recording sends out a regular newsletter that details client sessions and projects, maintaining an ongoing positive image.

Keeping the Power Station On Line

Drawing on her experience as a personal assistant to artist Little Steven for 11 years, Zoe Yanakis has toured the world and its studios, as well as participating in mounting numerous charitable concerts and events.

Zoe Yanakis

Studio Manager

The Power Station

New York, New York

POWER STATION

Facility Three recording and mixing rooms, one post-production room, one overdub and film-scoring room. Studio A: 48' x 52', with 35-foot ceiling and a 40-input Neve 8068. Studio B: 20' x 30', with SSL 48 E Series and G automation. Studio C: 40' x 24' plus five isolation booths, 72-input Neve VRP with Flying Faders. AV-1: 25' x 23' control room, 80-input SSL, 6-channel Dolby Surround and mag projection. All formats of multitrack available. 28 full-time staff members, plus two interns.

Recent Projects Aerosmith, Al DiMeola, Akiko Yano, Sophia's Toy, Joshua Redmond, Bernadette Peters, post sound for *Beverly Hills Cop 3* and *The Hudsucker Proxy.*

Background Worked at the Power Station for a year and a half as an intern and then moved up to assistant engineer. "There weren't that many of us [women] and there still aren't.

"The unique perspective I brought to this studio was in having worked in so many rooms around the world as a client. That really helps me to know what a client wants."

Engineering "Maybe five percent of the sessions we do here are via house engineers, which is a complete about-face from the past, when there used to be eight full-time firsts on staff. These days, the producers always bring their own engineer. It's tough to be an independent these days. If you're not talented at going out and getting business, you have to have a manager and a plan. I think virtually every position in the studio is competitive right now. "

Balancing Costs "It costs much more to maintain, keep up and continue to be a state-of-the-art facility, and at the same time, our clients demand that we keep our rates down. For us, the rates have remained unchanged here for fourteen years. Some of our callers act shocked when we quote them our rate, but in truth of fact, there are a lot of other facilities in town that are quite a bit more expensive and we often get a return call from the same people, especially if they've been here before and know that they're going to get a lot of work done in a short amount of time. That's a real difference here. And it's due in part to our very competent maintenance staff, which is here 24 hours a day. Preventative maintenance is the key, because if something goes down you're out of business...the client's gonna go somewhere else; it's that simple."

Team Players "What makes this place so special is the design of the rooms [by owner Tony Bongiovi] and the staff, who we train from the ground up. This is great, because everyone has a respect for each other in the building. Everyone knows what they need to do, and people fill in certain areas when necessary. It's a team that we try hard to maintain. And we have a nice balance of state-of-the-art equipment, professional attitude and a very warm feeling. I always loved working here as a client."

Artist Development "We have the facility to develop any sort of artist you want, and Tony Bongiovi has a number of projects he's been working on. We find talent via word of mouth, live performance, and all the ways that a typical record-company A&R department would find fresh talent.

When we're doing in-house production, we look at it strictly like a development project,

Power Station's Studio

AV-1

which is to say in the best interest of the artist. It's taken very seriously. So we'll use both staff and outside talent.

"Success is pretty elusive. So now, we're reshaping that division of the company. We're quite serious about making a brand-new production company successful, so we're committing with new personnel and fresh ideas."

Philosophy "Obviously, our emphasis is on the client. We try to accommodate them in any way that will create the right environment for the creative process. Most important to me is having a happy staff, because when the staff's happy, the client's happy. I've seen it time and time again in other studios, where people are expected to work ridiculous hours...which can happen anyway, but to the point where they can't have their own life. I truly believe that if the staff isn't happy outside the studio, they're not going to be happy inside the studio. So I try my best to be as accommodating to their personal lives as their professional lives.

"On the other hand, it's critical that they're committed a hundred percent to their profession. Which doesn't mean they have to be here a hundred percent of the time, except for me—I'm the only one who doesn't get a break!"

Employees "More than anything, I look for attitude in future employees. They're either ready to do anything or I'm not interested. I'm after hard workers with an open attitude and a commitment to the field they're pursuing."

11
The Art of Scheduling

studio manager's prime responsibility is to keep the daily activity of the studio flowing smoothly and humming professionally. In a multiroom facility, that includes a full menu of jobs: session booking, staff scheduling, job bidding and negotiations, client shmoozing, cash-flow tracking and possibly bookkeeping, as well as making a host of "the buck stops here" decisions.

Sometimes the studio manager's primary job is traffic, and the job title may change to traffic manager because that's all there will be time to do. The designation really depends on the number of administration personnel; larger facilities can have a separate studio manager, traffic manager, bookkeeper and receptionist.

In traffic, what makes the work challenging is the barrage of last-minute changes that occur, and the mad juggling that follows. The changes come from both sides. Clients confirm dates and times, and then a day or two before the sessions call to apologize that the producer was just called out of town; could they postpone for an extra day? Or they say that the editor of the industrial showed the finished project to the company, which insisted on massive changes, and she's been up all night and can't make it by 10 a.m., so how does a 3:30 music-dub time sound?

Studio-side, the current session is going into its fourth overtime hour, with the next one already backed up and waiting. And the same thing that the tech couldn't figure out yesterday is causing track 24 on the 2-inch to sputter in and out. The spare card ought to work, but it's already caused 20 minutes of down time while the staff continues to try to figure out why it doesn't.

Those are the kinds of factors that make scheduling an art, consisting largely of guidelines, know-how and experience. To a great degree, it's also an art steeped in personality and charm. The idea is to keep everybody happy, which means for starters you have to at least *seem* happy yourself. That makes the individual a crucial link—the relationship between studio manager and client is the only real connection that exists outside of the sessions themselves.

If you set up a company policy for bookings, you have a baseline from which to operate. Combine that with some innate diplomacy, a non-volatile personality and a knack for, say, being able to juggle an orange, a bowling ball and a chain saw, and you've got the makings of a good management team.

SCHEDULING GUIDELINES

If you can agree on rules internally, then your business can be that much more effective at serving the needs of your clientele. Once you set your policy, it's important that you remember to inform clients of *their* responsibilities. This should only have to be done once: when the client books their first date. But learn to take a moment to give them a friendly tour through the rulebook. If there's a problem later on, reminding them of the fact that the policy was already discussed is a strong argument in your favor.

Many studios go so far as to print up contracts that clients must sign before the work begins. The use of policy contracts almost invariably follows a particularly unpleasant experience in which the studio suffers monetary or physical damage, and the owners vow that they'll never be taken again.

In fact, studios that use contracts report that they do solve most of the problems. Some working examples appear as illustrations in this chapter.

But with or without contracts, here are some general guidelines that many studios regard as standard policy:

1. All session bookings are assumed confirmed within 24 hours of the session start time.

It's the client's responsibility to show up and make good on his commitment. In the event that a client cancels more than a day ahead of time, the studio takes it on the chin and tries to fill the vacancy. If the client cancels less than 24 hours before the session, it's his or her responsibility.

Technically, that means the client should be required to pay in full for the time booked and then canceled, because it's too late to fill that spot, and your business is all about selling time. Convincing your client to pay that fee is quite another story.

Reaching a Fair Settlement

You don't want to be so tough on someone that they'll hate you for prevailing and never show up again. But you should be able to work something out that at least compensates you in part for the lost income.

A *kill fee* is a negotiated settlement paid by the client to the studio when the client has canceled at the last minute and left the studio control room with nothing but an air-conditioned breeze blowing through it. The fee represents a negotiated sum that ultimately seems reasonable to everyone. Factors that come into play include how long you've been working together, the length of the current project and how good an excuse they've got.

Once you've gently but firmly informed them that they're not allowed to simply disappear, most clients will feel guilty enough to at least apologize and swear to be good Scouts forever after. It's at that moment that you should tell them how much you appreciate the sentiment, and that you'll also need to be compensated for your loss of business.

The most important point to get across is that this is a major no-no, and that it won't be tolerated (you should, however, stop short of rolling up a newspaper and banging it on the floor). From that point on, you need to go by instinct.

What's a fair sum? It depends on who the client is. Is it a major company that wouldn't tolerate the same mishap if it were reversed? Charge 'em full price. Is it a new client who has a ton of work coming up and wants to book it at your place? You may feel it's best to let the whole thing slide, reschedule and hope that the point has sunk in.

Maybe your client is a film editor who calls in embarrassment an hour before he's supposed to show up to report that the company he's working for decided to change the music at the last minute. That puts the two of you on the same side: It's both the studio and the editor against the film company. In that case, ask the editor what *he* thinks you should do.

The lead guitarist of the group that's block-booked the room for two weeks has come down with the flu? Try to talk them into doing cleanup work or other overdubs, reminding them the place is theirs.

You'll certainly have to swallow a few frustrating cancellations, but it's a good idea to at least spell out your cancellation policy right on your client contract. Then, with policy in hand, you can at least come out of your corner waving your constitution righteously.

Best-Guess Diplomacy

Recently, a production company that was a new but enthusiastic client at Interlok booked a six-hour, top-dollar session to work on a major film. The morning of the scheduled session, the company called to cancel and apologize. The producer left word with our receptionist that they were sorry, and to please call to make arrangements for rescheduling and whatever fees might be involved.

My studio manager and I discussed the situation for several minutes. Here was an important and fairly new client we'd finally won over from another studio, who seemed very impressed with us and was booking a lot of work. They were also a little difficult to deal with, being prone to frequent, though not quite last-minute, changes. This was the first one that had come in under the 24-hour mark.

To complicate matters, they had sung loud praises about what a good job we were doing with their very demanding projects and how good it was to have finally found a place where they could really work with professional people who understood their scheduling problems.

We finally decided that although we'd lost virtually a full day's income, as a grand political gesture of goodwill we'd tell them not to worry about a kill fee, but to please try and give us better notice in the future. We felt very wise and benevolent about all this, and called the producer at the company, who we thought would be waiting nervously.

"You guys!" she laughed. "That's really nice of you, but we canceled because *our* client rejected the stuff we did and ordered a complete re-edit. They've been driving us nuts on this project and we hate the whole company! Send us a bill for the full amount and we'll make *them* pay it!"

So much for my U.N. ambassadorship. Next rule:

2. Minimum session bookings are two hours.

Any less than that and you may wind up prepping the room for longer than the actual session itself, so it's a fair rule. That doesn't mean that you shouldn't do the occasional half-hour session. But if you tell your client that the minimum is two hours, he or she will often agree and find some more work that needs to be done.

Short sessions are a scheduling nightmare in a busy studio. If a regular client calls in just to do a quick transfer from 1/4-inch to cassette, ask her if she can be a little flexible on the time that day and wait until there's a break in the action. Then give her a call 20 minutes before a lunch break or between clients so that she comes in at *your* convenience.

And if it truly *is* a short session and she's a good client or someone you want to do business with, give her a smile at the end and tell her it's on the house. People love freebies, the cost to the studio is negligible, and there's no better way to win gratitude and loyalty.

3. New clients should pay for services upon delivery of the finished tape. Regular clients should be billed Net 10.

Tell your clients up front what the billing arrangements are to be, if they don't ask you first. New clients usually expect to be asked for payment at the end of the session, and until you establish an ongoing relationship, it's fair to politely insist on immediate compensation. If the project is to last several days, it's fair to ask for half up front and the rest on delivery.

Sometimes a new company that you don't know, maybe one that you found through your ads or mailings, may have a project in mind that will take several days. Their internal accounting may be set up to pay bills at the end of the week or some other time period. In that case, ask the client to fill out a credit application and return it to you at least a few days before the first session, and then check the references. (See Chapter 7 for details on designing and following up on your credit application.)

If you are unable to get a reasonable referral or two on your potential client, you may want to ask the client for other referrals. Or you can politely insist on cash payment. If your client finds this unacceptable and does not propose another solution that guarantees you payment on delivery of the first project, *pass on the project.* (Read this paragraph again. It could save you a lot of money in the future.)

Finally, if business is slow, and you feel like gambling on a flaky producer whose referrals have warned you about him, confront him with the negative feedback you've gotten from his references. If he insists he's good for the money, let him at least promise to pay by signing a purchase order specifying the expected charges and a schedule of payment. Get as much of a guarantee as possible in writing before you begin. That's always the time when things look the rosiest to your client and you are at the strongest business advantage.

Most people who are anxious, if not desperate, to get to work will agree with almost any reasonable solution you proffer, as long as the negotiation takes place before you begin. Once tape starts to roll, you will not have anywhere near the same clout or personal wherewithal to negotiate any further points. Plan ahead and make a fair deal that you will feel comfortable insisting on later, then shake hands and get to work.

Bear in mind that personal referrals can be troublesome, too. We once extended several thousand dollars in credit to a low-budget film producer who came to the studio via a freelance engineer who'd done a lot of work with us over the previous year, a very likable and trustworthy fellow.

Our freelancer actually did all the engineering for the project, wrapped it up, gave us all the billing information and went on his way. Trouble was, so did the new client. After about 90 days, it became pretty obvious that we were getting stuck for the bills. Our only course was to go back to the person who'd vouched for the client—our friend the freelancer. Needless to say, he was taken aback that his client had flown the coop. What was worse, we felt we had no option but to continue to turn the screws on him in order to get paid. We didn't go as far as demanding money from the engineer. But we did wind up getting burned for the majority of the money, and in the process watched a perfectly good relationship go sour—our only conversations with our former engineer from then on involved politely but adamantly insisting he help us get our dough.

In the end, he actually delivered the client back to us. This was a guy who came to town when he needed post-production work and otherwise lived 5,000 miles and many, many court jurisdictions away. The client's self-serving solution to paying up was to bill another film production company for the new audio work he wanted us to do and then tack on an extra 30 or 40 hours' worth of time to get us caught up from the previous sessions.

We debated that scam for a while, decided that when you consciously do slimy business with slimeballs you become one yourself, and passed. Instead, we opted to try to put our differences aside with our former friend, the freelance engineer, who learned as much as we did from the whole affair. In the end, I'm sure the client didn't have any trouble finding another facility to start anew.

4. It's reasonable to charge overtime on late-night dates.

Overtime rarely exists on music and record dates, though it is sometimes charged against the first or second engineer's time, but it's standard practice on audio post sessions. Overtime hours can begin after eight consecutive session hours, and are billed at 20% to 50% more per hour. Lines of demarcation are quite varied—one studio may kick into overtime at 6:00 p.m., while another might define overtime as after 12:00 midnight and on weekends.

So here we have another interesting inequity. The music studio makes a block-rate deal, expecting to go until dawn or into the morning rush hour, while the audio post studio borrows from the film trade and adds extra hefty charges on a specific daily schedule.

Of course, in post, the studio is most often providing engineering staff, who will be billing the studio time-and-a-half or double-time beyond their normal 8-hour shifts. With music dates, the producer may well be bringing his or her own engineering talent and have a separate or contract deal with them. On the whole, both practices seem pretty well dug in.

Using Overtime for Leverage
Overtime can be used as a tool to help end a session that's dragging on while another is waiting, or as a technique for granting a favor (by not adding it on when it's understood that it's supposed to be charged). It's also a good negotiating tool.

If a client is planning a long session using in-house staffers, you can "settle" for your asking rate by intoning the arrival of overtime and then lowering or dropping it on the condition the rate remains the original one you proposed. The client gets a favor, and the studio winds up billing a higher overall rate.

In general, most clients are apologetic about going overtime. They perceive it as a favor, and often try to be as accommodating as possible. A good studio manager will often negotiate an increased rate at the onset of overtime, or make some arrangement in which both parties acknowledge that overtime has begun and that fair compensation needs to be found, such as a higher rate or a concession that might include moving to another room to make way for the next booked client.

Each situation is unique and needs to be played with care and fairness. Remember that a good client relationship can last for years and that the soundest approach to a given situation is to consider your future relationship with that individual or group. Profits come most easily in the long run, not the short. So rather than looking for a quick buck, work to protect your long-term goals.

5. Booking "time on hold" is standard procedure.

Very often, clients will ask that a block of time be put on hold in the schedule book and promise to confirm the time after their own scheduling is complete.

Most studios agree to hold time until someone else calls with a firm booking. If someone else does call, inform the person that the time is on hold. Then call the original client and ask if he or she is able to confirm the time. If not, apologize and explain you need to give it to the new caller, while suggesting an alternate hold time.

It may take you a few minutes or an entire day to locate the original client who put the time on hold. But during that time, you should politely but firmly decline to confirm with the second caller until you reach the first, even if it's a great booking.

Explain that you promised to notify the first caller who has the time on hold before letting it go, that you're committed to taking the best possible care of each of your clients, and that you'd do the same for the second caller if it was she who had time on hold. Your clients will respect you for maintaining a high standard of ethics and will learn that they can count on you.

Conversely, it's fair to leave two or three

phone messages over an agreed-upon time period, and then to release the time to the second caller if the first doesn't return your call. Your clients need to be responsible too. I know of at least one world-class studio that gives its top-dollar clients one *hour* to confirm a hold when there's a live booking at stake. The studio staff informs clients that they expect to be able to contact them efficiently and gets an agreement up front. Since so many people wear beepers, it seems to be a reasonable policy, one that works especially well for the platinum class.

Standing Firm on Policy

Here's the printed policy that Interlok Studios' clients agree to. Bear in mind that Interlok is a multibay audio post facility that often accommodates three different sessions in each bay per day, so timing is of the essence. In music facilities, you may find a lot more leeway to accommodate telephone changes.

TIME ON HOLD

Client agrees to remain in close communication with the Facility when placing future session time on "hold." In the event another party attempts to book the Client's held time, Client agrees to respond to a telephone message from the Facility by 6 p.m. on the same day, if the message is left prior to 2 p.m., or by 12 noon the following day if the message is left after 2 p.m.

Facility may, at its discretion, cancel Client's time on hold if no response is forthcoming after leaving such messages at an agreed-to number, and make the time available to another party.

6. Client-owned 24-track reels should be dropped off at least two hours prior to session time for alignment and biasing.

If your client is going to be working on a tape that was recorded elsewhere, or is using a different brand or formulation than your house tape, it's going to require a partial or full alignment that may take from ten to 60 minutes.

It's the studio's responsibility to be ready on time and to not charge for re-alignment if the client drops the tape off early. If the client brings it at the start of the session, the studio is enti-

tled to charge the regular hourly rate while the alignment is being done.

This policy just makes sense: A responsible client gets an expected free service; an irresponsible one shouldn't be allowed to penalize the studio for lost billing time. As more equipment becomes auto-alignable, this rule may go the way of the buffalo, but as long as it takes an average of 30 to 45 minutes for a complete alignment, your clients need to understand that they must play by the rules.

7. Tapes left on the premises are done so at the risk of the client.

You can't assume full responsibility for the safekeeping of a priceless work of art—who can say how much it's worth, and who'll pay if it's lost in a fire? Of course, the chances are that your clients' tapes will be safer left in the studio's "vault" than being dragged back and forth, and that holding onto the tapes provides a considerable convenience for clients, not to mention a subtle psychological factor pulling them back.

But you need to protect yourself from an unlikely disaster. In this case, your best insurance (besides your paid-up commercial insurance policy) is a disclaimer at the bottom of your invoice absolving your business of responsibility if something happens.

A typical disclaimer states: "Materials and equipment left on the premises are the sole responsibility of their owner."

PROBLEMS & CONFLICTS IN SCHEDULING

Putting scheduling and traffic guidelines into the real world of running a studio is, of course, an entirely unpredictable challenge, and one that makes the business mighty interesting. It takes time to develop a feel for the unspoken messages your clients are sending you between their words. And it takes experience to develop a style that helps you adapt to the ever-changing level of stress that occurs from day to day.

One thing is certain: The traffic manager forms the crucial communication link between the client and the studio in between session bookings. So the job brings with it the responsibility of keeping the relationship between the two as healthy as possible. The traffic manager plays a major role in projecting the personality of the studio and the service it's offering. Teach a client that he can depend on being taken care of on the phone, and he will be that much more likely to keep coming back.

But the obstacles can be formidable. Even when professional clients are being responsible and playing by the rules, last-minute changes are inevitable. And they can wreak havoc on a schedule that looked as if five different dates were in perfect sync an hour before.

Booking time on hold carries the added weight of having to double back to the original caller every time another potential client calls in and wants the same time. And internally, staff engineers may wind up working wildly uneven shifts, with 18-hour days and odd morning off-hours leaving them exhausted and unhappy.

Some Rudimentary Juggling

Here's a simple challenge: The Fabulous Tyrodoctyles call up to book Tuesday from 12:00 noon to 4:00 p.m. They've been referred by another client who raved about your place and they want to try some overdubs in advance of a big project to see what the room feels like. They put a "firm hold" on the time, pending the confirmation by the drummer, who was last seen in the parking lot of the club the other night wandering off with a blonde and muttering about checking in later.

An hour later, Dweeb Productions calls to ask about availability on Tuesday from 2:00 to 8:00 p.m. They're a steady client, and they're always on time. The studio has done a lot of scheduling favors for them, moving other projects around so that they can be accommodated, and they've occasionally agreed to be moved to accommodate the studio.

The studio manager calls the Tyrodoctyles and asks about their hold time. Is there any room to slip back a couple of hours? Or perhaps change to that night, or another day? No way. This is the only time we can make it. We'll let you know as soon as we can confirm. Click.

Back to Dweeb. Any flexibility there? Not this time. Their client is flying in for the session, and it's the only time they can do it.

To the Fab T's two hours later: Any news? Nope. It just has to be this way or we'll find some other place that can take care of us.

Getting the Message

By now, something should be telling you that there's trouble ahead. Those "fabulous" musicians may have a big project in the works and it may be worth a good deal of time and money.

But they're unwilling to even *talk* about any kind of flexibility, in spite of the fact that they refuse to confirm their own booking. Right out of the box, they're being flaky and adamant at the same time.

Dweeb is a professional outfit (anybody with a name like that *has* to be). They're good people and a steady gig. They don't bring in as much work as this other project has to offer, but they're reliable and they act like they care about other humans. And if this is any indication, the Tyrodoctyles are going to push and pull the schedule on a regular basis without allowing for any give and take on their own part. That means frayed nerves at best, and at worst lost business from otherwise reliable clients who are trying to book time but are being bullied by this group of prima donnas.

However, it's still a good policy for a manager to never say 'no.' Perhaps the best way to handle a troublesome client like this is to politely insist that you can take care of them as long as they're willing to play fair and share the sandbox with the other kids. And in this case, they need to be taught that lesson right away.

That puts the ball in their court, where they can decide what to do next. And their decision will be the right one for the studio, whichever way they go.

A Workable Time-On-Hold Policy

A recording studio bases its income on the selling of time. With that in mind, one learns quickly that the concept of holding time is a two-edged sword. On the one hand, professionals need certain elements to come together before they can effectively use a recording studio for their work. The music has to be ready. The players must be available. The video has to be in some stage of completeness for lockup.

But the other side involves the risk of booking time on hold when other clients are ready with firm schedules. That's where things start heating up in the traffic office. Do we book the sure thing, or do we pray that the guys on hold are going to come through?

One eventually learns that, in terms of studio bookings, prayer is not the answer—responsibility is. And to that end, you must give some serious thought to fashioning a time-on-hold policy that will work for both you and your clients. It's either that, or get hung out to dry.

We've tried to be firm but reasonable with our policy at Interlok. And for the most part, our clients respect and understand the rule. The most important thing, of course is to make sure they know the rule exists. To that end, it's written in boldface on the contract that every client signs prior to their first session here. (See this chapter's "Scheduling Guidelines," point 5, for the text.)

The rule pretty well makes it clear that we'll honor our clients' needs if they honor ours. Otherwise, we'll do what we need to do in order to run a proper business.

Some people get very put out when they feel they deserve extra privileges because they've been longtime clients, or have run into a difficult situation. And we do everything we can to honor those relationships. But experience has taught us that we need to insist on professional behavior from the people who hold us hostage to their own time-on-hold schedules, however legitimate they may be. And that nearly all the time respect, however grudging, is the result of professional follow-through.

That's *Juggler*, not *Jugular*

Scheduling is an unpredictable job. You never know what kind of craziness may be lurking on the other side of the telephone line. No matter how prepared and organized you are, you can expect to play politician, psychologist and seat-of-the-pants policy-maker in one difficult to downright impossible situation after another.

The challenge and the frustration is in attempting to keep each client happy and to run a profitable business at the same time. And the truth is that sometimes there's just nothing you can do but make a judgment call, hope you don't alienate the wrong person, and look forward to getting into bed and pulling the covers up over your head.

Here's a true story that has repeated itself enough times in various incarnations to be called "typical."

TRYING TO PLEASE EVERYONE, ALL THE TIME: A RECURRING STORY

A couple of years after we started Interlok as a one-room operation, we were getting enough conflicting requests for bookings to decide that a second 24-track room would be a pretty reasonable gamble. We sank every available dollar we had into building a small but very pleasant and efficient room to work in, and agreed to switch to a diet of beans and bread crust until we pulled ourselves out of the financial dark.

Naturally, as soon as we completed the room, the demand for it completely subsided. Now we had two professional rooms, and for the most part, in spite of strong marketing and promotion, one sat silent for days on end. But the few days on which both rooms were filled were heady and exciting. And in anticipation of the increased business, we had begun soliciting resumes from first engineers for our on-call list and had been holding informal familiarization sessions with them.

One day, as we were discussing the very empty upcoming week, the phone rang with a full day's booking from a trailer production company that we'd worked hard to turn into a client. Call them "Acme." We'd done substantial business with them in the past at a very good rate, but they'd been unhappy with the amount of time it had taken to do a complicated project about a year ago and had decided to go elsewhere on subsequent dates.

Months later, I'd found out the reason they'd disappeared, and wooed them back with a promise of free time and a different approach to billing. We would bid the jobs as if they were complete, large packages and guarantee them a fixed price. Now they were back with us and beginning to book a lot of work with my partner and chief engineer, Mike.

"Bijou," a new film company with an ongoing TV series, was also a past client. The TV series producers had hired them to do just the "coming next week" trailers.

Bijou had been in once before and liked working with us. Now they were calling back to arrange a regular time to come in each week, a nice little 2-hour booking for the next 30 weeks. Bijou called 15 minutes after Acme and requested a booking for the same day with the same engineer (Mike) who'd taken such good care of them before.

"Cirrus" was an industrial film company. They too were fairly new clients, had completed a couple of good-sized sessions with us, had happily kissed their old facility goodbye, and were ours. All they wanted was to book 6 hours on the same day with the same great engineer they'd worked with in the past. Uh, that would be Mike, right?

Back to the Present

So here, in you-are-there format, is the problem: Acme needs 14 hours to cut and mix a trailer package, Bijou needs a mere 2 hours for its TV previews, and Cirrus needs 6-8 hours for a truly exciting sales industrial introducing a new low-induction plastic-tubing chemical compound.

All have killer deadlines, all are squeezed into a one-day window, and all want to work with Mr. "Once you work with him, you're gonna be spoiled for anybody else," Mike (the standard client pitch, but absolutely true).

We begin by calling each company. Is there any flexibility in your schedule? Would it be possible to do a portion of your session the day before or the day after the one you're requesting?

"Sorry, it's got to be that day at that time," says Bijou. "We called you first because our producer liked working with Mike so much. But if you can't give us that specific time, we'll have to go somewhere else."

"I appreciate your calling us first," I say. "And we can accommodate you in Studio 2 at the time you'd like, but Mike's already committed for the day. However, I have another first who's truly great, and who I know you'll enjoy working with."

"Well," sighs Bijou, "let me run that past the producer. He's out right now. I'll call you back in an hour."

Okay. Maybe that'll work. Let's wait before we go and shake anybody else's tree. But when the call comes through: "He's sorry, but he only feels comfortable there with Mike. If Mike can't do it, he'd rather go to the other studio we use and work with his other favorite engineer, Zazo."

Zazo? Great. I can't *give* Studio 2 away, and I'm being threatened with competition that sounds like some kind of foaming cleanser. It's time to call Acme.

Look Mom, I'm Dancin', I'm Dancin'!

"What do you mean, change days?!" snorts Acme. "I thought we had the day locked in. What, is somebody else more important than us?"

"Not at all," I smile, silently drowning. "But as you know, we're a very family-oriented studio, and we try to do everything we can to accommodate each of our clients when they're under pressure. And someone else is pleading for the same time, so I promised I'd give you a call to see if I could help them out." Trying to lay in a little guilt: "But the time is yours, and if you can't move, I'll work it out on their side."

"Hmm," says Acme, catching on. "Well, lemme check with the editor who's going to be

producing the session. But I'm pretty sure she has something else to do the next day, and I know she doesn't like splitting sessions in half, not to mention the deadline. I'll get back to you."

Terrific. So now I get to start aggravating the same people I've been courting for a month by trying to move their date after they've locked it in. I know Acme's editor, and she really *doesn't* like to split the day in half.

He calls back a few minutes later. "No go," he says in a somewhat annoyed tone, free of whatever short-term helpfulness had been there before. "She needs to get it done that day. So we're all set, right?"

"Definitely. Right."

That leaves Cirrus. We call and ask if they wouldn't mind starting at 8 a.m. instead of 10. No problem.

Fine—all I have to do is convince the engineer that 16 consecutive session hours are no problem for *him*. But he'll go for that. He knows that this stuff happens. And after all, he *is* the fabled Mike.

Solution Fantasies

Amongst ourselves, we discuss the time conflict with Acme and Bijou. They're both important clients, we're broke, it looks like an awful week, and I can't budge either of them. There's gotta be a way to make this work.

I flash on a great idea. Book them both in Studio 1 and 2 and start Acme with another engineer for the nuts-and-bolts half of the session. He'll type in the edit-list numbers, set up, and lay in some simple effects, while Mike starts Bijou at 10 a.m., finishes by 4, then takes over for the other engineer and does the lion's share of the job and the final mix.

This makes sense to me. It works perfectly in my best-of-all-worlds mind. I have successfully stepped out beyond the nine dots. I feel fine about this logical executive decision for about as long as it takes to talk the Studio 2 building contractor into waiting for another week to get the final check we owe him.

Fifteen minutes later, I realize I can't keep the switch a secret. I need to call Acme and tell them that we're going to start them with another engineer, but that we *will* be finishing with that flyin' finagler of the faders, Mike!

I realize that if I wait until the session and just spring this inspired bit of change on them, they may be more than a bit perturbed. I take a deep breath and dial the number, asking for my friend, the film editor. I cheerfully explain the plan to the same woman whom I'd laughed with through lunch on the company card earlier in the day. "Everything's gonna be all right. I've worked it out so that you'll be well taken care of," I say in my most fatherly tone.

For some unfathomable reason, there is no joy in her voice. "I'm sorry, but this really doesn't work for me," she says quietly. "I'm the kind of person who likes to know who I'm working with, and I know Mike."

I smile confidently through three paragraphs of hype-ridden reassurance. She listens, considers and reluctantly gives in. I hang up the phone with teeth gnashed. This is eating me alive, and I know it isn't even over yet.

I'm Melting, I'm Mellllllllllting!

After a few minutes, the manager at Acme calls. "What's this I hear about getting switched to your 'B list'?" he demands. "We're not important enough to get your best guy? How do I know we're not gonna get burned with this guy? What if he doesn't know the room and it winds up taking forever? My editor's upset, dammit."

"Look," I plead. "We bid your job for a fixed amount just so the time problem wouldn't come up. And the engineer I'm setting you up with is a great guy who has the room down cold."

I'm lying. The room's brand-new, and nobody but Mike has it really sussed. "If you really feel that you need to work with Mike the whole time, I'll get him for you, but I promise you're going to come out with the same product either way."

"Ohhh-ka-aay" he says in a sing-song, I'll-see-you-in-court tone, and hangs up.

Now I'm really coming unglued. I've got an important client whom I once lost and then spent months reeling back in, who's unhappy about a session that's still a week away. He's got half a dozen house editors who each pick the studios they want to work in, who are going to hear all about this, and I've just *lied* to the guy, which is something I *never* do (OK, *rarely*).

And if something *does* go wrong on the session, any little thing, people are going to point at me and yell, "See, we knew it!" I'm not handling this well, and there are some very dangerous vibes floating around in the Land of Lost Future Business.

Crawling Out of This Comic Strip

I realize that as badly as we need the few bookings that have come in for the week, Acme's business is the most important part of the puzzle. And I am sure that my editor friend is going to anticipate her session with doom for the entire week leading up to it and discuss her feelings with anyone who'll listen.

It's time to be cool. And smart, if that's still possible. I walk into my office, bang the desk out of frustration, hurt my hand and call Acme back. "I've got good news," I proclaim cheerfully. "The other company rebooked for the following day, so I can get you Mike for the entire session! I'm sorry for all the hassle. Sometimes it gets a little out of control when you're trying to satisfy several people at once."

"Hey, that's great!" he says, smiling through the phone. "I knew you could do it. My editor looked like she was gonna worry about this all week." So my intuition was right about her. I just wish that I'd been smarter about it from the start.

Of course, I've lied again. Bijou hasn't moved their session at all. I've only said this so that Acme won't be left with any guilty feelings about forcing us to do it their way and blowing off other business (which could lead to more negative feelings about working with us in the future).

I call Bijou and tell them we can't squeeze them in. "Well," they intone wistfully, "maybe next time," and hang up to book their former studio with their old pal, Zazo.

I'm left with Studio 1 booked for 14 hours while Studio 2 sits eerily still, like some spaghetti-western ghost town, the wind softly moaning as an occasional tumbleweed blows through.

I keep reassuring myself that Acme's account and future business is worth it.

I hope.

THE SCHEDULE BOOK

We call it the booking book. Some people call it the Bible. Whatever name you give it, it's the book that most strongly controls your life in the studio. And anything that important needs some rules and guidelines of its own.

First off, there are any number of configurations to a scheduling book. Many studios opt for ease and convenience, purchasing a daily or weekly appointment book of the stationery-store variety.

We used this type for quite a while. If you buy one that displays a full week on two facing pages, you can quickly see what kind of shape you're in at a glance. The only problem with weekly books is that no one seems to have anticipated the studios' need for a large format with extra space for appropriate booking information. Just think of the money a printing company could make on a special format like that! (Well, maybe not.)

There are larger books, but most are called "professional appointment" books and are intended for use in doctors' offices. They offer lots of room but are usually set up with one day per page, with each page carved into 15-minute intervals between the hours of 8:00 a.m. and 6:00 p.m. Not exactly a comprehensive studio outlook.

Some studios forgo a book completely and work from a large easel-sized marking board or sheet of paper. Sometimes it's hung on the wall (which is hard to work on), and sometimes it lives on a desk or a special slanted table with a sheet of weekly pages that can be thumbed through.

We're getting into the custom stuff now, which is where one seems to inevitably drift when one is in need of a special solution. All of the above methods work, but if you want it to work just right, consider designing a form for yourself. In this case, all that means is whipping out a pencil and ruler or sitting down with a computer page layout program. Let an hour or two bring out the design genius in you, and you'll find yourself making multiple erasures in your very own made-to-order scheduling book

before you can say "Whaddayamean, cancel that orchestra?"

Here are a few guidelines that will help keep peace in your trafficking:

1. Always write in pencil. Murphy's Law states that any time a booking is written in pen, the start time will change at least twice. Then there are all the other people who try to sneak in for an hour, change the talent around at the last minute, etc. Keep lots of erasers on hand. Invest in electric sharpeners. Pens are the enemy.

2. Leave the scheduling duties to one person. It's much less confusing when one person is handling incoming calls. He or she may be waiting for one call from someone before writing in another session that depends on that call. Everybody develops their own sense of this, which means that someone else who walks in and takes over is at least going to need some briefing. Then there's the idea of getting used to the scrawl that's supposed to be legible, handwriting being the personal signature that it is.

Obviously, a booking that comes in when the regular person isn't around has to be handled. But you'll cut way down on the confusion if they are the one who gets briefed the next day, instead of the other way around. It's not going too far to even say, "Let me take the

This custom design is 8-1/2" x 14" and is mounted in an accounting binder. The traffic manager prints out a month's pages in advance, keeping the template on file in the computer and altering the dates. House engineers' initials provide a quick reference for their daily report times and studio assignments. Note that Studio 3, an edit room, requires less space for planning.

Monday, July 11, 1994

Studio 1	Studio 2	Studio 3	Studio 4	Studio 5	ENG IN STUDIO
					JS
					JH
					VC
					TC
					KN
					JR
					VG
					PN
					JB
					AC

Tuesday, July 12, 1994

Studio 1	Studio 2	Studio 3	Studio 4	Studio 5	ENG IN STUDIO
					JS
					JH
					VC
					TC
					KN
					JR
					VG
					PN
					JB
					AC

information down now and have our traffic person get back to confirm with you after lunch."

Multiperson booking free-for-alls create a sloppy book that can become confusing, unreadable and potentially disastrous. You'll also avoid an inordinate number of arguments and help maintain a far more peaceful atmosphere by making that one special person the Book Czar. One person, one brain.

3.   Keep the book in one place. A simple rule, right? It's midnight and a regular client calls in with a couple of schedule changes while you, the engineer, are virtually alone in the middle of a mix. You run and grab the book, bring it back to the control room, make the changes and keep mixing.

The next morning, the traffic manager calmly walks in and begins to slowly squeeze his fingers around your neck until you begin to realize that he is in fact trying to kill you, because he spent 20 minutes frantically trying to find the book when the first call of the day came in—five minutes after you left, at 8:30 a.m.

Better to sit at his desk next time, play with the schedule and then go back to work. But here's a tip for non-perfectionists: Make the cover of the book a bright color (like neon pink) for the times that you forget, so that it can be spotted from across the room.

4.   Agree on language and abbreviations to be used. Use these same notations all the time—you may even want to include a key (a written explanation of all signs and abbreviations) in the front of the book. Take a lunch meeting with the staff and figure how best to state the items you want to include.

This may be as simple as agreeing that the book will only show the client name and booking time, and the rest of the information will be recorded on the work order. Or that a double check-mark means the booking is firm (or the word "firm" means firm). Once you figure out your system, everyone will know how it works.

5.   Write legibly. Nah, too dumb a rule. Never mind.

Never Saying "No" to a Client

With policy firmly in hand, Susan Skaggs has built a reputation on letting her clients know that no matter what the circumstances, they can count on her to get the job done.

Career Roots Started working for an investment company, enrolled in a recording class, then got a job in administration at Wally Heider Studios. Went into partnership with the chief engineer at Different Fur and financed the purchase of the business in a private deal for part cash and part continuing studio time with the owner, guitarist Pat Gleason.

Facility One studio, with SSL 4056 E/G Series console, two 24-track Studer analog decks. Studio: 25' x 35'; Control room: 17' x 21'. The studio name came from a poem, in which 'different fur' refers to something out of the ordinary.

House Staff One managerial assistant who doubles as receptionist and PR/marketing/A&R consultant. Three on-call seconds. Chief engineer/partner. One upstairs tenant who runs a separate MIDI room.

Primary Focus Music for records, film and TV, as well as artist management.

Notable Artists Stevie Wonder, Faith No More, The Whispers, George Winston, Bobby McFerrin and Starship.

Rates Variable. "If you start out on a hard line, and you're negotiating from the first moment, you're already in an adversarial position with your client. I try to determine what his particular needs are and then design a schedule and budget to fit those needs. One of the things I've been successful at is clearing my mind of the competitive aspect, and just concentrating on how to make the best possible deal.

"Every time I talk to anyone and quote a rate, even if it's a one-second conversation, I have a book in which I write their name and any other information I get from the conversation. I quote so many different rates, based on trying to fit their particular budget, that it's a great help to refer to this."

Different Fur's live room

Marketing By reputation, press release, direct mail and telephone.

Embracing ADAT "Many of our clients now like to come in here to overdub to their home ADAT tapes, or to mix down. So we're now adding our own ADAT decks to make it easier for them. As far as it affecting us ratewise, I still ask people where they are in their budget and try to figure out a way that they can work here."

Booking Policy "The one thing I learned from the start was never to say 'no' to a booking. If you look in the book and you see three firm bookings and then someone calls and wants the same time, don't say 'no, it's booked.' I've always followed that."

"The first time I did that was back at Wally Heider's. We got a call for a 20-voice Samoan choir, and I booked them into the smallest room. When the senior manager found out what I'd done and explained the size of your basic Samoan, I panicked. But by the time of the session, the whole book had changed, and we were able to move them into a much larger room. Bookings really flow in and out, like the tide. Of course, we had the advantage of having four rooms to play with.

"Nowadays, I just have one room to book, but I follow the same policy. I may have a date completely booked. When that happens, I first say that I'm holding that date for a client and ask them if they can work on an alternate date. If there isn't, I still give them hope.

"I try to find a way by methodically talking to everyone about the potential for moving around, asking them if another day would suit them as well. By taking some extra time, you can usually accommodate all bookings that come in. If all else fails, I'll recommend and personally book them into another facility that meets their needs. That kind of good will always comes back to you in the end.

"I'm also booking for another studio in town from my office here. We get a commission on each project I book there."

Philosophy "You can spend thousands of dollars in advertising, but you can never take back the damage caused by one person having a bad experience in your studio.

"Never say no. Never take no for an answer."

BOOKING AND WORK ORDERS

Once the phone rings with a booking, it's necessary to write down the details of the session, and using a printed form called a *booking order* is a good way to cover all the bases.

First, you need information that includes your client's name, address, phone number, and P.O. number if applicable. Then you'll want to know what kind of session is being planned—is it a live date, an overdub, or a mix? Is there any setup involved? What kind of tape will be used—yours or theirs? Will there be vocals? Is there picture? Are the formats compatible? Do you have to rent any special equipment? Who's going to engineer? Why am I here? What is the meaning of life? Dammit, Jim, I'm a *doctor,* not a miracle worker!

There are lots of questions, but they're necessary ones, and they also give you a chance to get a little more intimate with your client, to show that you're on the ball and that you care. And they also make sure that you'll be ready to deliver the needed goods.

Cutting Down on Confusion

The method that we developed at Interlok was to print the booking order on the other side of the *work order*. This has reduced the amount of loose paper around the studio by 50% and simplified long-term record-keeping.

Once the booking order is filled out, the session engineer is free to look it over at his or her leisure. Just prior to the session, the studio manager puts the work order on the engineer's desk in the control room. That way, the engineer has all the information about the upcoming session close by for reference. Then, during the session, the second flips it over to start filling in the work order.

The Importance of the Work Order

The work order is a summary of the work done in the session. It serves a few essential purposes. First, it specifies exactly what was done in how much time and is later used as a summary sheet when the invoice is written. Second, it is a signed contract between the client and the studio that says the two are in agreement on what was done. And third, it is a detailed permanent record that can be referred to when reviewing how a project has shaped up, or when a client needs a detailed breakdown of

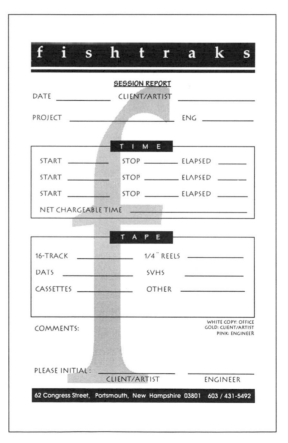

Surreal Studios, in Anchorage, Alaska, incorporates a track sheet, DiskMix, EQ settings and session log into a unique, stylized 8-1/2"x11" sheet.

Fishtraks calls their work order a Session Report and keeps it simple.

paid time to justify expenses.

It's imperative that the work order is signed at the session's end. By signing the work order, your client agrees that the work was done and accepts responsibility for payment. Without a signature, it's your word against your client's that they owe you money. A signed work order is proof that the multitrack god is on your side.

A work order should include space for the

Interlok's booking and
work orders

INTERLOK
1550 Crossroads of the World Hollywood, CA 90028 213/469-3986

Booking Order

Session Date

Time   Studio

Client

Billing Address

Project

Contact Person & Phone

Producer/Supervisor

Format	Transfers
Client's existing format:	From: To:
Laydown:	Time Code: Reshape ☐ Drop ☐ Non-Drop ☐
Layback:	Address Track ☐ Window ☐
Length of show/s:	Start Time : :
	Noise Reduction: Dolby SR ☐ Dolby A ☐ None ☐

Talent	Track Assignments
Voiceover: Sync ☐ Wild ☐	
To:	
Time:	

Tape	Buy	Rent	Client Stored	Client Bringing	Video	Buy	Client Stored	Client Bringing
2" 24 trk analog	☐	☐	☐	☐	D2	☐	☐	☐
1/2" 24 trk digital	☐	☐	☐	☐	1"	☐	☐	☐
1/2" 4 trk	☐	☐	☐	☐	Beta SP	☐	☐	☐
1/4" 2 trk	☐	☐	☐	☐	3/4"	☐	☐	☐
Analog Cassette	☐	☐	☐	☐	VHS	☐	☐	☐
DAT Cassette	☐	☐	☐	☐				

Notes

INTERLOK
1550 Crossroads of the World Hollywood, CA 90028 213/469-3986

Work Order

Date   Time

Job #

Engineers

1 Client

3 Titles/Show #

PO#   2 Studio

4 Studio Time					Tape
	from	to	=	@	5 Rental 24 Tk Stock: None ☐
	from	to	=	@	Serial No. Analog ☐ Digital ☐
	from	to	=	@	6 Purchased Stock: None ☐
	from	to	=	@	Serial No. Description Stored
	from	to	=	@	/ Y ☐ N ☐
	from	to	=	@	/ Y ☐ N ☐
	from	to	=	@	/ Y ☐ N ☐
	from	to	=	@	/ Y ☐ N ☐
Totals					/ Y ☐ N ☐

7 Session Log

8 Client / Re-use Stock: None ☐
Serial No. Description   Stored
/   Y ☐ N ☐

9 Rentals / Misc. Charges
Extra Machine: Yes ☐ No ☐
Type:
# of Hours used:
Type:
# of Hours used:
Other:

Signator is authorized to sign for charges billed and agrees the above information
is accurate. Interlok will endeavor to secure materials or personal property left on
the premises, but is not responsible for any damage, loss or theft.

10 Signature

Date

---

client and session name, time worked, tape used, rentals, general session notes and any special services rendered. It's normally the task of the second to write up the work order and make sure the client signs it before departing.

You may need to ask your client to stay an extra moment or two while the final entries are being made, but it's important to teach them that their signature is part of the required routine. Even if you are paid at the end of the session, get a signature. It's indisputable proof of payment and good for record-keeping.

Designing Your Own

To the left are the booking and work orders that have evolved here at Interlok. Each is about the fifth revision—as time passed and things changed, we wanted to change and update the forms we used.

If your forms are computer-generated, keep them on a disk, so that changing them is as simple as starting with what you have and then taking it from there. An 8-1/2" x 11" format makes it a snap to run off a couple hundred copies at the local copy center.

We do ours on light blue paper. As with the pink scheduling book, the color stands out and makes the page easy to spot in the control room. We hole-punch the sheets and neatly arrange them in a looseleaf binder after use.

INTERNAL SCHEDULING

The other half of a smooth operation is making sure the machine runs well from the inside. Pulling that off is often as challenging for the studio manager as juggling the last-minute panic calls of your most quixotic client.

The Scheduling Board

The best way to get a good picture of who's on first is to hang a large erasable marking-pen board on the wall. Stationery stores sell them in different sizes, along with spools of pencil-thin lining tape, which you can use to custom-create a permanent week-long box graph with spaces to write in the daily hours of each staff member.

Using a wall board allows you to glance up at it while you're working on a cluttered desk, or when you have the schedule book open. It's also important that staff members have easy visual access. When everyone knows where the board is, there's no time wasted in asking or looking for the schedule. Engineers can take a quick glance at the board and then efficiently get right down to the task of arguing with you about how unfair their schedule is this week.

Playing Solomon

A good way to avoid arguments is to set up your weekly schedule while as many staff people as possible are in the room. Also, have individual discussions with each person to figure out what days and times are the easiest and most difficult for them to work. As you go through each day of the coming week, the staff can actively participate in working out their own hours according to their individual outside commitments. It's true that as the days go by, the schedule will probably be transformed several times, but at least there'll be some basic agreement to start from.

When the schedule does change, consult the people whose hours will be altered. They'll usually be better at working the changes out between themselves than being forced into abrupt turnarounds. At least, that's the way to play fairly.

But when disagreements become heated, fingers start getting pointed and accusations start to fly, it's time to take back the control stick. It's the studio manager's job to set the final schedule, and there will be times when those decisions won't be popular.

Try to keep the lines of communication open and have meetings with your staff to discuss methods that will cause the least amount of resistance. But be sure that everyone understands that the work has to get done and that the manager has the final word.

One way to make an unwanted order more palatable is to promise extra consideration next time, or to rotate the unfavorable dates from one person to another. Play fairly but firmly, and you'll at least generate grudging respect.

PLANNING FOR A MARATHON SESSION

Marathons usually occur when there's a deadline that has to be met and there hasn't been enough work done to meet it in a civilized fashion.

The record company is insisting on a dance mix of the original single and has promised to ship it in 24 hours. The TV special was held up in editing pending the outcome of the final scenes shot the day before. The talent got the flu and is a week late coming in. Or the thing just won't get itself finished because the groove wandered off to the 7-Eleven last night and hasn't been heard from since.

This is the land of loony-tunes—something happens to people when they reach the 12th or 18th hour of a session that won't end. You never know what to expect. Waves of personality changes come and go. Somebody gets giddy and starts a giggle binge. The producer gets emotionally frazzled about something, and the whole vibe in the room turns black. You break for a meal, and the room goes comatose for two hours while stomachs deal with 4:00 a.m.

Different Fur adopts the open-space-for-whatever approach.

Platinum Island combines work order and invoice into one super-informative page. Note the detailed breakdown of service charges and spaces for long-distance calls and food delivery.

pepperoni pizza. Worst of all, somebody walks in fresh from the outside, takes one listen to the work at hand and says, "Are you guys kidding, or what?"

Planning Intelligently

It's important for a manager to know who's capable of what stamina on the engineering staff. If you have a seasoned pro who's got the grit to go the whole distance (no chemical cheating, please), then it's your job to make sure his assistants are going to back him with vigor. You'll need to relieve your seconds for optimum performance. While the first engineer is constantly on, the second is probably going to be waiting around quite a bit, making sleep a constant danger.

If your first is something less than Superman, plan in advance with both engineer and client how and when the switchover will occur. Maybe the first shift will do the vocal overdubs and the next will start in with the vocal combines. Use the replacement engineer's "fresh ears" as a selling point. Twelve hours later, the original first can come back rested for the final mix.

Welcome to Our Home

During a marathon, your clients are going to be living in your building for an extended period. Are you ready for that? At Interlok, the one thing we insisted on when we added more space to our facility was a small shower room just for these occasions. When sleep isn't an option, there's nothing like washing a day's work off so you can move on to the next one.

But aside from major plumbing, it's wise to keep a few items on hand. A couple of airline-type blankets will give comfort to the clients who can't stay awake all night (and who don't need to). Some packaged cereal or oatmeal will keep for months at a time and is a nice substi-

tute for breakfast when you're rummaging around for a pick-me-up at sunrise. If you've got a vending machine, have a heart and stock it with a few healthy alternatives to the Snickers bars and salted peanuts. And by all means, take a detailed look around your neighborhood and assemble a book of take-out and all-night restaurants that are convenient or that deliver.

Finally, be sensible. Know when the session has reached a point of diminishing (or invisible) returns. It doesn't make much sense to go on if everyone is too exhausted to realize they need to leave the building for a while. Extra billing time aside, your clients and your staff may appreciate your fresh managerial face walking in at 10:00 a.m. and suggesting that everyone take an 8-hour break.

In terms of billing, lean toward your client's side when you're adding up the hours. It's rare that a client plans for or can afford a marathon, and a compromise will bring future loyalty and work. Round a 40-minute dinner break to an hour, and if the staff had some problems, be generous with non-billable time. There'll still be plenty of extra money in the end.

Taking Care of Your Ears

One important and classic caveat is to keep the overall monitor level at a moderate-to-low volume. High decibel levels are highly fatiguing over long periods and invariably mask the true

This type of wall board is easy to see and wipes clean in seconds.

nature of the average listening level. Any good producer knows that in order to approximate the listening levels of the average living room, you need to simulate the relative volume most people turn to. By nature, that's a comfort level that allows people to do other activities while listening, and doesn't wear them out in the process. Sure, there's a proper time to set the knob on "stun," but those times should be the icing on the cake, not a normal operating level. Stick to the near-field mini's, and you're more likely to be able to look at one another at 6:00 a.m. without hypno-spirals whirling around in your eyes.

The other factor, of course, is the amount of physical damage one can do to one's eardrums with loud music. They just aren't made to withstand the level of a jet fighter at takeoff for more than a few moments. So be farsighted in your thinking. If you're the type that is used to high-level dosages, consider the health of the other people in the room as well as your own. Try turning down to 5 and see what it's like for a few sessions. It's a good bet that your whole perception of the music will change, from the amount of work you feel like you're doing to the quality of the product.

But the strongest argument may come from the business side. Your client, the one who's basically paying you to go out and buy cool equipment for the rest of your life, is going to be far more comfortable in a room where the sound levels are not oppressive.

Okay, you say, but what about block bookings where the producer either brings in their own engineer or insists on keeping the listening range at concert levels? Well, that's another thing entirely. You can't really insist that the level be turned down, so the best advice is probably to get the heck out of the room. However, if one of your staff engineers is on the date and complains to you about the ringing in his ears, you owe it to him to approach the producer and calmly discuss the problem. If the producer remains intractable, then you should give the engineer the option of removing himself from the project. Anything less is at the very least uncaring and insensitive, and at worst is a personal-injury lawsuit or workers-comp claim in the making.

PROJECTS FROM MARS

It's only happened three or four times in our history. But there have been people and projects that were so difficult to deal with that in spite of their money, clout or potential for future income, we've opted to fire *them*.

One recent learning experience involved a freelance engineer who made his living recording Foley for TV series. Foley is the live recording of sound effects to picture and is one of the few remaining "ancient" arts that's unlikely to disappear in the foreseeable future: You just can't get every human nuance neatly packed onto a sampler's hard drive and key it up with any sense of believability, at least for anything beyond the cartoon genre.

Anyway, Blaine had been doing this sort of thing for several years when he came to us with a very attractive package. He had a network dramatic series with a full year's commitment and needed a good Foley stage to work on 20 nights a month. He worked with his own Foley walkers (the artists who create the live effects) and would do the engineering himself. All he needed from us was a receptionist and an assistant to get him started each night. After that, as far as he was concerned, we could all leave. He'd lock up at night and pay a fair hourly rate within ten days of billing.

This sounded like a dream client to us. We were looking at the next eight months of second-shift billing at maybe $20K per month, and the guy didn't even need an engineer!

But things started to go wrong, fast. First, we needed to extensively modify the stage to his personal satisfaction. That meant digging new pits (holes in the floor, about 3' x 4', to be filled with various materials like dirt or rocks to re-create the surfaces actors walk on in the picture), adding storage space, and moving other equipment that we regularly used out of the way. Second, he insisted on using some special and somewhat arcane pieces of electronic equipment. These were devices that he was used to and worked best with, but which were only available through one source and were very expensive. Our total outlay for everything was going to be about $15,000, up front.

Fair enough, we thought. We'll improve the studio and gain some nifty equipment.

Getting Down to Business

We completed the improvements and the bookings started, but we also began to run into some really difficult problems. First, our studio was doing double duty: During the day it was a sweetening and mixing room; at night, it was a Foley stage. That meant that the whole place had to be torn down and set up again in time for a 6:00 p.m. start each night. However, most of our daytime clients were used to booking the studio and going overtime when they needed to—they'd gladly pay the extra charges, just as long as they got their work done. Now we had to kick them out at 5:30 to madly change the room over in time. And about every other day, I'd get a worried call from the traffic office informing me that it looked like they were going to go over and we'd have to bump the day client into another room. (When we had a room to bump them into, that is.)

The clients had no intention of moving their whole operation for the last hour of work and made that assertion very clear to us. They expected to be treated just as professionally as the next guy, especially when they'd been in all day.

Our solution was to book sessions that would end earlier, at 5:00 p.m., so that there'd be enough time for them to go a bit over without incurring any problems. When that didn't work, we tried 4:30. But now the out time was getting way too early for the amount of work our regular daytimers needed to do. And we were starting to lose substantial money from the extra time the studio stood vacant during the changeover.

Meanwhile, Blaine had begun to make numerous requests and criticisms about our preparation. He insisted, and rightly so, that the studio be swept clean to the walls, so that each night he'd walk into a pristine room that was ready to be trashed by his people, as they moved props ranging from fish tanks to car doors around and tramped up dust-storms of dirt and grit. This was all legitimate Foley work, and to be expected.

At the same time, a major equipment problem had emerged. We'd bought him a SMPTE controller that locked the tape and video machines together, but it turned out not to like the electronic chain we placed it in. This was a piece of equipment that we didn't want to use during the day, because it didn't do the things our engineers were used to, so we'd disconnect our normal keypad and hook this one up. This would work fine for a while, but about 15 minutes after the tech went home for the night, it would freeze up and raspberry the session. This happened maybe eight times.

This made everybody, including Blaine, crazy. On top of that, in spite of our best efforts, we were batting no better than .500 in motivating our daytime clients to get the heck out of the room on time for the nighttime changeover. Which meant that Blaine was getting started

half an hour to an hour late, while his highly paid Foley crew watched TV and ate pizza in the lounge.

We offered to pay the talent for the lost time, which was extremely costly, but that didn't solve the related problem: This was their second full working shift of the day. Blaine was less concerned with the cost, however substantial, than he was with the end of the night, when his talent would start to crash from sheer exhaustion. The deal was that they'd start at 6:00 p.m. and get out by 1:00 a.m.; any longer than that and they'd lose their sense of humor and work effectiveness very quickly.

Damage Control Becomes Business as Usual

Naturally, no one stood still during all of this. We went through a period of daily 30- to 60-minute meetings, trying to figure out what was going wrong, no sooner plugging one leak than watching another spurt up. Blaine had long since lost his sense of humor and was becoming positively adversarial, despite his knowledge of our continuous efforts.

To make matters worse, he revealed a Jason-like attitude toward our traffic manager. He'd refuse to discuss anything until 5:00 p.m. the day of the session, insisting he was off before then, wouldn't return phone calls and began accusing the office of *sabotaging* his sessions. He'd say, "I've never been treated so unprofessionally in my life. Who taught you how to book time?" And Shelly's favorite: "Wait till I tell your boss that you're the one who's going to be responsible for blowing this entire account because of your amateur behavior!"

That was enough to completely alienate him not only from the traffic office, which was his lifeline to the studio, but from all of us. Granted, there was no question that we'd run into one difficult problem after another. But each time, we'd compensated him with gratis time and talent payments. We'd spent time sitting in, bringing in pros to try and figure out why the lockup system had problems and had finally solved them, and had maintained the highest form of interaction we possibly could short of sitting in every evening.

But Blaine had nonetheless become the enemy, and a bitter one at that. And in spite of the hefty billing his account promised, he was offending our staff and indirectly causing us to drive our other happy clients wacko with continuous daytime scheduling problems. We finally realized that it was either us or him, cried over the lost revenue and invited him to book his project elsewhere. It was a wrenching decision.

And then a funny thing happened. We snapped back into being an efficient multiroom facility with happy clients and a humming staff. Daytime mix sessions went into the mid-evening and replaced a fair portion of the lost second-shift revenue. And everybody got some well-deserved sleep.

In retrospect, we certainly shared the blame for all the problems that had occurred. But unfortunately, our client had given up on us before we'd given up trying to make things right. And it was at that point that we knew that the old maxim "The customer is always right" no longer fit. What was true was that the customer is always the *customer*, and nothing more. Without his continuing effort alongside of ours, the situation was lost.

12
Keeping Track of Things

Tapes, videos, log books and edit lists tend to flow in and out of the studio at a regular clip, which depends on how busy the schedule is and what sort of work you're doing, and your clients will expect you to take reasonable care of the materials they leave with you.

For example, if the tapes for a record session were originally cut in another studio, you need to know the brand, bias and alignment, so that your machines will be properly aligned before the start of the session. That means someone, usually the artist or the producer, will be dropping the tapes off a few hours or days earlier. In the case of audio post, the tapes may arrive before the client by messenger from another location, such as the video online studio or editing facility. They may also be picked up by a service after the session is complete.

When this happens, your client should notify you that they are sending someone who is authorized to handle the materials. If there's any doubt, a phone call is the easiest way to clear up any confusion about who the person at the door really is.

The best way to keep track of the coming and going of materials is with a simple tape log book. Ours is printed on 8-1/2" x 11", 2-sheet NCR (carbonless) paper. The forms are hole-punched and kept in a permanent looseleaf record book. When a tape is dropped off at our studio, the receptionist fills out a blank form, signs it and tears off the copy underneath to give to the person who dropped off the tapes. That leaves them with a receipt, which gives the client a little peace of mind. It also provides us with a record of exactly what we accepted.

Then, when the tapes are shipped out of the studio, the person walking out with them signs the right side of the form, indicating that he has everything that was originally left with us. It's not necessary to give him a receipt. The client now has his tapes back, and we have a permanent record of the whole story.

THE TAPE VAULT

The term "vault" originally came from the old film-studio libraries, which really were bank-type vaults. Nowadays, "library" is used just as often, though some of the older recording facilities still do have 500-pound doors that open into lead-lined storage rooms.

You can get pretty much the same effect with a locking steel office-supply closet, which is useful for client tapes in current use. But any studio that's been in business for a while quickly builds up a need for a room (or at least an expanse of wall) to act as a storage facility. One way to maximize the use of space is to build floor-to-ceiling shelves against three of the walls and use the fourth as the corner for a simple shop bench or storage area. That way, until you have so many tapes that you need to start building aisles, you create a multipurpose room that's fully utilized. (Just don't turn on any bulk erasers while you're sitting at the shop bench.)

As you grow, you may find that you need more space for your library. You may have many clients who record with you on a regular basis and expect you to store their tapes on the premises. They'll also assume that you'll keep their tapes safe from loss and damage. These are reasonable expectations, but they can also cause devastating results if you don't protect yourself. There are three ways to do that.

Protecting Your Rolls

The first way is to include a disclaimer on your work orders and tape storage forms that says something like, "We are not responsible for materials left on the premises. Signator hereby releases studio from any and all future claims."

With that disclaimer on the work order, along with the client's normal signature at the end of the session, you should be able to sleep peacefully. You don't have to write a book's worth of conditions and considerations; the courts tend to interpret "layman's languaging" of legalese in the spirit that it was written, which means as a layman would understand it. So that one simple sentence should go a long way in stating your intent.

Nevertheless, as a business offering professional services, you are expected to take professional care of the tools and materials of your trade. So the second way you should protect yourself is by making the tape library reasonably secure. Using a separate room means that you can put a lock on the door. That's enough to stop any casual individual from wandering down the hall and into a room where he doesn't belong.

A reasonable lock should also protect you from a client who wants to spirit his tapes out of the building before the bill is paid, or before you've agreed to let them go. Just remember to turn the latch each time you leave the room. Our main "vault" is a small room we built within an office, so that it could be lined from floor to ceiling on both sides with a narrow walkway in the middle. It's got its own door with a special combination push-button lock, so that staff members don't have to fumble for keys when their arms are full. They just give the mechanism a couple of jabs and they're in. The door closes and relocks itself on exit. Everyone understands the combination is something to be protected, and so far, no bodies have been discovered inside.

Finally, missing or damaged tapes are another excellent reason why you should have a solid commercial insurance policy in place, just in case something goes wrong with points one and two. For more on that, see the insurance section in Chapter 6 (p. 65).

There are also studios that spell out their policies in the "Terms and Conditions" section of the contracts that clients sign. This is good policy, because it makes the terms explicit. Criteria Studios in Miami includes these paragraphs in its paperwork:

"Criteria shall not be liable for loss or damage to client's tape, instruments or personal property stored in the studio. We advise our clients to obtain proper insurance against these risks.

"Criteria will store Masters or Safeties in the building for one year after completion of the record. This is without charge or assumption of any liability for damage or loss, and at your option. Upon release of the record, all outtakes or roughs must be recovered, or will be destroyed at Criteria's option. It is the responsibility of the client to acquire the appropriate insurance for tapes left in Criteria's library, and for property left in storage. All shipping charges will be assumed by the client. No tapes or disks will be released without payment in full."

That sounds like the kind of policy that must have evolved over years of experience!

Maintaining Order

You need to devise a system to keep a few hundred tapes in order so that you can find them when you need to. The simplest and easiest way is to arrange them alphabetically, by client. Anticipate the addition of more tapes in each section so that you don't have to rearrange a whole wall when two new boxes of 2-inch are added to the Major Migraine Productions space.

An effective method we've devised at

This tape log provides a quick and easy point-of-delivery record-keeping system.

Material In/Out Log

Client

Address

_____

_____

Phone

_____

Project

Description of Materials

_____

_____

_____

IN	OUT		
Quantity _____ 2" Audio Tape		Quantity _____ 1" Video Tape	
Quantity _____ 1/2" Audio Tape		Quantity _____ D2 Video Tape	
Quantity _____ 1/4" Audio Tape		Quantity _____ Beta Video Tape	
Quantity _____ Audio Cassette		Quantity _____ 3/4" Video Tape	
Quantity _____ DAT		Quantity _____ 1/2" Video Tape	
		Quantity _____ Other (See Above)	

Date/ Time   Name

Signature

All materials left on the premises are stored at the client's risk.
Signator hereby releases Interlok from any and all future claims.

1550 Crossroads of the World   Hollywood, California 90028   213/469-3986

Interlok is to subdivide client tapes when the same client is doing more than one project. We simply use different-colored highlighters to indicate which projects go together by putting a colored stripe on the spine of each box. Each color represents one unified project or show.

We also maintain an "in use" space or shelf for projects that are currently in process at the complex. This section is in the spot that is easiest to get to, and doubles as a parking spot for tapes that have yet to be coded or vaulted. But you need to be vigilant, or the space quickly piles up with a jumble of unfiled items.

Some studios use a numbering system and log book to keep track of the coming and going of each tape; others set up databases on their house computers. Some even set up rows of private metal lockers, give one to each of their clients, and let *them* deal with the whole problem. But the best solution is to keep things as simple and orderly as possible.

One challenge that's arisen in recent years has been devising a good storage system for DAT masters. The paradox is that the seemingly minuscule size of the medium implies ease of

storage, yet the reality is that it's nearly impossible to get any pertinent information on the 1/2" x 3" spine.

About all you can fit on that small a piece of real estate is a title or a company name. We've opted to place each separate DAT in its case in an 8-1/2" x 11" manila envelope, with full details on the front of the envelope. That also provides a storage space for track and take sheets, as well as creating a package that's much less likely to get shuffled aside by mistake.

NUMBERING SYSTEMS

Some people swear by them; others simply don't see the need. But wait—they're both right! Basically, a numbering system works if you need one, and that's up to you to determine.

The purpose of such a system is to help keep better track of the paperwork and tape piles at the studio. Some items require consecutive numbering, like invoices. That's easy: All you have to do is to remember to tell your printer to be sure and number the invoices when the job is printed.

It doesn't matter what number you start with—you can choose 001 or 1001 or 45273 as a starting point. Choosing a four-digit number makes you look like you do a lot of invoices, so maybe that's a good place to start. As long as they're numbered consecutively, you'll have a simple way of keeping your invoices in chronological order.

You can do the same thing with work orders. Choose any starting number, and then have them printed consecutively with the printing order. There's usually a very minimal charge for numbering.

Job Numbers

Consecutive numbering will give you some rudimentary help in keeping your papers in order. But a coded system can add a lot more useful features. The purpose of a job number is to display the most information in the smallest possible space. For example, the number 53-940944-2AT is packed with references that everyone on our staff can read at a glance:

53 is the number assigned to the client, which is stored in a separate computer file along with all pertinent billing information.

Some big studios like Criteria have thousands of square feet of library space and use detailed forms to keep track of the entire history of each tape.

- offsets the client number.
94 refers to the year, 1994.
09 is the month, September.
44 means it was the 44th session of the month (this is a good way to see at a glance if any tapes are missing from the pile).
- separates the timing from the description details.
2 means the session was in Studio 2.
A is the house code for 24-track lockup to picture.
T stands for video transfer.

So by looking at a few numbers, we can get a pretty good idea of not only when the session occurred, but what kind of session it was.

You can create a simple code for just about anything. With ours, B means an audio-only session, C means mixdown from 24-track to 2-track, D means a 4-track session, and E means 2-track.

There are several advantages to using a system like this. The first is that a job number is a failsafe method that can be very helpful when an invoice or work order gets lost. When the job orders are listed at the end of each month, the missing paperwork becomes visible as a number. Second, a phone inquiry from a client regarding a particular past session can often be handled just by looking at the job number. The client asks what you did on the 6th, and a glance at the job number gives you a solid reference point without further searching.

The third is that you can easily categorize and collate sessions by type, giving you a good idea of what your monthly trends are. This can be instrumental in making marketing plans and developing advertisements.

And the fourth reason is that you have a permanent reference number on each session that gives you instant information a month or ten years later about the kind of work that you were doing.

Tape Numbers

You can use a portion of the same job order code for numbering tapes that are stored on the premises. For example, 53-1 simply means the first of client number 53's tapes on the shelf.

Write that number in three places: on the spine of the tape, on the tape hub and in a log book with a master list or database of all the client tapes in the building. For long-term storage recordkeeping, you can give a separate

DIFFERENT FUR *RECORDING*

415/864-1967
3470 Nineteenth Street
San Francisco, CA 94110

FILE #

CLIENT

ARTIST

SONG TITLES

MASTER	SAFETY
OUTTAKES	IPS
TAPE	LEVEL
TONES	RECORD PAD
ENGINEER	ASST. ENG.
REEL #	
DATE	

This label for 2-inch tapes puts all the information on the box spine—a real time-saver when you're lost in the library.

page to each client in a looseleaf notebook. Draw two wide columns to the right of the page and call one IN and the other OUT. Then write in the date that each tape is left. When your client takes them back, enter the date and have him or her sign in the OUT column.

Keep the tape log either in the tape library or with the receptionist, and make sure that each time a tape is dropped off or picked up, someone signs for it. You can win a lot of arguments with a signature, and you can see at a glance whether or not the tape you're looking for is in the house.

One of the few similarities between the service business of the recording studio and a retail operation like a department store is that both are subject to what retailers call *shrinkage*—shoplifting or theft.

There are two ways that equipment and accessories can take an unscheduled trip outside. The first is unintentional: The guitarist gets one of your connecting cords jumbled up in his own tangle, or the cartage guys mistakenly swipe the SMPTE converter box that's been set up on the synthesist's rig by a second. The second way out is a result of our less-than-perfect civilization and the relative ease with which an expensive microphone can be packed into an instrument case at 2:00 a.m.

In the first instance, the mistake is usually acknowledged by the pro session player, and the item is returned with apologies. In the second, you realize that you *are* capable of murder after all, if you could just figure out who to point the shotgun at.

Protecting Your Stuff

Organization is one of the keys to maintaining control—in short, know what you've got! Contrary to what you may think, you can't keep it all in your head, so start by making a master list of everything you own. A detailed inventory list may be required by your insurance company. But you also need it to figure your net worth, and in the case of theft, to have a record of ownership and a serial number to make positive identification.

You should mark your equipment with your studio name; the least expensive method is to engrave them with an electric marker. When space permits, write something like "Property of Nano Matter Studios, DL# [state driver's license number] N3234501."

You can also buy property nameplates customized with your studio name and sequential serial numbers. They're available from identification products businesses, listed in the Yellow Pages. These metal tags bond permanently onto your equipment and are very difficult to remove.

With either system, you have a visible deterrent to a casual thief. In the studio, that may be someone with his own home studio who'd love to own an AKG 414 but just can't afford one. A mic that size can be unclipped and dropped into a briefcase in seconds. But a would-be ripoff artist should and could be turned off by the prospect of displaying a mic in his studio that is prominently identified with someone else's ID. And a pawnshop isn't likely to overlook such an overt sign of illegitimate acquisition, either.

As for the more ruthless break-in thief, the vast majority are either too wasted or too desperate to deal with altering ID tags on stolen property. When we were ripped off in 1986, a burly and overzealous cop fairly burst into my apartment after I'd dragged myself out of bed to answer the door one aprés-marathon morning. He nearly knocked me over with an armload of recovered equipment, striding into my living room and loudly proclaiming, "See? It really does pay to engrave your stuff!"

Naturally, it was all the ten-year-old home stereo equipment that the thieves hadn't fenced yet; the brand-new thousand-dollar synth that we hadn't gotten around to engraving was never seen again. And faced with a $500 deductible on our policy and the certainty that our premium would go up if we claimed the loss, we chose to eat it. Aaaaargh! They did, however, throw the suckers in jail for, like, *months*.

Not Flaunting It

The best way to limit pilferage is to make the least amount of easily transportable equipment available. The thieves' two favorite must-have items are microphones and headphones, both of which are small and easily concealable. So use only the number needed for each session and keep the rest locked securely away in a locker (usually a closet in the studio where mics, cords and headphones are stored...and protected). All you need is a simple doorknob lock that automatically locks the door when you close it. Then, when the session is over, make it a policy to pack up mics and headphones first, leaving them exposed for the least amount of time.

The vast majority of players who come to work at your place will respect your equipment. The problem is with the occasional person who eyes an item all day and then can't resist the ease of spiriting it away. Teach them that those items are accounted for by your staff while the players are still packing up, and you'll provide another sober deterrent to being caught red-handed.

When the Worst Happens

In spite of your best efforts, you're likely to be victimized. When you are, there are difficult choices to make. Remember that the basis of a successful studio business is repeat business, so think diplomatically. You can do more harm than good by making emotional accusations, so consider the circumstances carefully before taking action.

Determine as closely as possible the day or time that the gear was last seen. Talk to everyone in-house who was there on the day it happened. If you feel certain of the thief's identity, there are ways to deal with him outside of calling the cops. Call him and tell him you're afraid someone at the session may have inadvertently packed up a piece of your equipment by mistake. Would he please ask around and get back to you? Tell him you're spreading the word and that you're sure it's just a mistake. You're simply interested in recovering what's yours; no names or circumstances need be explained.

That way, you've informed him that you suspect he's connected to the disappearance, but that you're willing to give him a way out without pointing a finger. You've also told him that you're talking to other people who know him, people who will recognize that piece when they see it in the future, especially if it's prominently marked with your studio name.

When he realizes he's cornered, but there's a way out, the odds are good he'll cooperate. The key is to stay calm and not point any fingers of blame. It's all just been a mistake, and mistakes happen.

But if diplomacy doesn't work, you should take further action. First, be certain that the equipment is missing! Make a thorough check of the premises again. You might even find something *else* that's been gone for a month.

Then, when you're sure, call the police and make a report. And if you're certain about where the equipment wound up, tell them of your suspicions. This is serious stuff. You're about to lose a client (who, if guilty, you want out of your face forever anyway), and you may be in for some angry rebuttals or counter-accusations. But that's no reason to suffer the loss of a $900 mic, especially if you're absolutely sure you know who took it.

Figuring It In

Unfortunately, the loss of equipment often goes unnoticed for days or weeks after the fact. At that point, it will probably be useless to try and determine what happened.

If the loss is under a thousand dollars, it probably won't pay to report it to your insurance company. You may recover some of the money after your deductible, but your rates may be raised as a result of the report. That's the way insurance companies stay in business.

So you may be left with a feeling of emptiness and frustration, the prospect of paying out a lot of money to replace what you already own, and a feeling of resignation that this world is still an imperfect environment in which to raise children. In the meantime, we are individually the best source of protection for the ones, and the things, we love.

13
Politics & Psychology

Maintaining good client relationships is a challenging art, both in and out of the studio. And in the studio business, you're going to be dealing with a wide-ranging group of sensitive, creative people who want more than anything else to express their artistic vision in the most spectacular and successful way possible.

Your clients also want to achieve these miraculous results in the shortest possible time, often while up against severe budget restraints and deadlines. With that in mind, it's no wonder that musicians, producers, songwriters, film editors and singers can be counted on to run the full gamut of emotions during the course of their work.

Being aware of the pressure they must endure should help you relate to their needs and behavior. In a pressure-filled situation, moods are often dictated not by personal interaction but by how the work at hand has been going. So engineers learn pretty early on to maintain their composure when a client becomes angry or frustrated.

Unconsciously, your client may be depending on just that—to be able to vent his or her emotions in a safe and permissive atmosphere, one conducive to getting the job done regardless of the obstacles the clients themselves toss into the fray.

SETTING THE SCENE

One of the vitally important precepts of good studio management is to remember to look at your studio with a client's eye. If you were working there as a paying customer, what would you see, in terms of the value you were receiving? And don't just think from a results standpoint, but also from a perception of the place as a whole. Would that perception register as a conscious observation or

as a subconscious feeling? And how would it affect your future dealings with the people there, and with the facility as a whole?

The overall look of your studio will affect each person differently, but you can ccunt on it to ultimately create a complex set of stored impressions in each person's mind. For instance, the style of decor in a room has a definite relationship to the mood it sets when you first walk in. And a perfectly maintained room will create two entirely different moods, depending on whether the lighting is garishly bright or subdued and shadowed.

There's something a little mystical about a dimly lit room—the soft shadows, the quiet and satisfying sense of power emanating from the glowing equipment lights and the soft hum of the exhaust fans. Here, people actually tend to lower their voices, feel their tensions ease and shake off a bit of the outside world. This, you might agree, is a good subliminal message to transmit at the beginning of a high-pressure session.

Making Observations

Look around the room: How do you feel being in it? Relax, sit back and stare ahead, much as your clients do, hour after hour. What do you see? Could the place use a new coat of paint? Is there a crack in the wall next to a $60,000 digital deck? Has the dust muted the sheen on the console, or is a broken fixture sitting in the open? When you sit at the producer's desk, do you have a clear and direct view of the inside of the trash basket?

Keep looking. How are the sightlines into the studio? Is there a mini-monitor placed directly in the way of the client's view through the control-room glass? How about the producer's chair itself? Is it solid and comfortable, or does it tilt and squeak whenever it moves? Is there enough desk space to put a few personal things in front of you without getting in the engineer's way? Are you comfortable and at ease?

All these conscious observations on your part may never pass the subconscious level in some of your clients' minds, but you can bet that their moods and attitudes will be affected by them, and that you'll be dealing with whatever comes out of those minds during the course of the day. You'll certainly be doing both yourself and your clients a favor by leveling the playing field instead of inadvertently creating extra obstacles.

Consider the kind of impression you want to make and then try to follow through with as much preplanned physical design and execution as possible. And when you've created the kind of environment that you feel will be the most effective, keep an eye on it. Buy a couple of ultra-soft dust brushes and give the room a good dusting at least once a week. Dust is the bane of sensitive equipment. Left unchecked, it can make everything look dingy, not to speak of the equipment damage.

You can put a schedule of "mood mainte nance" together with very little effort. Make the once-a-week dusting a regular duty for yourself or a staff member, and then, once a month, take ten or 15 minutes for some real *detailing*.

That's what we try to do every so often at Interlok. Two or three of us walk into a control room and studio together, look around, and discuss what could be done a little better, or made a little more comfortable or clean. And then we try to take care of it on the spot. It only takes a few minutes, and the room benefits from it every time.

In Session

Once sessions get into full swing, it's easy for the control room to get pretty torn up. When stacks of tapes and reels are lying about and track sheets are in piles among a dozen mostly eaten takeout containers on every available surface, the date is obviously chugging along. But it's a good idea to have someone keep an eye on the physical buildup.

Food, trash and leftovers should be hauled out before you're buried in them, and after a midsession meal, a quick cleanup will help shift the mood back to the work at hand. Try to keep open tapes and boxes in one specific area, so that the room looks good, and so that *you* don't look bad when you can't find the reel you rewound an hour ago.

In acknowledging subconscious impres-

sions, it's best to pay particular attention to keeping the mixing console free of debris. The console is usually the most impressive piece of equipment in the room, and your client will be staring at it for hour after hour. If you can keep the console clean, that should go a long way in making the rest of the room feel good. Most studios have a no-drinks-on-the-console policy that is politely intoned by the engineer whenever necessary. I once saw a giant tub of buttered popcorn get spilled from its precarious perch atop a Neve meter bridge onto the main section of the desk. Watching three panic-stricken people desperately blotting at a puddle of liquid goo as it seeped into the fader glide-paths was enough to make a permanent impression.

As for the lighting, if you're designing or remodeling the room, well-placed track lights with high-quality, non-buzzing rheostats can't be beat. They're literally the way to dial a mood.

It seems like everyone has a different idea of what that mood should be. My partner tends to lean towards night-game stadium brightness; I prefer a little mystery in the shadows. Maybe my mood is a good way to start and his is the only way to stay awake after 12 hours. Whatever your preference, dimmers give you the option of choosing a level that feels right.

Playing House

Make sure the trash around the studio doesn't pile up. Make it a part of the daily routine to empty all receptacles in the facility, preferably before they're bursting at the seams.

Recycling has become such a normal part of the landscape that it's both practical and conscientious to set up some clearly marked bins for cans and bottles. If you're in a commercial area, you can accomplish two good deeds at once by befriending one of the needy people in your neighborhood who you see regularly scouring the dumpsters for recycleables and arranging for him or her to pick up yours. You'll be getting a free service while helping preserve the environment and benefiting someone in need.

Keep an eye on the restrooms. Maintain a supply of extra towels and toilet paper, and keep the room itself clean and sanitary. If you've hired a cleaning service, the restroom should be their primary focus. And if they're not performing up to snuff, make it clear that you expect better work, or you'll be shopping for a new crew.

Also keep a supply of eating utensils and dishware on hand. Some studios prefer real cutlery and dishes, while most go the disposable route; we decided to eliminate foam cups some years ago in favor of real mugs. We had them imprinted with the studio logo and made their washing and maintenance part of the job description for the receptionist. If you go the plastic-utensil route, keep a couple of real utensils, including some good cutting knives and serving spoons, on hand for handling special jobs. The more like home your lounge becomes, the more comfortable people will feel, especially as the days and hours of work grind on.

And don't forget the great outdoors. Your location should make no difference to your resolve to keep your entrance and front walks swept up, hosed down and generally inviting. If the surrounding properties are similarly kept up, then a lack of effort on your part will cast you in an unfavorable light. And if you've chosen a warehouse district or are on a less-than-savory street, your care and upkeep will make you stand out as a welcome place to arrive.

DEALING WITH PERSONALITIES

Although everyone comes with their very own DNA, certain basic types of personalities are certainly encountered pretty frequently. If you know what you're likely to encounter going into a session, you ought to be a lot more ready for it when that behavior actually occurs. Here are some observations based on my own experience and discussions with engineers and managers from around the country.

Just one note before we get started though: Everyone's entitled to their own opinions. Draw a generalization about anyone or anything, and you're likely to walk into a hornet's nest of retorts and accusations (or at least some spirited debate) from someone who has irrefutable proof that it just ain't so. But if everyone knuckled under to that kind of pressure, there'd be nothing left to argue about in the world. So with that in mind, let's get on with it.

Session Players

A pro player's main goal is to transfer his or her best performance onto tape effectively and in the shortest possible time. That means the player's primary concern is going to be what the mix sounds like in his headphones. It isn't easy to satisfy a live rhythm section—each key player has his or her own idea about what the mix should be like. But there are a few obvious solutions.

First, it's a great help to have at least two cue mixes to send through the phones. That way, the drummer and bass player can concentrate on the crash/boom and the guitarist and keyboard players can monitor more rhythm and melody. There are even devices on the market that go a giant step further, by providing a separate 8-track mix in a 3" x 5" box that each player can set to their own liking. This is a nice idea.

Secondly, it's important that you, as the studio manager, realize that the mix is an endlessly subjective topic of discussion. It may be that the players are simply not going to be able to agree on what sounds best. Anticipating this problem should help you and your engineer maintain calm while making each change that may be testily requested by the players as the session goes on.

Some players are easy to please; some are not. Most are able to reach a compromise and get on with the job at hand if they realize that the booth is doing its best to give them what they want. The operative words are patience and cooperation, when the complaint comes back that the bass player still can't hear the bloody kick drum.

The other physical challenge when doing live sessions is the readiness of the room. It's important to leave enough time beforehand to prepare for the session. Normally, the client should be guided by the traffic manager at the time of the booking as to how many players to expect, what the specific instrumentation will be, and often, what track assignments or special miking may be requested. The more prepared you are, the better the session will run and the happier the client will be.

At the very least, have the room properly prepped: Chairs and gobos set for each player; mic lines, phone mix boxes and headphones alongside stands or booms. A room that's been cleaned and freshened from the previous session, yielding an atmosphere that invites the next creative ideas. Fresh coffee in the lounge. An alert and awake support staff. And a welcoming atmosphere, one that makes it a pleasure to arrive and anticipate the work ahead.

Soloists

Good overdubbers, recording guitar or sax solos, for instance, really earn their pay. They're under intense scrutiny by the artist or producer, who often want a performance to be just so. If you've ever wailed on a solo until you satisfied someone else's taste, you know how frustrating it is to get a total thumbs-down from a brain-dead producer on the best solo you've played all year, and have to swallow it while they erase it and re-record two dozen more.

If you're on the staff or administrative end, watching this happen before your eyes, stay out of the way when the vibe gets that intense unless you're specifically asked for help or an opinion. Egos can overshadow normal reasoning or logic in the heat of it all, and maintaining your calm may be the critical thread that holds the whole session together.

And if you just can't take it and realize you're the only person in the room who knows the answer to the problem that's making everyone else lean toward the hysterical, take this advice before you offer your pearl: Leave the control room. The moment you intrude on the process, you'll find to your amazement that you'll be perceived as being just as mistaken as everyone else. Part of your job is to maintain a degree of professional distance, and you'll have just blown it.

Record Producers

Record producers are an emotional lot. To begin with, their job title is one that has no particular definition set in stone. They're present to somehow make the record come out well, but the way they get there can run the gamut from schooled conservatory arranger to drug-crazed Gameboy wizard. Some producers walk in knowing exactly what is going to get done on a given night. Others walk out wondering what, if anything, happened at *all* that night.

What they *do* know is that ten thousand other people would just love to have their job and get a shot at the big time, that their own tenure is often dependent on the success of the project that they're working on at the present.

If this all sounds a little flaky, it often is. However, an inspired pro can really make it all swing his or her way, resulting in a session run with military precision.

In most cases, the producer's personality tends to be a little paranoid, a little standoffish, and a bit regal. They are likely to demand that a recording be made in one particular way, which may go against everything holy in the mind of the engineer.

Handling Incompetence

When an engineer encounters a producer who's headed for trouble, the best politics are to wait for the right moment and then calmly suggest an alternate technique. When the producer insists he knows what he's doing, it's your job to go with orders and to attempt to make the uphill journey as comfortable as possible. This way, the studio has done its part in attempting to help but has relinquished responsibility to the person who's in charge of the session.

The hardest part about handing over the reins to someone who has just insisted that everything you know is wrong is to then support that person's method. A bad situation gets worse if the staff develops their own attitude problem at the hands of an incompetent.

The place to air your frustrations is out of the control room, and out of earshot. You may swear you'll never work with this jerk again, or roll your eyes in disbelief as a producer digs a deeper and deeper hole for himself. But if it's been made clear that this is the way the work is to be done, then give thanks that not everybody is this dumb and make the best of it.

The operative word is "neutrality": Stay cool, don't make visible or verbal judgments, do your job and learn something as you observe someone else's mistakes. It's situations like these that put the concept of "service" in a whole new light, but that's exactly what's called for. And there's a great deal in life to be learned by sitting at the side of someone who is teaching you an indelible truth by negative example.

Doing it right should mean that when the session or project wraps, your client will have no finger of blame to point at anyone else. And that's a cornerstone of protecting your own and your studio's reputation on the street.

On Time and Money

The producer most often sets the tone for the whole session. Some like to hunker down to work, and others love to hang out and tell stories all night long. From a management point of view, storytelling at a good hourly rate makes extra dollars. But the record company may become very unhappy with the pace of the project if they see little getting accomplished. And that could result in a lot of pressure on the producer, and subsequently on the studio and staff, later on.

It's a tricky managerial decision whether or not to suggest that the group get back to the work at hand. Getting a feel for when to butt in comes with experience, but taking a more assertive role may be much appreciated later on when the money starts running out. One way to check the waters is to hang out with the producer after the session wraps. Who knows—they may well loosen up or become an entirely different person at the end of a long day and surprise you by specifically asking you to stop them tomorrow if they insist on doing more than two retakes once they announce they like something.

In the meantime, if you notice that the producer of your latest album project has a fondness for goat cheese and rye crackers, why not have a mini-platter made up every so often? They could wind up liking you for that alone.

Film Producers and Editors

The film producer or film editor, on the other hand, is all business. Yet in the area of sound recording, he or she tends to be technically naive or uninterested. The film producer is primarily focused on end results and staying within the budget, and the audio mix is usually the absolute last item on the list. Since every other part of the film or video must be complete before the final audio mix is laid in, you'll be working with people who may be exhausted from months of intense work, and who are up against a killer deadline to deliver the final print.

The one item that'll keep a picture professional happy and out of your hair is the telephone. Through the phone, he or she is connected to the rest of the whole project, which is usually in the chaotic throes of lining up the premiere or air dates and wrestling with maddening last-minute changes. Your phones are likely to ring the most when you're on this kind of project; there is often constant communication needed between audio- and picture-sweetening sessions, and between all the editors, the actors who need to be re-recorded and the top brass.

Make sure there's a receptionist for the length of each session to handle incoming calls and arrange for long-distance outgoing (as well as keeping a diary of the date and numbers that aren't called with clients' calling cards, to be billed back to them later on). Keep the coffee fresh and the staff alert. And be ready to explain patiently why transferring the DAT elements to hard disk is going to take an extra half-hour and can't be avoided. You need to garner trust in these situations.

Once you have earned that trust, you may be largely left alone to do the job in your own way. Do it well, and your film and TV people will bring you everything they've got. The one thing they want is to have an established list of ser-vice people and places they can depend on to deliver the goods and thus make *them* look good.

Preparing for Post Work

Professionally, your engineer needs to be on intimate terms with the house sound-effects library, its limitations and the available alternatives. The producer or editor tends not to care *how* a sound effect is created; their concern is that it *sound* right.

Likewise with technical procedures: The "doingness" is left to the engineer. That's why it's smart to anticipate the needs of the project before the session begins, so that you'll be ready when the requests are made. If you're ill-equipped to make the kind of transfer called for, it's not a problem as long as you're ready with rates, runners and information on the closest facility in town that can handle it for you.

Know which places are capable of what, and keep a list of rates and rental charges on hand. That way, when the request comes, you can handle it with surety and speed.

At Interlok, we've developed a relationship with dubbing and transfer facilities nearby. When the need arises, we make a call, quote the figure, send a runner with the elements over to our neighbor, have them bill us, and then charge the client at our cost on the final bill. That way, they know they're getting as good a deal as they would on their own, and there's no threat of their changing facilities for that reason. In the meantime, we come across as a full-service studio.

There is often so much communication outside of the studio to be done on post dates that it's an advantage to have a private room or lounge where an assistant producer can spread out his paperwork and stay on the phone. By creating a separate nook or place for him, you'll be taking a lot of pressure off the producer and your own engineer to get their respective jobs done, both of whom will appreciate the relative privacy and quiet.

Advertising-Agency Brass

You gotta love these guys. It seems like their whole lives are hanging in the balance of how well their 30-second Pampers spot is going to do on a *Brady Bunch* rerun.

Agency producers tend to run in packs. They show up in groups that usually include an account exec, an editor, a writer, an art director and a client or two, plus significant others and an occasional personal trainer. It's not uncommon for half a dozen people with some kind of power to be present for one session.

This is a double-edged sword for a studio manager. On the one hand, all these people need adequate space to spread out, take over your phone system and make threatening gestures at each other. On the other, if your engineer can stand it, their endless bickering and creative differences can easily stretch what should be a 90-minute slam-dunk into a 12-hour marathon.

Breathe deeply, stay out of the fray and bill 'em at full rate. They know it's their own fault and the high cost seems to make them feel more important. Go figure.

Composers

Composers tend to be pretty responsible, professional people. They have to be, because music is invariably the final link in the film or video production chain, and they are often presented with a delivery date of three to six weeks from receiving a print they can work with. On top of that, most non-feature-film productions tend to have low music budgets. And producers like to make deals for the delivery of the entire score for one fixed price, which the composer agrees to and then must use to pay for studio time, musicians and tape—the profit is whatever's left.

So they usually arrive with a specific game plan in mind and with written parts ready to go. A great number of projects are now recorded in project rooms, but whether they come in just to mix or to start from scratch, experienced composers often bring in their own engineers, who'll need efficient assistance from your best seconds. There is rarely any wasted hangout time. (But they can take forever to get the music to sound the way they hear it in their heads!)

With composers, it's especially important to be clear about who's paying the bill and what the rules are involving overtime and extra services—such as what happens if a music-only session is booked, and a higher picture lockup rate is requested four hours later. It's hard to talk business in the midst of the heat. Be clear about it beforehand.

Also, established composers work under enormous time and client pressure, and tend to demand a high level of service. That means equipment that runs reliably and a staff that responds with efficiency. Down-time doesn't

stop the union clock, so a composer still has to pay all of the musicians for sitting around reading the paper while you're fixing a broken multitrack. Keep a strict and regular equipment-maintenance program, and you'll go a long way in keeping the positive side of the politics in your corner.

If you have an in-house synth setup, it's wise to have someone on staff who's adept at programming. Whether you just need a last-minute change or all the keyboard work is done on your own stack, few composers are as familiar with MIDI techniques as pro keyboardists are. You may be asked to help with MIDI and sequencer software or drum programming, or to find a patch that pleases. If you can, that's a powerful draw for return bookings on future projects.

Orchestral sessions are the most exciting, and naturally the biggest headaches, of all. A composer who takes on the conductor's chores is going to spend most of his or her time coaxing the best performance out of the ensemble, fixing copying and arranging mistakes and firing orders and questions into the booth at the engineer and the film producer. Again, stay out of the way when the feathers fly.

Give the composer a separate talkback mic to make communication easier. Keep a stash of extra pencils and some loose manuscript paper at hand. Tape the long mic wires down in the studio to avoid injuries, and try to anticipate the next logical request by a conductor who's much more concerned about the musical dissonance in the woodwinds than the electronic distortion in the brass.

Figure out the maximum number of live musicians your room can handle and be frank with someone who is anticipating using a larger number. If your room can't handle the size of the group, it's much wiser to recommend a place that can rather than try to shoehorn an inordinate number of professionals into a box where they'll be unhappy.

Once you do establish your limit, equip yourself with half a dozen more chairs, music stands, lights, booms and mics than you'll need when the room is going full-tilt. You'll need that amount at the very least for breakdown insurance and instant replacement during the heat of the session.

Recording Artists

Then there are the individual artists, the people the recording session is all about. As a group, they're the most difficult to profile. Some are in for the first time, and need all the help they can get. Some are highly experienced, straight-ahead professionals. And some are highly experienced bumbling idiots, or worse, broken people whose lives are in shambles.

The pros will immediately set the tone for the session; just follow their lead. The amateurs will either ask for help or stumble around not knowing *how* to ask for help. That's when it's appropriate to suggest politely that your experience might be beneficial to them, and would they be interested in a suggestion or two (or five)?

The answer is almost invariably yes, and you're suddenly thrust into the position of taking over and producing the session, which may be the best thing that could happen for all concerned. It's a creative opportunity for you, and one that can turn a torturous evening into a productive one. Just be sure to test the waters, going one step at a time so as not to suddenly find you're pushing artists in a direction they're unhappy with.

The Less-Than-Professional Professional

In the case of the out-of-control artist, once again, you're best off following the artist's lead. If you find yourself dealing with someone who's wrestling with a heavy alcohol or drug dependency, or whose mental faculties are less than

secure, keep an eye on him or her, but keep out of the way. You'll have a lot stronger case inquiring how the bathroom caught on fire if you weren't in it when it did.

What you do in terms of future bookings with difficult people is a decision you make for yourself. If you do continue the relationship, maintain a diplomatic immunity and distance, and make sure your facility is secure on the inside and out. But experience teaches that these are not the kind of people who will further your dreams. Exercise care when choosing your continuing clientele and you may go a long way in controlling any number of other factors that contribute to your happiness and sense of purpose.

POST-SESSION POLITICS

One of the most important political jobs for the studio manager is to make sure the client leaves feeling good about the session. To a great extent, the responsibility for this rests on the engineer's shoulders. But whenever possible, it's a very positive custom for the manager or owner who hasn't been in the room the whole time to step up and check in.

Just approaching a client and asking how things went is to say that you really care, and that your service extends beyond the usual nuts and bolts. But more to the point, you'll likely get an accurate measure on just how well things *did* go, and whether anything else is needed.

The solution to handling a truly difficult client? Well, no. But playing back the sounds captured during a cocking-and-loading sound-effects session might help to make a point!

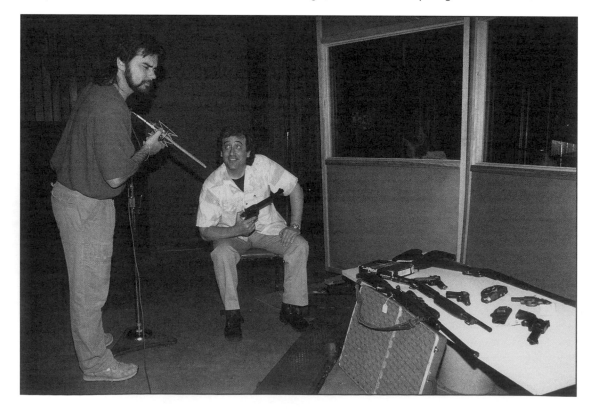

Hopefully, your clients will appreciate being approached, tell you how happy they are about the work that was done and assure you they'll be back soon. Conversely, if there have been problems, this is the absolute best time to get their side of the story.

Blocking the Door

If something's gone wrong, whether real or imagined, *now* is the time to take care of it. Your client may have been sitting in the control room for the last six hours fuming with anger, yet was too polite (or calculating) to say something in the midst of the session. Coming in as a third party, looking the client in the eye and asking sincerely if everything went all right is the best way to change a negative experience into a positive one. As a manager or owner, you have the power to turn things around right on the spot.

It's amazing how many problems a client will walk out the door with, not mentioning a thing: The second wrote down 20 minutes less time for lunch than actually occurred. The engineer wasn't responsive enough to a panning request. There was too much noise in the hall. The monitor system didn't sound right. The tape cost too much. How come they used that mic? The engineer took too many breaks. *The mix doesn't sound good!*

You can work out every one of these problems *before* your client leaves the building and some real damage is done to your relationship, let alone the word of mouth the client will generate.

Understanding What the Truth Really Is

As a rule, it doesn't matter if the fifteen minutes of down-time has been accurately noted or not. The truth is that your client is sure he's getting ripped off. Letting go of a few dollars now may make you a lot more later.

If the client is dissatisfied with the engineer, you need to know that *now,* and why he or she feels that way. Then you can assure the client that appropriate steps will be taken so that the trouble doesn't occur again. Occasionally, someone will be really upset with an engineer's performance. This is the time to make concessions and try to reach a satisfactory agreement, not a week from now.

It doesn't really matter what the problem with the engineer was, certainly not as much as finding out what will make your client happier. Is the mix bad? Offer a remix. Was the engineer unresponsive? Offer to talk with him and to get back to your client by phone later (thus avoiding an embarrassing confrontation between the three of you now).

Call back when you have the facts and work out a solution. Promise better treatment next time, explain what the misunderstanding was, or in extreme situations, suggest another engineer altogether. You may even have to offer to go back to the beginning with someone else and pick up the tab on another free session.

But since you as the studio manager are making the rules and the only likely expense will be for labor, the result could be turning a disaster into a reasonable success. Your clients may not love you after repeating the work twice, but they'll definitely respect you for standing behind your business.

Icing on the Cake

Make a note of the deadline or delivery date on a project that had a bumpy ride at the studio. Then, a week or so later, follow up with a call to the client and find out how things went. Time has a way of smoothing things out, and the odds are that they'll have calmed down and that the project will have worked out for the best. And if not, there may be more that you can do, or at least say, to smooth the way to the future.

With that in mind, your client, who was ready to cuss on your mother's grave before being nabbed by you in the hallway, will thank you for checking in, and appreciate the extra time and effort that you spent fixing the problem. And that's good for everybody.

WHEN YOU LOSE A CLIENT

Best efforts and intentions aside, client attrition is a fact of life that every studio must expect. There are two broad categories of loss.

The first comes as a result of customer dissatisfaction, which as we've seen, can be controlled to a great extent with good follow-up and inspired intervention. The biggest client-killer is probably disorganization, which is a pity. Good businesspeople should be able to virtually eliminate these problems by just paying attention to what's going on around them.

A client-killing session might begin with a late start, since the room wasn't prepped for the intended start time. Then, the assistant shows up late and is unaware that the 2-inch was supposed to be biased for the client's brand of tape and begins the process five minutes before the downbeat. Half an hour later, under the chilling stare of the waiting artist, it's finished and ready. This is ultimately management's fault, either for not making the session setup requirements clear to the engineers or for allowing such a lax policy on timely preparation.

As our star-crossed session lurches forward, other things begin to unravel. After experiencing a half-hour's worth of lackluster drum miking, the assistant is sent out to see what can be done by shifting some of the mic stands around. The aging reverb unit sputters in and out of the signal path, indicating there's a short in the wiring, which no one has had the time to repair. The house engineer on the date looks tired and slightly bored, responding to the producer's requests only after they are repeated, and nothing seems to be EQ'd to taste.

The producer doesn't like the sound of the mic the singer is using, requests another, then another, questioning why the studio doesn't own some of the classic models. Three hours into the date, the multitrack goes down, just like it has on four other occasions in the past month. It takes both engineers 20 minutes to nudge it back to life while the entire rhythm section sits on their hands and the artist fumes.

That night, the producer slaps a reference cassette of the day's work onto his home unit, and it plays back at a much faster tempo, a half step higher: The studio's cassette machine hasn't ever been calibrated and is running slow in Record mode. When the bass part jumps way out in front of the mix, not at all like it sounded on the big speakers at full volume, it's the last straw. That night, the producer angrily calls another studio, asks them a couple of facetious questions, like "Do you have any engineers who know what the hell they're doing over there?", and books their room for the rest of the project.

If this sounds like a case of extremes, it is. This is 20-20 Hindsight 101. Yet all of these completely preventable (and predictable) occurrences happen all the time in the so-called "professional" studio world with frightening regularity. And it's no wonder that professional artists and creative people refuse to put up with that kind of incompetence.

Losing Business Through No Fault of Your Own

The other kind of client attrition involves human nature and outside events over which you have

no control. Your client decides to try another room because he or she heard they do a fine job and thinks a fresh take might be interesting. A competing studio makes a cold call and offers an irresistible deal. A new group member raves about the house engineer at another place, who's offered a free night session just for fun. An editor finds a studio that is much more convenient to home, or invests in a home-studio setup. Or, after completing three successful TV projects in a row, your client decides to try a completely different recording environment just for fun.

It's frustrating and emotional to lose a client with whom you've grown friendly, to whom you've consistently delivered the goods, and whom you have begun to count on for business. But you need to remember that human nature often gravitates toward change simply for its own sake. And after reviewing your performance with your staff and your client and finding nothing lacking on your part, what's left is acknowledging that people are people.

But the upside of quixotic flight is that, handled correctly, the bird will often come back to the nest. A good manager learns to sense the departure of a client on good terms with the studio as a *fait accompli,* and to back off and allow it to happen without further resistance. In doing so, you're letting go of a client who leaves with a positive and successful experience of the studio, and who may return with more work in the future. It may take years, but in the meantime, that client will have good things to say about your facility to inquiring friends and associates. And sooner or later, something positive will come of it.

We recently had one former client call us from out of the blue after a three-year absence, explaining that his TV production company had been politicked into using another studio for a multiyear project. They had done a satisfactory job, but he had often wished he'd been working at our place instead. Now that the project was complete and a new one was about to begin, could we discuss a deal?

In the interim, we'd stayed in touch with the company, sending news of the studio and occasionally calling to check in, so we knew about the project he was describing. It was good to get them back. After the first show wrapped, I stopped into the bay where he'd been working for ten hours to see how everything had gone. He was tired but pleased, smiled at me and said, "It's good to be home again."

Staying on Top of Music Row

Hired as an engineer in 1976, Glenn Meadows moved up to become one of Nashville's premier facility owners, assembling a unique complex that features tracking, mixing and mastering under one roof.

Facility Both a recording studio and mastering facility. 12 full-time employees. "We literally can go from live tracking all the way through overdubs and mixing and then on to mastering, so that you walk out with a finished CD reference in your hands."

Equipment Two mastering rooms and two tracking/mixing rooms, designed by Tom Hidley, including "the only 20Hz control room in the U.S., where the monitors are flat to 20 cycles with no EQ at all. It takes a large cubic volume in the room to be able to generate that kind of low-frequency energy."

One tracking studio with SSL 4000E/G hybrid console, completely re-engineered by in-house staff and connected to an AT&T parallel-processing computer console with 120 32-bit, floating-point DSPs. One very large mixing room with 64-input SSL. Otari DTR-900 Model II 32-track digital decks.

Clients Tammy Wynette, Reba McEntire, Vince Gill, Patty Loveless, George Strait, Lynyrd Skynyrd.

Booking "The room has been running solid, booking 75 to 95 percent of the time since 1986. What you hear on the large monitors is what you really have, and that makes working in that environment much more enjoyable.

"I wanted to go backwards [from mastering] down the chain and generate an environment where people were comfortable and the sonics were accurate. I saw people building inexpensive rooms and throwing the equipment in and figuring, 'Oh well, that's the best we can do.' Then we'd get the tape in for mastering and think, 'Hey, this thing needs work. Why can't they get it right when they mix it?'

"So the room we built at the time was the most expensive room in Nashville to work in. We decided to stake out the high ground for the front-line artists who had the budget, could afford it, wanted to indulge themselves in the best and know that their product would be the best they could make."

Tracking vs. Mastering "We do have to be careful from a business standpoint to make sure that the studios that feed mastering business to us don't feel threatened that we're going to pitch their clients to mix here. We also don't want clients to think, 'Gee, I can't mix at Masterfonics because they're going to pressure me to master there.'

"For a while, that was a difficult line to walk. We've now solved much of that problem in that we've split the mastering and the studio operation and given them to two separate managers. So we try to maintain them as separate entities.

"For instance, there's a producer in Nashville who enjoys the work we do but prefers to go and master at a lab in L.A. This is where personalities get involved, and you have to get past holding grudges when somebody goes somewhere else. You have to be above that and just not worry about it. There are people who will move from place to place every six months just to try something new."

Digital City "Nashville has, to a much greater extent than New York or L.A., embraced digital audio. I'd venture to say that at least 95 percent of the product that comes out of Nashville is at least digital 2-track. And at least 75 percent is digital multitrack. That's probably due to Jimmy Bowen at MCA, who realized in the early '80s the potential of digital master mixing.

"He introduced it to the country-music community at the 2-track stage. He then went on to embrace the Mitsubishi 32-track digital deck and then produced virtually the entire Warner Brothers roster using that technology, keeping two and three studios booked 200 days a year. That made Nashville stand up and take notice. More people bought in and it spread all over town."

The Local Scene "Nashville is a very compact recording community. We're right down the block from the new Warners office building, on the corner is Sony Music, on the opposite side is BMG and Arista, and a block and a half down is MCA Music.

"There's room here. The town just absorbs each new facility. But there's more of a friendly atmosphere of competition here. We have the perception of New York and L.A. being a dog-eat-dog, cutthroat competition for studios. You get into massive rate wars and steal other projects at the drop of a hat.

"There are at least one or two facilities that have opened here with their owners operating under that scheme. But the people they're dealing with at the production coordinator level are backing off and saying, 'Wait a minute, I don't like the way this guy treats his people. I'm not gonna book here again.'

"So initially they may be very busy, and then the way they treat the clients will drive people away and all of sudden they'll find themselves empty for a while. That's the way it works in this town."

Rates "Our mix room came on line in 1986 at a card rate of $1,900 a day. A lot of facilities will do a 12-hour day and then charge you per hour after that. But I know full well that I'm not gonna book that room the other 12 hours you're not in there, especially if you're doing a two-week project. So I don't care how many hours you want to stay in there; if you want to work 16, 17 hours, that's no skin off my back. The gear's there, the equipment's there, it's powered up, the facility's yours 24 hours a day.

"We're still charging the same rate, because the room made sense economically in 1986 and still does. And of course, the construction costs and purchase costs for the console and equipment are paid for now.

"Everything works, we have on-staff maintenance here all the time, the rooms sound great, the consoles have been upgraded and it's a world-class facility. There are other places that have put Neve and SSL boards in rooms in which the monitors don't work as well, modules are down all the time, and the room is not as acoustically capable as what we're able to do. They're the mid-line studios, the guys that are sluggin' it out at eight or nine hundred dollars a day.

"So we're high-end for Nashville. Which isn't that high compared with other major cities. But there's this mystique here. You can't have a 2 as the first digit in your rate."

Principles "I always strive for excellence. Mediocrity and 'good enough' doesn't cut it with me. When the facility was under construction, people would ask, 'Why are you putting all this concrete in here? You don't need to do all this, it doesn't need to be this big. You can get by with it this way...'

"And I'd say, 'Yeah, I'm sure you can.' But we feel that this is better. If you talk to producers and engineers who work here, they'll tell you these rooms are far and away the best in town. And it's because we didn't cut corners. We treat our clients as if they're paying five thousand dollars a day."

14

Equipment, Money & Strategy

O nce you spend all the money you have in the world—along with a lot from parents, friends, aunts and angels—and you've actually managed to get your studio up and running, a really rotten thing is going to happen: Your equipment is going to get outdated.

It's not that it's going to malfunction and break down (which it probably will do as well). It's that it's going to become the *old* model, and fast. And before you know it, it's not going to be able to do all kinds of things that you never realized it needed to do. You're going to need to keep up with the technology, to keep up with the trends in the business, and to keep up with the Joneses. Then, quite naturally, there's the matter of your own insatiable lust for bigger, better, newer, shinier and niftier stuff.

Admit it: One of the prime reasons you love this business is that all that incredible equipment, with the lights and the numbers and faders and switches, is so totally cool, so buff, so cutting-edge, so awesomely powerful...ya just gotta have it, right? Right! And so do your clients.

Buying new equipment on a regular, unending merry-go-round of investing, leasing and borrowing is the reason that the most successful studio owners in the business lament, "I hate this business. I'm always broke." What they don't tell you is what a thrill it is to own a thriving studio that's chock-full of the neatest backlit, full-color, multiline, computer-generated displays in town.

CHOOSING THE RIGHT EQUIPMENT

U pgrading with new equipment is a serious business, however, much more so than one might expect at first glance.

To illustrate this, consider the "Workstation Shootout," a very impressive event sponsored by SPARS that has become a regular, traveling major-city event. At the most recent shootout, about 10 workstation manufacturers were given the opportunity to present their wares in a controlled environment that attempted to level the playing field for the benefit of potential buyers. All the equipment was placed in one large convention room, the audience was seated facing a stage, and each company was given exactly 20 minutes to show off. Live TV cameras looked over the shoulders of the operators and shot the image onto a ten-foot screen while company spokesmen explained the features and play-by-play. It was fascinating, enlightening and entertaining.

What became very clear was that each brand was attempting to simultaneously match and outshine the other. They would each demonstrate their ability to perform all the usual nonlinear tasks, and then would concentrate on the superiority of their latest software revision, or the quintessential hardware that only they made. And each made another promise: Just wait until next year. Then we'll *really* blow you away with what's coming!

A participant summed it up with a question that has stayed with me: "With all this moving-target technology, how am I supposed to choose the system that will work the best for me today and tomorrow?" The plaintive buyer's cry, and a great term for the '90s and beyond: moving-target technology. Ready, aim, quick—try to stay current.

Dealing With Change

What all of us who've invested serious money in this business have learned in the past few years is that with the rampaging advances in computer and digital technology, it's anybody's guess what's going to show up just a few months down the line. And that's a fundamental change that has occurred in all high-tech businesses in the last several years. Where once you could count on amortizing a piece of gear for eight, ten or 15 years, now it seems that a piece's relative lifespan depends on the timing of the next breakthrough, be it three years or three months away.

The most important lesson we've learned at Interlok is that unless you have a firm commitment from a trustworthy client who absolutely requires the gear in question, *nothing* is worth buying the minute it hits the market. It may be a great temptation to be the first in town to own the revolutionary new recording format and proudly display serial number 0003, but the benefit of nearly immediate competition and improvement pales against the premium price you pay for being first in line.

Experience has taught us that it pays to wait a year or more for the inevitable hardware and software enhancements. It doesn't take a crystal ball to predict the rush to the marketplace of competitive and improved product and the steep decline in price that always occurs.

The introduction of the D2 digital video master recorder is a perfect example. When it arrived around 1990, the TV industry flipped for it and the major post houses invested a fortune in gearing up. At the time, the low-end D2 model cost about $75,000 (plus tax) and was very finicky about the signal you fed it. We began to believe there might be one in our future but opted to wait, for two reasons: One, it was way too expensive, and two, no one could predict whether it would really become a standard and necessary broadcast format.

But client demand stayed steady. And what's more, our post clients were willing to pay a premium for the use of the machine. We negotiated good deals with two local equipment-rental companies offering D2 for about a year and a half, renting them at about $450 a day. The rental companies picked up and delivered, kept the machines in pristine condition, sent techs when we couldn't get them to link up right and swapped one deck for another when real trouble persisted. Meanwhile, we billed our clients the entire cost of the rental. D2 wasn't costing us a cent, except for the paperwork and setup hassles.

About a year and a half later, the format had indeed become a mainstay, and rentals were becoming more costly. Our clients had grown used to using D2 regularly, and they were working at other places where the day rate was just $200 to $300. We began matching the reduced rental fees and negotiated a lower rental from one of the companies, but we were beginning to lose money, eating a hundred or more a day to stay competitive.

Also, the hassle of connecting up, then disconnecting and shipping the units was getting very intrusive. Meanwhile, most of the glitches in the operating system had been solved with internal hardware and software updates and there were lots of new machines out.

We put out the word to used-equipment brokers and dealers that we were looking for a good machine, and about two years after the introduction of D2, bought a used one through a dealer, who added all the new updates and sold it to us, including his profit, for $30 grand.

We immediately lowered our D2 rates, to the satisfaction of our grumbling clients, installed a house machine that stayed put, and began billing double our monthly payments right out of the gate. We made a bet, based on steady client demand and its general acceptance as one of the new industry standards, that D2 would be a good investment. And it more than paid for itself, once the initial phase of its introduction gave way to its further development.

Playing Safe

You won't always be able to employ a strategy like this, but it's a good idea to consider it whenever you can. Remember that the idea of being in business is to become and stay profitable for the long run, not to just play catch-up and pray for profits.

Equipment-rental houses are a great way to try out new products, assuming they exist in your city. Another way is to go right to the manufacturer and ask for a one- or two-week on-site test. Many have demo units that they move from studio to studio for just that purpose. But that still saddles you with the prospect of buying new. That may be good for the economy, but it may not be so good for you.

Unfortunately, the desire to buy new and shiny toys runs strong in human nature. For example, many of our staff members are just getting started in their careers and are in their early to mid-20s. They don't make a lot of money, but over the years I've watched several show up at various times proudly parking and displaying their brand-new cars. It seems like the most exciting day of their lives, driving up in a gleaming chariot that only set them back, say, $17,000.

What a job the American Dream has done on these people! They've committed the better part of a year's salary to an icon of success and power, but at what cost? How seriously will those payments impact the quality of their lives? And is it worth it to be seen in something shiny and new, when they could spend a third the amount on a fine piece of rolling stock with just as nice a paint job and a good limited warranty, and maintain a far safer and more secure financial position? Some folks would say, "No! A new car is an important status symbol that brings success with it." But I think that wringing the greatest possible bang out of each buck serves the prudent entrepreneur in both business and private life.

So think twice about major purchases. Scrutinize your numbers. Watch for trends. Wait for a certain level of surety and be aware of the cost of killer competition. Let *other* people's money forge new paths and wait and see if they get eaten by the lions. The '90s present the most hostile business climate since the Depression, so think lean and long-range.

BUYING INTELLIGENTLY

Equipment-purchasing technique starts with setting long-range acquisition goals and then finding a logical pace that works for you. I've found that a good way to determine the proper amount that is affordable for each individual can be derived from this simple formula:

Assuming Yearning (y) exceeds Fear (f), then Lust Levels (LL) should outweigh late-night Cold Sweats (C) by a factor of at least three, or

$$\text{if } y > f, \text{ then } LL >= 3C$$

Use this formula as a handy way to gauge how well you'll be coping with your significant other screaming obscenities about eating beans for dinner again this week.

Eating aside, once you know what you want, you can begin to plan how fast you can afford to get there. Contrary to the majority opinion, there *is* life without a 96-input automated console that brews fresh coffee and offers a five-minute shiatsu massage option. It may not be quite as exciting, but an awful lot of owners seem to be having a pretty good time without one.

Look Before You Leap

Whenever you spend a lot of money, you should seek the help and advice of people who are experienced and knowledgeable in the field. A new console, for instance, may be the most expensive gadget you ever buy. So by all means, make an extra effort to be sure you're acquiring the right one.

Ask your clients, associates and peers what kind of console they like to work with. Talk to as many other engineers and producers as possible, and you'll begin to get a broad sample of what the trends and attitudes are about the consoles in your price range.

If you own a project studio, seek out other musician/engineers who can give you insight on the brands and features that will give you the greatest return. You'll undoubtedly get a wide sampling of opinions and suggestions, but you'll also begin to get a sense of what most people look for and appreciate. And don't neglect the trades. *Mix*, *Pro Sound News*, *Keyboard* and *Electronic Musician*, among others, are full of ads and reviews that you should pay close attention to. Getting a broad overview like that will make you both knowledgeable and focused, as you begin to hone in on the few models that meet the majority of your artistic and financial needs.

Next, go to the sellers. You'll find the world-class manufacturers in three places: their own dedicated showrooms, professional dealers and annual industry conventions. Lower-cost professional lines can be found in the same places, as well as a wider range of pro instrument dealers. And all are floating around on the used market.

If you're serious about buying expensive new equipment, you owe it to yourself to attend a show. There are several, and they move around from city to city, year after year.

Attending a Show

The granddaddy of them all is the Audio Engineering Society convention, better known as the AES show. There, in one location, is all the latest gear on the planet, with hundreds of experts and manufacturers demonstrating, answering questions and taking orders from mildly to wildly enthusiastic players.

There's simply no better way to see, compare and discuss your serious equipment needs than at a show like this. If you're about to spend 30, 50, 200 thousand or more, there's no excuse not to take a few days and a few hundred from the kitty, fly to the host city and immerse yourself in an intense educational experience. You'll find great benefits in choosing the right gear, while you shmooze and attend seminars and functions with the top people in the field.

When AES or other shows, like SMPTE or Showbiz Expo, come to town, they're usually closed to the general public. But it's easy to get tickets: Just call your local dealer or a manufacturer whose equipment you're interested in and ask for complimentary passes. You'll stagger out of these shows a little dazed, but you'll be leaving with a year's worth of valuable hands-on experience and updated knowledge that has been expertly presented for you, the studio owner or manager.

Shows, by the way, are also an excellent source for used equipment. It's quite common for a studio to sell a major piece from one city and ship it to another, either across the country or across the ocean. And shows are a great networking opportunity to find out about what's out

Selling or trading is another way to raise cash or credit towards the purchase of another piece of equipment. Most major cities have brokers who network as far as overseas to keep tabs on what's currently available in the used market.

there and available. Just talk to everyone you can: the reps, the dealers and the studio owners and engineers. If you're really brave, write the words "I'm looking for a good deal on a console" in large print on an extra name badge, clip it onto your other lapel and see what happens.

Deals for the Short-of-Funds Set

Another way to acquire equipment is to *trade* for some of the equipment you want. Remember, you've got a commodity that musicians, producers, singers and media people want: a studio where they can ply their craft. Most of these people have equipment of their own, and often, it may turn out to be the kind you're after. If you know someone who already has that rack-mount sampler you've been after, so much the easier: Ask him if he's interested in trading it for a good deal on studio time.

Another way to go after a particular piece is to check your local used-merchandise paper. In major cities, there is often a pro musical equipment category. Call the numbers listed, be friendly and find out if the owner is a working pro. If so, you may be able to make a deal trading for time instead of money, or some of each. You may also wind up getting new prospects interested in your studio who might otherwise have never heard of it.

Calling people who list equipment in the paper isn't the easiest way to get what you're after. You may run into some rather gruff responses; there are a lot of different personality types out there. But many people are open to intriguing ideas if they're presented in a calm and friendly fashion. Check and see if there's a section in your local Pennysaver devoted to swapping or trading, in which people specify the kinds of non-money exchanges they're after. My favorite actual listing from a few years ago was "Will trade entire advanced Scientology library of hardcover books for used gun collection."

And don't forget to check with your barter company (see Chapter 4) for leads. The point is that you can get very creative in finding solutions to a variety of problems, and bargaining with studio time is one of them. If you're willing to stretch a little and take a few chances, the rewards are often well worth the trouble.

Client Cash Advances

Say the producer of a low-budget movie calls your studio with his best pitch. He says that you come highly recommended by another client who you've done your usual sparkling best for, and this is a great opportunity for you to get the credit for doing the audio or the score on a feature film. All you have to agree to is an absurdly low package price for your services.

Well, you figure, bookings have been light, and we could use the film credit, not to mention the experience. The problem is, your old 3/4" VCR has long seen its best days, and you're aching for a new one (unless you're a qualified tech, VCRs are better bought new or with good warranties).

The normal procedure for payment on a full-scale project like this would be a third or half up front, with the rest coming during, or at completion of, the work. But you both have something the other wants. If you agree to his price, will he advance two-thirds of the money up front? "Why?" he asks.

"Because I'm up for doing the job, but my old VCR isn't. If you'll advance me the money, I'll put half of it into buying a new one, I won't have to charge you for extra rentals, and we'll both get what we want."

"Okay, but I can only come up with half up front."

"Can't do it. Your budget's too low. I appreciate your calling me, and I'm agreeing to your price. But I have to have the two-thirds to be able to deliver the kind of quality you want."

"Well, let me think about it..."

This may be stretching the boundaries of win-win negotiating a bit. But there's no reason why your clients can't do a little work for you while you take care of them. If this deal works, you'll get your badly needed equipment and a fresh credit, and your client will be on-budget.

Your client may say that the extra money will be hard to scrape together, but the chances are it's already budgeted. You may not like working for a considerably lower rate, but you'll feel a lot better looking at a shiny new 3/4-inch machine than you would have with the potential dead time you were facing in the first place.

The Christmas Club Technique

Barring these kinds of deals, the best way to acquire new equipment is to keep a separate equipment account at your business bank. It's nearly painless to develop a habit of depositing, say, 5% of your gross income into a savings account that's devoted strictly to new gear purchases.

If you average $7,500 a month during your first year, that translates into nearly 5,000 fairly painless dollars in 12 months. Hardly a king's ransom, but enough to acquire another 8-track module and a few prudently researched pieces of useful and tasty outboard gear.

It's also a comforting feeling to have a little nest egg stashed away when money gets tight during a quiet period. The idea isn't to spend your equipment account on helping to pay the rent during a difficult month, but it sure feels a lot better knowing that there's some stashed away in a secret place if all else should fail.

The method of building an account like this is to be firm in your resolve to keep the deposits coming. Just make it a regular part of your routine to make out two slips each time you go to the bank. Let it slide a few times, and months will begin to slip away before you decide you can afford to divert an extra hundred into your "old" savings account. Instead, think of your savings deposit as a separate monthly expense that has to be met. And in moments of weakness, visualize the payoff.

Watching the Market and Networking for Profit

Based in a 100-year-old opera house, Baird Banner uses his hands-on experience as a consultant for local music and equipment store owners, who send him to shows and solicit his advice.

PROFILE

Baird Banner

Owner/Chief Engineer

Kludgit Sound

Cerrillos, New Mexico

Career Roots Started as an musician and engineer in L.A. Moved to Santa Fe in 1977 because it offered more elbow room and a diversity of artistic creativity, not to mention much lower real-estate costs.

Facility The studio was built in a hundred-year-old, cut-stone opera house and an old post office next door, which was remodeled as a MIDI room and guest quarters. Offers a Sound Workshop 3046 console with ARMS automation and an Otari MTR 90 24-track. Studio 35' x 22', control room 18' x 15'.

House Staff Owner/manager and three "full-time independent" on-call engineers.

Booking Policy For new clients, no session is firm until there is a 50% cash deposit on the estimated time. Client gets a session proposal, plus a session contract. "I still like playing the bar scene as a musician, but I find I have to be pretty serious with the people who I might have jammed with the night before. A lot of people seem to think that you're still just playing at running a studio."

Marketing Mostly word of mouth. "We advertise sometimes. But we do demos at music stores and classes at the community college, which we found to be much more effective than actually taking out advertising.

"It isn't possible to really specialize because there's such a diverse number of projects and cultures going on out here, so we try to be ready for anything. People book us for our musical and production talents more than some incredible array of equipment."

Buying Equipment "We've got an interesting relationship with several of the music stores in the area. They actually pay us to go to the national merchandise shows as consultants, because we're the ones who are really using the stuff, and most of the smaller owners don't have the time to go themselves. They say they more than pay for our tickets by avoiding the purchase of turkey products for their stores.

"If you're not in an urban area and you're technically astute, the store owners are pretty grateful to meet you. It's been a real good thing for us, and with several stores behind us, we carry some real clout at the shows."

Traffic "We get a pretty amusing mix of people at different levels of success. A typical scene is to have one of the local superstars arrive in a Rolls, do a session and then on the way out, bump shoulders in the hallway with an incoming speed metal band. The picture of a mink-drenched wife, complete with babe in arms and nanny, being introduced to a leather guy with a ring in his nose and chains has a sort of breath-holding nature to it."

Growth Plans Has just found a large church downtown with 25-foot ceilings.

"For a while, I was becoming increasingly uncomfortable with the explosion of small 8- and 16-track rooms that people were setting up in their homes. Then I realized that most of them didn't have any good outboard equipment, didn't have professional engineers and didn't have accurate monitoring. So we're setting up a small-format 16-track studio that offers a

great mixdown facility for all those home projects."

They plan to move the 24-track equipment into the larger church and install the 16-track in the opera house. They've also found an investor who's become a limited partner, along with an ad agency and a computer graphics company, to finance the installation of a video mixing bay, so that an entire post-production facility will be available under one roof.

Philosophy "Unfortunately, you can't tell people that you need a couple of weeks off and expect them to wait. I try to accommodate people. Service is what does it. If you don't go an extra mile and get personally involved with people, I don't think your business is going to go as well as it might."

The studio interior reflects the local Southwest culture.

FINESSING SIZABLE SUMS

Whether you start out big or small, a year or two down the line you're going to come up with some indisputable justification for the purchase of some big new piece of gear. It may be a new 32-track, an editing workstation, D5 video or an automation package.

Whatever it is, unless you have an unlimited source of funds, you're going to find yourself short of the money to pay for it. But there are several ways you may be able to get the money you're after.

1. Give your original lender a second chance.

Now's the time to pick up the phone and call the place that got you on your feet when you first started up. They obviously believed in you enough then to take a chance. And since then, you've been an *exemplary* customer!

You've made virtually all your monthly payments on time (if you, uh, "forgot" a couple of months and made some triple payments to catch up in order to avoid repossession, you might just want to skip over to the next section), the original term is more than half over, and your business has grown.

Your banker or leasing officer will, at the very least, be pleased to talk to you about your new plans. He or she will politely demand an up-to-date financial statement (prepared by your accountant, of course), review your payment record and be more than casually available for meeting and/or pleading. If your business shows positive growth, and you've increased its net worth, you stand a chance of getting more money.

Once again, a lot of what happens in the end will depend on the gut feeling of one officer, which is the best argument for staying on good terms before, during and after any business loan you get.

2. Approach friendly lenders who originally turned you down.

Try going back to the two or three people or places who were really friendly and loved your business plan when you originally pitched them, but turned you down because they were gun-shy of new business ventures. If the same officers are still there, they'll remember the impression you made, and the somewhat genuine sorrow they felt in turning you down.

Eighteen months into our business, my partner and I went back to a bank officer we'd shmoozed to death in the beginning. He was a big, straight-arrow, middle-aged guy who seemed more interested in watching women walk by his desk at the bank than in crunching numbers, and he liked our plan and the studio glamor factor we brought with us.

From what we had learned about on his personality the first time through, we had calculated that our best bet would be to spend the rest of our second meeting watching women with him. Later, he had finally called us, apologized and said he just couldn't make the loan fly, but to think of him in the future (bankers like to tell you that).

So we gave it a shot. We called his bank, and the receptionist told us that he no longer worked there. He'd been transferred to another branch across town and been made president!

He remembered us right away, smiled at our modest success, and okayed a $40,000 loan at prime rate plus 2% in less than 48 hours. We used the money to buy a wide-ranging assortment of used equipment from a single source at a killer price.

We made the monthly payments a priority and paid the loan off without a single late payment. That set us up for the next loan we needed a couple years down the line. And all that good "luck" came out of connecting with one person.

3. Consider adding a partner.

It may be another partner, or it may be your first. Either way, it can be a very smart move to bring in new blood—and new cash—at a critical time of acquisition or expansion. Partnerships can take several forms.

An *investor* is primarily interested in a good return on the money he or she lends the business. The easiest kind of offer to make is to approach someone with an attractive loan proposal. You can approach an individual with the same proposal you'd take to a bank, and should get some serious conversation if you ask for, say, a one-year, $10,000 loan at six or seven points above current bank CD rates.

This is an attractive offer to the right person. You can use the same proposal you'd bring to a bank, or approach people you know who trust you.

Making the Deal Attractive

A one-year or 18-month term makes sense for

several reasons. From the investor's point of view, it's a quick return, which lowers their risk. And from the owner's side, you're taking on a short-term debt that you should feel good about being able to handle.

Most banks, if you can find ones that will talk to you, won't give you a one- or two-year term. There just isn't enough money in it for them. But to an investor looking to get in and get out, that kind of term is just right. You're actually much more likely to encounter resistance from someone if you propose a longer term. A private investor is likely to think of too many things that can potentially go wrong in a longer period. Going with a short term is also a good way to keep from getting too greedy. The payments are going to be hefty on a year's contract, which tends to help people act more sanely when they're planning their monthly expenses.

You may also be able to find this kind of deal through your friendly lease-company contact. You may be surprised to find that some of the smaller companies actually solicit individuals to provide funding on some leases.

A couple of years ago, we bought a used 1-inch video recorder to act as a backup machine when lines had begun to form at the end of the day for the one we had in our machine room. All we needed was about $15,000 for this older machine to pick up the overflow, and I offered to make it a one-year lease term with our regular company, rather than putting up all the cash at once. We signed the lease papers a few days later, and when the first payment became due, the coupon instructed us to make the check out to one Irving Blatsky.

I called the lease company. "Who the heck is Irving Blatsky?" I asked. "Oh," said my old friend. "He's my partner's boyfriend. He likes to get in on some of the smaller deals we occasionally do. Good rate, huh?"

Well, yeah.

Coming To Terms

If you arrange a private deal, you can work out all the terms between the two of you, although you'll want your lawyer to take a look at the final document you draw up before you sign it. If you're buying a specific piece of gear with the money, you may be asked to include it as collateral in the loan. That makes sense from the investor's point of view.

Here's a simple letter of agreement for a short-term loan:

Mr. Michael Eisner
Dwarf Building
Disney Studios
Burbank, CA

Dear Mike,

This is a note to formalize the terms of your $15,000 loan to Financial Reality Studios, Inc.

We agree to repay your loan of $15,000.00 to us at 12% interest over a 12-month period, per the following schedule:

12 equal payments of $1,332.73 on the 15th day of each month beginning Nov. 15, 1994.

FRS agrees that the following equipment shall be used as security against this loan, in the event of default:

1 Acme XR7 analog 19-track tape deck (very rare), serial # S0443L1

We agree to pay a late fee of $50 if payment is received more than five days past the due date, and define default as a period of 60 days in which no payment has been made past the due date.

Thanks for your belief in us, and for the discount coupons on admission to EuroDisneyland. If you ever need to spend a couple hundred million on studio time, do look us up.

Sincerely,

J. Cricket
President

4. Find out if the manufacturer of the equipment you want can offer its own lease or finance plans.

Many of the majors do. And often their terms are the best in the market. That makes sense, since they're profiting directly from selling you their own equipment. Manufacturers can be also be more flexible, because if you default they can take their own equipment back, refurbish it and restock with the least amount of hassle.

The companies who don't offer their own financing often have ongoing relationships with leasing companies who are already educated and experienced in dealing with them. The advantage is that, again, the company is interested in finding the lowest terms to make the deals more attractive to their customers. So the shopping is done for you.

That's not to say that either the manufacturers or the leasing companies are going to give the store away, but they may be the most likely to smile on you if your qualifications fall a little short. Which brings me to another true story.

When All Else Fails, Start Tap-Dancin'

Right from the start, my partner and I embraced the audio post beast as our business specialty. Michael was a natural for it, with all the skill and the taste for the challenge. I loved the added dimension of working to picture, and the challenge of trying to sell filmmakers on transferring to video so they could bring their work in.

As we began to get our name out there, and more work started coming to us, it became apparent that we were losing out on a lot of bigger and better projects because we didn't have a 1-inch master video recorder, the final format of choice at the time. I would pitch my best about personally taking the finished mixes to neighboring studios and transferring them at cost, but it just didn't work for many of our perspective clients. They wanted the convenience and the advantage of working in a place that offered the full service, from 1-inch laydown to 1-inch layback.

It got so frustrating that we talked a rental company into dropping off a 1-inch for a couple of months at only $1,500 a month (a real bargain), but even that low amount of rental was killing us. In three months, we'd paid out nearly five grand and were just barely breaking even.

Meanwhile, our business was growing, but slowly, and as fast as the extra money came in, there'd be something important to spend it on. We had a small savings account with a few grand in it, but that was it.

Making the Rounds

We tried the banker and leasing routes and got turned down everywhere. We asked a couple of people we knew if they'd like to invest in a piece of equipment with us but didn't get any bites. We called the manufacturer and pitched its leasing department, and even *they* turned us down, citing our financials, which showed us just breaking even.

By the time they turned us down, I'd personally spent the better part of a month on the phone, pounding the pavement and banging out proposals to a dozen different companies. I had

put my last hope on the manufacturer's own leasing department giving us the go.

When they didn't, I got really upset. I remember putting down the phone and banging my fist on the desk. And at that moment, I decided not to take "no" for an answer.

I was sure I'd convinced that equipment company to lease us the machine through their own program, and they'd just turned us down. I decided I had nothing left to lose, and that I'd try contacting them one more time. Except this time, I'd make sure they'd at least notice us.

On the following pages is a copy of the actual letter I sent. I knew I had nothing to lose, and that a standout performance was in order.

Going on Instinct

I don't know what made me think that the photo was a good idea, but I spent half an hour convincing everyone to snarl at the camera while I went through two packs of Polaroid film, trying to get just the right sort of warmth. The above shot is pretty close to the one I sent, but Meredyth, our studio manager, looked a bit more striking in that one.

I threw every piece of literature and hype about the studio into the biggest manila envelope I could find, with the sort of forced carefree attitude that you try to wear when you're about to go skinny-dipping in a pool full of piranhas at gunpoint while you try to prove to the guy who's making you do it how cool you are.

Not Breathing

I tried holding my breath, gave up and waited five days.

That morning, a secretary from the company called and said Paul would see us at his place on Tuesday. As we drove over there, my partner kept saying, "Now, tell me just once more what you put in that letter again..."

We were kept waiting for half an hour. Two guys left the office looking ashen-faced and silently walked out of the building. Finally, we were shown in. Paul was a portly, fiftyish, cigar-chomping tough guy in a gray business suit, with half a head of hair. He was bent over a stack of spreadsheet reports on his desk and didn't look up.

While we stood there, I noticed that the group photograph I'd included in the package was on top of the stack. At last, he tilted his head up and silently stared at the two of us. He scowled, took a wheezing breath, and with a tobacco-laced throatiness muttered, "Geez...you didn't bring the broad?"

The equipment was delivered a week later.

Mr. Paul Dudeck
First Universal Bank
Fourth Street Annex
Memphis, Tennessee

Dear Paul,

Welcome to your custom-tailored Interlok dog and pony show, the one that gets to prove that we may not be big, but we certainly have a nifty little operation and the spunk to make it keep on growing.

First, I want to restate that the primary reason that our Profit & Loss numbers may have looked a little depressing is that a) we keep re-investing all our profit, and b) we have, perhaps to our detriment, a scrupulously honest accountant. Should you have someone of more dubious repute to recommend, I'd be pleased to take him to lunch.

That said, kindly direct your attention to the center ring displaying these numbers for the last half of the year:

Studio Income by Month

(Here, we listed our actual income during the past six months.)

Definitely has that look of steady growth when compared to last year. Comes from people liking the way we do business. Good marketing and promotion. Healthy here today, here tomorrow kind of feel to the place. People who love their work, that sort of thing, what?

AND NOW,
OUR SECRET PLAN
FOR MAJOR GROWTH THIS YEAR:

Buy that 1-inch video we've been renting for 2 to 3 grand a month while we attract new business that we couldn't get without it!

Wow...Logic like that just kinda takes your breath away, eh? Because here's what's been happening: Companies that wouldn't give us the time of day three months ago are booking weeks at a gulp, now that we can lay back to 1-inch at 4:00 a.m. when the session ends.

Since September, we've billed Ace Films $12,000 doing weekly preview trailers for the hit TV series "My Mother Escaped from the Circus." Their producers come in once a week for half a day, lay it back and send it off. And in December, we billed Ecstasy Productions $15,277.70 to do the audio post on the hour-long TV special "Oriental Secrets of Napkin Folding," based on the best-selling novel. The pivotal deal point was having a 1-inch for the hour's worth of layback they needed at the end of each of the six nights they were here.

Right, OK, so the 1-inch isn't the only reason we're getting these great projects. Our talent, experience and ability are playing a marginal role in attracting and keeping these guys from going elsewhere. **But the 1-inch is the missing piece in the puzzle,** and its

Snarling mad-dog INTERLOK professionals form protective Circle of Death around *rented* 1-inch VCR.

mere, yet awesome, presence is going to make us a lot closer to becoming rich and famous this year as we trudge ever upward on our vision quest towards that California pinnacle of perception: **TRUE SIGNIFICANCE!!**

Why, just look at this clever promotion that went out on Jan. 1st to 250 hand-picked, personally called, qualified and interested production-company leads we've made our studio manager suffer miserably over in the last few months [we enclosed our two-page mailer]. Could you, with a hot little project in your hands that needed some touching up, possibly resist a deal like this? Of course not! And then, once you worked with us, you too would be ours!

Because we are *truly awesome dudes!*

SO HERE'S WHAT WE WANT:

One New Acme 1-inch Video Deck With All The Trimmings

AND HERE'S WHAT WE'RE WILLING TO DO TO GET IT:

PAY 20% DOWN + TAX + 1ST
& LAST IF WE HAVE TO)
That's about $6,800 + $2,100 + $600 = $9,500. Down.

**Why, just think about the kind of vacation
your whole family will enjoy!**

BUT SERIOUSLY:

We hope that we've at least caught your attention with all this silliness. It's just our way of trying to tell you how important this purchase is to us, and how much we'd like to do business with you now (and later, too).

I'd be glad to meet you anywhere in town during your next visit to say hello, and would be delighted to show you our facility, located in the very unique Crossroads of the World complex in the center of Hollywood.

Thanks for keeping the door open. Hope we'll hear from you soon.

Sincerely,

JM

BETA-TESTING: A WEIGHTY ALTERNATIVE

In 1989, we signed our first full-blown TV series, "The New Zorro," which lasted 78 episodes over a three-year period on The Family Channel. It was great fun and a fascinating experience, posing many new challenges, as we faced the ongoing deadline of delivering a weekly show that required precision planning, execution and about 90 hours of work per episode.

One immediate decision we made was to commit to a nonlinear workstation for all the dialog and music editing. Those were relatively early days for audio workstations—we looked at everything out there, decided it wasn't worth the 100K+ that the best ones were asking and settled on a powerful, cost-effective alternative—let's call it the Wondro.

One of the reasons we ultimately bought the setup was that I was so impressed with the rep who had brought and showed it to us, Ron Franklin, that I offered to buy the box on the condition that he edit the show. The timing was right for both of us, and we made the deal.

Ron was experienced at editing music and dialog, a process that takes some serious experience and talent. He was also totally at ease with the unit, having given demos in facilities across the country. It was for those reasons that I felt confident in purchasing what was to turn out to be a pretty early version of this new and sophisticated whiz-bang box.

We began running into problems within days after its installation. The software had some rough glitches and when the memory got close to full, big parts of it could suddenly up and disappear. The company was made aware of the problem via us and Ron, who maintained his status as a rep on their payroll, and they responded with a high degree of integrity and support. Each time something unexpected occurred, they were there to analyze it and attempt to fix it. The problem was that we were losing a lot of time waiting for solutions to appear and were becoming increasingly wary of the unit.

Other editors were coming in for sessions too, and there were times when the entire contents of the hard drive would suddenly vanish in the midst of an operation. One of our staff editors was so surprised and enraged when this happened (having backed up internally and thus lost eight hours of work) that he smashed his fist into the wall behind him in reaction and broke his hand! Poor Eric walked around in a cast for six weeks after that, a sad reminder of the throes of raging technology.

Unknowingly Signing On

What had occurred at our studio was that Interlok had become an unwitting beta-test site for a largely unproven system. Beta-testing is research in the field on a piece of equipment once it has largely proven itself at the factory. Most manufacturers seek out facilities in which to place their equipment for real-world workouts before they begin to sell to the general public, keeping a close eye on the machine to see how it handles its chores.

The normal deal is that the studio gets the piece for an extended period of time at no charge, in return for enduring likely crashes, system errors, malfunctions and a lot of site-to-manufacturer communication. At the end of the shakeout period, some kind of option to buy is struck; the studio gets the piece at a deep discount or for free, or perhaps simply returns it.

In our case, it felt like we'd become the nerve center for the manufacturer. They basically dedicated a couple of their techs to the cause, and every time we experienced difficulty they rushed one of them over to ponder the challenge. The problem was that many times, there was no immediate answer, which caused some pretty tense situations. Ultimately, we wound up with a system that did the job in a smooth and impressive manner, but it was a long and bumpy road that took us there.

In the end, the company was more than accommodating, staying in touch and spending what must have been thousands of dollars on tech time and equipment swapping, all at no charge to us. And when it was time to purchase another system for our newest bay, they were very generous in their offer to sell us a new and *proven* Wondro Plus! Based on their offer and the kind of support we'd gotten from them, we took them up on it and were very pleased with the results. This time, it was made clear to us that the system had already been extensively tested, and with a few minor adjustments, it soon became the reliable and impressive center of our newest tapeless bay.

Determining the Risk

To be a good candidate for beta-testing, your studio should have at least one person who is at the very least an excellent troubleshooter, if not a component-level tech.

Bear in mind that beta-testing is by definition a symbiotic relationship between facility and manufacturer. Be sure that you have adequate backup to get the job done in the event of any serious problems. And don't volunteer just for the sake of getting some cutting-edge technology for a free ride. More often than not, there'll be a lot more commitment on your part than you may want or have the patience for.

A Pre-Studio Programming Service

Providing a notable alternative to the standard studio, Mark Shifman has the facility and the know-how to offer his clients a money-saving step between composing the music and putting it down on tape.

Mark Shifman

Owner/Engineer

MIDI Lab

Los Angeles, California

Career Roots Worked as a staff and independent engineer for ten years, his last staff position being an engineer for a small record company. In the mid-'80s, the company started using a lot of MIDI gear.

"Suddenly, the artists were walking in, handing me a disk and saying, 'Here, put this on tape.' "

The Idea "I began realizing that a lot of people wanted MIDI power without having to learn exactly how to use it. Even people who were familiar with it would often get frustrated with the mechanical aspect getting in the way of the creative flow. So I decided to set up a place where people could come in, be creative and just play, while they took advantage of all the things that MIDI could do for them."

Facility One room, located next door to another independent 24-track studio. Two Tascam M216 mixing boards totaling 24 inputs and an 8-input Boss BX800 for effects returns, Ampex 4-track, keyboards, samplers and outboard gear. Total investment: about $20,000.

House Staff Just Mark himself.

Dual Focus Independent engineering and pretracking sequencing for composers and songwriters.

"As an engineer, I'm able to start by doing the programming. But that's also the beginning of doing an entire project. I've mounted most of the equipment on a rack and made it available for rent. That way, the equipment and I can follow through in a choice of studios, and clients get the continuity of my knowing what's going on in the project. People get comfortable working with me here and as their engineer in the studio."

Rates "I keep the rates down so that the people can afford to spend more time in here. I like working and doing this, and doing it right.

Marketing "I've never done any advertising, but I'm considering it now. I feel this is a personal service and that people work with specific engineers because of who they are as individuals. My business has always come through personal references. People call me because they believe I can do a good job. However, I've begun to consider a direct-mail campaign to help broaden my existing client base."

Pros and Cons "The biggest advantage I have is the flexibility to prep a project and then take it to any studio I feel is appropriate. I don't have to feel tied or obligated to a particular studio. But that also means a lot more work for me, and a lot of drudgery in setup and take-down time."

Problems "My original plan was to set up tie lines between my room and the studio next door. At one point, I was working with another engineer. He'd be there and I'd be here. We'd talk on the phone, getting everything set up, and then I'd come over and start recording. But they've since become an audio post facility. Now, in order to work there, I have to do a complete alignment from scratch, do the session, (which is often only two to three hours), then realign the machines back to the way they were. It's just not worth the time and trouble. So

I've turned to several other local studios where I can be set up in 20 minutes."

Plans "This is a good room to work in for composing, because the sound is kind of 'hype-y.' So it's exciting, it's punchy, it feels good and it inspires creativity. Business has gone from good to very good. I'm not sure what's next, but right now I'm really enjoying what I'm doing."

15
On Being the Boss

Yessir, I mean no ma'am, I mean r-r-right away, boss!

If this is your first experience in giving orders, you may be in for a giddy ride. There are any number of nervously funny sides and situations to being the person in charge. If you're somewhat reserved, you may find it pretty embarrassing to ask someone to take out the garbage for you, or duplicate the Rolodex. Or to stand right there and tell your receptionist to tell a caller you're not there.

On the other hand, if you've always been a little brassy, or if you started a business because you were sick of getting pushed around, then you may have the time of your life taking charge and soaking up the power, the options and the glory.

Everyone develops their own style of giving orders. For some, it may be sweet revenge after years of resentful fetching. For others, it's a chance to finally set up a shop in which everyone is treated fairly, like human beings. And for others, it's just plain terrifying. The idea is to learn how to be comfortable, to manage effectively and to remain somewhat human at the same time.

So here, for anyone who's interested in an outsider's opinion, are a few suggestions to mull over in your ivory tower.

How To Play Fair and Stay in Charge

1. Be reasonable, consider both sides, solicit input and remember to do unto others...

2. Be polite when you're giving orders. Say "please" and "thanks." Politeness promotes mutual respect and truly makes a difference. It also sets the tone for the way both you and your staff members conduct your business and relate to other people.

3. When an employee really knots things up, don't reprimand him or her in front of others. Go somewhere private, and then read 'em the riot act, if that's what's needed. Keeping it between yourselves, even if it's anger, promotes bonding instead of burning, because it tells your employee that you care enough to protect his or her dignity.

And there's more: Arguments between management and staff members are always sensitive and can be taken personally. What may seem petty or inconsequential to you may strike the recipient of your consternation as the coming of Armageddon. For that reason alone, just the act of inviting the perpetrator into a private area may give you enough time to think a little more about what you're going to say and to temper your words with an eye toward the future. Just as you need to fix your eyes on the horizon driving at night when some idiot comes at you with his brights on, you need to look at the longevity of the relationship you're dealing with at each high emotional point.

Finally, our litigious society advocates threats and suits at every turn in the road these days, and it is advisable and important to maintain an air of civility and care when chewing out an employee. A stressful lawsuit is the last thing you want to be dealing with; it's a good reason to develop a style of support rather than malignment.

4. Let your people know you care about them. Hold regular company meetings and encourage everyone to participate and let their opinions and feelings come out. And let them know that they can come to you in private as well. Be accessible and you will avoid a multitude of potential confrontations, behavior and policy problems.

The corollary to that accessibility is to give each ensuing meeting your attention and respect. Become a boss who is respected for that and you'll have gone a long way in promoting company spirit and personal loyalty.

5. Don't pinch pennies and don't rip off your employees. All you wind up with is extra pennies. Expect a certain amount of breakage and wear and tear as inevitable. Pick up a lunch tab once in a while. Give your assistant a couple of extra hours off on the day of the big concert he's been looking forward to. Reward extra effort with occasional bonuses or favors. And don't ever haggle with an employee about properly earned overtime.

6. Respect people's personal lives. Let a reasonable amount of phone calls and personal interaction take place, as long as it's not disrupting the system. Avoid criticizing lifestyles and keep your nose out of other people's relationships. In an employer/employee context, that's none of your damn business. Promote an air of tolerance couched in professionalism and you will go a long way toward earning and preserving real mutual respect.

7. Set policies and rules that people can agree to live by. Then, with you as the example, insist that they be followed.

8. Acknowledge achievement. Congratulate an engineer for a great mix. Compliment a receptionist for handling a tough client. Give a high-five for a job well done. Let people know how much you appreciate their accomplishments. Share your pride.

9. Set the company example. Be conscious and exemplary in the way that you dress, deal with a client, engineer a session or handle a problem. Observe the way you handle punctuality, etiquette, communication, follow-up and leadership. Walk a mile in the shoes of your employees and decide whether you like what they see when they look at you.

Also, solicit input from peers and other executives you know. If you find out something about yourself you don't like, work hard to change it.

10. Be a strong leader. Stay in charge, but always be within reach. Make the decisions, but be available for input. Treat your people like the family they are and let them know you're standing behind them with all the support they may need.

And when you've got all that down, run for office: The rest of us need all the enlightened politicians we can find.

PAYROLL ETIQUETTE

The privilege of being the boss brings with it a host of rules, responsibilities and judgment calls. Perhaps the most obvious is that in return for your employees spending 40, 60, 70 or even 90 hours a week practically killing themselves for you, you're agreeing to do them the honor of actually paying them real money on a regular basis. Unfortunately, this basic "care and feeding" tenet may be a bit more challenging than you anticipated.

Studio bookings and business have a funny habit of going from hot to suddenly cool to just plain nonexistent at times. When that happens, you may find yourself doing some pretty sweaty tap-dancing to keep your creditors happy and the VU meters swinging. The fact is, during your first few years of operation, the only time you may see an abundance of money floating around will probably be the day the wind blows the cover off the Wheel of Fortune play-at-home-version game box.

With that in mind, be sure you can afford to pay the salaries that you've agreed to hand over to the people who believed you when you promised you would. And then be sure to do it—on time and without excuses.

Keeping Your Word

Nothing is more important in creating trust and company morale than for your employees to be able to depend on getting the money you've promised to pay them. Make payday a no-nonsense affair, and you'll have gone a long way toward creating a professional and trusting environment that is the foundation of a successful working team.

There will be times that doing this won't be easy; the chances are that your studio will have to weather some pretty shaky financial periods. But your employees are the last people who should have to pay for those problems.

One way to keep that from happening is to maintain an emergency bank account, one that's earmarked for real emergencies only. You can just throw a few grand into it when you're flush, or earmark, say, 3% of your income on a regular basis and direct it into the account. Either way, having a few thousand stashed away can give lifesaving aid when you just need to hang in there for a couple more weeks, until that big check you've been expecting comes in.

That should help you avoid withholding employee salaries. Postponing paydays, even if your employees agree to wait, trades away some of the mutual trust and respect that keeps a business internally healthy. By making paychecks a given, you're telling your people that they can depend on you, and that you expect the same from them. Tease them or plead with them, cajole or dance around them, and company morale will slip through your fingers like so many digital ones and zeros.

When Money Gets Short

If you're short of funds, pay the rest of the bills a week or two late—employee paychecks should come first. Pay yourself last, if there's anything left: It's your business, not theirs. Even if it isn't true or doesn't seem like it to you, they figure that you're the one who at least gets to keep the equipment. Somehow, it just doesn't look that good to have all that stuff and still be claiming poverty.

But if you take care of them first and they know it, you'll have a track record to stand behind if things really do get bad. Then, if your receivables are late, if you're out of cash and you're looking at a power shutoff or an eviction notice and you've got a real emergency on your hands, you can call a meeting and ask the people whose paychecks you've always put first for a little faith and patience.

Hopefully, something that drastic won't happen more than once in a great while, but if you've made every payday before that one, and the guy from the electric company is standing in your doorway with a wrench in his hand, your people will understand. They'll believe you and support you with the spirit you've always shown them. And together, you'll have a fighting chance to recover and make things right again.

COMPANY MEETINGS

One of the best ways to stay in touch with your employees is to call regular company meetings. Given the haphazard nature of studio booking schedules, it's crazy to try and schedule something for the third Wednesday of every month, but it should be easy enough to arrange a sit-down every so often when a hole miraculously pokes through the schedule.

Company meetings are like town meetings, where the people of the village all get together and talk about the issues that are most important to each of them. As the boss, a good way to run a meeting is to be the person to begin the discussion.

You might start with an overview of the previous weeks' events and add some observations about various clients and upcoming projects. This is also a good time to give a little praise for a job well done in front of the group.

There may also be some problems on your mind. One may be pressing enough to begin to discuss right away, but it's often more constructive to pass the focus on to others after a few opening remarks.

That's because the best meetings come from your employees sensing a willingness on your part to listen to *them* for a change. Chances are, the problems you have in mind will be the same ones they want to talk about. Giving others the floor gives you a chance to listen to a fresh perspective, without first coloring the room with your own.

After letting others take the lead, you can then help steer the discussion in the direction you choose, if you feel the necessity to do so. That way, you become a moderator instead of a debater. This is another subtle way of delegating responsibility while maintaining ultimate

Elements for a Successful Meeting

1. A company meeting should preclude all other business. Give everyone enough notice and then don't take 'no' for an answer. Company meetings are not only the glue that helps to create morale, they are often the site of germination for new ideas, policies and projects.

2. Make the setting conducive to work. Don't allow outside distractions to interrupt your meeting. Turn off the stereo and TV. Take the phone off the hook, or appoint the newest staff member present to answer the phone in another room when it rings, informing callers that the person they're trying to reach is tied up in a meeting and will call them back. Make it understood that everyone is there to focus on the job of running the company for the next hour or two.

3. Choose a good location. The simplest and most obvious would be within the facility environs. But you can also add some pizazz by hosting a breakfast at a nearby restaurant. Find a place that offers a private dining room or wing that is both quiet and relatively private. Explain your purpose to the manager and arrange for meal service at a specific time, usually at the beginning of the meeting. It's easiest to arrange for one check for the entire table and makes for a nice, inexpensive perk when you to pick up the tab.

Important: Do not consume alcohol during a company meeting!

4. Solicit employee feedback before the meeting. Let staff members know you're interested in their opinions and ideas about the way things are done at the studio. Employees have a far better perspective on operations you may be totally unaware of, and are in a position to be creative with solutions.

You can even offer a prize in the form of a cash award, a bottle of wine or a couple of tickets to the movies for the best idea of the meeting. Little rewards like these are very inexpensive, yet mean a great deal to employees.

5. Keep the floor open to discussion. Even in the best of companies, there still exists an adversarial relationship between employer and employee. Remind your employees often that their input and opinions are important and valuable. Pause between topics during meetings. Ask for more input or ideas. Let them know you really mean it.

6. Be poised and diplomatic. Don't demean employee suggestions. Respect the bravery of a staff member who speaks up at your behest, only to offer something that sounds silly, useless or redundant. These are the most telling moments of a discussion: When someone offers up a gaffe, your reaction will be critically tracked by the rest of the staff. Their subsequent behavior and participation will hinge on your diplomatic reaction.

7. Offer praise and agreement often. The more positively you react to your employees' suggestions and input, the more they will trust you and one another, resulting in a company with high morale and sense of family. You don't have to go overboard; just remember that people are social beings who are very dependent on interfacing and feedback in a work environment. Taking an engineer aside and praising his mix, or even just asking about his life, can mean a great deal to someone who is stressed out from his personal workload or responsibility.

authority. When the debate finally reaches a place of agreement, you can act as the leader to interpret the solution that's been worked out. That's also the point when you can offer a differing opinion or further refine the ideas on the floor.

Keeping a Loose Structure

Company meetings should be simple and informal; this is the best atmosphere to promote discussion. Most of the time, they'll pretty much run themselves. Just keep a casual eye on the focus of the meeting—if it begins drifting to the basketball playoffs or an upcoming concert, you can help to casually steer it back to the subject at hand.

But a relaxed setting is very conducive to stimulating an atmosphere of openness and trust that helps promote sincere communication. If your employees know that they can say what they feel without fear of embarrassment or protocol, important emotions and ideas are bound to come out and benefit everyone.

So sit back and listen. Schedule enough time for everyone to participate and speak their minds, and let the focus go where it will.

Getting the Most out of the Meeting

If you've got a lot on your mind, write your ideas down so that you don't forget any important points. Let everyone know that there's going to be a meeting tomorrow and encourage them to think about what they'd like to discuss. During the meeting, have someone take notes so that you can review the discussion afterwards.

Try to meet at least once a month. By letting the time float, you can schedule more easily the day or morning before. Make sure everyone in the company attends; company meetings are too important to miss. That applies to part-time or on-call personnel as well. If someone is unable to be there, consider rescheduling.

Great things come out of company meetings. Problems get solved, policy gets refined, employees get recognition and people get closer to one another. A company meeting is one of the special activities that help make a family out of a group of otherwise separate people, by encouraging them to share their feelings and ideas together.

Getting Out of the Studio

There is a great deal to be learned about running a successful studio business by examining the way people handle themselves in the corporate business world. One effective example is the desirability of a company outing. If your studio involves more employees than just yourself, there are great results to be had by taking your partner, an engineer or a small group of employees away from their workplace once in a while and doing something else as a group.

Bonding is an abstract concept that connects people to one another on a more intimate level, which affects their performance, trust and

level of integrity. People bond in any number of ways, but it certainly occurs in a studio situation. You spend long hours together working creatively on something you hope will be successful (in a number of ways). And in the end, you listen to the results and judge the quality of your individual and cumulative efforts.

But people need more than high-stakes drama and responsibility to form a good team. They need something far more important—they need to have fun.

There's no doubt that this business can be as fun as fun gets. Nevertheless, if you're paying an employee to work for you, there is always a fear factor involved in the workplace: My job depends upon my turning in the good results; I'd better be careful with what I say to the boss; if I make a mistake while we're fooling around, I could really blow the whole thing; etc.

You need to get out of the building together once in a while to escape that kind of pressure. And you'll be glad you did.

The Studio That Plays Together...

There are a number of simple ways to get outside. All that really matters is that you are enthusiastic about making it happen, and make sure your staff catches the buzz. Do it successfully once or twice, and you won't have to be enthusiastic anymore; your staff will bug you about the next activity. Here are some ideas.

1. Play ball. Organize a softball game. Invite staff friends and families to participate. Do it in a park on a Sunday afternoon and make it a picnic. As the boss, do something special, like bringing a giant cooler of drinks or a big bucket of chicken.

Go one step further and inform everyone that lunch is on the studio. Reserve a picnic area and lay out a spread. The cost is minimal and the payback is genuine appreciation for doing something special for your employees.

Be sure and participate in whatever activity you arrange. You don't have to be any good at it. Looking dumb and human in front of your staff provides a strong, intangible connection that will serve everyone with goodwill.

2. Go bowling. A bowling party is a real blast, much more fun than you may realize. It's indoors, there's bar and waiter service on the lanes, it's noisy, and you're surrounded by lots of other people having a good time. And it's easy to put together at the spur of the moment.

Last year, my studio manager walked into my office, closed the door and said, "You know, with us losing that client because of the scheduling snafu, and the equipment problems causing us so much grief in the last few days, morale is really in the pits this week. What should we do?"

We decided to break out and go bowling. We invited everyone to bring their significant others, picked up their burger and lane tabs, and for three hours whooped it up in a way that would never have been possible in the studio.

The high scorer of the night made it to 154. By the next week, both the equipment and the company morale were fixed.

3. Do something special around Christmas. Maybe the easiest and most logical way to test the outing waters is to plan something extra for the holiday season. If your staff consists of just one or two other people, take them out for an intimate dinner. If there are more than half a dozen, plan a special event.

We've done parties both in-house and outside with great success, simply because we've devoted some time and effort to making the evening fun. It's grown into a real extravaganza over the years, with a mock awards ceremony parodying the Grammys and "honoring" something personal and funny about each staffer. We sing custom comedy songs, hand out special certificates and have a riotous gift exchange that never fails to elicit applause.

All it takes is a conscious effort to connect with the people you're chained to in the workaday world. The rewards are immeasurable, from your own sense of pleasure to the very real meaning you bring to the people whose lives you touch, especially the ones who would otherwise be alone during this important time.

If there's only one time of year you feel moved or obligated to do something out of the ordinary with and for your company, let it be during these holidays, whatever your religion. And spend a little dough. A box of cookies and some soft drinks won't cut it and may foster more resentment than appreciation (both of which can last for months following the event).

4. Get out of town. In 1987, we had one studio and three employees, one of whom was part-time. We had just finished an exhausting album project, had a little extra money in the bank and were in dire need of some R & R. We decided to all go somewhere together to celebrate and crash.

We thumbed through the local AAA guide,

found a nifty-sounding hotel in the mountains about two hours away and booked a two-night weekend stay, inviting couples to go together and picking up all room charges. It was a great time, and all we did was relax together—eating, drinking, swimming, dancing, sitting in the Jacuzzi, watching TV, the works.

By the time we returned, we felt relaxed and recharged. We'd had some riotous and special moments together, and we knew each other as friends.

That was the start of a yearly tradition known here as the Interlok Outing. As the years have rolled by, we've grown into a substantial company, but we've never missed a year—our staff won't let us! But the experience is worth the cost. And we've figured out a few ways to keep it affordable, in spite of having to book ten or 15 rooms at a time.

First, we found a couple of destinations that offered special rates for groups, to which we've returned over the years. Second, we found that hotels are negotiable about the hours you book. We changed the length of the stay from two nights to one (Saturday) but arranged for early check-ins and late checkouts. Employees are given a list of rooms and asked to double up and make their own arrangements. We split the cost of housing significant others if they stay overnight in a private room with their partners.

That means that staff can arrive at noon on Saturday and remain till 4:00 or 6:00 p.m. on Sunday. Depending on the hotel, they will charge you a percentage of an extra day's rate for this, or throw it in gratis if the rest of the deal is right. Our tradition also includes hosting a champagne brunch on Sunday, but we notify everyone that they are on their own for other meals.

Finally, we schedule activities for everyone to attend (a real necessity for a successful event): a company volleyball game, pool party hours and a company meeting at the hotel. It's a full schedule that still leaves plenty of time for privacy and free time. And although the whole thing only lasts about 30 hours, it's a great out-of-studio experience that our staff buzzes about for months. Approximate cost per employee is $80, well worth the return it brings in loyalty, morale and work ethic.

TAKING RESPONSIBILITY

Things are going to happen in the studio that you are going to wish never had: An engineer is going to erase a master take. The second is going to show up late on a

Saturday and keep the client waiting outside a locked door shivering in the snow. Between two days of big-band sessions, the roof is going to leak overnight and fill up the bell of the antique alto sax with half an inch of rainwater.

The mail will get lost, the receptionist's dog will bark in middle of the only good take the has-been singer had a prayer of getting away with, the record company P.O. won't arrive on time, a homeless family will take up residence outside your load-in door, and someone will undoubtedly vociferously complain that yesterday's mix sounds like warmed-over doo-doo.

Guess who's problem it is, boss. Don't run away and hide. It won't work, and anyway, they'll find you. It's far better to stand still and let it blow at you with the force of the hurricane in the Maxell tape ad. Because the chances are, if that first blast of hot and humid air doesn't knock you down, you're going to survive, whatever the problem is.

SOME PERSONAL PHILOSOPHY

A few great truths have come to me over the course of my life and career, inspired by example, experience, and ultimately from simply surviving the passage of time. Here they are.

Burn Clean

Live your life as close to the truth as you can possibly stand. Stretching the truth, exaggeration, fibs, white lies, masquerading and out-and-out slander all have their place in life. But the more you rely on them, the more explaining and looking over your shoulder you have to do later on.

Telling, and *living*, the truth is one of life's most difficult challenges. But it is undeniably its own sweetest reward. It touches you in everything you do, every moment of the day, from the way you feel about yourself to the way you are perceived as a planetary citizen.

The truth may get you into temporary trouble, but it almost never lasts. It forces you onto the high road of integrity and puts a sheen on everything you touch, everyone you meet, every deal you make, every love and hate you experience.

It's no easy thing, this truth business. You will find yourself severely tested on a regular basis. But the more you live it, the higher your

How to Take Immediate Action

1. Express genuine concern: "Oh, my goodness."

2. Repeat the problem to whoever is standing there and screaming at you, in a way that will make them see that you understand what's happened: "Okay, I can see that you're covered with dozens of cold squashed melon balls that were launched at you when that Marshall stack fell over and crashed onto the buffet table."

3. Sympathize: "Gosh, that must feel awfully yucky..."

4. Apologize: "I'm really sorry about this. I hope you're okay."

5. Take charge of the situation: "Let's get some of this goo out of your hair. Danny, get some towels from the bathroom. Zoe, see if there are any clean Reeboks in the clothes closet. JJ, call the deli and tell them to get some fresh cheese and crackers here right away..."

6. Stick around until everyone calms down. "Everything's gonna be all right, folks. There's nothing more to see now. You clients and musicians, just move along now and go about your business. Let's slip back into that funky house groove again, shall we?"

7. Find something clever to say and change the subject. "You know, Mr. Farnsworth, now that I've seen you in it, light green is a fabulous color on you. Have you ever had your colors done—you know, where they test different colors against your skin tone to find out what 'season' you are? Well, my Aunt Myrna in Kansas City once had the funniest experience..."

self-esteem will grow and the more you will love your life and, most importantly, yourself.

Stand By Your Word

Once you tell the truth, you need to do some consistent follow-up management. It's one thing to be sincere, and quite another to be reliable.

When you agree to attend that meeting next week, make sure you arrive when you said you would. When you promise to deliver a mix by Tuesday afternoon, arrange your schedule so that there are no excuses, come dusk. When you promise to call back, back up an associate, get a bid out, take out the trash or pick up a quart of milk on the way home, make it a natural fact of life. Then get on to the next thing.

And don't forget to give yourself a silent pat on the back each time you do the things you say you will. It's no easy accomplishment to pull this stuff off with regularity.

Honesty in Business

In a small business, a shared vision built on a foundation of trust can weather misfortune and adversity far better than corporate might or more money. But this honesty is an elusive quality in a wealth-worshipping society. As a business owner or manager, you will no doubt find yourself in a position to profit from illegal or shifty disbursements or transactions that land in your lap regardless of your intentions.

A client winks and hands you $200 cash for a low-rate nighttime session that the boss doesn't even have to know ever took place. You add a $300 home receiver onto an equipment package and conveniently forget to tell your partner. A big client pays an invoice that contains an unintentional $600 overcharge, which you discover and decide to keep.

None of these things, you reason, are really hurting anybody, and there's some real monetary gain to be had here. And so, as the years slip by, you fall into a pattern of finagling and keeping your "fair share" of the extra pie.

But it comes at a price, because in doing so, you are robbing yourself of your personal integrity and self-esteem, and of the regard that others hold for you. It doesn't matter that you're slick enough to avoid detection; people sense characteristics about others that go way beyond factual data when they're making unconscious assessments. Think about the last time you said to yourself, "I dunno, I just don't like that guy. There's something slimy going on there."

It's hard to burn clean. It often looks like nobody else is, so why should you? But there is a sweet reward from making the extra effort. One of the luckiest things that ever happened to me was choosing my partner Michael when I started my business. Right from the start, his integrity was so high that there were times I found it exasperating. He certainly played an important role in raising my own personal standards.

Over the years, a great deal of money has flowed in and out of our company. Hundreds of individual client deals have been struck, relationships tested and promises made. And through it all, we've made the extra, difficult effort to remain as aboveboard, forthcoming and painfully honest with one another—and with our associates and clientele—as we insisted we should.

The result has been that after all these years, neither of us carries the heavy baggage of subterfuge or deceit. When the phone rings, we're ready to talk without screening for enemies. When the IRS sends a threatening notice, we're ready to respond with clean and sober paperwork. When a client stays with us year after year, it's in part because he's never felt suspicious. And when the lights go out at night, we both fall asleep in our homes in peaceful exhaustion.

I'd trust my partner with my life at any given moment. And I've never had to agonize or waste my precious time trying to cover my tracks or worrying that he might discover the secret transaction I made six months before. Because there wasn't one.

It's hard maintaining that kind of level of truth—you get tested by the universe all the time. But the payoff is that your relationships, be they with your most intimate partner, spouse or friend, or with associates and clients, *burn clean*. And with that comes an inner peacefulness, satisfaction and self-love that makes life a joyful thing. Amen.

Bring Your Whole Self to the Task

Don't just get it done to get it over with. Do the work at hand with the highest personal involvement and effort you can muster.

When you agree to create the background score for a chemical-additive industrial that only three pimple-faced junior execs are going to see, make it the best music you ever wrote. Rewrite a business letter until it looks like a publishable manuscript. Spend an extra ten minutes on a guitar lick that's almost but not quite yours.

Make every project you tackle a special event, and when you look back, your accomplishments will sparkle and fill you with a sense of pride and achievement. That's what makes for a superstar.

Make Sure You're Having a Good Time

Check yourself and your life out every so often. Are you doing things that make you happy and feel good? If not, you need to sit down, take as much time as you need and figure out why.

Most people get stuck because they're either too busy to notice, too scared to change or too victimized to believe they can. You may have ten good reasons to explain why things aren't better than they are, but the bottom line, my friend, is that this is *your* life.

From moment to moment, year after year, *your life becomes what you say it is*. And along the way, there's a giant menu of choices at every crossroads and decision you make. It may take courage, sweat, heightened consciousness or virtual heroism to break yourself out of your chains and go after your dream, but ultimately you and you alone are the only one who can say yea or nay.

Every so often, sometimes every day and sometimes weeks apart, I think to myself, "How am I doing? Am I on track with the vision of my perfect life? Do I know what my goals are now? Am I getting there?" And then I try to be as real with myself as I am with everybody else.

And I remember to repeat the most powerful mantra of all: *This Is It!* Not last year, not next year. Right now, right here: *THIS...IS...IT!!*

HANGING IN THERE

Owning and managing a small business is a pretty big deal. No, make that a *very* big deal. You've committed yourself to spending a great deal of time doing the one thing that you felt sure was right for you and would make you happy on a day-to-day basis.

In the meantime, you've most likely put your savings, your credit, your intuition and your whole future on the line. And that's the way it should be. Because there's no getting around the seriousness of the endeavor you've chosen.

The cold facts are that two out of every three new businesses go belly-up in the first five years of operation. Maybe that's because people are so often surprised, shocked, amazed and frustrated when the reality of the business world hits them squarely in their schedule book.

Taxes seem neverending, absurd and unfair. Equipment needs to be updated a month after you make your last payment. Competition is intense and relentless. Clients are difficult or just plain impossible. And the hours go on, deep into the night...

Resolving to Win

So don't lose track of the positive. Don't forget to step back and look at the facility you dreamed up and pulled out of thin air. Don't forget what a thrill it was when a really great mix came roaring down the sweet spot in front of the console and you and the producer looked at each other and knew you were geniuses.

Look at the accomplishment. At your achievement. At the people who come to work with you and who come back time after time because they want to be there. Look at the new piece of gear you just bought by being good enough to earn the money. And at the sense of pride you feel when you lock up at 3:00 a.m., knowing you really pushed it to the outer edges of the envelope today.

You chose this crazy business because it's what you really wanted. Of course it's hard—most everything worthwhile is—but it's a challenge you can turn into a success if you keep calm, stay focused, use your brain, work really hard and just plain hang in there.

That's what life is all about. And believe me, it's worth it.

☥, Paisley Park & Professionalism

As a freelance mixer, flying nationwide, Tom Tucker started his own operation in Minneapolis in 1985. After Paisley Park opened in '87, he found himself doing more work there than at his own place, and was subsequently offered the job of both making the recording division profitable and becoming its chief engineer.

Facility Three recording studios plus 12,000-square-foot shooting stage with 45' ceiling.

Studio A: 50' x 35' live room, with granite stone room for live drums, SSL 8000 88-input G+ console with Ultimation, Studer 48-track digital deck, two Studer 800s.

Studio B: 35' x 35' live room, two Studer A800 Mark III analog decks, API 48-input DiMedio console with GML moving-fader automation.

Studio C: Soundcraft TS24 with MCI 24-track deck.

Staff 27 full-time studio employees, including half a dozen house firsts. The second floor is mostly business, with 110 employees, including record, video, tour, accounting and publicity departments. 65,000 square feet overall.

"It's really nice to be in this environment for young engineers coming out of Berklee or Full Sail. A facility like this can really kick off their career."

Market Niche Caters to major-label business, including REM, Stevie Wonder, George Clinton, Fine Young Cannibals, Madonna, Moody Blues.

The Vibe "This is a wonderful facility, and the staff here is second to none, in part due to ☥ being a demanding boss. It takes a good crew to keep him happy, because he tends to work around the clock and likes to work real fast. So we get a lot of comments on how well-groomed the staff is here and how speedy we are.

"Some major artists have come out here to have ☥ produce a tune. Minnesota is pretty much crime-free and it's not at all like L.A. or New York. It does get cold in the winter, but overall, it's a distraction-free environment. And the artists sometimes like to get away from the record companies, too."

Staying Profitable "We work hard to keep this environment very, very world-class and keep it available to artists who want the best. That's an on-purpose business decision. And that's particularly because I don't think the middle-range facility has any kind of real future in this business, unless you're doing a lot of commercial or post work."

Dueling Job Titles "This is one of the more creative times in my life. There's a lot of hours to be worked. But I think it keeps me really in tune with all the business problems from a creative level, particularly in terms of the staff and knowing creatively what I think is appropriate to buy or not. I pretty much delegate authority, but it really makes it possible for me to avoid getting sidetracked with the kind of detail work that used to slow me down."

Future Focus "ADAT-type rooms, be they studio or project, are the future. We have artists who might come and do the original tracks here, then bounce them onto their own ADATs to work on them at home and then bring them back here to mix. Mid-line 24-track analog rooms are a thing of the past.

"I think that all videos are headed for Surround, and we're geared up for that with the new equipment we've brought in. We're only a few years away from as many consumers having Surround in their living room as VCRs. Remember there was a time when not many people had VCRs and then over a very short period of time, it was as if almost everybody in America suddenly had one? All those videos are available with Surround that you can rent in

the video shops, so it's like, why not in the music business? With all the artists doing videos, the potential market is huge.

"So I definitely see the posting side marrying more in the future. CD-I is gonna be a really big deal. Fiber-optic lines are going to be a household thing, with producers hooking up all over the country. You'll be able to just call up and fix a vocal overdub or put a sax solo on a tune."

Choosing Your Path "I think we're turning more and more into a world where you need to be pretty much a specialist. Oftentimes, the direction of a studio needs to reflect that. You need to be very good at the top of whatever you're trying to pursue, businesswise. Whereas in the past, we've seen more studios that catered to everything.

"If you know a lot about records, then you should try and pick a market, like Atlanta, here, Austin, Seattle, San Francisco, develop relationships and get into the record business. If you don't really have a knack for music, you can seek out people who have business relationships in place, offer them money or partnership and start your business with clients.

"Back in '74, my partner and I started out with no money. So we found a couple of non-music-biz investors and talked them into putting up all the money. We just put up all the labor. So there were four of us, and we paid back their share out of the profits. But it's all gotta center around business relationships. You've gotta find somebody who has clients if you want to be in business."

Philosophy "I'm always at home with the best gear, best musicians and people who know how to really play and engineer. High quality. Just being one of the best there is at what you do.

"Being able to really deliver the goods has been what's always worked for me."

16
Hiring and Firing

A lot of studios get off the ground with little or no outside personnel. The owner or partners split up the workload, agree to worry about money later, and get down to it. But with a little time, a little luck and some natural growth, the need for a staff becomes more and more pressing.

Choosing the people with whom you'll spend most of your professional time is a serious task. You need to find like-minded, enthusiastic supporters who are dependable and trustworthy, who complement your style of work, and who you can afford to pay on a regular basis.

When you think about each of those qualities, you may begin to sympathize with the big-company personnel director in the cartoon strip who wearily sits behind his desk as a parade of people with spaghetti in their ears inform him they're perfect for the job. It's a funny situation to look in on, but you're probably going to find yourself in the same predicament from time to time as the years move on and positions have to be filled and refilled.

HIRING A RECEPTIONIST

If you're answering the phone yourself, reception may be the first position you become desperate to get out from under. If you start up a business by answering the phones yourself, you'll quickly find that at best, the responsibility is an annoying distraction and at worst, it's a crippling time-gobbler. If you're at the mercy of your own ringing phone, you are going to be constantly forced to abandon the task at hand in order to serve someone else's completely unrelated needs.

An adept receptionist will free you of this burden, as well as screening all incoming calls, routing them to the proper people when necessary, and taking care of most of the routine tasks that roll through each day as well. He or she will also act as host for the bodies that actually walk through your door and will try to make everyone feel at home.

As you know, there's a fine line between being a receptionist and becoming a studio manager. Sometimes the receptionist grows into the part, and sometimes it's understood that studio management is included with the job. In larger facilities, the receptionist only has time to be just that—the front-room receptionist. But if you have management in mind, you're going to need someone who can do more than just answer the phone.

Choosing the Right Person

The primary qualifications for receptionists are that they be reasonably organized, have a clear and pleasant speaking voice, and be dependable and trustworthy enough to open up in the morning and lock the doors at night.

For a receptionist/manager, you'll need to add some other important qualifications: good people-management skills and a solid understanding of the workings of a recording studio. Add to that a familiarity or willingness to learn computer operations and the ability to take some major responsibility in the day-to-day running of the business. Obviously, someone with managerial potential is going to be harder to find, train and keep happy than a receptionist, but that person will be well worth the extra effort and salary.

There are several ways to look for good people. If you're in a major city, a classified ad in a local entertainment-industry paper should bring dozens of responses. Entertainment jobs are highly prized and sought after for the glamor factor. If you run an ad, it doesn't have to be very prominent—you should be reasonably assured of getting between respectable and overwhelming response with just a few lines of copy.

Try to be specific about the kind of person you're looking for and what the job entails. The more factual you are, the fewer unnecessary calls you'll get. For example, this ad:

Receptionist

Recording studio, full time,
experienced, salary negotiable.
Call Heather, 555-1234.

would probably pull a huge volume of calls, leaving you inundated with the time-consuming problem of scheduling and interviewing.

But this ad:

Rec. Studio Receptionist

Mid-town loc., permanent pos.,
experienced, up attitude, nonsmoker, full-time, $1,600 mo.
Call Nelson bet. 2-4 PM 555-2345

would probably go a long way in cutting down the field. This ad mentions the studio location, eliminating people who live too far away. "Permanent position" should help discourage the type of person who prefers to work a while and then collect unemployment, or who's just looking for something to get by on while they look for a better job. You'll also get respondents who are very anxious to find a solid gig.

An "up attitude" says if you're shy or withdrawn, don't bother. If you're concerned about smoking, "nonsmoker" eliminates anyone who does, and the printed salary eliminates embarrassing questions as well as the people who want to make more than you can afford to offer. Finally, by specifying the time to call, you'll hopefully be freeing up most of the rest of the day to do other business.

Another factor to consider is the amount of intrusion an ad like this may cause in your workday. If you're too busy to answer a constantly ringing phone or just aren't in a desperate hurry, you can specify that job-seekers send their resumes to a printed address. That may also help weed out the people who aren't as serious or well-prepared with their resumes. It also gives you the opportunity to make some critical judgments based on their paperwork before you talk to anyone.

HIRING AN ENGINEER

It isn't easy finding good engineering talent. You can try the classifieds, but the response may be disappointing. The best sources seem to come from either professional referral or from hiring and working with interns, some of whom will rise to the position later on.

So here's a perfect example of the advantage gained in making friends and contacts with the competition. A personal relationship with other studio owners and managers around town may be instrumental in digging up the talent you're looking for. If the relationships aren't there, why not use this as an excuse to help make one?

Make a few cold calls to neighboring studios, introduce yourself and ask for names. In the process, you'll be making yourself known, and in the future, you may be able to refer business back and forth. So use your reason for calling as a way of finding out what sort of business your competitors are doing, share some insight on your own and leave the door open for future communication.

It's quite possible that the owners you talk to may not care to share their talented people with you. That's their prerogative, and in the future, it may be yours. But you can bet on some people being a lot more helpful than others in any endeavor, which means that if you hang in there long enough, the time spent on the phone should turn out to be profitable.

Other Sources

Record and publishing companies often use independent engineering talent. So do music and jingle companies. What better way to pitch your studio services than to tell them that your studio's doing so well you're looking for extra help with all the work that's coming in? A rap like that paints an attractive picture of a successful business, and if the person on the other end of the line doesn't bring it up, you should be able to turn the conversation around to finding out more about their needs before you hang up.

Engineers, like other employee candidates, keep updated resumes. Expect to get one from a job applicant. It should list experience and schooling and then go on to list projects and artists worked with and familiarity with different kinds of equipment. Once again, be sure to check up on references. Don't rely solely on a photocopied letter of recommendation or the listing of a big-name group.

Call and find out what people thought of the engineer's performance, skill and final mixes. What's he or she like as a person? How about musical sensibilities? Can he read music or follow a chord chart? Is her handwriting legible? Do people enjoy working with her in the studio?

If an engineer has had staff affiliation in another studio, find out about reliability, honesty and loyalty. Was he punctual for session start times? Did she have keys? Did he take any clients when he left?

Be careful about that one. You're not going to be very happy if you hire someone full-time and give them your best clients to work with, and then have them quit and take those same clients along with them a few months later.

Looking for the Right Chemistry

You don't just have to rely on gut feeling. Ask people who've worked with the engineer you're considering: Why did he leave his old job, and what happened after he left?

Most good engineers are creative and talented people, and as a result, are far less predictable than typical office personnel. Most maintain a professional demeanor, which also encompasses a sense of protocol and ethics. Include a conversation in your interview about client/studio relationships, and you'll make yourself clear to your prospect while you get a better idea of where she's coming from.

Ultimately, a house first engineer is going to have a lot of power in your business. They'll be spending long hours alone with your clients. Their mixes will speak for themselves and carry great weight in the area of repeat bookings. They'll be responsible for cleaning up the mistakes, whether that means down time, repairs or replacing tape. And they'll have a master set of keys to the building, so that they can open and close at any hour.

So it pays to be careful. Know who you're hiring and trusting with your business. Check references. Talk to people they've worked with in the past. And be up front about what you expect from your employees. Do your job well, and chances are you'll wind up with a real pro.

On-Call Engineers

If most of your engineering is getting covered and you only need occasional help, an on-call engineer is the answer.

There's always a good talent pool to choose from, and many professionals actually prefer to float from one project and studio to another. The obvious advantage to the studio is that you only have to pay for the actual time you need extra ears. Usually, those ears come with a higher price tag. But they're worth it.

The trick is to be ready to handle extra demand before you need to. That means that you shouldn't wait until the last minute to figure out who it is you're going to be calling to help out. You can find people the same way you'd hire a core staff, but you should keep one important point in mind: On-call engineers brought in to take care of your valuable clientele should be made familiar with your room *before* you let them loose on the clients who are paying the day's billing.

There are two simple ways to let freelancers get intimate with your studio. The first is to ask them to attend a working session at your place when the type of project you're likely to need help with is being done. A good engineer will pick up most of the techniques and styles of the in-house first in a couple of hours of observation. That way, he or she will know what's expected when stepping in to take over.

You should also schedule a free hour or two when they can meet with your house first or an assistant to go over patch points and signal paths in the control room. Then they'll feel familiar with its workings and be confident during a real paying session.

The Easy Way to Introduce a New Engineer to Your Room

The other method is to simply let your on-call engineer have the room for a free session of their own. Most engineers have either friends or ongoing projects that need studio time. Give them a house second and an evening, and they'll become thoroughly familiar with your console and patch points.

Schedule these "training" sessions sooner than later. The scene you want to avoid is introducing your client to a last-minute engineer substitute who's never seen the room, bidding a pleasant evening to all and hoping for the best. For some strange reason, clients don't appreciate playing the role of guinea pig while the qualified but room-ignorant first tries to figure out why he can't get that darn reverb to fold back.

The other thing to bear in mind about on-call engineers is that they're on call for other projects and studios as well. This simply means that, to improve your odds of finding help when you need it, you should try to assemble a list of several potential call-up people. This is going to mean running through the same observation/ break-in-the-room routines with each one, which is a time-consuming effort, but necessary and worthwhile.

There is a nice payback to all this. First, you'll be able to breathe a lot easier knowing that your rear is covered when you need it. And second, all these engineers traipsing through your studio are going to think of it when they have independent projects to record and the choice of where to go. So the by-product of expending all this time and energy is some very effective promotion for potential future business.

LEARNING THE RULES

IMPORTANT: *Please note that the following opinions are those of the author, and are not to be taken as legal doctrine when interpreting state and federal law. It is vital that you consult both your own state agencies and your attorney for specific advice and counseling regarding all forms of potential discrimination.*

There are, by the way, things you usually may *not* mention in a job description ad, either by law or by the house rules of the publication in which you advertise. One is specifying that the applicants be either male or female. Another is that they have to look a certain way, whether fat or skinny, gorgeous or ugly. Age is also an illegal bias. And you may not specify religion, marital status, race or ethnic origin.

For that matter, it's really uncool (and also illegal) to ask about age, race, religion and marital or parental status on the phone or in person during a job interview. The applicant may volunteer the information, but equal-opportunity legislation makes it illegal for you as a potential employer to ask those questions flat out. That makes a lot of sense, this purporting to be an enlightened age in which we are the ones purporting to be enlightened.

If you have always felt little twinges of prejudice or preference in choosing the people you want around you, you may find interviewing candidates a very broadening exercise. If you play by the rules, many people whom you might have passed by will sit across from you and surprise you with their ability and aptitude. And in the process, you just may take a few chances on the growth opportunity that's there for *you* in trying something new.

Ignorance of the law can be a little embar-rassing. A well-informed applicant with some experience may inform you flat out that it's illegal to ask the question you just did, and then either smile or begin murmuring veiled threats. Every situation is different.

But the idea behind equal opportunity is to give more people a chance at the work for which they are qualified. And the result is that you'll wind up talking to a wider variety and more interesting mix of people than you may have imagined, and in the process, learn a lot about yourself as well.

Discrimination and the Law

Here's a list of specific items on which the state of California prohibits employers from basing any employment decisions. Although it's a state list, most of these topics are also covered by federal legislation that is either now in place or pending. Check with your own state Department of Employment for other stipulations, and have them send you printed literature for clarification.

The California Fair Employment and Housing Act:

Prohibits harassment and sexual harassment of employees or applicants.

Requires employers to reasonably accommodate physically challenged or mentally disturbed employees or job applicants in order to enable them to perform the essential functions of the job.

Permits job applicants to file complaints against an employer with state departments.

Prohibits on-the-job segregation and requires employees not to discriminate against any job applicant in hiring, promotions, assignments or discharge.

This is serious business. Rights counsels, class-action suits, the media, the courts and individuals have steeply accelerated the pace of legal reform in the area of people's rights. And rightly so: The days of good ol' boys, cultural boundaries and casual or self-righteous discrimination are a relic of the past. Those who think differently are being hauled into court on the losing side of crippling lawsuits that applicants and employees are filing with government encouragement and backing.

Employers can no longer be cavalier about fairness without subjecting themselves to potentially serious consequences. And the end result is that America is steadily increasing the opportunities for its people in groundbreaking waves. In the wake of all this legislation, the shining path that has emerged is for employers to become far more vigilant, equitable and unbiased in their treatment of employees. Or else.

The Law and the Studio

While the majority of the high-visibility cases you read about in the paper tend to come out of faceless corporations, you shouldn't be too quick to write off the potential impact on small businesses. So let's look a little closer at the rules that might affect a studio operation with, say, half a dozen employees.

The most clear-cut is personal discrimination. You may not discriminate against an applicant or employee in regards to sex, race, color, ancestry, religious creed, national origin, physical disability, mental disability, medical condition (including HIV, AIDS and cancer), age, marital status or family care leave.

While the temptation is to hire the perfect employee, an applicant who has AIDS, for instance, but is otherwise well-qualified for the job has every right to expect that he or she will have a fair chance at it. And while the majority of discrimination cases stem from larger corporate hiring practices, there is nothing to stop an HIV-positive applicant from filing a legal complaint alleging that he or she has been turned down solely on the basis of revealing a physical condition (if, in fact, he or she chooses to do so).

An employer's attitude must be fair-minded and mindful of the law. But an employer is *not* required to make concessions that would cause any substantial hardship or financial impact on his business.

For example, if an otherwise well-qualified engineer applicant is unable to navigate his wheelchair up and down numerous staircases or narrow hallways, an employer is usually not required to alter the building to accommodate them. The law states that if the improvements necessary would impose undue expense and resulting hardship to the business, they are not required. However, if all that's necessary is the installation of a ramp or handicapped bathroom fixtures, that would be considered reasonable and necessary.

It is also necessary to exercise caution in presenting these potential obstacles to a physically challenged person. It would be potentially illegal to simply state, 'Sorry, but we can't accommodate you without undue physical hardship,' or even, 'Do you think you can get around the building all right?' Think about how you'd feel if you were the person in the wheelchair

going from one interview to the next, being asked those sorts of things.

The more appropriate action, according to the recommendations of one prominent labor attorney, would be to take the applicant on a tour of the studio, so that he could form his own opinions about the layout. An even better precaution is write out a detailed description of the job and ask the applicant to read it. The more detailed, the better. When the applicant has finished, it is appropriate to ask if, based on what he has just read, he feels that he can satisfactorily perform the listed duties.

What you have now done, is to hand a completely nonbiased description to one and all, and to begin to responsibly weed out those who feel that they would no longer qualify.

Sexual Discrimination

True or False: Nowadays, off-color sex jokes are forbidden in mixed company in a professional studio setting. Answer: Both. In some workplaces, it's true. In others, it's false. And there, in a nutshell, is how vague and confusing federal and state sexual discrimination laws can get.

The general thinking runs along very human grounds: Each situation is different. Every workplace is enveloped in its own vibe, its own sense of family and decorum, its own insulated relationships and degrees of permissiveness. In the studio business, many clients and employees are creative, dynamic individuals, who tend to express themselves with more, shall we say, *vigor* than many rank-and-file corporate clerics. Even if your workplace is sexually mixed, it may be quite normal and acceptable to retell the latest Andrew "Dice" Clay jokes verbatim and receive applause and encouragement for more.

The trick is to be sure that no one is being offended. And the usual course of discovery takes place over a period of time, when people working together get to know one another on various levels of intimacy. If a female is telling the joke with relish to an assemblage of approving males, it may be perfectly okay to accept the challenge of one-upsmanship after the applause dies down. But it's up to the employer to bring a heightened sensitivity to the workplace and look for potential signs of uneasiness.

The law is pretty specific about action. Employers must respond to and take seriously any complaint from an employee about potential harassment. This may require some sensitive listening, further quiet investigation and some ultimate action, such as identifying the concern and warning the offender to alter his or her behavior. An employer should also keep a written record of all such events, in the event that a court action is filed later on. Such records demonstrate the willingness and the efforts of the employer to counteract the problem and attempt to solve it, which should satisfy most accusations later on.

Adjusting Your Attitude

The other component is to exercise care and restraint in your own interactions with people on the job. There is no longer any place for casual innuendo or physical contact that could be construed as sexual. What strikes you as simply a normal display of affection or reinforcement may wind up being interpreted in a completely different way by the recipient.

To avoid these problems, you need to be conscious of what may have been an offhanded remark or gesture, and instead consider the potential implication before going for the laugh. And whenever in doubt, ask. Ask a co-worker if what you just said offended them. Offer a further explanation of a remark that could be taken as a come-on and ask if it was. Get to know the people you work with and their levels of tolerance and comfort.

The laws on sexual harassment are meant to protect people, but not necessarily at the expense of human interaction. It's just that now, you're required to respect the feelings of others with a heightened sense of awareness, decorum and care.

INTERVIEWING

You should expect, at the very least, to get a typewritten resume from a job applicant. A person who's looking for an office or engineering job without one is, in almost every case, waving a red flag in your face. At best, they're saying, "Resumes aren't important to me; it's who I am that you're hiring." More likely is that, for whatever reason, they don't have it together enough to present themselves for a crucial meeting in a professional manner, which means that there's a good chance they won't be ready later on either.

Standard elements of a resume include a name, address, phone number, schooling and work history, hobbies, interests and references. When one is handed to you, you're holding an instant insight into the workings of the person sitting across from you. It's an interesting 45 seconds or so, as if a program has just been inserted into your computer brain, and after a quick scan you're filled with useful information in deciding where to take the conversation.

It's also quite an advantage. A mildly anxious human has just bared his career story in all its glory to you, while you sit there, secure, mysterious and omnipotent, the sunlight streaming in over your shoulder, glaring in his squinting face. He cowers slightly in the footstool you've parked him on so that he must tilt his head upward above the desk at your regal silhouette seated in the high-backed chair of judgment in which you luxuriate, scowling over his puny inadequacy, wordlessly gloating, almost as if to slowly tear the worthless flesh from this vile excuse of a creature that dares to beg for an audience with the majestic royalness that has deigned to endure yet another insignificant...

Uh, sorry. Got a little carried away there. Ahem. The point is, you at that moment are holding all the cards. So do try and make your applicant feel comfortable in the beginning of the interview.

Developing a Rapport

Find something interesting in the resume and start off with some conversation about his history or hobbies, or about a listed company you're familiar with. If you take a moment for casual conversation, you'll show him a little about who you are, which should make it a lot easier to talk in specifics and get answers when you really get down to them.

A good interview should reveal the answers to three basic questions: 1) Does this person qualify for the job? 2) Do you feel good about the prospect of depending on him or her? and 3) What's it going to be like spending half of your waking hours together?

A piece of advice: Hold out for "yes," "good" and "tolerable." But don't be fanatical; there's plenty of room in there for interpretation.

An assistant engineer, for instance, may be fully qualified for an upcoming second position, having had three years of hands-on experience. But a fresh recording-school graduate could be as good or better a choice. Consider that three years' experience means that his work habits are ingrown, and that he's probably more interested in first engineering than assisting. On the other hand, the grad may not be a seasoned pro, but will probably be more enthusiastic about working hard, as she learns your particular routine the way you teach it.

Or, a professional office manager may whip your shop into shape and singlehandedly rewrite your accounting software. But a former publishing company receptionist may be ready to move up, and a lot less likely to get bored and quit four months and a hundred hours of training into the job.

A Couple of Other Things to Notice

Remember that you have to live with the choice you make, at least for as long as it takes you to realize your terrible mistake. This means that if you wind up with a dud after all and it's time to start a new search again, at least you can take advantage of everything you've unhappily learned at the hand of your latest protégé. So if the experience and the acumen is all there, but during the interview the candidate ends every other sentence with "Ya know, man?", take a long view on what murder weapon you're going to use on him at the end of a typical 650-sentence work day.

Another telltale problem sign: gallows humor. If your applicant keeps saying things like "I'll probably really screw something up two weeks down the road, ha, ha," he may well be belying his true history and work pattern. If he repeats an utterance like that more than once, it should be a bright red flag.

Common sense comes into play throughout the interview process. Focus on this: You're entering into a mini-relationship with each applicant you meet. Traits you notice now, under what for an applicant is at best an important situation (and at worst, highly stressful), will most likely come to bear with a vengeance if the person becomes a full-time employee.

So when you've shaken hands and said goodbye, sit down for a moment and think back over what was said, and how some things that may have been casually mentioned or glossed over may manifest themselves in a long-term relationship. That could mean finding some insight into a person's untapped potential, or a chasm of bottomless trouble.

More Interview Principles

When you interview, put aside a couple of specified days and schedule people about every 30 minutes. It's not that you need to talk to each of them for a half hour. But the process is exhausting, and people often show up late, or not at all. With some, you'll make up your mind within seconds after they walk in. But even if you're turned off at the start, you still need to be reasonably civil. It just isn't polite to take one look, spin them around and steer them out the door, repeating "Sorry, job's filled!" over and over.

Try to walk a mile in their shoes. Make some conversation, and then, if you know there's no chance, do them a favor and *tell them what you're thinking*. When I meet someone I'm sure I don't want to hire, I make a point of ending it cleanly, right then and there. I look them in the eye and say, "To be honest with you, I don't feel that you're the right person for this job, and there are a couple of other people I'm seriously considering," and then give them a reason.

That doesn't mean telling them what I think their problem is, as in, "Frankly, you smell bad and you're awfully stupid, aren't you?" Rather, I will describe an attribute of another applicant they do not possess, such as a couple of years' hands-on experience. Choose something that's genuine and you'll help that person to be better prepared for the next interview.

People really appreciate that. They thank you for being straight with them, for not wasting their time, and for not keeping them on the hook with a vague promise of "I'll get back to you when I decide" and then never calling. It's also a great technique for you, as the person who's hiring—the interview is complete and you don't need to do anything else. You just move on, unburdened, to the next prospect.

You should be able to get a bead on someone who is worth considering in ten or 20 minutes of conversation. At that point, unless you've fallen in love, it's a good idea to write down some notes (I like to write on the resume so everything stays together) and promise a follow-up call in the near future. Bob Walters, retired co-owner of the Power Station, swears that he offered the chief engineering job at his old studio to Tony Bongiovi, who later became his partner, less than three minutes after they met. He says he just knew he was perfect immediately.

Anyway, you can always arrange a longer callback interview for a serious prospect, and you may be surprised to find that you like many of the applicants who show up. So get an overview first. At the end of a day or two of interviews, you'll probably be exhausted from the whole process, but you'll also have one or two standout candidates in mind.

Call the two or three you like best and schedule about an hour with each on the same day. That way, the impressions they make will be fresh in your mind for comparison, and you'll complete the whole process with efficiency. Tell your callback people that you're down to two or three finalists, and then in the second meeting, try to get into the real specifics of the job. This is the time to hand them a written and detailed description of the job, so that you both have a clear understanding of what's needed. If there are unpleasant aspects to the job, such as multiple runs to the city dump, ask them if they're prepared to assume those responsibilities. You might discuss an ongoing problem with a client they'll have to deal with, or ask for their approach to a difficult assignment.

Be yourself and be real. Relax, let down your guard so that they'll follow your lead, and look at the human being you're dealing with. Does he reflect the attitude of your company? Does her personality seem to relate to those who are already in the family? Is it a good bet that he'll be enthusiastic about showing up the day after you hire him?

Once you feel good about those answers, be sure to do the most important part of your homework: Check their references.

Putting Your References on the Table

Resumes tend to either list reference names and phone numbers, or simply say "References on request." By all means, request them! Don't kid yourself into thinking that you're insulting someone by going behind their back, or that you can simply trust your own basic instincts. You are in fact, complimenting them by saying "I'm seriously interested in taking the time to find out more about you."

Former employers can provide a gold mine of insight on your job candidate. Many are very cooperative and honest, because they make the same reference calls to other employers when they're doing their own interviews. It only takes a moment or two of conversation with a couple of reliable people to find out if your candidate was a treasure or an anchor around their necks.

Tell them about the kind of job you're offering and ask for their opinion. If you're really sold on one candidate and you get a negative report, call him up and ask them why one of his references was so unhappy! You have nothing to lose, and more information to gain.

We had a prospect for a receptionist position who we liked very much. She was bright, qualified and had a kind of sixth sense that seemed to put answers in her mouth before the questions were asked. Everything went well until we called her references. Two people claimed they'd never heard of her, and one said that she'd ripped them off!

We told her what they'd said. She was totally puzzled and stared at her own resume, and then realized that she'd listed her maiden name because she'd recently been divorced, but had been known by her married name in the past. When we called back, the employers remembered her immediately and gave her good marks. The third was as surprised as we were. He'd employed someone else who, coincidentally, had the same name.

We all breathed a sigh of relief and happily hired her. Three months later, I fired her because I couldn't communicate with her and she had a lousy attitude. And so it goes.

Making Nighttime Showtime

O ccupying a cavernous building, Bo Reusch manages a business that's taken full advantage of its capabilities, turning a first-class studio into a full-sized concert club as night descends.

Career Roots Partners started out playing in a party band. As their reputation grew, they decided to cut a couple of songs for a demo. After recording in a local studio, they became very unhappy with the way they perceived the studio scene was being run.

"We decided that if each song was going to cost three or four thousand dollars a piece to get right, that for an album's worth of material, we could buy a whole studio of our own. So we did."

Facility Started with a home 16-track setup, made the album, got ousted from the basement studio by one partner's growing family, put a plan together and found a commercial location to open for business. Went 24-track in 1987, using cash supplied by a wealthy partner.

They built the sound stage a year after moving in and started renting it out as a function room. In 1988, they guessed that there was a need for more entertainment outlets in the area, got a liquor license and opened as a live music club. The company is now booking name talent, who sometimes hire the studio to record the dates, and turning a profit as an entertainment venue and studio.

Amek Angela console, Studer A80 24-track. Main room: 135' (!) x 35', including five isolation booths. Control room: 18' x 20'.

House Staff Two full-time people who do everything. Part-time bookkeeper. Three on-call engineers who double as live sound people for the concerts.

Primary Focus Country, religious, rock and heavy-metal music.

Terms Half of the payment down when the project is booked. Second half at session end.

Marketing "We're very aggressive. What we're doing reaches across a five-state area. We've become a legitimate concert club with the ability to record the acts. Mitch Ryder is coming in this weekend, and we got him at a reduced rate in trade for recording his sets on Saturday night. He's got some new tunes he wants to get down on tape."

Creative Overview "I've come to the conclusion that the sole reason for having a producer rather than relying on a capable engineer is to screw up everything you can. Any engineer who's worth his salt is gonna be producing the session anyway. I've seen a lot of bands who could produce themselves a whole lot better than most producers could."

Lessons Learned "We've been burned by the nicest people you'd ever want to work with. Always get payment first. Never let your tapes walk."

Plans "We're going more and more toward live music venues. We're really into doing the club scene, using the studio to lure the bigger names in with, and being mindful of major changes that are on the way."

Bo Reusch

Manager/Engineer

Big Dog Studios

Wichita, Kansas

Big Dog's unique layout lends itself to a wide variety of concert and recording situations.

At 12"x18", this ad serves as both a mailer and a poster.

INTERNS

Internship is a clever and valuable way for both the studio and the young beginner to get what they're after: work. By definition, an intern is a person who is willing to trade time and effort for the opportunity to be in an environment that will take him through the critical next steps in learning his craft.

The intern agrees to work a set amount of time each week, usually between 20 and 40 hours, in return for being taught more about the job. The business agrees to teach the work on condition that the intern helps with whatever is needed and expects little or no pay.

Played fairly, internship is a good deal for the intern and the business. At Interlok, we interview graduates from the recording schools in our area, as well as reviewing applications that come in during the year. Even though there's no pay in the beginning, a lot of people apply because they see the value of the program. What we look for is a serious attitude along with a basic familiarity with equipment, usually gained in school, and the chemistry to fit in with the other people in the company.

Our "program" averages one new person about every nine months. We tell them that the amount of intern time averages two to four months, and that if all goes well, a paid position will follow. It's worked well for us. By choosing intelligent people who are eager to learn, we're getting fresh talent that we can train to work effectively in our environment. Several have gone on to become full-time second and then first engineers, adding pride and long-term success to our family.

Dealing Them In

An intern brings a responsibility to bear on the part of the studio. In return for the free labor, he or she rightfully expects to get a reasonable amount of personal training and guidance. Most of that will come from the other assistants, as they work together to keep the operation running smoothly. But management and firsts should also take time to help with the training.

In a good program, the intern should be exposed to all the goings-on. That might include reception, gofering and sweeping the floors, but should concentrate on a fair amount of assisting the second, machine operation, alignments, logging and setup.

If you take on an intern simply to get a free employee, you're missing the point, and more importantly, you're not playing fair. If you need a full-time runner, hire one. With an intern, you should be working with a level of respect due someone who's willing to run the gauntlet in order to become an integral member of the team.

Try to work out a schedule that acknowledges the no- or low-pay situation the intern is in. Many interns either live with their families or take a part-time job to survive their internships. You'll know when the free time is coming to an end: You'll start feeling confident about putting the intern on dates as an unsupervised assistant. When that happens, it's time to start paying livable wages.

We try to ease our interns into that phase. We start by paying a token salary when they start to take on some professional responsibility and, assuming things go well, raise that salary on a monthly basis by a couple hundred dollars for the next few months. By then, six to ten months have passed, and the successful intern has become a trusted and valuable second engineer, earning a full salary.

There is pride and satisfaction in teaching and helping someone enter the professional world, and a valuable bond is built as it happens. Our interns have become true family members with whom we expect to nurture long-term relationships. That kind of connection doesn't just walk in off the street; it's built with mutual trust, respect and hard work.

PEOPLE PROBLEMS

There's a lot to learn about working with other people on a close and daily basis, especially if you're the person in charge. You can't expect people to be perfect or to do exactly as they're told all the time. And you can't expect someone who's there day and night not to fly off the handle, lose their temper, or break down in tears once in a while. It's the stuff we humans are made of.

Being the boss of a small company is a lot like being a parent. You're expected to set an example, to make sure everything runs smoothly and to deal with each problem as it arises in an authoritative manner. Each boss finds his or her own level of tolerance and enlightenment. Each boss finds his or her own method for getting opinions across, whether the practice includes love, might, ignorance or fear.

You'll develop your own sense of right and wrong and a style with which to implement your own philosophy. And ultimately, that should be one that reflects the kind of connection we all share on this particular planet.

Two Kinds of People

I try to give people the benefit of the doubt. Unless someone walks straight up and tries to whack me in the head, I tend to think that they'd prefer to live in a world where people respect and take care of one another.

So I believe that there are two major groups of people: those who want love and approval, and those who (claim they) don't give a damn. Personally, I think of myself as a good enough judge of character to feel that I can spot a "type 2" with a fair amount of accuracy from...oh, 50 yards or so. At least, I try to keep them at that distance when I'm looking to fill a job spot in my studio. That hopefully leaves me with a room filled with people who care about helping one another whenever some kind of trouble begins to become visible.

The reason that major corporations send their employees through alcohol rehabilitation programs or pay for personal therapy usually isn't because the unions have demanded it of management. They don't have to—the corporations know that it's far more cost-effective to make the effort to help an employee who does the job well than to fire him and have to start training someone else from scratch to do that same job.

By the way, California state law makes it a dubious proposition to fire an employee who is addicted to drugs. Since drug addiction is generally classified as a disease, this falls under discrimination legislation dealing with physical conditions. However, if the addiction leads an employee to break the company rules, you're generally okay in letting him or her go, as long as the addiction *itself* isn't the cause. Of course, as with alcoholism, rehabilitation of a valuable employee can sometimes be a better idea in the long run.

This kind of thinking makes sense in a three-person company as well, and the effect is even more pronounced because you're all so much closer together. Which is why in a small studio operation, everyone not only becomes essential to getting the job done but must also be able to trust one another on a regular basis.

That kind of efficiency and professionalism must be nurtured and guided over a period of time. Taking care to choose the best possible associates and then setting and maintaining the standards you expect will go a long way in accomplishing that goal.

Once you begin down that path, it's up to you to determine which forks in the road to choose (they have a habit of springing up around every corner). So it's important to develop a philosophy and style that you can call your own, and that you can use to make your business successful. One outgrowth of that philosophy is a company handbook. See Chapter 17 for details.

SALARIES AND EGOS

We tend to agonize over what we're paying every individual in our company on a regular basis. The agony comes from judging the quality of a staff member's performance vs. what we're paying him or her, vs. what *they* feel they should be getting, vs. what we can *afford* to pay them.

The easiest factor to consider in setting someone's salary is to look at what the going rate around town is. You can get a feel for that by asking prospective employees what their salary range was elsewhere and by talking to other owners and managers at business and industry gatherings. Rates are different in each part of the country and are often reported in trade-sponsored surveys.

Next, you have to consider the individual's level of experience and his or her potential value to the studio. Then you need to be realistic in determining the cost of living and the value of any benefits, such as health insurance, that you're adding to the package. Finally, you've got to figure out if you can afford to pay the figure you've come up with, or if you need to begin all over again.

A studio's costs tend to be high, and the amount of work that comes in is usually hard to predict from week to week. Long ago, we determined that we could add real value and respect in our relationship with our employees by guaranteeing them a weekly draw, no matter what the bookings were. We said, "We're not going to pay you top dollar, but we promise that you can count on the dollars we pay, come rain or come shine, as your base wage. Work overtime, and you'll make more. Work less, and you'll make that base."

We add a great health-insurance package for all employees after 60 days with the company, which is long enough for both parties to determine whether or not the relationship is likely to be long-term. And when a staff member hits the three-year mark, he or she can choose to participate in our company pension fund, to which we make additional contributions.

We know of many studios that pay on a per-hour or independent contractor basis. Some feel they have to, and some feel it's the best deal for the business to pay as you go. We believe it's bad for morale to hang a carrot out on a stick and say if we dip it in front of you, you can take a bite. I believe that a steady paycheck is a real show of respect and a great morale-builder for a company.

There have been times when my partner and I have had to forgo our own pay to make ends meet, but in all the years we've been together, no employee has ever received a pay envelope with an IOU in it. And that goes a long way in relieving the stress and tension of making ends meet for every individual on the team.

Raises

As time moves forward, everybody expects to do better, or at least keep up with the cost of living. At Interlok, we have regular employee reviews in which performance and salary are discussed with each staff member about twice a year on a one-to-one, confidential basis. Our staff knows when reviews are coming and that they're the best time to discuss money. We listen, evaluate and try to make intelligent decisions, but you can't please everybody.

Problems arise that make the system less than perfect. Depending on your current or seasonal situation, a raise may run headlong into a studio's period of financial doldrums. Or an employee may feel entitled to a raise when, unbeknownst to him, you've actually been giving serious consideration to letting him go due to his unsatisfactory performance.

The best approach seems to be to try to remain open and honest about the relative health of both your company and feelings about the performance level of each employee. It doesn't do anyone any good to arrange a review, only to skirt an uncomfortable issue or fudge the truth in order to make the conversation more palatable.

Good or bad, most people prefer a straight dose of truth to sugarcoating. If you're dissatisfied with an employee's attitude, it's your responsibility to inform him of such in a mature fashion, especially if it's formal review time; anything less is unfair to the employee. That doesn't mean you need to clunk him over the head with a barrage of accusations—management carries some difficult responsibilities, and one is learning how to impart a level of criticism that hopefully empowers an individual with the knowledge and desire for change, rather than destroying his ego from outright hurt or embarrassment. That kind of skill takes time, thought and courage to develop.

Making Promises

On the other hand, if an employee is entitled to a raise but the money isn't there, he or she at least deserves some frank discussion about the chances for getting something more in the foreseeable future. And if you believe you can follow through, you can postpone that reward now and set a date months in advance to follow through. An employee who knows she is being treated fairly and reasonably will be willing to share the hard times along with the promise of better times in the future.

But be careful not to make promises you can't keep, and be sure to follow through on the deals you do make. It's a good idea to keep a file for each employee on their work history, successes and failures; when you make a promise, writing it down will remove any doubt about what was said months later at the due date.

People want to be treated fairly and honestly. Often, that's a more valuable commodity than plain dollars, and one that makes for long-term, successful relationships.

WHEN TO RAISE A SALARY

The second time she pulls a new client in from out of the blue and helps make them a regular.

When you realize he's a terrific bargain, and before he begins to look elsewhere for a commensurate income.

When someone you've learned to count on reaches their next anniversary as your employee.

When he's more concerned with the quality of his work than with keeping track of the overtime.

When you find yourself constantly appreciating the extra effort she makes.

When he asks for it, and you know he deserves it.

When all hell breaks loose, but you know she's got it totally under control.

When he pulls himself out of a performance slump and changes the way he functions on a permanent basis.

WHEN TO FIRE AN EMPLOYEE

When he repeatedly tries his best, gets all the support he needs and fails on a regular basis.

When you find yourself doing the work she's supposed to be doing.

When he is chronically missing at the times you need him the most.

When she badmouths you behind your back to your clients.

When substance abuse leads him to violate company policies repeatedly.

When she doesn't care about what *you* care about.

When clients begin to politely insist on a different engineer in the future.

When you realize that her negative attitude has changed the personality of the whole company.

When the problems he keeps causing overshadow the real problems that need solving.

When she clearly violates company policy after repeated reviews and warnings.

When he insists that he's leaving enough time to get to sessions early, but cites a different excuse each time he's late.

DEALING WITH SUBSTANCE ABUSE

KAA-BOOM!

"What the hell was that?"

"I'm not sure, man."

"'It, it sounded like an *explosion* in the control room."

"...Could be."

"Waddaya mean, *could be?!*"

"Well, the group in Studio 1's been doin' a little freebasin' with, um, one of those blowtorches..."

"Ohmygod..."

"Hey, mellow out, dude. Want me to go check?"

Remember the Fabulous Furry Freak Brothers Comix? That scene would be a riot in pen and ink. But as an employer or manager, substance abuse may be one of the most difficult and heart-wrenching problems you encounter if it turns up in one of your employees' lives.

It happens almost everywhere. You're hip, you're happening, life's a party, and everybody loves you. And then somebody walks up and throws *this* in your face.

Here's a true story about a first engineer who was headed for real success...

Too Hip, Gotta Go

Charlie came to us with some powerful references. He'd worked at some of the top facilities in town, his former employers had good things to say about him, and the music he recorded sounded world-class. On top of that, he was a nice guy. He cared about his work and he cared about the people around him.

We started him off on some minor jobs, but within a couple of weeks, he'd won our trust and was working with our top music clients. They really took to him, insisting on him when they booked more time. The guy was building a client following, the best thing a staffer can do for a studio.

Then he started getting sick. At first, he'd just miss a day, calling in with a migraine and sounding awful. Soon the one-day absences turned into two days, then three. One morning, I arrived at the studio to find a message saying that the session from the night before had been canceled because he hadn't shown up. The client was really upset but rescheduled and made his deadline.

We were alarmed and worried. We really liked Charlie and had already begun thinking of him as a member of the family. I sat down with him and found out that he was very depressed. He said that things were going badly with his family at home, that he couldn't bring himself to talk about it, but that he'd definitely get a grip and be more reliable in the future.

The following week the same thing happened: another no-show. Except this time, a little later on, his mother called. She told us he'd OD'd the night before and was in the hospital. As worldly as we felt, we were shocked to find that cocaine was at the center of the problem. Sometimes when you believe in someone and want them to succeed, you don't look hard enough for the real truth.

Taking Care of Our Own

One of our staff members had reached dangerous levels with coke in the distant past. She had long since cleaned up; she liked Charlie and offered to help. She volunteered to take him to C.A. (Cocaine Anonymous) meetings twice a week and partner up to support him in staying sober. He went for it, and a week later, feeling concerned but hopeful, we reinstated him.

Two weeks later, Charlie woke up in the hospital again. His family pleaded with us to help, saying that we were all that he lived for.

His clients wanted to know where the hell he was and when he would be back. And the studio lost the second half of a project he'd been on, with the producers muttering about reliability.

He cried real tears, pleading for another chance. And we *still* felt sure we could handle the problem. We didn't want to lose such a talent.

We put together a system of *relentless* support. Several staff members went to regular C.A. meetings with him, we stayed in touch with his family, and for a while things seemed to stabilize and get back to normal. But we'd begun to look over our shoulders a lot.

One night, a shady dude came to the studio door asking if Charlie was there. The next day, Charlie disappeared, along with a couple of expensive condenser microphones from the studio locker. When we realized what was happening, we got scared.

Something happened to my partner and me at that moment. We started thinking about taking care of *ourselves* and changed the cylinders on all the outside locks that afternoon. Two days later, we got word that his dealer had swiped his car for payment, and that Charlie had wound up nearly dead in the hospital again.

This time, even *we* knew that he was beyond our help or understanding. We recovered the mics and fired him. I had gone from confusion to compassion, to anger and back to confusion, not fully understanding the depth of the problem. I felt like he'd personally let me down. I was vexed and frustrated that he couldn't hold himself together. And I was really upset about losing a major account stemming from a third no-show.

Charlie was so far gone that his overriding emotion seemed to be bewilderment. But he was one of the lucky ones. His upper-middle-class family loved him and paid thousands of dollars for in-patient treatment at a top-flight care center for a full month.

One Step at a Time

After *another* relapse and *another* month at the center, he got clean and stayed clean. He lost weight and started looking healthier. This time, although we'd long since fired him, he maintained communication with us in the form of a casual call every so often to see what was going on at the studio where he once worked.

Then one day he called and asked if I had a few moments to see him. I was glad to say yes by that point. He came over, looking straight, fit and carrying a lot more wisdom from his experience. He said, "I'm here for just one reason. I want to apologize for the trouble I caused you and thank you for all the help and support you gave me. It just took a while longer than anybody would have liked for me to get to the point where I feel like I'm back in control.

"I'm not asking for work," he said. "I just want to set things straight." Then he handed me an envelope with $100 cash in it. "This is for the locksmith," he explained, looking me in the eye. "I hope it's enough."

It wasn't, but it was good enough for me. That predictable action that is one of the essential 12-step ingredients for recovery signaled that he was indeed getting his life back on track. A couple of years later, he was still in touch, and we hired him to do a complete project, which he pulled off with all the talent he'd once displayed.

The last time I saw him, he was still straight and freelancing around town. He'd found the strength and the courage to pull himself and his life back together. And in the process, we'd all learned a lot about counting on one another.

Being Aware

What we learned was that there's only so much you can do for someone who's stepped outside of his own control. Also, that it's important to know where to draw the line—to know when you've reached the point of diminishing returns and the wave is about to fold back and drown you.

Drug addiction is a disease. People can be helped, treated and cured, but you're probably not qualified to be the doctor. Be kind and compassionate, but get educated.

Talk to people who are experienced, and learn what you can and cannot do. You can try to save the world, but you're probably going to get kicked around by a lot of people who aren't ready to be saved by you or by anyone else, at least not yet. And when you're running a business, the risks can be a lot higher than in friendship.

Think about it. Keep communicating. And keep your eyes open.

17

The Employee Manual

t's up to the owner or day-to-day manager of each facility to set the tone and an example for how business will be conducted. So it may be that a written contract that lays the rules out in black and white strikes you as a bit formal. We lived without one at Interlok for quite a while.

However, one difficult employee may be all it takes to realize that you need to make the studio's rules and regulations clear. What pushed me into writing one was a hired hand who approached authority with a loud rebel yell. He was a pretty good worker, but there was something in his mind that tended to make dealing with orders an irresistible challenge.

I'd ask him to do something, and he'd glare at me and say "Why?" or "Not now," or "Maybe later." I'd say, "Here's how I'd like you to do this," and he'd say, "Why do I have to do it like that?" Or I'd ask, "How come you haven't done what I asked you to do?" And he'd say, "Because I'm doing something else."

It wasn't that I was making any outrageous demands; he just liked having someone to rail at. The problem was that he'd been with us for quite a while, and for the most part was a dedicated, hard-working employee who we all usually liked.

Nevertheless, we got into some pretty intense arguments. Physically, he was taller and a lot stronger than me, and there I'd be, finding myself moving in on him as his challenges escalated until we were virtually nose to nose. In the heat of it all, I'd begin wondering if I was being as stubborn as he was in not backing down, and if the day would ever come when he might just take a swing at me.

Writing Down the Rules

What was happening was that two strong egos were confronting one another, and I was

damned if mine was going to shake loose first. The Interlok Employee Agreement came out of one of those confrontations.

Joey didn't care much about his appearance. He was a young guy who liked to party hearty and would often make it to work in the morning within seconds of his check-in time, careening his Harley into the parking lot at 40 miles an hour.

Well, *I* cared a lot about what he looked like. We cater to a professional TV and movie production clientele who often dress to match the level of their expensive sessions. Once or twice a week, despite my warnings, Joey came in with a day-old beard that made him look more like a wino than a good second.

Finally, one afternoon, we had an absurd argument about his right to look any way he pleased. That time ended in my threatening to fire him the next time he walked in with a day-old beard.

I remember him staring at me with hate in his eyes, incredulous that his job was being threatened over something he insisted was an essential part of his lifestyle, and therefore his right. He stormed out of the room in mid-argument. It was as if he'd gotten the last lick in, before the fight was over. I didn't know what to expect next, but I'd begun to feel more and more like a hapless parent facing his delinquent offspring, and I wasn't having fun anymore.

Half an hour later, Zack, one of our other seconds, came and told me he and Joey had talked it over and had decided to go in halves for an electric razor to keep at the studio. I was amazed that something so fundamental could have caused so much trouble.

The next day I came to work inspired to write down the rules and regulations that seemed obvious to me. I figured that if I put them to paper, we could all sit down and discuss each one during a company meeting, get everyone to agree that the rules were reasonable and necessary, and sign at the bottom to seal the deal.

When we convened that meeting, it lasted two hours, with lots of spirited conversation. We made a few adjustments, and in the end, everyone signed the paper.

Since then, life's gotten a bit easier. People seem to know what's expected of them and what will and won't be tolerated. Granted, it took some passion and strength to get there, but under the circumstances, it seemed like that's what was called for.

Maybe something this formal strikes you as "old school." It's true that I don't know of many studios that use such an agreement. But I've always felt passionate about my place. I'm proud of the way we do business, of our employees, of the level of quality in the product we turn out, and of the success we've made in such a competitive town.

It might be just as effective to let common sense make the rules, or to sit down and just discuss what is and what is not appropriate behavior. What is important, I think, is to set a conscious company policy and to live by it. Leaving it all to chance, at least with someone like Joey around, seems a little risky.

The Employee Handbook

What follows are the major portions of the Employee Handbook for all staff members at Interlok. We took a lot of care to tailor it to our own situation: The book started out as a three-page document and now runs nearly 50, a product of a great deal of thought, employee input and refinement. And I find that I need to update it on a regular basis.

Sometimes, when I glance at all the policies, they seem obvious, petty or unnecessary. And sometimes, when I realize that they've made a lot of vague concepts much more clear, it really makes sense to have written them out.

You should also seriously consider your state's employer/employee rules and regs when assembling your own handbook. In these lawsuit-happy days, with screaming attorneys on daytime TV urging everyone to dial 1-800-SUE-THEM, an employee handbook can serve as a potent and powerful tool in determining just whose rights have been violated. It's also a clear and concise method of explaining your position to all of your employees.

Each of our new employees gets a copy of this manual sometime during the first week they sign on. They are asked to read it carefully,

urged to discuss any matters they question, and then required to sign the last page, agreeing that they will abide by the rules.

As we have grown, I've tried to impart as much written philosophy as rules and regulations. When a new staff member signs the last page and turns it in, I know that I have imparted a lot more than just a number of do's and don'ts: I've given a real sense of where we're coming from and how I expect new employees to fit in.

Our handbook also makes clear a few very important agreements. First, by law, that working for us is an at-will arrangement, meaning that either the employer or the employee may terminate the position at any time. The importance of that, from a court standpoint, is that you are making it clear that no verbal promise of employment longevity exists on either side.

Second, we clearly define wage scales, behavior and ethics codes and discipline policies. This precludes having to verbally explain every detail to each person and assures us that we've covered everything in detail in the book and that our new staff member has accepted the responsibility of comprehending each policy.

Finally, the handbook conveys the pride we have in our business and encourages each employee to embrace the vibe we've worked so hard to build. Once a new staff member has finished reading it and has signed their name on the dotted line, they've officially begun a very special relationship with a group of handpicked, dedicated professionals who'll welcome them as a new family member. Knowing what to expect from them, and what they can expect in return, is a great advantage and a real comfort to all.

An Important Note

The Interlok Employee Handbook has been developed and revised over an eight-year period, with additions and updates as needed. It is a unique and singular work created strictly for the use of Interlok employees and should not be construed as anything but an example of what a good handbook *might* include.

<u>PLEASE DO NOT DUPLICATE ANY PART OF THIS DOCUMENT FOR USE IN ANY OTHER BUSINESS,</u>

Read it, think about it and then *create your own.* Writing a handbook is a personal and highly productive experience. There are excellent books to use as references, and you may want to also contact your state's Chamber of

Commerce and/or your attorney for more help on the subject.

Think about the guidelines that will work best for *you*. Then write them down and generate policies that will help you find greater success at your own facility.

THE INTERLOK EMPLOYEE HANDBOOK

Welcome to Interlok. The following is a handbook of rules, regulations and guidelines of the company. We encourage your input and comments in helping us to grow, to learn and to work effectively with one another.

For quick reference, this book is arranged by subject in alphabetical order.

Authority, Chain of

The partners carry equal and final authority.

The studio manager is the authority in charge of both internal and external scheduling and the day-to-day running of the premises. The assistant manager is second in command to the manager.

First engineers are in charge of their own sessions and have authority over assistants on the session.

Interns assist both first and second engineers.

Reception is responsible for client care and for securing the building during working hours.

Assistant (Second) Engineers

All assistants are members of the Blue Team, which meets on its own to discuss work-related problems and challenges on a regular basis. Blue Team meetings are paid when conducted on the premises. Meetings are scheduled by the team leader, who also conducts the meeting and reports to and from management.

The purpose of the Blue Team is to create a forum for problem-solving and to encourage harmony among fellow staffers. If you feel a problem exists that needs discussion, you are encouraged to approach either your team leader or management to begin the discussion process.

One of the prime reasons for having team meetings is to help increase your knowledge and skill in equipment operation and maintenance. Very often, your own personal questions may turn out to be shared by other co-workers. When we discover weaknesses regarding tech-

nical knowledge, we often arrange special equipment clinics that help to enlighten everyone.

EXTRA DUTY

We do not employ runners, food preparation people or production assistants. Instead, we try to share the occasional extra duties among both assistants and office staff. These may include running errands, helping to set up an area for a meal or function, picking up materials or checks, etc.

When errands require a car, you should use a company vehicle. These jobs generally fall to the day's "floater," if there is one, or to anyone who has the time available. Neither assistants nor interns are expected to do any regular janitorial duties. We have a service for that. But you *are* expected to assist in taking out the trash, keeping studios, lounges and common areas neat and in order.

Communication When Off Premises

Because the nature of this operation requires that the company schedule somewhat unpredictable work days and times, employees need to stay in professional contact with the company, and to make themselves reasonably available for work.

Therefore, you agree to maintain a reliable answering service or answering machine at all times, and to answer a message left by the company within 12 hours of that call being made. This does *not* obligate you to work at any day or time, but *does* require responsibility for maintaining communication on a reliable basis.

Failure to answer a message requesting a check-in within 12 hours may result in your having to forfeit the number of hours' work and pay equal to those paid to a substitute or independent contractor brought in to do the work in question.

Company Meetings

We consider company meetings to be essential to our growth, communication and family spirit. Meetings include discussions of pressing projects, problems and reviews and are always thrown open for input from all.

Our policy is to have regular company meetings with the entire staff present. This is no easy trick and is impossible to schedule more than a day or two in advance. If you are the one person who is being contacted by phone and being asked to come in for a company meeting, please consider the difficulty of finding an appropriate time for all, and make your best effort to join us. We strive mightily for 100% attendance.

The CPOV

CPOV stands for the Client's Point of View. And one of our prime objectives is to pay close and continuing attention to it. In doing so, it has helped to create the unique atmosphere our clients enjoy and desire to be a part of.

You should learn to instinctively check the CPOV several times per day. All it takes is common sense and a desire to provide ongoing, conscious service.

Some examples:

What does the producer see from his chair? A clear view into an open-topped garbage pail? A near-field speaker blocking his view to the live room? A plant in front of a video monitor?

Improve his view, which will raise his comfort level.

What does a voice-over person need to do his job? Is there a squeaky chair? An empty water jug? A light that's burned out?

Double-check these items and eliminate predictable requests.

Why is the singer at the mic continually gesturing wildly, trying to get someone's attention in the control room?

Set up a separate room mic that opens an easier line of communication between artist and engineer.

What does a tour visitor notice in the client lounge? Overstuffed garbage pails? Empty lunch bags and papers? Four-month-old magazines?

Take a moment to make the room home again.

Help us make and keep our facility professional, warm and friendly. Don't take your own view and routine for granted. Learn to look from the CPOV. And if you see a problem or have an idea for improved service, share your thoughts and recommendations with management.

Decorum and Consideration

ANSWERING THE PHONE

Incoming calls should be answered with a greeting, followed by "Interlok," such as "Hi, Interlok" or "Good afternoon, Interlok." The greeting is the first thing clients hear when they want to communicate with us. Keep the emotion or attitude of the moment out of it.

Incoming calls should be handled with either a neutral or positive businesslike tone. Maintain a courteous and professional attitude when taking messages or transferring calls.

When taking messages, it is your responsibility to deliver the message to the intended recipient. If you can't verbally relate the message immediately, write it down and either hand it to the proper person or leave it in his or her message box. Please do not trust your own memory with someone else's business. Part of the trust we have developed among each other here is to be able to count on each staff member individually.

AS A STAFF MEMBER

Our philosophy is to live and function as a family. Employees are expected to be considerate of one another and to coexist with professional courtesy.

Noise from personal music or discussions should be confined in a manner that does not offend or interfere with other people or the performance of their duties. In general, you're expected to act with a consistent level of respect and consideration due each member of our hand-picked staff.

WITH CLIENTS PRESENT

Personal problems or circumstances involving other projects should never be discussed within earshot of another client. That's private business that should not be aired in front of anyone else.

Abusive language is not permissible during a session with a client present, and in keeping with a professional attitude, should be kept to a minimum at other times. *Professional behavior in all client relations is an absolute.*

CLIENT POLITICS

You are expected to maintain a professional demeanor in all dealings with clients and visitors. In this context, that means allowing the client to set the tone of the communication, as a rule.

Although the atmosphere at the studio is casual, it's important to maintain a certain "distance" in client/employee relationships to help maintain a good business relationship. This would be evident in an ongoing level of politeness and reserve, unless it becomes obvious that a visitor is at ease in being more casual with you.

Very occasionally, we run into a difficult or abusive personality. If you feel that you are being given a rough ride by a client, avoid being sucked down to his or her level of behavior. Maintain your aloofness and try to set a better example.

If you are unsuccessful or remain uncomfortable, excuse yourself for a moment and inform management of the problem at hand. The last thing you want to deal with is a client who has a bone to pick with you while you're trying to work together. Let management take the reins and act as your agent in dealing with the problem, so that when we find a comfortable solution, you can return to the work at hand with impunity.

DEALING WITH CELEBRITIES

Celebrities, in particular, should be given extra space and privacy. Avoid causing them the kind of discomfort they might feel if they were, for instance, to be approached by a fan in a restaurant where they were trying to eat in peace.

Don't stare or linger in their presence. Resist the temptation to ask for autographs or pictures. We occasionally ask artist representatives for permission to take photos for the company, and endeavor to include staff members whenever possible. But we must present an environment of safety and ease if we are to continue to work successfully with star talent.

Decorum amidst star-power is an important quality to develop, and one that is best approached by erring on the side of conservatism and propriety. In general, outside of a smile and a 'hello,' do not speak to a celebrity unless he or she speaks to you, or there is a specific purpose in your communication. Many of them are friendly and open, but there are those who become very put off or simply want their privacy. Follow their lead, and you'll avoid embarrassment for yourself and the company.

Disciplinary Procedures

Several policies described in this Handbook contain attached disciplinary procedures. Please note that all such policies are only guidelines, and are not all-inclusive. They are not intended to apply to every possible situation, but are instead presented herein as guidelines for procedures we may choose to follow. Management retains the right to discipline an employee for any or no reason.

References to termination and discharge are merely examples that management, in its sole discretion, can refer to and rely on. The employer retains the sole discretion to determine under what circumstances discipline and discharge are appropriate.

Dress Code

Your appearance must be neat and professional. Casual wear is the norm. Clothing should be clean and pressed, shirts tucked into pants, shoelaces tied and hair combed. We do not permit bare feet, sandals without socks or profane T-shirts.

Our dress code is based on one simple philosophy: When our clients look at us, they should see the embodiment of a professional who can get their job done with efficiency and integrity.

With that in mind, it is necessary to show them a neat, alive and adult presentation. Clothing reflecting that attitude is washed, pressed and comfortable. It should not look like the same stuff you wear on the weekend when you relax at home, even on studio days when you don't expect to be in session. On those days, when you expect to be doing technical or manual labor here, wear the work clothes you keep here for that purpose (there is a designated storage area for changes of clothing).

What you should wear to work:

- Your choice of moderate or dressy styles.
- Shirts must have collars and buttons if they are worn alone.
- Belts should be worn on pants with belt loops.
- Casual and athletic shoes should be clean with laces tied.
- Hair must be combed and neat. If your hairstyle does not lend itself to a tailored look, then you need to alter it in some way: either with rubber bands and hairpins or by cutting it in the line of more mature '90s fashion.
- If you wear a T-shirt, you should wear a jacket or vest with it. T-shirts without jackets or vests are not permitted.

Men: Non-bearded employees must report to work clean-shaven daily.

Women: Makeup and accessories should be applied in moderation.

Please do not wear:

- Torn jeans, old clothes, lone T-shirts, dirty shoes or old sneakers.
- T-shirts with loud or outrageous imprints.
- Midriff-baring tops, short shorts or any overtly sexual items.

Your appearance should be neat. A look that clearly states you are at work, not play.

Remember:

- You're here as a paid professional.
- We expect you to look like one, *every* day.

Drug and Alcohol Usage

No alcohol may be consumed on the premises during work hours. Marijuana, cocaine and other illegal-substance possession or usage is strictly prohibited at all times.

Evidence of alcohol or drug usage while at work will result in an immediate 3-day unpaid suspension, followed by a review of the circumstances. Pending the outcome of that review, the company may opt to reinstate or dismiss the offender, depending on prior history.

A second episode will result in immediate termination.

Employment Policy

If you're a new employee, we expect you to make a reasonable commitment of time and effort to becoming a long-term employee. We wouldn't have hired you otherwise.

However, whether you are a new or long-term employee at Interlok, it is specifically understood that your position on staff is an "at-will employment relationship," meaning that your employment with the company is for no specific duration and may be terminated at any time at the will of either the employer or the employee for any reason or for no reason at all. In the case of dismissal, the company may, at its sole discretion, give some notice of its intent to dismiss an employee, but the company is not required to give any such notice. Nor is it required to provide any severance pay.

This may sound like a harsh and uncaring policy. But please understand that it is based on California law and exists to protect both employer and employee. It simply means that you are not compelled to work for the company for any specific length of time, nor is the company entering into any contract of employment or guaranteeing your position.

It is both time-consuming and expensive for us to find talented, quality staff members. When we do, our intention is to make the association a long one. To that end, we pay special attention to new staff members when you join us.

We solicit your questions or discussion about any conflicts or problems. We talk to other staffers about how you are matriculating into our environment and system. We keep a heightened watch to make sure you understand and abide by company policy. And we encourage you to succeed.

During your first 30 days, our basic philosophy is to determine whether the job you've been hired for is right for you. We think of this time as a trial period, from both your side and ours. Again, we encourage you to come forward with any difficulties you may be experiencing, so that we can find solutions together that work the best for us all.

Your being hired is our strong show of faith in you. We want you to succeed.

Engineer Session Rules

IN SESSION
In the past, we referred to engineers who are slow on the uptake but who get the job done as "secret weapons." That referred to the fact that even though they were doing a less-than-professional job, the project was getting done *eventually,* and we were billing the client for the longer hours it took to get there.

We're beyond those days now. We no longer want any unintentional secret weapons on staff. So learn to anticipate the next logical step in the session process. Stay alert and "in the room." Think from the Client's Point Of View as to what you would like to see happen next, and then prepare to do it. Anticipate the need for extra tape, equipment or special needs and get them ready before you're asked. Help make our clients loyal by not simply doing the job, but by going the extra distance to let them know that we value their time as much as they do.

And help us change the meaning of "secret weapon" into something that explains why our clients keep coming back time after time.

LOCKING UP
If you are present when the studio is locked up for the night, it is your responsibility to make sure that the premises have been thoroughly straightened up and are ready for the next day's sessions. This includes zeroing of the board in the bay where you have been working and emptying of all garbage. You are also responsible for turning off all lights and lowering air-conditioning to overnight levels.

SECURITY
We consider ourselves lucky to have only been broken into twice in the past nine years. Those break-ins have made us very security-conscious and have fostered liberal use of alarms with

armed response, barred windows and a system of locked rooms.

With one exception*, most commercial ripoffs occur during the night. For that reason, be alert and aware of suspicious behavior and for your own safety as well. If you are relatively alone during a night session, lock all unnecessary doors around you. Most studios and hallways can be deadbolted, which helps to minimize any potential breach.

Think defensively and overcompensate. We've never suffered a physical assault here. Let's keep it that way.

*THE SECURITY EXCEPTION

The other problem all studios experience is theft by clientele. The prime hardware that turns up missing is mics and headphones. For that reason, *it is essential that mic lockers stay locked.* There is no reason for locker doors to be left open or unlocked other than from an uncaring attitude.

RELEASING TAPES

The same common sense applies to our tape vaults. Keep them locked and secure. If a client asks you to release a tape to him, make sure that management is made aware of the client's request and the client's bill is paid in full. A held master is often the studio's trump card in getting a final bill paid.

You should also be aware that there is ample legal precedent for maintaining such a stance. Do not be intimidated by any client threats of legal action.

As a rule, *always check with management first before releasing any master. Do not take management into your own hands!*

THINKING FOR YOURSELF

We encourage innovation, imagination and individual autonomy. Before you ask a question or decide there's a mechanical or electrical problem you can't find an answer to, take another moment and think again. Quite often, the answer will be there, looking right back at you, just waiting to be noticed.

If you do need to ask a question or get help, stay with the person you've gone to and make sure you understand the answer and subsequent application. And then, mentally "eat it." Make it a part of you, so that you'll understand the principle in the future and be able to implement it yourself.

Often, that may mean taking some extra time to pull out a manual, or stay after work, or get down on your hands and knees and crawl around in the wiring. Do it.

We recognize and reward enthusiasm, extra effort and inspiration just as much as we recognize laziness, lack of concentration and poor comprehension. Learn not to have to ask the same question twice, and you'll be on your way to becoming a valuable team member.

Engineer Rules and Guidelines, Assistant

BEING THERE

It's the second's job to make sure that the session runs smoothly from a preparedness point of view. Depending on the work at hand, you may be run ragged, or at times, find yourself crashingly bored with the lack of action. Whatever the case, you need to be "in the room." Assistants have a depressing habit of wandering out, going to the bathroom or just plain disappearing at exactly the times they're needed the most.

It's not always a glamorous job, but remember that you're being paid to be there. Make your trips out quick and efficient. And then get back in there. Your first needs you, and your client expects to be getting the service he's paying for.

PREPPING TAPE

All tapes recorded at Interlok MUST start with a minimum 2-minute house-generated tone roll, including 30 seconds each of 1K, 10K, 100Hz, and when applicable, Dolby NR.

Proper forms must be filled out detailing type and formats.

Company policy dictates severe penalties or outright termination if you are found negligent in this all-important process.

CLEANING UP

Post-session cleanup routine includes the following:

1. All tapes must be removed from all machines, put in boxes and put away.
2. No tapes may be left in a control room from a previous session.
3. All machines should be taken out of record.
4. Null the board.
5. The room must be left clean and neat, ready for the next session.

READING

In general, reading material for assistant engineers is prohibited during paid sessions with clients present. A book or a small magazine in a corner of the room during a long session with nothing to do is permissible if handled with discretion, and if you are able to stay in touch with the job at hand. But regard this exception as just that—an exception. The vast majority of sessions will require your complete attention.

Reading newspapers, because of their size and noisiness, is prohibited in the control room at all times when clients are in session.

SEATING

If a client is present on a date, you may not sit in any chair in front of the console, unless specifically requested or invited. That position is always to be available to the client, whether he uses it or not. Couches are strictly off-limits as well. They are reserved for clients and visitors only.

Never sit on a couch with clients present. The proper seating for you is in a separate chair that is out of the line of sight between the client and engineer, studio or video monitor.

Pay careful attention to your position in relation to the client's. It is your responsibility to stay out of his way while making him feel as comfortable as possible. Do not create your own CPOV problem!

WORK ORDERS

Work orders are the lifeblood of our business operation. They document exactly what went on during the session, who engineered, how much time was taken and what supplies were used. The work order is used both for invoicing and for proof of the work having been done. It is your responsibility to make sure that each session ends with a work order that it is complete and signed by the client.

Careless omissions of tape, hours or rentals from the work order can result in costly billing losses to the studio if they are not caught by the studio manager or invoicing department. Likewise, a missing client signature greatly weakens our position in the case of any client disputes over billing.

You must, therefore, *be scrupulous and professional in filling in and maintaining accurate work orders.* A missing signature, time, tape or equipment rental entry means a potential loss of income as a direct result. To err is human. To err repeatedly is grounds for termination.

Remember these work order rules:

1. Fill out work orders *as you go.*
2. Log materials as you use them. Don't wait until the end of a session to figure out what you did and what you used.
3. If you are relieved in mid-session, make sure that both the person replacing you and your work order are fully updated.
4. Be sure all ten numbered items on each work order have been addressed.

IMPORTANT: STRICT POLICY REGARDING TIME SHEETS AND WORK ORDERS

1. Employee time sheets may not be turned in late. This is strict policy. You have until 9:00 a.m. the following business day to deliver your daily completed time sheet. As a rule, you should be turning them in before you leave at the end of each work day. The 9:00 a.m. deadline is a grace period.
2. Work orders must be picked up prior to each session for review, and be filled out *as the session progresses.* They must be returned to the work order book immediately following the completion of the session. You may not pull a work order the day after a session to fill it in. It must be completed during and immediately after the actual session has occurred.

Failure to fully fill in all sections, obtain a signature or return the work order to the work book in timely fashion will result in disciplinary action.

DISCIPLINARY ACTION

After the first infraction, you'll be given a warning. Thereafter, failing to follow these rules will result in a schedule of *unpaid suspensions.*

After the second infraction, you will be relieved from duty for an eight-hour day, to be scheduled at management's convenience, and your pay forfeited for that time period. That means that eight hours' worth of regular pay will be deducted from your next paycheck, reflecting the length of your suspension, whether you have worked more or less than 40 hours during the week in question.

The third infraction will result in a 2-day unpaid suspension.

The fourth, a 3-day suspension.

The final action is termination.

Please get the message. We don't want to penalize *anyone.* We just want you to be professional. If you can't hack that, you're going to be held responsible in a big way.

Guests

One of our prime marketing methods is to give guest tours of the facilities. We encourage you to bring industry-related friends for a tour of the studio.

Our policy on *social* guests is that they are welcome for short visits when you are not in session as long as they do not impede the work at hand. Guests are not permitted to sit in on paid client sessions unless the client requests their presence. You may not ask a client for permission to bring a guest. Instead, ask permission from management first.

Please support this policy by using common sense when inviting friends to drop by, in order to avoid potentially embarrassing situations.

Health Insurance

Medical insurance is provided as a benefit without charge to all full-time employees beginning on the first of the month following 60 days of continuous employment. You may also add spouses and dependents to the plan at cost, which will be automatically deducted from your paycheck.

Our present company offers you a choice between using your own doctor and covering 80% of the bill, or using one of the company's approved physicians at just $10 per visit. The plan also includes local hospitals at 90%. A prescription card is also included.

We're proud to be able to provide this great plan to all our full-time staff members. The management office will provide you with all necessary forms for claims and will work with you to get any problems satisfactorily resolved.

The Interlok Philosophy

Interlok is a professional service company catering to a wide range of entertainment industry companies and individuals. Our philosophy and goal is to provide creative, world-class, good-natured and utterly reliable recording services and follow-through. You are expected to embody that philosophy from day one, and have been hired because we feel you have the ability to represent the company in its best possible light.

To that end, be polite, try to anticipate needs and requests, and maintain your professionalism by putting forth a can-do attitude to our clientele.

Don't reply to a client, "It can't be done."

Say, "Let me see what I can do about that."

Don't answer a client's question with "I don't know."

Say, "I'll find out."

In doing so, you'll help us make our clients and visitors feel comfortable and catered to, which is one of the fundamental reasons we do such good repeat business.

THE CLIENT'S EYE

Look at the premises with a client's eye and help keep it clean and inviting. Move a monitor speaker that's blocking the producer's view of the studio. Empty a trash can that's stuffed with ugly garbage. Pick up a cigarette butt that's sitting on the ground. Straighten out a magazine table. Put another roll of toilet paper on the dispenser.

You haven't been hired to be a janitor, but we do ask that you help preserve the unique, homelike atmosphere that our clients appreciate so much. Put some pride in these mundane items that speak volumes about who we are, and feel the pride in yourself as well.

FAMILY TIES

During the past nine years, we've expended a great deal of energy finding, encouraging and nurturing the talented people who make up our staff. We try hard to stay aware of both the caliber of work that is being done by them and the emotional spirit in the air from day to day.

If you have a problem with a client or another staff member; if you feel you're overworked or aren't being given the chance to reach for your full potential; if something strikes you as wrong or unfair...tell us. Individually, you are our greatest asset, and we are fiercely proud of you for that reason.

Bringing a problem to light is the best way to get past it. And Interlok is a small enough company to be able to devote the personal attention any given situation needs.

We want you to be a happy, long-term family member here. Help us achieve that goal by speaking up in a company meeting, or requesting a private one whenever you feel the need.

Keys

Employees who are given keys to the building agree that none will be duplicated and are liable for their replacement cost if lost.

Lateness

Our services are paid for by the hour. Clients expect to start on time. Therefore, *we simply do not tolerate employee lateness*. With that fact in mind, here are the rules:

It is imperative that all scheduled personnel arrive at least 30 minutes before any session is scheduled to begin. Circumstances preventing session start-time arrival should be communicated to the studio while en route.

In the event that you are personally scheduled to open the doors for the first session of the day and you realize you're going to be late, you must immediately contact the studio manager at home and notify the client, if possible. You may also phone other employees to try to find someone to meet the client at the door on time. If you can't find anyone, make sure you get a call through to management notifying them of your estimated time of arrival. All studio personnel are required to carry the staff master phone number card in their wallets at all times. The phone card is your link to total communication with the rest of the company.

Being scheduled to be the first to open the studio for a client carries the full responsibility of showing up on time, without fail. Inability to shoulder this responsibility may result in your finding yourself on a search for employment in a company that has a more tolerant code of responsibility.

It is your shared responsibility (between first and second engineer) to ensure that the studio is 100% ready to work at the stroke of the session start time. Late starts are a lousy way to begin a session and will not be tolerated. They make us look sloppy and unprofessional. They also justifiably anger clients, especially those who are used to paying for first-rate service in other facilities.

It is also your responsibility to be sure of your next day's start time! Make it a habit to double-check that time just before you leave for the day. Times may have changed since you last looked. While it is management's responsibility to notify you when those changes occur, sometimes circumstances get in the way. Double-checking is a way to help make the policy nearly failsafe.

As long as we can maintain a competent base level of performance and integrity, we're satisfied with the more casual level of lenience that prevails here. However (one more time for dramatic effect), you MUST report to work on time.

If you run into a problem that prevents you from getting here when scheduled, *call in.* If you're stuck on the freeway, get off at the next exit and call. If your dog eats your homework, if a rival studio fires shots through your window, if the microwave oven blew up all over your schedule book or you just plain overslept, CALL.

Calling may not absolve you of all sins, but is necessary so that we may take appropriate action to assure our clients the full service they're paying for. We'll review the circumstances later. The only excuse for not calling in if you are going to be more than ten minutes late is that you were unconscious at the time (preferably at the bottom of some ravine so that you don't get in trouble for oversleeping).

As for oversleeping, it's your responsibility to cure the problem. Ditto for car troubles, significant other emergencies, all-night jams, etc. Almost all other lateness can be similarly cured by planning ahead professionally. Which is exactly what we expect from you.

DISCIPLINE FOR LATENESS
First time: up-close and personal review of circumstances with owners and manager.

Second time: 30-day probation period, in which subsequent tardiness carries immediate penalties.

First time during probation: one-day unpaid suspension from work. You will likely be sent home that day.

Second time during probation: two-day suspension and final warning.

Third time during probation: termination.

Recommendation: Make promptness a regular part of your integrity. That way, you'll have more time to spend worrying about important things, like what you're having for lunch. And whether the client is paying for it.

Leisure and Personal Time

Reasonable breaks at logical times may be taken at your discretion. During non-meal session breaks of over 15 minutes, you're required to check in with the studio manager to see if other work needs to be done.

Personal time is often granted when the schedule permits. Personal time is unpaid and should be deducted from time sheets if more than a half-hour has been taken in a pay period when extra hourly billing is due you. If you are on the clock and need to leave the premises, you must notify the studio manager before departure so that we know where you are.

Meals

You're entitled to a half-hour meal break each day. When time permits, that break can be longer. When working on a session in progress, your break must coincide with the session's. Meal breaks are not to be taken less than one hour after reporting for work, unless the session also breaks for a meal.

PAYING UP FRONT

At times, you may be asked to front the money for part or all of a delivery bill for food that has been ordered by several people. Whether you front the money or ask someone to cover your own bill, please honor this convenience system, and reimburse one another within 24 hours. It only works if we trust each other to be responsible for individual expenses, with a minimum of game-playing.

CLIENT TABS

Clients occasionally offer to pick up the tab for a meal break. If you are working on such a session, you may accept without the need to reimburse. Employees outside of the session may not piggyback onto a client's tab.

Pay Policies

Employees of the company are paid every other Thursday. An independent payroll service deducts all applicable taxes and miscellaneous deductions.

TIME LOGS

Every hourly employee is responsible for keeping an accurate time log. Forms are obtained from the manager's office. It is your responsibility to accurately fill in the hours worked, along with project names, dates, rate of pay and overtime due on a daily basis.

Time logs must be completed and handed in on the Monday morning preceding the coming Thursday payday. Logs are spot-checked by management for accuracy and honesty, but the basic tenet of the company is that you are being trusted to report your hours in a scrupulous and professional manner. This code is part of the bedrock from which we operate.

WEEKLY DRAW

As a full-time employee, you are guaranteed a certain number of base pay hours per week in wages. That means that whether you work 80 hours or only 10 hours in any given week, you will always be paid at least your hourly rate times your base guarantee, at minimum.

All hours worked, regardless of overtime, count toward the total. Thus, whether you work three 14-hour days or six 7-hour days, your minimum is the base number that needs to be reached.

HOURLY DRAW

If you prefer to be on less frequent call, you may elect to work on an hourly basis exclusively. In this case, all your hours are worked by mutual agreement between you and the company, and you are paid for no more or less than you work in any given week. In this case, there is no wage guarantee.

You must choose your preferred method of payment for periods of at least three months before switching from hourly to weekly or vice versa.

HEALTH INSURANCE ELIGIBILITY

If you are hired as an hourly employee, you must work two 120-hour months in row to become eligible for company health insurance. Once you meet this "full-time" requirement, insurance payments are figured as above.

OVERTIME

Overtime (paid at time and a half) begins on the ninth consecutive billing hour of work. If your base rate of pay is $10, then beginning on the ninth hour, your pay will be $15.

Overtime hours are included in totaling your base hourly work requirement. That means that a 14-hour day counts as 14 of your guaranteed base hours. You simply get the overtime amount paid in excess of the base for the time worked starting on the ninth hour. So, if you worked 14 hours on a single day, all 14 would count towards your base, but 4 would be paid to you at time and a half and 2 would be paid at double time.

Note: Overtime is never at the employee's discretion. It shall only be incurred at the request of the management or when a paying session continues into the ninth hour of your day.

If you expect to go into overtime on a project other than a paying per-hour session, you must inform management that you will be billing overtime hours for the work at hand and obtain permission to continue.

OVERTIME IS ALWAYS PAID ADDITIONALLY

Overtime is always paid in addition to any guaranteed minimum weekly draw. Thus, if you worked only 25 hours during one week including 3 hours of overtime, but were guaranteed a wage based on 40 hours' pay, you would receive:

40 times your hourly rate, plus 3 times the difference between your regular and overtime pay.

At $10 per hour, that would mean:

40 x 10 = $400.

15 (OT Rate) - 10 (Regular rate) = $5

5 x 3 OT hours = $15

400 + 15 = $415 gross pay.

TWO-TIER PAY SCALES

We sometimes pay two different rates for engineers qualified and needed for both firsting and seconding. At the company's election, we may set up two separate rates of pay if you are doing two different jobs. In that case:

1. Your individual weekly guarantee remains in effect.

2. You must detail each day's work at the proper rate of pay on your time sheet.

3. You will earn in excess of your weekly draw when your combined pay rates *exceed* it.

Example 1:

You earn $10/hour as a second and $20/hour as a first. Your weekly guarantee is $400. During one week, you work 22 hours @ $10 and 14 hours @ $20.

22 x 10 = $220

14 x 20 = $280

220 + 280 = $500 gross pay.

Example 2:

You earn $10/hour as a second and $20/hour as a first. Your weekly guarantee is $400. During one week, you work 7 hours @ $10 and 13 hours @ $20.

7 x 10 = $70

13 x 20 = $260

70 + 260 = $330.

You automatically make your draw of $400 gross pay.

PAY RAISES

There is no formal review, performance appraisal or annual schedule for pay raises. They are instead based entirely on employee performance as perceived by management. You may receive several raises within a year or none at all.

We expect professional, high-quality and enthusiastic performance from every individual at Interlok. Those who show follow-through and consistency will be rewarded for value received.

PAYCHECKS

Paychecks are issued only by management. All matters involving payroll should be referred to the studio manager. Please respect people's privacy regarding pay.

It is strictly forbidden to access pay records or to disburse your own or anyone else's paychecks without express permission from management.

Personal Recording Time

We encourage engineers to hone their skills with free studio time, when available. You may engineer any live music project of your choice providing that:

1. You ask and receive permission to record on a specific date we are made aware of.

2. You are contributing your services to the project free of charge.

3. It is understood by all that the session may be bumped at the last minute by a paying session that is booked in, which you may wind up engineering.

4. Working on these elective projects does not interfere with your paid duties from a scheduling or fatigue standpoint.

5. You assume responsibility for maintaining the security and cleanliness of the facility during and immediately after the time you work on such sessions. Since we rarely have a receptionist at these times, this includes keeping all access doors locked at all times.

Guests must be made aware of these policies, because the responsibility is yours.

PERSONAL FOLLOW-THROUGH

We expect you to treat the facility with extra care when it is entrusted to you for personal use. Lack of follow-through may result in a suspension of all free session privileges.

Personal recording time is a privilege, and we want to re-emphasize that you must be aware of, and agree to abide by, these rules:

PERSONAL ARTIST PROJECTS: BOOKING

You may record free of charge with the *one* group you call your own. You must, however, book all sessions with the studio manager before the fact, and you *must* fill out a work order detailing the work that was done.

Failure to either book a session ahead of time or turn in a work order will result in a 30-day suspension of personal recording privileges.

ENGINEERING FEES

You may *not* charge personal project clients for your engineering services. The idea of allowing personal projects is to enable you to work on your craft. If your client can afford to pay you, arrange the billing through us and we will be glad to see you get your fair share.

ONE AT A TIME, PLEASE

We want to encourage everyone who wants to, to book project time, and to follow through on completion. Therefore, we allow only one project per engineer at any given time.

Complete that project, and you may then be given permission to move on to another.

It is your responsibility to learn and abide by these personal session rules:

1. Sessions must be booked ahead of time.
2. Complete work orders must be filed for every session.
3. Access doors must always remain locked. You are responsible for security and cleanup.
4. You may not use fresh house tape without advance permission.
5. You must engineer the session. No outside engineers are permitted to operate the board or machines for personal sessions.
6. You must balance your personal time responsibly and report to work the next day looking and acting alive and alert.
7. Visitors may not make long-distance phone calls and must not enter offices or other studios.
8. No drugs or hard liquor are allowed on the premises.

Office of the Controller

This job centers around invoicing, check-writing, form-generating and tape-labeling.

In general, invoices are to be generated and mailed within 48 hours of the completion of a billable project. A file of receivables is to be maintained and updated when payments are received.

A statement detailing income, outflow and receivables is due to management on the first of each month.

Labeling needs to be accomplished in as efficient a manner as possible. Our goal is to prevent our clients from having to wait after

their session in order to receive properly labeled tape boxes. Therefore, you need to work closely with assistants to get the correct information in time to deliver your work efficiently.

Accuracy is the other important component. We strive to maintain a high degree, so that names and projects are spelled correctly. We have all agreed that incorrect spelling is a powerful turnoff to a tired and stressed-out client.

You are also expected to cover phones and reception when the receptionist is not present, which means that you need to maintain a close and personable working relationship with the front desk.

Client invoices should not be left on-screen for anyone else to see during the day. Rates are individually negotiated and are no one else's business. Hard copies need to be filed and sent out immediately.

In general, unless invited, you and other office personnel should not be in any control room during sessions with clients present.

Receptionists

Besides regular job duties, the receptionist is in charge of daytime housekeeping in the client lounge. That entails keeping the refrigerator stocked, coffee fresh and the bathrooms supplied with paper, and clearing any client (not staff) leftovers from the tables. Our night cleaning crew will do the rest.

Your job includes regular supermarket runs and preparing of goodie baskets for daily client sessions.

You also share responsibility for tape labeling and the daytime in- and outflow of client materials and rental items with the other front office person.

Remember that all tape deliveries and pickups must be logged in the Tape In/Out Book!

Because of the front location, the receptionist is involved in many personal and interoffice communications and goings-on in the front building. That means there will be times to exercise discretion, to take matters into your own hands, and to maintain a level of diplomacy.

In particular, this applies to your interfacing with other staff members. Be aware of the CPOV when clients are present. How do your conversations and actions appear to them? Your body language? Your visible personal space?

And be aware of the long-term relationships you need to maintain with other staff members. That may mean withholding certain personal judgments in favor of group harmony, and taking care to maintain a certain level of neutrality in order to avoid finding yourself in the middle of a dispute.

Retirement Benefits

The Interlok Pension Fund is a company-administered IRA plan that extends special benefits to employees who have been on the payroll for three or more years.

Our company retirement plan takes the basic IRA several steps beyond what an individual is allowed to do. The plan we have chosen is called a SARSEP IRA, which stands for SAlary Reduction Simplified Employee Pension plan. This is a government-sanctioned plan that is only available to small businesses whose employers and employees are willing to participate.

Participation in this plan is voluntary and open only to 3-year-or-more employees. At least 50% of all qualified employees in the company must choose to participate in order for the plan to remain viable. Once you as an employee commit to participating, you are presented with a veritable smorgasbord of investment choices.

First, you must decide how much of your gross wages you would like to invest on a yearly basis. You may choose to invest anywhere from 1%-15% of your pay. Second, you need to pick a qualified investment vehicle in which to place your money.

And third, upon committing to this unique plan, Interlok will *also* contribute tax-deferred money to your personal IRA account. The company will contribute an amount equal to 3% of your gross pay per year. This is the one of the best benefits of the plan, because it will make your account grow faster with the higher influx of employer-contributed dollars.

CHOOSING AN INVESTMENT VEHICLE
We will be glad to assist you with facts and information that will help you choose the right fund for your investment goals. In addition, plan investment brokers are available for personal consultations at their offices whenever you wish.

This plan is 100% vested in the employee from inception, which means that all of the money in your account belongs to you from the first dollar that goes in. Should you leave Interlok for any reason, the entire balance of your account will be turned over to you without charge or impediment. The company's only involvement is to qualify individuals for the plan, administer it and add to each participant's

investment as a special benefit of employment. The company charges you no fee whatsoever.

We encourage you to contribute as much as you comfortably can to this great personal plan. At current inflation rates, the cost of living will double in 20 years and triple in 40. The government has made it clear that the best tax breaks come to long-term investors who are willing to plan ahead, and that by the time you reach retirement age, you're going to be more or less on your own financially.

Retirement savings are completely deductible, which means you pay no tax on the portion of your earnings you contribute. Plus, the interest you earn on your investments is not taxed until you begin withdrawing money at retirement. There is no better investment for long-term planning on the planet.

Retirement may seem light-years away now, but the magic of tax-free compounded interest and contributions over a 30-year period is quite astonishing. According to a recent projection done by Merrill Lynch, the average American starts saving for retirement at age 38. But if he'd started ten years earlier, he could *stop* by age 38 and still come out ahead. For example, if you save $4,000 a year for 10 years—a total of $40,000—you wind up with $72,219, if your investment earns 10% a year. But if you instead contribute $1,000 a year for 40 years (the same $40,000), you'll have $562,986!

Start now, and you can wind up a genuine millionaire later on.

Scheduling

The studio manager carries the final authority in all engineering and office personnel scheduling. It is the manager's and assistant manager's responsibility to set hours with reasonable advance warning. It is every staff member's responsibility to check in and be available for communication on a daily basis, excepting weekends and holidays.

The studio manager and assistant will make their best effort to maintain fairness, but there are times you will feel unfairly put upon. This is inevitable; unpredictable and chaotic tangles are part of the studio norm. We ask for your understanding and willingness to bend when the stress hits the fan. We'll try to make it up to you.

SCHEDULING CONFLICTS
Experience has demonstrated that the only sane way to coordinate client traffic is to allow only

the studio manager and assistant to enter sessions in the schedule book. By focusing on these two people, they become the keepers of the "invisible book" as well, the one that juggles all the quirks and client requests that are never written down, but kept in mind.

For that reason, unless you have been specifically instructed to by management, *never* attempt to schedule a client for a session. Always refer the client to the studio manager for scheduling. If management is unavailable, tell the client that someone will get back to him shortly with an answer.

Sick Days

Since schedules are flexible, we endeavor to work around times you may be sick or unavailable by making up the time on alternate days. If additionally necessary, up to five days of paid sick leave are permitted each year. After the fifth day, calling in sick becomes unpaid leave.

Smoking

Smoking is not permitted on the premises.

Studio Manager

The management office is the central hub for all the business-related activity of the studio. The studio manager is the day-to-day authority in charge of client relations and booking, staff management and scheduling, payroll, bookkeeping, project bids and most any problem or challenge that may come your way. The studio manager may either participate in or control the hiring and firing of employees, employee disputes and negotiations.

The studio manager is also the company's General Manager, and as such is entitled to executive privilege beyond the scope of some staff rules. With that privilege comes the responsibility of rising to a given occasion, be it keeping late hours, accepting and dealing with after-hours phone calls or taking the initiative as he or she sees fit in a given situation. The manager carries a pager and is to be paged if not otherwise available when an important situation arises.

The studio manager is also the final authority in staff scheduling. You may discuss your needs and preferences and plead your case at times, but once the decision is made, be well advised to refrain from whining.

Studio Manager, Assistant

The assistant manager is generally in charge of client booking (traffic) and session record-keeping. The assistant also carries staff-scheduling power and is empowered to direct the day-to-day activities of staff members. The assistant manager works in concert with the studio manager and is directly responsible to him or her.

The assistant manager becomes the officer in charge when the studio manager is not present and is required to be accessible at most times via beeper.

Technical Bulletins

Interlok Technical Bulletins are released on an as-needed basis. Their primary purpose is to alert staff to new operating procedures, updates or quirks in our existing system. They are usually issued in the form of one-page announcements, and are distributed to all engineering personnel, as well as being posted for a period of time.

All engineers are expected to read and understand the information contained in the bulletin. We encourage you to ask questions, request more information or suggest topics for future bulletins.

Telephone Calls

Everyone is entitled to a private outside life, but please be reasonable about your use of the phone. That means explaining to friends that we would prefer they leave messages on your home machine as a rule, and make their calls to the studio brief.

CALLS DURING SESSIONS
Incoming calls to engineering personnel who are in session are not forwarded. Reception will inform the caller that you are in session and take a message, which will be left in your box.

LONG-DISTANCE CALLS
We constantly review our phone bills, which are enormous due to client usage. Most phones are blocked for calls out beyond the local area.

Please respect your privileges here. Occasional long-distance calls of short duration are a reasonable perk, but frequent ones are not. If you need to make frequent or expensive long-distance calls, either use your personal calling card or inform management and arrange to reimburse the company when the bill arrives.

The Top 10 No-No's For Good Client Relations

1. Never say "no" to a client request. If you're stuck, say "Let me find out."

2. Never discuss rates with a client. Always refer them to management.

3. Never deliver a master to a client without getting management's permission first.

4. Never let a tape out of the studio without double-checking for tones, accuracy and documentation.

5. Never discuss studio, equipment or time problems within earshot of any visitor.

6. Never wear clothes that make you look like you don't care about the service you're performing.

7. Don't cross the conversational boundaries of decorum until a client leads you there.

8. Don't forget that work orders are legal documents. Always fill them out in 10-part detail.

9. Always look at your session considering and caring for the CPOV.

10. Never act like anything less than the professional you are.

Vacations

After one year's employment, you are entitled to one week's paid vacation. After two years, two weeks. We will be as flexible as possible in scheduling paid vacation time in any manner you choose. In return, please give us as much notice as possible of your plans. Minimum notice is two weeks.

ACCRUED VACATION TIME
You must take your vacation within six months of becoming eligible for it. Otherwise, you will lose the time earned.

NATIONAL AND RELIGIOUS HOLIDAYS
We close for the following holidays: New Year's, Easter, Memorial Day, July 4th, Labor Day, Thanksgiving and Christmas. These are paid holidays, within the scope of your payment guarantee.

If your beliefs require other special days off, we will endeavor to grant them, with the understanding that you may be asked to make up for the lost time or take it as unpaid leave.

We occasionally book desperate clients for session work on national holidays. Holiday pay is at least time and a half, depending on the circumstances. We ask for volunteers first. If none are forthcoming, you will be asked to work your fair share of the time as needed.

EXTRA DAYS OFF
Management may, from time to time, also grant three or four consecutive paid or unpaid days off in addition to normal paid holidays. This may occur as a result of a marathon being completed, off-season doldrums, or personal merit.

In Conclusion

Interlok is a people-oriented company. We partners truly care about you as individuals and as members of a special family. We ask only that you return the level of respect and integrity we strive to maintain, and that you take the same pride in doing your job as we do in providing our services for the industry.

Our door is always open for consultation or problem-solving. Give us your best, and we'll give you everything we can in return.

We're glad you've become a part of us.

Connecting the Global Village

The founder of the Record Plant and past president of SPARS, Chris Stone has forged an alliance among some of the finest studios in the world, weaving a continent-by-continent connection and networking them into an elite and eclectic association.

Chris Stone

Founder & President

The World Studio Group

Los Angeles, California

Q. *What's the primary purpose of the group?*
A. To maintain the mothership. When we started SPARS, every studio was an island. Studios didn't talk to each other. You couldn't get any meaningful information from one. We now have a worldwide network in which we can check out anything and everything and then share that information, because our members do not compete! They share. Everybody wins, and everybody makes money.

We're also doing market research for manufacturers. For instance, we're working with 3M, who want to introduce a new tape formula. So they'll send me 40 reels of tape, we'll get them out to 40 facilities around the world, and within 30 days we get 3M all their answers.

Q. *Can you explain what you mean about the "mothership philosophy?"*
A. Well, you have the large conglomerate facilities and you have the little guys who need to work them. By now, everybody's learned it's a lot simpler to work together. The larger studios can provide services to the smaller ones, and continue to come to the facilities to which they've developed relationships.

Without the motherships, the major manufacturers in our industry would have no reason to continue their R&D in product development, because we are a filter-down industry. The top guys try and buy the new equipment, and then it filters down to the mainstream.

So I decided that we needed to develop an association of big guys. I actually got the idea from SPARS. I decided to assemble the top studios, mostly two per major market, moving down to a single studio in a minor market, in the world.

Q. *How does the organization work?*
A. We currently have 40 members, and are growing to a goal of 50. What we try to do is to book sessions between members. So you call me and say, "Chris, I've got a client who's going to Tokyo and then London. Here's his budget, what can you do for me?"

The receiving studio pays a 10% commission on time only, and the referring studio splits it with our office. So everybody makes money. This is not only a private and elitist organization, but everyone makes a profit. It helps to keep these people on top, buying new equipment and keeping the filter-down happening.

In addition, we've stumbled onto the global village, which is getting incredibly sophisticated. For instance, we're a natural for becoming our own little digital network. We've also become a worldwide emergency service center for ADAT. And since everybody from Sting on down carries those with them and likes the idea of sending a tape around to put another instrument on, they can now look at the listing directory and find a place in the network just about everywhere they go.

Q. *How do you choose your members?*
A. We choose those we consider to be the best in their market. For example, we've got a studio in Ecuador that would qualify to be a reasonable project studio in Los Angeles, but it's the only thing in Ecuador. So in that location, it's the best.

I've had some trouble explaining this to people. You don't have to have three Neves, two SSLs and four 48-tracks—it's more about what your position is in your market. If you're the best, then we'd like to talk to you. And in terms of Ecuador, they have several very specialized Indian percussion instruments, as well as a record label and recording school.

Q. *How does the booking tend to go?*

A. The majority of our bookings are outside the country, for a few simple reasons. Most people don't know the area or the studios. They don't speak the language, and the people don't know them. So if you tried calling one of the members cold and tried to book some time, you'd have to go through the whole new client application process and probably pay in advance.

But if we call, say, to our location in Capri, we can simply say, "Hey, Quinto, we've got a friend who needs to record there for a week. Give me a price and put this time on hold." And it's done.

Q. *How do you maintain live interaction among members?*

A. For meetings, we get together at AES New York, Europe and Tokyo. The tough part is that I also personally visit every member once a year! I love to travel. That's where the membership fees ($1,000 per year) go. So I'm on the road about four months a year.

Q. *What changes have you seen in the cost of running a world-class room?*

A. When we built the first Record Plant in 1968, we built and totally equipped one studio and did all the major construction on a second at a total cost of 85,000 dollars. The day we opened, we were booked for three months at $85 an hour. Compare that to today, where the same quality of studio is $1.5 to $2 million and you're getting $175 to $200 per hour, if you're on the top. It just doesn't make sense.

So the answer is both the mothership philosophy and diversification. As the project studios start to affiliate with the motherships to provide them with the services they need, the projects figure, wait a minute. If this guy will give me, say, a D2 digital video layback service, then why should I go and spend the enormous amount of money on the cost of one? I can go to a large facility, get the stuff done that I can't comfortably afford to put in my own place, and they'll give me a special rate because I'm gonna do this on a regular basis. Then we can both survive!

Q. *How are your members coping with rising costs and shrinking rates?*

A. Well, you just have to keep beating your head against the wall until you find something that works. Often that's called diversification. You examine all the different possibilities and come down to a formula that works for you.

I think you need to run a recording studio in the same way that a supermarket runs: What is the productivity per square foot? It's simply a matter of setting up a multiroom complex as a series of separate profit centers. And if that doesn't justify each room's existence, then you have to find something else for that room to do. People are doing this worldwide and pulling down good profits. The key is to properly structure your debt service.

Now on the other hand, take the case of a fellow named Mike Cordell, who owns The Time Machine in Vermont. So far, he has spent 12 million dollars. He has two control rooms and one small studio. He decided to go up into the wilds of Vermont and found this beautiful ridge that overlooks three ski areas.

He now has eight buildings on it, including a recreation building that has a huge pool; a regulation racquetball court; male and female steam, sauna and exercise rooms; a conference room that looks out at the view; and on the side of the mountain, he's dug himself a soccer field. He's 26, and his parents are extremely wealthy.

Now some people like that, you throw out everything you know. So he doesn't need the money and is using it for his own musical projects. In a sense, it's the world's most palatial project studio.

Q. *But back to reality…*

A. Well, the world-class rooms are developing specialties and profit centers that offset the enormous costs of equipping themselves. And they do it with style.

Take Rick Stevens, who bought the Record Plant, who does very well in spite of the enormous multi-million investment he's made in the place. He does music recording, and music recording only, but he does it beautifully.

For example, when ♀ comes into the Record Plant, Rick brings in a designer, who *does* the room. And it's different every time ♀ comes in! And he'll drape different materials and create moods and everything, and of course, Rick will charge ♀ for it, but it's the old story. You make the client comfortable, and he'll stay longer. At the top of the line, money is not the object. *Comfort* is the object. Comfort.

Q. *What about diversification?*
A. That's the key. Take John Fry at Ardent, in Memphis. He's been there 28 years, with the aura of Presley and all the old legends that have come out of there. He attracts clients from Europe, and all over the U.S., because they want to come over and get the Memphis sound. And that's what he sells.

He also has a production company, a little boutique label and manages seven or eight engineer/producers and has a facility that's spread out into a lot of little rooms and works beautifully.

Or take Bad Animals — a classic example. Steve Lawson started out as a garage studio in Seattle and hooked up with Heart, who built his premier studio for him, called Studio X. Now they do music and post, he's the best in his marketplace, he's got a lot of little rooms so he does a lot of editing, bought himself some Post Pros, does duplication, was one of the first to get on EdNet and does a lot of talent-booking using it. He'll get you various character voices or foreign-language artists for dubbing and has built a beautiful operation.

Q. *How are facilities planning on exploiting the digital highway?*
A. The major trend that's coming at us is a vast increase in communication. You're going to be able to be a composer in Wyoming and have every service you want, via digital technology. The world is getting smaller and smaller.

So you'll be able to sit in your control room in Brazil and be able to say, "You know, I want that guy from Tibet who plays that incredible instrument on this record that I'm working on," and you'll be able to get him by phone!

Q. *How does an entrepreneur work up to world-class?*
A. If you want a single word to describe your status in this business, it's your phone book. The people in it are the people who'll take your calls, and the bigger your phone book is, the more important you are in this business.

If you have the reputation and you treat people fairly, over time, everybody will talk to you because they know you're not gonna mess with them. You're gonna take care of their needs.

Business negotiation is one thing. But by the same token, if it's done within the rules of business propriety and ethics [laughing], which differ from country to country, by the way, then that's the long-term person who's going to have the biggest phone book and who's going to be able to get the most done with a single call. If people know that you're going to treat them fairly, they'll flock to you.

Q. *So how do you do good business today and tomorrow?*
A. The key is proper management. Take off your blinders and look at every possible way to make money. You need to become more efficient, you need objectivity, so you can benefit from outside consultation. You tend to become ingrown and small unless you join organizations, talk to your competitors and do everything you can to avoid allowing your vision to become narrow. And to get that value, you really gotta get down with people. You gotta live together a little, have dinner, have a few drinks, loosen up and really talk and reveal something about yourself.

And without that outside injection of objectivity, you're doomed. Doomed! Because there's no way that you know everything about your business. So one of the ways to get more profitable once you're in a professional organization is to get it to really work for you. That's the way to stay connected and keep moving forward.

18
Coping With Disaster

There are times when things don't just go wrong—they blow you over with gale force, leaving you a little stunned. Your first plan of action should be to remember to breathe. With the oxygen swimming smoothly around in your brain once again, you should then be able to begin to assess the extent of the previous moment's events. Often, that's when stars are born.

What follows are a few stories that are just too crazy to have been made up. In fact, they all actually happened. Read on and give thanks that you weren't there at the time. (Or were you?)

THE CLIENT SPILLS
HIS DRINK ON THE CONSOLE

Bo Reusch, from Big Dog Studios in Kansas, has a story about a group of "glam rockers" who spent a lot of time parading around the room all decked out in glitter, makeup and Spandex when they weren't slashing away at C chords for the album they were producing themselves. They block-booked a week and virtually moved into the building in order to concentrate and get the job done.

The lead singer, who was also the group's principal writer and producer, spent a lot of time in the control booth struttin' and sputterin', and as the band worked into the wee hours, he drank a lot of coffee to stay alert. Bo had warned him a dozen times not to hold his coffee over the console as he talked to the group, but to the singer, it was an unconscious act, and he just kept drinking and swaying over the board throughout the night.

By about 4:00 a.m., the group had gotten pretty cranky and had begun to complain about not finding the groove and quitting for the night, but the leader wouldn't hear of it. He really wanted to press on, and in an emotional outburst, managed to both yell at the group over the talkback and spill an entire cup of coffee right into the center fader mains.

In the stunned silence that followed, everyone watched as the board started crackling and throwing sparks, followed by wisps of smoke. The smoke did it—Bo jumped up and shut down the power for the entire room, and everyone just sat there in the dark, dumbfounded.

Bo went down the hall to the maintenance shop, came back with a toolkit and a roll of paper towels, turned the lights back on and proceeded to remove about half of the fader modules, from the center of the console outward. It could've been worse—coffee is a little acidic, but at least it's not sticky or gooey. He started blotting the cards dry, which didn't pick up the droplets trapped beneath the various resistors, and then looked up at the guys in the group, who were just sitting there watching him.

"Now you know," he said in measured tones, "why this session is gonna take all night. I want each of you to pick up a few modules, go and get your electric hair-stylers, and blow-dry each one of these suckers as if it were a perm you were frosting for an appearance at the Coliseum."

With that, the group left, came back, and spread the modules out across the control-room floor, styler pistols blazing. By dawn, the console was back to normal, the lead singer had forever changed his producing style, and a half a dozen tired boys headed for home to get some sleep for the next day's session.

A FISTFIGHT BREAKS OUT
IN THE CONTROL ROOM

George Conurs was working on two album projects at Avalanche Studios in Denver. One was with a local Christian heavy metal band. They worked during the night. The other, no lie, was a bona fide Satanic Heavy Metal Band. They worked each day.

About the only contact they had with each other was to wave a wary hello between sessions. But that's not what the story's about.

The Satan buddies were a roadwise, professional outfit, all business and no hanky-panky. It was the Christian group that looked like trouble. The problem was that the guys had been fighting among themselves from the beginning of the project about how to properly produce the album. There seemed to be a lot of animosity between them, and the air stayed thick with insults and barbs.

By the time the final mix sessions began, the hot vibes hit the boiling point. It came to a head when the singer and the guitarist squared off on the relative volume of their parts in the mix. Suddenly, without any warning, the singer threw a roundhouse that knocked the guitarist flat on the floor. And then all hell broke loose.

George, the engineer, jumped up and heroically threw himself between the fighters and the console. The second ran into the room and moved over toward his compatriot, and the two men methodically but firmly began to edge the furious fighters out of the control room, through the doorway, and onto the street, fists flying all the while.

It had been a long night, and the next shift had begun to arrive to take over, while the ruckus raged on. Not recognizing who they were, one of the people arriving—the drummer from the Satanic group—called the cops. When they arrived, the Christian guitarist ducked into the studio, and the singer just took off.

That was the end of his membership in the group. The rest of the guys finished the project by dividing up the vocals, paid their bill and disappeared.

By all accounts, George turned out to be the hero. He was the one who finished both projects and protected the console.

THE SPECIALLY SHIPPED GEAR FOR THE SUNDAY SESSION GETS LOCKED IN THE WAREHOUSE FOR THE WEEKEND

Different Fur owner Sue Skaggs had an important client who wanted a rather esoteric piece of outboard gear that needed to be rented from out of town. It was flown in, and she'd scheduled the only person available—herself—to pick it up on Saturday, but she was so busy when the day came that it slipped her mind.

The next morning, the second called from the studio to ask where the equipment was. Sue realized she'd completely forgotten about the gear, called the airline freight office and found out the warehouse was locked up until Monday. She was told there was no way the gear could be removed, and that calls like this came every so often, but there was nothing anyone could do.

Several calls later, she found a manager with a sympathetic ear. "I didn't let him get a word in for the first three minutes. I just filled him up with half of my life story, and romanced him about the studio business." The manager agreed to meet her at the warehouse himself.

She met him at the airport, where they went inside the giant warehouse, and spent the next fifteen minutes trying to locate the two large cases. Finally, they spotted them at the top of a 12-foot stack. There were no ladders, no way to get to them.

The manager shrugged and apologized, figuring that was that. But Sue had spotted a dormant fork lift, jumped in, and started up the engine. That was enough to panic the manager into offering to drive it instead, all the while praying out loud that the union would never find out about this.

She made it back to the studio, gear in hand, with ten minutes to spare. Everything went smoothly after that. Later, when the producer thanked her for going to the trouble of renting the special equipment, she sighed, smiled and chirped, "No problem."

THE ENTIRE 30-MINUTE MASTER GETS ACCIDENTALLY ERASED

Blair Wilkins' Studio West in Canada became successful in large part due to the wide range of marketing campaigns he developed. One of them included soliciting clients from all over the country and plugging his retreat-like setting in central Canada as an ideal place to get away from it all.

That made sense to a trio of musicians who had been hired to do the score for a half-hour documentary which needed virtually wall-to-wall music. It was a government-sponsored project, and the coordinator figured out that they'd actually save money if the group flew 2,500 miles from their home in Nova Scotia to take advantage of the studio's offer of high quality and competitive rates.

They worked for three days and nights on

the project, got it all down on tape, and according to plan, flew out the next day, leaving the master to be mixed by the producer of the project.

It had been a long weekend at the studio, and the night staff smiled a weak hello as the new shift arrived the next morning. The night crew finally dragged themselves out of the studio and went home.

The room's next session started immediately. It was a song-demo date for a group who'd asked to work with used tape to save money. The new engineer put up a roll of 2-inch, which had been mistakenly put into the wrong box, and rolled it in RECORD from top to bottom, 24 red lights blazing, to clean it for the session while they set up.

It wasn't until that night that anyone realized that the entire scoring project tape had been transformed into a bluesy bar-band performance master. When the facts did become known, and everyone finally decided against slitting each others' throats, management sat down to sort things out.

They decided that the engineer, who everyone liked, was entitled to one mistake like that in his life (that was three years ago, and his scorecard is still clean). Then Blair closed his office door, took a deep breath, and made a long-distance call. He broke the news to the flabbergasted group, and then made his best offer: A free round-trip flight back to the studio on the following weekend, and a complete re-record on the house.

"I couldn't just hang them out in the wind," he said. "We were just as blown away by the whole thing as they were."

The group naturally accepted the offer; they really didn't have much choice. And the studio rolled out the red carpet and made them as comfortable as possible.

One unexpected development did unfold: About halfway through the re-record, the group started to smile again. Their new performances were beating the pants off the ones that had been removed from the planet the week before. And this time, the mix made it back home.

THE PRODUCER DECIDES THE MONITORING SYSTEM IS UNACCEPTABLE

Part of the promotional package that Criteria Studios in Florida sends out contains two typewritten, single-spaced, two-column lists of a few of the artists who have contributed to the studio's list of 150 gold

albums. When you get up to that level of performance, the fabulously successful talent can be rather unpredictable in its studio behavior.

Mac Emerman remembers one household-name group whose flamboyant producer set the tone for food-fights and room-trashing whenever they came in. In keeping with mellow studio policy, Mac would shake his head, keep out of the room and calmly bill them for every scuff mark they left.

One particularly long night, after the group had finished throwing plates of spaghetti at the video monitor during a concert broadcast by a friend, they filed back into the control room and hunkered down to mixing their latest tune. Hours went by, but it just wasn't getting done. The producer couldn't find the feel in the overall balance that he kept rolling back to find.

Suddenly, he cocked his head, took his feet off the console and sat up straight. With an air of divine revelation, he announced in his loudest, most proprietary voice, "You know what the problem is? It's these damn monitors!" With that, he pulled out a .45 automatic and emptied a full, deafening clip into the center of each woofer.

There was a stunned silence in the room. Nobody breathed for 30 seconds. Finally, the assistant engineer gamely smiled, stood up and began moving a couple of speaker stands in front of the console.

"Well then," he offered, clearing his throat. "Perhaps a pair of near-field monitors would be more to your liking!"

And the session lurched forward.

THE SUPERSTAR BOOKS A SESSION AND THEN HAS HIS OWN DISASTER

Baird Banner works with a wide variety of clients at Kludgit Sound in Cerrillos, New Mexico. Several have come from the west to escape the L.A. industry grind from time to time. So it was to his delight that after receiving a few long-distance phone calls and participating in some amiable negotiation, he block-booked his room to Stevie Wonder for an entire month.

Stevie had been on his usual heavy schedule of records and commercial jingle recordings, and was more interested in a comfortable room than the equipment that was there. His plan was to bring a digital mastering room with him, installed in a mobile truck.

The day before he was to begin, Baird got a call from Stevie's manager. They had arrived in a small town 30 miles away, stayed the night and prepared to make the trip over that morning. But when the truck driver had given the truck the gas, the rear axle had suddenly snapped in two.

They were very apologetic to Baird, but they didn't know what to do. The nearest service station was miles away, the replacement parts were in another state, and the show had to go on.

Baird also happened to be something of an auto mechanic. He decided to drive to their location, fix the problem and save the day. But when he arrived and looked at the truck, he realized that the worst had really happened. The axle was truly in pieces.

"Naturally, it was a big disappointment for me," he said. "I'd always been a really big fan, and I'd been looking forward to hangin' out at the sessions." He couldn't see the logic in charging a cancellation fee. It wasn't anybody's fault, everyone was apologetic, and the parts would be two weeks in coming.

The producer made an executive decision. The whole cast and crew would set up where the truck had broken down, which happened to be right outside a small dance club that they immediately block-booked. The crew had brought along all the keyboards and computers that were necessary.

As a small consolation, Baird got to hang out at the sessions in the new "studio" all he wanted, and because he had a healthy business to begin with, managed to rebook most of the lost time. "Hey," he said. "I still got to be buddies with the guy. He was just as friendly as could be."

THE STUDIO GETS SOME UNEXPECTED PUBLICITY

Joe Gottfried (who died unexpectedly in 1993, leaving a great legacy behind) knew that something was wrong the minute the ringing phone jolted him out of dreamland. It was 6:00 a.m. and he'd been fast asleep at home in bed. "Turn the TV on, to channel 11," groaned his studio manager on the other end. "You ain't gonna believe this."

About a month earlier, a guy with a strange personality had walked in off the street to inquire about booking time at Joe's Sound City in Van Nuys, California. It was strange enough that he'd done just that—the studio is located in an industrial complex way outside of town, and he didn't have a car. But his request was rea-

sonable enough: Would they let him record an album of his original songs performed on a standup bass during a three-day booking the next week? He'd be glad to pay full rate.

The dates went down, the studio was paid and the guy turned out to be an okay songwriter. The material was a little strange, like him, but not bad. When the mixes were done, however, he wasn't too happy. There was something about them he didn't like, and he told the engineer he'd take them home to listen there and then make up his mind about what to do.

It was two days later when Joe got up out of bed and turned the TV on. There, live and in color, was a floodlit outdoor shot of the studio, surrounded by a police patrol cars, medical emergency vans, news crews and half a dozen members of the L.A. SWAT team with automatic weapons drawn.

That strange little guy had decided he didn't like the way the songs had come out, and since they were his suicide love ballads to his girlfriend, he'd come back, armed to the teeth, to demand a remix.

Everyone had been evacuated from the building except for one engineer who'd been taken hostage. The songwriter demanded that the cops recite the Lord's Prayer with him before he finally surrendered himself and his handgun, but not before he used the studio for a little target practice. Later on, the cop received a medal of valor for saving the engineer.

By the time Joe got to the studio, everyone had gone. It was as if it really had only been a dream. It wasn't until the next day that he found the bullet holes from the night before. His Accounts Receivable file cabinet had been shot dead.

A PLUMBING PROBLEM GIVES "SURF'S UP!" A WHOLE NEW MEANING

According to Peter, the engineer who opened the door that morning, it was the closest he'd ever been to being in a Looney Tune: A wave of dirty water rushed out and damn near knocked him down. Naturally, it was in the complex's most expensive suite, a 48-track digital surround sound mixing room, featuring a custom-built Quad Eight board mounted in a nice, deep chassis.

Sometime in the early morning hours, a two-dollar plastic pipe fitting under an upstairs bathroom sink burst and started spraying a steady stream of water onto the floor. Eventually, the growing beast found itself a path that led right down through the ceiling over monitor fader number 19 on the Quad Eight.

We (yeah, we—this happened to *my* studio!) were running some pretty heavy amperage through that room, and Peter, realizing it had the potential to become its own killing field, bounded off to shut off the power and then get on the phone. By the time I arrived, a crew was using pumps and vacuums to suck up the wave, and our landlord was sloshing around in bare feet with his pant legs rolled up, looking like a guy at the beach who hadn't brought his trunks.

The console chassis had filled up with, oh, about eighty gallons, and it took a double-shift crew of four techs eight days to hand-dry and clean every module and card, most of which had corroded into a metallic mass of crud in just a few hours underwater. The bill for Blue Shower cleaner alone totaled about $1,500.

Naturally, it was the busy season and the facility was booked to the gills. Two of Interlok's five bays, plus a hallway and the central machine room, were soaking wet. The clients in the dry rooms clucked about fate and went on with their work. The clients getting bumped from the wet rooms queued up in the manager's office and demanded to know just who in the hell the dry-room clients were, and how come they were more important?

We did our best to stay cool. We put in extra shifts, ran ourselves ragged and tried to be philosophical. On the bright side, the insurance company rep arrived the day of the flood and calmly intoned the magic words: "Do whatever you need to get back up and don't worry about the money." It took ten days to virtually rebuild the console, tear down what was left of the ceiling and walls, remodel and replace them, dry out the carpets, buy new equipment and furniture and calm the last skittish client down.

Two days later, my partner arrived fresh and rested from a fabulous three-week vacation he and his wife had just taken in Italy, and pronounced it the best time they'd ever had.

19
Betting on the Future

unning a business is risky. And in spite of all the giant leaps in technology, predicting the future is just as murky a subject as it's ever been. The best you can hope to do about figuring out what's going to happen next is to educate yourself, by doing as much reading and research as you can stand. And then make informed decisions that you hope won't trip you up a week down the line. It's a risk that no one can really ease.

Consider this amazing bit of truth: Twice a year, the Wall Street Journal does a feature in which four top-performing investment portfolio guru/advisers are asked to pick six stocks they feel are the best bet for profitable returns during the coming year. Any stock traded on any major exchange is fair game. Advisers can use any form of computer software, their full research teams, whatever it takes to pick six winners over the coming six months.

The Journal then pits their picks against a randomly chosen staff writer who hangs up the newspaper's stock-exchange listing pages on a bulletin board and throws six darts at them from ten paces. Where the darts land determines the Journal's competing portfolio of stock. It's a world-class contest between Wall Street's heaviest hitters and a handful of flying serendipity. Believe it or not, the darts win nearly half the time. I *love* it when that happens!

There's two things to learn from that exercise: Don't let *anyone* tell you that there's only one way to do something, and as Reverend Ike, the irreverent televangelist, used to say: "When you comes to a fork in the road, and ya just can't figure which way to turn...just deeee-cide, my friend, just dee-cide..."

Equipping Yourself for Change

There is exhilarating change going on every-where you look in the field of technology. One of the more remarkable leaps is in the way we simply learn about things.

It's been said that between 1800 and 1900, the amount of sheer information on the planet literally doubled. It doubled again between 1900 and 1950. By 1980, the prediction was that a doubling of planetary information would occur every ten years. And now, researchers say that the total amount of information in the world is doubling every 20 *months*.

So about the only reliable prediction anyone can make is that things will continue to change at a breathtaking pace. In the recording equipment arena, that's meant a revolution in the capability and affordability of both the most fundamental and the most sophisticated gear, from data storage to a virtually infinite menu of audible manipulation. One no longer needs to invest $5,000 to get great-sounding digital reverb; units that virtually duplicate that performance now cost just a few hundred dollars. Digital tape and disk recording systems cost as little as a tenth of what professionals paid for similar performance five years ago. And computer mixdown has become commonplace in low-end, high-output home project rooms.

Certainly, quality will continue to improve, performance levels will increase and prices will go down, as the marketplace quickly assimilates each new generation of development. So the smart investor will need to look for gear that is adaptable, upgradable and affordable.

Choosing a location will become simpler and cheaper too. Mixing consoles on the low end now deliver broadcast quality, yet have shrunk to a fraction of the size of the giants that used to rule the day. The era of the professional tabletop studio is upon us, and with it, the era of the corner-of-a-bedroom, CD-quality facility.

But just as surely as the trend toward miniaturization progresses, so goes the evolution of the world-class room. Spectacular boards with transparent digital signal paths sit in the midst of pristine, tuned environments that accommodate a dozen superstars in luxury, as they listen to a mix in a multimillion-dollar setting. Instead of tape, they preview a custom-created CD of the evening's work on a variety of monitor displays, and try retakes in enormous, high-ceilinged live rooms with motorized wall tiles to tune the acoustical response.

And so, the gap widens even as it narrows, uniting both high- and low-end creators through feature-differentiated, but always digital, parity. And interestingly enough, in creating that parity, strong symbiotic relationships are being forged, as both micro- and mega-studios find they need one another to remain strong and vital.

Trends that Look Like They Aren't About to Disappear

The loudest and most obvious trend that's occurred in the recording business has been the melding of sound to picture. Blame it on MTV, if you must. Before that, we were more purist, concentrating on producing music solely for the pleasure of the listening. Many of us over 40 miss those days, but gone they are, solid gone. With today's torrent of visual images married to everything that makes a noise, sound and picture have become one solid object.

Add to that the explosion of cable TV and "57 channels with nothin' on," as Mr. Springsteen observed, and where once music fit into a neat little variety-show category of visual images, there is now a screaming demand for virtually tons of product to feed an insatiable beast.

And that's not all. As multimedia, interactive, mega-channel cable enters the fray, you can bet that demand will increase many fold. If we are in fact going to be dealing with cable networks of 500 channels, *someone's* going to have to put the sound to the visuals.

When my partner and I started up Interlok in 1985, we bet most of our resources that audio post was going to provide a major percentage of our income. We were wrong. By 1989, it was providing practically *all* of it. At the same time, one venerable recording studio after another in L.A. was feeling the downward pinch of dealing with reduced demand and the accompanying reduced rates as one after another home project studio popped up, leaving the majors to deal increasingly with final mixes of basement-recorded tapes.

Looking for the Middle

Just as we are becoming a society of rich and poor, with a declining middle class, so the studio business has become one of world-class giants versus thousands (soon to become tens of thousands) of home project rooms. In major cities, coast to coast, the middle-class music studio of the past is becoming just that—of the past. Squeezed out of the picture by changing politics and technology, old-style midrange entrepreneurs have either woken up or given up.

But out there in Smallville, what passes for big-city midrange has a mighty appealing, upscale look to it. From secondary markets to the Great Plains, the opportunities are rife for midrange music studios. And with the advent of multiple digital networks and the increasing big-city-to-small-town migration, the U.S. is poised for a spreading out and sharing of wealth.

Studios from New Mexico to the Dakotas, and from Mississippi to Maine, are finding new opportunities for growth and maturity, as they become focal points for vibrant cultures and the creation of local products. As people flee the big cities and go looking for their ideal of satisfaction and safety, we can expect to see areas that may once have been far from the beaten path become mini-centers of artistry and change; witness the emerging prominence of Austin, Richmond, Bangor and Branson.

It's quite conceivable that one person with a dream can cause a dramatic impact on an entire small town. And the need won't be for world-class spending. It will be for the vision to bring a capable enterprise to fruition.

So the midrange studio isn't dead. It's just relocating.

THE WRITING ON THE WALL

Meanwhile, virtually all the major music rooms in big cities are equipped for lockup to picture, if for no other reason than to allow their clients to watch their videos in the studio. But the more compelling reason to go to audio for video is the purely economic fact that with each passing day it becomes cheaper and easier to record broadcast-quality music at home.

That points the way to either broad diversification or micro-specialization. A diversified studio has a much better chance of success offering a variety of services, from music recording to duplicating services to dialog editorial to mix-to-pix services.

The other intelligent alternative is to develop one specialty, like dialog or music editing, and exploit the daylights out of it. Obviously, much of each entrepreneur's decision is going to be based on his or her current financial status, but that's all the more reason to develop a carefully executed plan based on local market research, extensive reading and a lot of discussion with other professionals. (If there are consultants in your area, call and use them.)

Coming Soon...

There are great things in store for this business of recording. As of 1994, there were no fewer than 15 digital workstation systems, four digital cassette multitrack systems and an explosion of new hybrids that did everything from audio/video editing to full-on post production mixing.

Meanwhile, industry reps and pros constantly raise a clarion call of breakthroughs that continue to amaze and humble us. In 1988, a digital 24-track recorder cost $120,000. Today, you can buy three linked ADATs in a good music store and charge them on your American Express card. In 1988, it took a million bucks to assemble a credible video online bay. Today, an Avid will run you $80 grand and will cost even less next month.

As all this raging technology bursts onto the scene, a new trend has become more and more evident: The leaps are happening simultaneously in the high and low ends of the business. You can get into 8-track digital with a Mac for a couple grand, or you can spend 100K on a high-end supersystem. Both are revolutionary advances: the low end in its incredible capability for the money, and the high end for its incredibly *superior* capability for the money.

Finding Your Own Way

The smartest approach may lie in the biggest-bang-for-the-buck method. Recent history has shown that raging technology begets multiple upgrades and new models, which begets tumbling prices. With that bit of historical truth, a formula emerges: Those who *spend* the least, *lose* the least.

At a recent meeting of the International Teleproduction Society, a panel of industry reps paraded their new picture-editing systems in front of a room filled with top video-post studio owners. Each rep brought a short demo tape that was exhibited, highlighting the amazing effects and capabilities of the new systems

they were heralding. When the panel began taking questions from the floor, it was evident that disbelief and gloom had descended on the participants.

"I just purchased a $900,000 paintbox system, and you're telling me that your setup can do the same thing for *ten thousand*?" asked one incredulous owner. "No," replied the panelist, smiling, "not *everything*."

"If this is the future of post-production, then what am I supposed to do with the $20-million-dollar facility I'm paying off now?" asked another. "Well, people are still going to need to come to you for all the fine high-end services you have to offer," said another panelist in a comforting tone.

I remember thinking two things at that moment: One, that I was very grateful not to be a major player in the video post field, and two, that the same technological advances were occurring in audio. But I also knew that at our own facility, our casual but steady and involved market research had kept us on top of those developments, and that although competition was becoming all the more fierce, that we had positioned ourselves as a strong and lean company.

As I've said over and over, service is a major component of success in the recording business. The other is the *way* you use your equipment, not necessarily the kind or amount you have, because what people are after is finding a *reasonable* solution to their needs. And going the most expensive route isn't very often the only road they're interested in taking.

Time and again, we've demonstrated to our clients that they can trust us to serve their needs, regardless of the brand of equipment we use. And with careful research, we've nearly always opted for lower-cost equipment that can do almost everything the expensive spread can without the very substantial risk that top-end gear with potentially crippling monthly payments entails.

So if money is no object, diversify. Offer an audio one-stop that caters to your world-class clients' every need and whim. But if you're counting every penny, specialize. Watch the trends as they unfold, wait out the first-generation waves and then buy prudently 12 to 24 months later, spending as little as possible.

Hug your TV. Go to the trade shows, even if it means getting on a plane once in a while. Join local and national professional organizations and participate on as high a level as possible. The more time you spend hanging out with other pros in your field, the smarter and more connected you'll get. Make efforts to seek out and both share and learn from experts. Do your best to surround yourself with them.

Read the trades. Check out your competition. And stay abreast of the unfolding and electrifying developments that will continue to make this one of the most exciting and creative businesses that you can be a part of. This *is* rocket science, you know. Approach it with all the awe, respect and excitement it comes with and you'll get one hell of a great ride.

20
The Manager's Quick Reference Guide

You don't need to be a qualified engineer to be a studio owner or manager. And you may not be quite as fluent in all the varying and specialized terminology that some of your clients use on the phone. I've put together the Manager's Quick Reference Guide to provide some instant reference and rescue during booking and information discussions in which the client is an expert (or thinks he is) and you aren't.

Using the Guide as a starting point, you should be able to get some grounding from which you can at least ask intelligent questions. I've paid special attention to the field of audio post and its accompanying film terminology.

Reading the Guide through is the first good way to check your familiarity. You might also consider photocopying it and keeping it with your studio's scheduling book for easy reference.

Address Track An extra track on a video tape for recording TIME CODE information.

ADR Automated (or Actor) Dialog Replacement. An ADR session is one in which live actors watch a scene on a monitor or projection screen in the studio and lip-sync the words. Used to replace poorly recorded or unacceptable takes, or to dub a film into another language.

AFI American Film Institute, a nonprofit organization that sponsors film festivals and offers a program for film students, who are granted small budgets for independent films.

AFM American Federation of Musicians, the musicians' union. Work under AFM jurisdiction requires written AFM contracts and SCALE wages.

AFTRA American Federation of Television and Radio Artists, the actors' union for radio and TV and the singers' union for radio. Work under AFTRA jurisdiction requires written AFTRA contracts and SCALE wages.

Animatic A film of still pictures or drawings, shot in real time, to better present an idea for shooting live action later. Often used by advertising agencies.

Announce Booth A film term for any live recording area in which an announcer records voice-over copy. An announce booth can be anything from a 3' x 4' vocal booth to a 60' x 90' orchestral stage.

Answer Print The first completed picture and sound print of a film that the director delivers to the producer.

Bay Film term for a control room, as in edit bay or mixing bay.

Beep Generator A synchronizer that produces a series of short beeps used to cue actors or sound-effects performers when they are recording to picture.

Bumper Extra time that is added to a booking, allowing a session to go overtime if necessary. Not charged unless used.

Composite Combination of music, dialog and effects tracks onto a single MONO MAG or OPTICAL TRACK.

Doughnut A commercial jingle that features music in the beginning and end, leaving an open space for copy in the middle.

Drop Frame The most common TIME CODE generation for videotape. So called because two timing frames are dropped from the count every 60 seconds to correct for mathematical discrepancies.

Dub A copy of an existing tape.

Edited Master The master 1-inch video that is the result of an online session. Laying back the master audio mix onto this tape is the final step in the entire production process.

EDL Edit Decision List. A printed list generated during an offline editing session, detailing all the picture edit points and their locations. Used in audio post sessions to find record and offset points quickly and accurately. Many INTERLOCK sync systems allow the engineer to type in EDLs and automatically advance to each successive point.

EFX Effects. Also SFX, sound effects.

Foley Live sound effects performed to picture in the studio; named after the guy who invented the art in the 1930s. Professionals use hundreds of unlikely objects to produce appropriate sounds and are called "Foley artists," or "walkers." One of their main tasks is to re-create the sounds of various footsteps on camera. As they watch a monitor, they walk in sync with the actors, and step on various surfaces in the studio. Pro sound stages build dozens of 3' x 4' pits into their floors and fill them with all the likely surfaces, from grass to linoleum to water.

Frame The smallest unit of time and picture measurement, a single still picture on a piece of film or videotape. On film, 24 frames equals one second of motion. In video, 30 frames equals one second.

Full Coat Sprocketed film stock with the entire surface coated with magnetic oxide for audio. Usually used for 3- or 4-track recording.

Holding The accepted practice of reserving recording session time without firmly committing to it. If another call comes in for the same time, the caller with time on hold gets first refusal for the booking.

IATSE International Alliance of Theatrical State Employees, the film trade union for behind-the-scenes workers, including recording engineers.

Industrial A film or video used for sales training or product presentation; not intended for public broadcast.

Interlock Synchronization of audio to video via an electronic or computerized system, so that the audio recording stays in perfect sync with the picture. Also used to refer to synchronizing any two or more sources together.

Kill Fee A fee charged by the studio for session time that was scheduled but cancelled by the client at the last minute.

Laser Drop Updated jargon used when NEEDLE DROP is carried out with music production libraries on compact disc.

Layback Transfer of a final audio mix from multitrack to the final video format, usually 1-inch.

Laydown The transfer of audio source material from the master 1-inch video tape to multitrack audio tape.

Live Tag Also called a Local Open-Ended Spot. A space left open at the end of a commercial for a live announcer to add local information at the time of broacast.

Lockup Same as INTERLOCK.

Looping Another term for ADR.

M & E Music and Effects. Refers to the separate tracks on a film or video, which exist independently of the dialog. Often used when dubbing into another language.

Mag Machine A machine that records and plays sound on 35mm film. Used for MAG TRANSFERS.

Mag Stripe Oxide coating on clear film stock, used for the soundtrack.

Mag Transfer Transfer of audio to the magnetic STRIPE on 35mm film.

Mono Mag Film stock with a single track of audio.

MOS A picture with no sound elements yet in place. Attributed to a German director from the 1930s who would say "Mit-out sprache" ("without words"). Colloquialized to "Mit-out sound."

Nagra A special tape recorder used for sound during filming in the field. It syncs to picture for playback using a special PILOT TONE, or the motor may be locked to the speed of a vibrating crystal (known as "crystal sync"). Nagra recordings must be played back on decks that can read this tone.

Needle Drop The use of prerecorded music as underscoring to picture. Refers to a phonograph needle dropping onto a record.

Nonlinear Refers to any format that provides digital access to information, including recorders and workstations that transfer sound directly to and from disk, thus virtually eliminating search time.

Offline In video editing, working with a non-master format, usually 3/4-inch video, to test and assemble all the edits that will be used in the master editing ONLINE session.

Online Refers to the editing and final recording of the master elements, usually to 1-inch video tape.

Optical Track A visible photographic strip printed on film that contains its soundtrack.

Pancake Audio (usually 1/4-inch) or video tape that is wound onto an inner hub without an outer shell or reel. This lowers the cost and allows easy transfer to a choice of reels.

P.D. Public Domain. Any creative work, such as a piece of music, in which there is no copyright, or whose copyright has expired, therefore allowing anyone to use it commercially without permission or payments. Most work written prior to the 1900s is P.D. The new copyright laws set protection for the life of the creator plus 50 years.

Pre-Dub A mixdown of several audio elements to a single track, done to make the final mix more manageable.

Production Audio Audio tracks that already exist on a film or videotape. They are transferred to multitrack as part of the first step in audio sweetening.

Production Elements (also Production Rolls) Separate 1/4-inch audio tapes recorded by the location sound engineer during filming or video

taping that may contain outtakes, extra sound effects or ambient noise associated with the scene. Often recorded on a NAGRA recorder, which requires a 2-track playback machine equipped with a pilot tone or center track head.

Protection Master A duplicate tape of the original, usually kept in a separate place as a SAFETY backup.

Rough Cut A rough, initial edited version of a film or video, assembled to get a general idea of what the work will look like.

Safety A duplicate of the master tape, recorded for security.

SAG Screen Actor's Guild, the union for actors, singers and voice-over talent for TV commercials and film. Work under SAG jurisdiction requires written SAG contracts and SCALE wages.

Scale Union term for a specific wage guaranteed to a member for services. The performance unions publish current lists detailing amounts, and will quote scale for specific projects over the phone.

Scratch Track In post-production, refers to a non-master recording used as a reference, usually done quickly and simply to get the general idea across and establish timings that will be replaced during sweetening. In music production, a reference track used as a guide for recording overdubs.

SFX Abbreviation for Sound Effects.

Single Stripe Or MAG TRANSFER, usually containing a composite audio track done on special stock with one small audio strip of oxide coating on perforated 16 or 35mm film.

SMPTE Society of Motion Picture and Television Engineers, which has set the code standards for synchronizing audio to picture.

SMPTE Time Code A system used for synchronizing audio or video, synths, drum machines and sequencers. When used on tape, SMPTE occupies one track on the 24-track master, usually track 24, and will also generate VISIBLE TIME CODE on a readout screen or monitor. Example: "01:02:52:27" means 1 hour, 2 minutes, 52 seconds, 27 frames.

Stage Film term for a studio, as in shooting stage or sound stage.

Stripe A thin ribbon of audio tape mounted on clear 16mm or 35mm film stock, used to transfer a tape recording onto film for editing.

Studio Manager The person responsible for causing impossible scheduling demands, cranky clientele and loudly moaning engineers to appear to be non-problematic.

Sync Pulse A timing signal used to maintain a recorder's speed consistency when the audio is played back, which takes up one track on the 24-track master. In film mixing, sync pulse is always transferred to a separate track of a 2- or 4-track tape to maintain the same synchronization in the final mix to film.

Sync Pop An audible beep on either tape or MAG STRIPE used as a common sync point to align picture and sound.

Telecine A videotape of a film. Picture and/or audio transfer from film to video. Also known by the machine's name, Rank Cintel.

Three-Stripe A sprocketed mag film format using three parallel audio tracks on 35mm film stock, containing separate soundtrack information, usually divided into dialog, music and sound effects.

Time Code Generic name for SMPTE TIME CODE.

Trailer A preview or coming-attractions film for a feature movie or show, so called because it is spliced onto the beginning or end of a feature film shown in movie theaters.

Tracking Musical-instrument recording.

Video Post Editing and enhancement done to picture following live production.

Visible Code Also known as Visible Window or Window Burn. On videotape, a small horizontal rectangle is superimposed over a portion of the picture, displaying TIME CODE numbers for production reference. A necessity for composers to get accurate musical timings and for editors and engineers who need a numerical visual reference.

V.O. Voice-over or announcing. A V.O. session involves an announcer recording either directly to 2-track or to multiltrack, usually along with picture.

Voice-Over See V.O.

Walla The sound of murmuring or background noises made by a few people or a crowd, in which individual voices are undiscernable. Also called Crowd Walla or Rhubarb.

Wild Track In film, a sound recording made separately or out of sync with the picture.

Window Burn See VISIBLE CODE.

Work Print A temporary print made of a film to be used for post-production. Also, a DUB of a film or video program used as a reference in the studio, thus protecting the master from possible damage.

Workstation A grouping of pieces of computer-based hardware that forms a complete production environment for recording and manipulating sound and/or picture.

CLEARING UP THE PICTURE

The steps involved in audio post can get pretty confusing, especially if you're trying to explain them to a film or video professional at the other end of the line who hasn't had a lot of experience in the recording studio. The following chart may be helpful in making a clear presentation to a client or explaining the process over the phone.

First, the edited master needs to be made compatible with the recording facility's video format. In most cases, that means that most of the actual work will be done using a separate 3/4-inch video workprint of the master, so as not to subject it to any unnecessary physical abuse. The master may be on film or one of many different video formats. Unless you're equipped for 35mm projection and lock, film must be transferred to videotape at a video post-production house. The process is called "telecine" and in most cases uses a machine called a Rank Cintel.

If your facility has master video capability, it's best to make the laydown (transfer sound from picture to audio tape) to that format. If not, a 3/4-inch video cassette is the standard. Both the production audio and SMPTE time code are transferred to the video as well, with production audio on tracks 1 and 2 and SMPTE on the address track.

From there, the audio is transferred to the multitrack master machine, with SMPTE usually going to track 24 and existing production audio going to tracks 1 and 2. That leaves 21 tracks open for sweetening.

Now comes the laying in of sound effects via sampler, CD, audio or videotape, and Foley (recording live effects to picture). If the effects or dialog tracks are complicated, the engineer may do a pre-dub, combining several dialog or effects tracks together and bouncing the resulting submix to one or more open tracks on the master. That can make for a more manageable final mix.

The music is first recorded on a different master multitrack, and the final mono or surround mix is then transferred to the 24-track master. The composer also works from a copy of the master with identical SMPTE code to ensure accuracy.

Finally, the mix is most often done to a 4-track 1/2-inch or digital master, with appropriate track assignments. If the production is also to be released in a foreign language, a separate M & E (Music and Effects) track is mixed. This usually requires some of the sound effects that are on the original production track to be re-recorded separately, without dialog. That way, all that's necessary is to re-record the dialog in another language, while all the sound effects exist on separate master tracks.

When the mix is complete, the engineer does a layback to the master, or the audio is sent to a post-production house for transfer to film.

A flowchart illustrating the audio post process.

PRO AND HOME TAPE FORMATS

Pro Analog Audio

2-inch The standard size of 24-track recorder tape.

1-inch Used on some current and older 16-track machines, such as the Otari MX-80. Also, the standard 8-track format of the late '60s and early '70s.

1/2-inch Used on 4-track recorders as a master for film and video mixes. Also occasionally used as a wide, 30ips 2-track master for record mixes.

1/4-inch The standard 2-track master mix format.

Pro Digital Audio

DASH Digital Audio with Stationary Head for Sony and Studer. Available in 2-, 24- and 48-track formats.

PD Professional Digital. 1/4-inch for 2-track, 1-inch for 32- or 64-track. Discontinued format for Mitsubishi and Otari.

Removable MO Magneto-optical cartridge for the Sony PCM-9000 recorder, as well as many digital workstations.

DAT Digital tape cassette that has become a standard mastering format.

U-Matic 1610 & 1630 Sony 2-track 3/4-inch. Used for mixing and CD mastering.

F1 Obsolete 2-track format that stored digital audio on Beta or VHS tape.

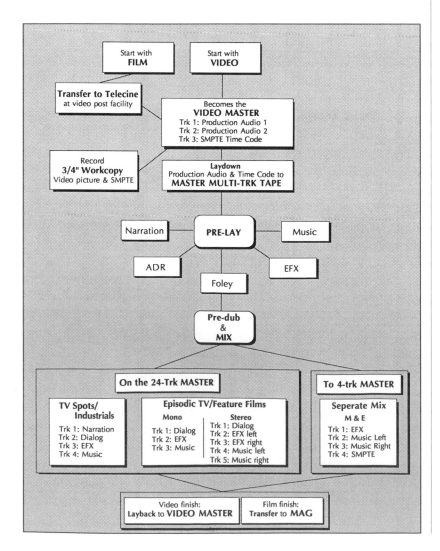

266

Brand-Name Digital Cassettes

Alesis ADAT 8-channel S-VHS cassette.

Fostex RD-8 8-channel ADAT format, S-VHS tape.

Tascam DA-88 8-channel Hi-8 metal-particle cassette (do not use Metal/E).

Akai A-DAM 12-channel standard high-grade 90-minute 8mm cassette.

Brand-Name Analog Tape

Tascam 8-track TSR-8 and Model 38: Standard 1/2-inch tape. Studio 8 model: 1/4-inch reel-to-reel. Cassette 8: Standard cassette.

Otari 8-track 5050 B/8: Standard 1/2-inch tape.

Fostex 8-track R8: Standard 1/4-inch tape.

Akai 12-track Akai 1/2-inch MK 20 cassettes.

Fostex 16-track G16S: Standard 1/2-inch tape.

Tascam 16-track Pre-'89: Standard 1-inch tape. Post-'89, including MSR16: Standard 1/2-inch tape.

Digital Data Storage

DAT Digital Audio Tape cassette.

4mm DDS Same mechanical format as DAT, with verified Digital Data Storage for archival backup, yields 1.2 to 2 gigabytes.

8mm DDS Yields 1.2 to 5 gigabytes storage (compressed).

D8 Magneto-optical cartridge in both 3.5-inch and 5.25-inch sizes.

CD-R Compact Disc-Recordable: A blank mastering format for write-once CD audio recorders, CD-ROM, CD-I, Photo CD and CD&G.

Pro Analog Video

U-Matic The commercial standard 3/4-inch video tape format.

Betacam High-grade 1/2-inch with luminance and chroma signals recorded on separate tracks.

Used extensively by news crews.

Betacam SP Uses thinner metal tape for increased performance and playing time. Compatible with Betacam machines, but requires Betacam SP decks for upgraded playback.

U-Matic SP High-quality U-Matic format. Compatible with standard U-Matic tapes.

1-inch C The standard for broadcast-quality video on 1-inch open reels. Requires a 1-inch video recorder for playback.

Video Formats, which come in the above tape configurations:

NTSC Stands for National Television Standards Committee. The standard video format in North America, Japan and most of Latin America.

PAL Phase Alteration Line. The standard video format for most of Europe. Incompatible with North American machines.

SECAM The standard format in France, Russia and parts of Eastern Europe and the Middle East.

Pro Digital Video

D1 4:2:2 component digital tape for a component digital machine used in a fully digital studio. The 4:2:2 refers to the sampling rate. The tape has four audio tracks, plus SMPTE and cue audio tracks.

D2 Composite Digital Tape. 3/4-inch cassette.

D3 1/2-inch composite digital video cassette.

DCT Digital Component Technology. Ampex digital 3/4-inch cassette.

Digital Betacam Component digital 1/2-inch cassette. Backwards compatibility allows Digital Betacam decks to play analog Betacam tapes.

Consumer Analog Video

VHS The standard 1/2-inch home video format.

S-VHS Doubles the amount of lines of resolution, for a greatly improved picture. Cannot be played on a standard VHS deck, but S-VHS decks can play standard VHS.

8mm Used primarily in handheld camcorders; a very small cassette that yields a high-quality picture and hi-fi sound. Requires 8mm deck or camera for playback.

VHS-C The other mini-camcorder tape. Can be placed in a plastic adaptor and played back on a regular VHS deck.

Hi-8 Enhanced, high-resolution format for Hi-8 camcorders, often used for ENG (Electronic News Gathering).

PROFESSIONAL ORGANIZATIONS

Academy of Television Arts & Sciences (ATLAS)
5220 Lankershim Blvd.
North Hollywood, CA 91601
(818) 754-2800

Association of Audio-Visual Technicians (AAVT)
PO Box 603
Farmingdale, NY 11735

Association of Professional Recording Services (APRS)
2 Windsor Square
Reading, RG1 2TH England
(73) 475-6218

Audio Engineering Society (AES)
60 E. 42nd Street, Rm. 2520
New York, NY 10165
212/661-8528

Canadian Academy of Recording Arts and Sciences (CARAS)
124 Merton Street, 3rd Floor
Toronto, ON M4S 2Z2 Canada
416/485-3135

Canadian Recording Industry Association (CRIA)
300-1255 Yonge St.
Toronto, ON M4S 2Z2 Canada
416/967-7272

Creative Audio & Music Electronics Organization (CAMEO)
10 Delmar Ave.
Framingham, MA 01701
617/877-6459

International Audiovisual Society (IAS)
c/o Dr. Paul S. Flynn
Western Carolina University
Cullowhee, NC 28723

International Teleproduction Society (ITS)
350 Fifth Ave., Suite 2400
New York, NY 10118
212/629-3266

MIDI Manufacturers Association (MMA)
2265 Westwood Boulevard #2223
Los Angeles, CA 90064
213/649-MIDI

National Academy of Recording Arts & Sciences (NARAS)
3402 Pico Blvd.
Santa Monica, CA 90405
(310) 392-3777

National Association of Broadcasters (NAB)
1771 N Street NW
Washington, DC 20036
202/429-5300

Recording Industry Association of America (RIAA)
1020 19th Street NW, Ste. 200
Washington, DC 20036
202/775-0101

Small Independent Record Manufacturers Association (SIRMA)
c/o Starvision International Records
2001 W. Main Street, Suite 205E
Stamford, CT 06902
718/529-7649

Society of Motion Picture and Television Engineers (SMPTE)
595 W. Hartsdale Ave.
White Plains, NY 10607
914/761-1100

Society of Professional Audio Recording Studios (SPARS)
4300 10th Ave. N., Ste. 2
Lake Worth, FL 33461
407/641-6648

RECOMMENDED READING

The following resources and more are available through Mix Bookshelf (800/233-9604), with the exception of the General Business section. Publisher names have been provided for General Business titles; most should be available through your local bookstore.

Music Business

Releasing an Independent Record
Gary Hustwit

Getting Radio Airplay
Gary Hustwit

The Musician's Business and Legal Guide
Mark Halloran

All You Need to Know About the Music Business, Revised Ed.
Donald Passman

101 Ways to Make Music in the Music Business
Bob Baker

Sound Advice: The Musician's Guide to the Record Industry
Wayne Wadhams

How to Make and Sell Your Own Recording, 4th Ed.
Diane Sward Rapaport

This Business of Music and *More About This Business of Music*
Shemel & Krasilovsky

Networking in the Music Industry
Clevo & Olsen

Successful Artist Management
Frascogna & Heatherington

The Art of Music Licensing
Al & Bob Kohn

Attn: A&R
Muench & Pomerantz

Power Shmoozing: The New Etiquette for Social and Business Success
Terri Mandell

Cash Tracks: How to Make Money Scoring Soundtracks & Jingles
Jeffrey P. Fisher

Music Publishing: The Real Road to Music Business Riches
Tim Whitsett

The Zen of Hype
Raleigh Pinskey

Studio Business & Design

A Complete Business Plan for the Small Studio
Al Stone

Studio Business Forms and *Studio Business Forms for Macintosh*
Kevan Patten

Building a Recording Studio, 4th Ed.
Jeff Cooper

General Business

All You Need to Know About Banks
John A. Cook and Robert Wood
Bantam

Growing a Business
Paul Hawken
Simon & Schuster

Marketing Without Advertising: Creative Strategies for Small Business Success
Michael Phillips and Salli Rasberry
Nolo Press

Starting on a Shoestring
Arnold Goldstein
Ronald Press

An Accounting Primer
Elwin W. Midgett
Mentor Books

Intrapreneuring
Gifford Pinchot III
Harper & Row

Swim With the Sharks Without Being Eaten Alive
Harvey Mackay
Ivy Books

Getting Past No
William Ury
Bantam Audio Publishing

Resource Guides

The Recording Industry Sourcebook
Cardinal Business Media

The Mix Master Directory of the Pro Audio Industry
Mix Magazine

The Official Country Music Directory
Entertainment Media Corporation

Technical Resources

Tech Terms: A Practical Dictionary for Audio and Music Production
George Petersen & Steve Oppenheimer

The Audio Dictionary, Revised and Expanded 2nd Edition
Glenn White

Master Handbook of Acoustics, 3rd Edition
F. Alton Everest

Modular Digital Multitracks: The Power User's Guide
George Petersen

Modern Recording Techniques
Bruce & Jenny Bartlett

Sound Recording Handbook
John Woram

Handbook for Sound Engineers, 2nd Edition
Glen Ballou, Ed.

Time Code: A User's Guide
John Ratcliff

Principles of Digital Audio
Ken Pohlmann

Audio Production Techniques for Video
David Miles Huber

The Technique of Audio Post-Production in Video and Film
Tim Amyes

On the Track: A Guide to Contemporary Film Scoring
Karlin & Wright

MIDI: A Comprehensive Introduction
Joseph Rothstein

The MIDI Manual
David Miles Huber

Index